TRAVELS BY NIGHT

The author at twenty-one, sketched by Michael Behnan

(See Chapter Five)

TRAVELS BY NIGHT

A MEMOIR OF THE SIXTIES

DOUGLAS FETHERLING

McArthur & Company
Toronto

First published in hardcover by Lester Publishing, 1994
First paperback edition published by McArthur & Company, 2000

Canadian Cataloguing in Publication Data

Fetherling, Douglas, 1949-
Travels by night

ISBN 1-55278-132-1

1. Fetherling, Douglas, 1949- . childhood and youth.
2. Canada - Intellectual life.
3. Authors, Canadian (English) - 20th century - Biography.*
I.Title.

PS8561.E834Z53 1994 C811'.54 C00-930256-5
PR9199.3.F475Z475 2000

McArthur & Company
322 King St. West
Suite 402
Toronto, ON
M5V 1J2

Printed and bound in Canada

10 9 8 7 6 5 4 3 2 1

The publisher wishes to acknowledge the financial support of the Government of Canada through the Book Publishing Industry Development Program (BPIDP) for our publishing activities.

BY THE SAME AUTHOR

The Dreams of Ancient Peoples
Variorum: New Poems and Old 1965–1985
Moving towards the Vertical Horizon
Rites of Alienation
Chinese Anthology
The Blue Notebook: Reports on Canadian Culture
Notes from a Journal
The Five Lives of Ben Hecht
The Crowded Darkness
Some Day Soon: Essays on Canadian Songwriters
Year of the Horse: A Journey through Russia and China
Gold Diggers of 1929
The Gold Crusades:
A Social History of Gold Rushes 1849–1929
The Rise of the Canadian Newspaper
A Little Bit of Thunder
Week-in-Review
Documents in Canadian Art (editor)

CONTENTS

CHAPTER ONE

JOE FEATHERS AND THE DRAGON LADY

A LOVE OF SECRECY was the most obvious trait my parents had in common. I was thirty-five before I knew my mother's true age, forty before I learned where she was born. My father's name was George Fetherling, but he worked for years alongside people who believed he was Joe Feathers, as he had led them to infer. Instead of taking his children to the doctor's office when we had colds or other minor complaints, he would lead us to a hospital emergency room. That way he didn't have to give our real names. To his way of thinking, the privacy thus preserved more than made up for the greater expense and the long waits in tragic surroundings. Both he and my mother kept their finances secret from each other and from the world. They put the very few dollars they had in a number of widely scattered banks, which they would change frequently. They did so to prevent bank employees from spying on them.

Such people were naturally circumspect about their own families. If pressed they would sometimes allude to skeletons in closets. On examination most of these embarrassments turned out to be small or long ago neutralized by changes in society. Like the farm girl in a thousand old ribald anecdotes, my maternal grandmother had become pregnant by a boarder. Two marriages and seventy years later, only my mother continued to be scandalized by the incident, which she would use as a taunt. But the darkest secret in my family was secret only in the sense that it was never mentioned. It didn't have to be spoken of, because it was the most blatant and pervasive and ultimately most damaging of all. It was the sin of exogamy. My father was a product of the upper middle class who through an unfortunate conjunction of circumstance and personality married a lower-class woman. The guilt he felt only increased her already considerable hostility and his own self-loathing. This, too, sounds archaic, like the plot of a Victorian melodrama, but the friction it produced was real enough to destroy lives. Anger born of class tension became the dominant element of my childhood.

The few records I have show that the Fetherlings were steadily miscellaneous in character; in the standard fashion of the nineteenth-century middle class, they were farmers, teachers, soldiers and merchants, with most of them having several such careers in sequence. It was only with my grandfather, Herschel Fetherling, whose life was divided in two by the turn of the century, that the pattern was broken for better and for worse. For reasons I have been unable to discover, a split in the family caused some members to assume variant spellings of the name. The schism, whatever it was, whether political, financial or romantic, pitted my grandfather against his brother Homer and may have pushed my grandfather away from the pack. He was a graduate engineer but an entrepreneur by temperament and a quite civilized fellow to judge by such evidence as has survived. He died more than a decade before I was born, but in my distorted view, based on the stories I've heard and the artefacts I've seen, he had been many places and done many things.

As I write this I look at two photographs. One is a *carte de visite* from perhaps 1890, showing him posing in front of a screen painted with Corinthian columns. One arm and one scuffed boot rest with studied insouciance on a stump-like pillar. In his face I recognize my own features, the same nose, the same heavy eyebrows and slightly slanted eyes. Only the ears are different, and the lips, which are full, like my father's. He wears striped trousers and sports a silk bow tie below his winged collar. He stares into the lens, one hand languidly holding an unlighted cigarette, the other stuck in the pocket of his inverness. His derby is pushed back off his forehead. He looks as though he's pausing in his conquest of the world. The other portrait was taken to illustrate some magazine article he had written. It shows a thinner-faced man of mature years with white hair and wire spectacles, but the eyes are vulnerable and full of sorrow. By subtracting the one from the other, I get the sum of my father's early years.

My grandfather washed up in San Francisco at some point before the 1906 earthquake and fire. He was an enthusiastic photographer, and among bundles of old pictures I now wish someone had saved were studies he had made of Chinatown. I remember images of men hurrying along the street with their hands inserted in the ample sleeves of their robes and queues protruding from beneath their pillbox hats. Grandfather seems to have been a bit of an amateur orientalist in fact. He had spent a lot of time in the Chinese quarter and once narrowly escaped involvement in a tong war. One day he was strolling with a Chinese man, he on the side nearer the street, the Chinese on the other side, by a wooden hoarding. A highbinder suddenly popped up over the fence and implanted a small hatchet in the skull of the Chinese, who crumpled to the pavement. As he related the story to his son, Grandfather knew that the man had died instantly and that his own best hope lay in continuing the walk as though nothing had happened.

It was this period perhaps to which belonged some of the curios and *objets d'art* I recall seeing or being told about. The house I lived in as a boy was stuffed with dime-store kitsch such as matador statuettes and gaggles of plaster geese in flight. My mother's taste was thus a marked contrast to that represented by Grandfather's sets of standard authors, a model he had made of Henry Hudson's ship *Halfmoon*, his china and silver and dinner gong, and especially his orientalia, such as a set of bronze elephant figures, designed and cast with extraordinary skill and set on a four-foot teak base. He had a weakness for inexpensive Buddhas and lacquered cigarette boxes as well. At one time he had also collected murder weapons. He would prevail on certain policemen to sell these once their value in court had passed. One was a pepper-box revolver, its wooden grips eaten away, which had been dredged up from the bay. Another, likewise used in some grisly crime, was a three-foot triangular rasp or file, which the villain had ground on a wheel to make a three-sided sword with razor-sharp edges, then fitted with a bleached ham bone as a handle.

I have vivid memories of Ethel Jane Abbott, my paternal grandmother. She had been born in London and after some family set-backs, not excluding a cruel step-father, had managed to attend one of those European finishing schools that imbue their graduates with a particular sort of English joviality, a quality that becomes a lifelong hum, never varying in pitch. It was sometime before the First World War that she and Herschel settled in Pittsburgh, the base from which he travelled about, selling electrical equipment to industry as a rep of General Electric. The city was then in the glory of its decadent modernism but still dominated by Carnegies, Mellons and Fricks, indeed must have been very much the way the muckrakers had found it in the 1890s: a place where frivolous mansions went hand-in-hand with wretched immigrant slums, and pollution from the mills turned the streets dark by late morning or early afternoon. It was at some necessary level a city for making deals, and in that stratum Herschel prospered, as when he made a famous $4-million sale to Ernest T. Weir, the steel baron. Eventually he set up a company that sold mining machinery and the like (I'm looking at the logotype, a fancy winged F, which survives on a piece of his letterhead). He became a clubman and kept offices in Senator George T. Oliver's Chamber of Commerce Building, an opulent early skyscraper, and a small but pretty home in the Beltzhover district that he wired with a complicated private telephone exchange of his own devising. More than sixty years later, I saw the bedroom where my father was born in 1915, when his mother was thirty-three and his father was approaching fifty.

I've sometimes speculated about the atmosphere in which my father grew up. Certainly his home life was very English, for quite apart from the anglicisms in his speech that so annoyed my mother he had, I feel, an essentially English character, so rare in an American. He must have sensed that, without quite realizing what it was that made him so out of place. The U.S. coastal cities such as New York, San Francisco and even Los Angeles, and certainly including smaller ones such as Boston or New Orleans, are often open to civilizing influences, in part because clusters of exiles and expatriates keep alive the historic links those places have with other parts of the world, but the vast interior has always been dark and barbaric. I've come to suspect that this is partly what forced or permitted him to create an imaginative world for himself, a sort of shadow life, but one that never found proper expression and got subsumed in a general pattern of emotional self-destruction.

When as a boy I would go exploring in the cellar or cubby-hole attic, I would sometimes come upon a doll my father had played with so long ago; it was wooden, stuffed with sawdust, and named Jimmie McFadden. It's easy for me to visualize him carrying it about, or to see him in short trousers and a cloth cap, rolling a hoop or (another childish diversion of that place and time) chewing the hot tar with which the brick streets were repaired. The earliest memory he related to me dated back to the Great War. Near his home, some soldiers were being trained in the use of the new queer-looking vehicle called a tank, one of those small rhomboid ones with all the treads exposed. It was driven up a steep bank until it was in a vertical position, whereupon it rolled over on its back like a turtle. He also remembered hearing a postwar lecture by Sergeant Alvin York, the former conscientious objector from the Tennessee backwoods who became a national hero after abandoning his pacifism and capturing a company of Germans. When the Liberty Tubes, the tunnels connecting downtown Pittsburgh with the South Hills, were opened for traffic in the 1920s, Father and a playmate found a large wooden spool, the sort used for steel cable, on the hilltop hundreds of feet above. Thinking it would make a giant yo-yo, they wound a line around the shaft and, grasping the free end of the rope, rolled the toy off the edge. Fortunately they let go before the slack played out and carried them over the side. When it hit, the device narrowly missed someone's flivver. They had to flee to avoid apprehension.

The old city directories reveal that Herschel's father, Cephas Fetherling, a veteran of the War between the States, was part of the household for some of this time, and pension records tell the sad story of his life. He had enlisted in 1862, just before his eighteenth birthday, and less than a month later was captured by General Kirby Smith's Confederate cavalry and held as a prisoner-of-war in Richmond, though quickly paroled. He was promoted from private to commissary sergeant, then reduced to private again, and finally made commissary sergeant a second time. It was in that capacity that he was accused of selling army potatoes to a civilian. His file states that hard marching and exposure gave him lung fever and left him deaf in both ears, though despite the handicap he would become a teacher as well as a merchant. He was discharged at war's end by reason of chronic dysentery and in 1867 married one Sarah Hollinger. They were divorced in 1917, when they were both seventy-three, whereupon he quickly remarried. No doubt his presence had some bearing on his grandson even though the grandson was only two at the time of the divorce and only five when the old soldier died. The great stock crash, however, was the more important factor in my father's early development, the turning point of his life in fact, though he was only fourteen at the time.

Herschel must have been speculating heavily, for my father always spoke of October 1929 with the disbelieving humour that disguises genuine horror. When the panic solidified into the Depression, there was suddenly no money coming in, but my grandmother continued to operate on the same budget as before. Her expenditures included large bills for milk and cream, most of which went unused in a domestic economy that had suddenly contracted and no longer permitted entertaining. When Herschel received some cheque in the mail—in one telling, it was the last of his receivables—he handed it to her with the derisive suggestion that it was just about enough to pay the bill from the creamery.

It was my father's ill luck to graduate from high school in the dismal year 1933. Going on to university was now out of the question. I've always felt that this accident of timing, by preventing him from even becoming aware of a creative community, ensured that he never developed his large linguistic gift or his slightly smaller visual one and didn't become a writer or some variety of artist, as his sensibility as well as his talent would have suggested. He did try without success to get on at the *Post-Gazette* and perhaps other papers and then drifted for a while. He started working for his father, which must have been awkward charity, as Grandfather was soon reduced to such bizarre ventures as taking over a warehouse full of department store mannequins. When the possibility presented itself, Grandfather helped him find a job with General Electric. This proved a rare opportunity, and at length Father became a sort of supervisory mechanical trouble-shooter. When disaster struck, he would go off on short notice to some distant mill or power plant where company turbines had been installed. It meant working with his hands—at which he excelled—usually in unpleasant surroundings. On one occasion he nearly died of appendicitis in a hotel room in a town that had been evacuated while he'd slept. But there was a certain romance to it and romance was a quality he valued. He was proud of his knowledge of good restaurants and hotels throughout much of the East, though the most important compensation for such a nomadic bachelor life was that it preserved some sense of belonging to the middle class. He played golf, for example (judging by the set of clubs, including a huge polka-dotted niblick, which later mocked his loss of status from a dark corner of our cellar). Photographs of the period show a handsome fellow with thick black hair combed straight back and parted in the centre, well dressed in the 1930s manner, with expensive commodious suits and short silk neckties that hung down like elongated diamonds. He had been living that kind of life for five years when he met my mother, Mary Emma Jones.

The Joneses came from Glandyfi, a lead-mining town in Cardiganshire, not far from where the River Dovey enters the Bay of Cardigan, and my mother's father, Owen, stands out in my memory for his Welshness. He was a big man, not tall but barrel-chested, who recalled the likeness of Andrew Jackson on the American twenty-dollar bill, what with his huge stalk of white hair set off here and there by streaks of urinary yellow. He had come to rest in eastern Ohio, in the coal-mining and steel-making region that also includes the contiguous parts of West Virginia and Pennsylvania. At twelve, he had gone to work in the same steel-mill as his father, who dropped dead at his side, and at some point he had boxed in the Moscow Golden Gloves. Another time he took a raft down the Mississippi to New Orleans. Later still, when my mother was a girl, he ran a saloon—Coates & Jones Double Six, it was called; he may have won it at poker—and was also a salesman for Red Top beer, a vile brew. These enterprises were all in Martins Ferry, one of the small Ohio cities opposite Wheeling, West Virginia. I had grown up believing that my mother had been born in Canton, Ohio, somewhat farther west. Only after she died did the truth come out: she had been born in Martins Ferry but had chosen Canton because it sounded to her so much more cosmopolitan. It was at that time that I also learned she wasn't a high school graduate. In any case, by the late thirties, Grandfather Jones was a gruff, taciturn fellow who had had a lifetime's worth of different jobs. I see him in his singlet, sitting on the porch of his old farmhouse (built over top of some early settler's log cabin), chewing Mail Pouch tobacco and staring out across the highway. Like Aldous Huxley, of whom he most assuredly never heard, he died on the day that President Kennedy was shot and was thus shortchanged in the amount of space the news of his passing was accorded in the papers.

Following her encounter with the family's lodger, my maternal grandmother, Effie Lee Halm, who for some reason was always called Bill, married a man named Ogden. They had a son whom my mother, his half-sister, resented intensely, in part because he clawed his way into the bottom register of the middle class, as a small-time public relations man with a weekly newspaper column. If it was a characteristic of the Fetherlings to split into ever smaller factions and sever all contact, the Jones style was to continue to harass blood enemies down through the years (the exception involved my grandmother's sister, whom my mother wouldn't visit or speak to, though she spent her last four decades in a nursing home only a few miles away).

When Bill and Owen were wed in 1907, then, it was her second marriage. They had six daughters, of whom my mother, born in 1911, was the eldest but one. To reach their house, outside Martins Ferry, one crossed a small stream, called a run, by means of a bridge that Owen had made from utility poles he had appropriated for this purpose. They owned a cow and each spring got a pig and had an orchard that was slowly being reclaimed by the woods. But Owen kept selling off bits of land, to the point where it made sense to let the spring-house collapse and convert the barn into a house for one of my aunts.

This grandmother, whom I came to admire, was a small wiry woman with only a grade seven education but a good deal of common sense. She had a likeable manner and a natural gift for drawing, and she was never seen except in running shoes whose sides had split open, revealing ancient toes. After Owen died (they'd been together fifty-five years) she carried on much as before. One day when she was in her middle eighties, a caller arrived at dusk and, after searching the house in fear she'd suffered an accident, chanced to glance up towards the crest of a hill. He saw her silhouetted figure chopping down a tree with a double-bladed axe and chopping vigorously at that.

In trying to write of these matters, I may be reading too much into photographs, but such are the tools available. One snapshot of my mother, for instance, shows a young girl in flapper clothes standing in a patch of mud, trying to look urbane and urban, pursing her lips and feigning a kind of sophisticated disinterest. The image seems to me a revealing one. From her earliest period of consciousness, my mother disliked her life and surroundings but lacked any means of improving or changing them, was bound to them, in fact, by the twists and turns of her personality. She had no patience for anything rural, including her parents and siblings. It must have been a special kind of torture for her to be a teenager in the Roaring Twenties, yearning to be part of

Flaming Youth but knowing that, though the popular culture found its way even to the hills behind Martins Ferry, there was no possibility that she could be a part of what it represented. So as soon as she could, she left home and got a job. First she worked in a printing shop in the Ferry and then made what seemed the big move to Columbus, the state capital, 150 miles away. Forever afterwards she would speak of Columbus, Ohio, as though it were Paris or Rio, much to the embarrassment or hilarity of others even a little more worldly. But she was apparently not wholly successful there.

In 1938 when she met my father, she was already twenty-seven and living back at the hated farmhouse with her parents and sisters. Though her manner wasn't suited to dealing with the public, she was working as a hostess at a restaurant in Wheeling when my vagabond father came in for lunch with some business associates. She was short and buxom with Rita Hayworth hair (the testimony of the camera once again). He looked a little like Dick Powell, whom he confused with another actor, William Powell, and so claimed to have known when the latter was a movie usher in Pittsburgh. She seemed to promise the anonymity he was seeking, the totally workaday world that would offer no reminders of what he was because it brooked no comparison with what he might have been. From her point of view, he was her ticket to the bright lights. Their expectations contradicted each other. The resulting disaster went on for more than twenty-five years.

My mother must have enjoyed the first leg of their marriage, when they would live for extended periods in apartment-hotels in places such as Philadelphia, but in time she must have come to dread the prospect of packing up and moving on. Father was still only in his mid-twenties but was perhaps starting to weary of the work in any case, particularly as he was having difficulty with one of his bosses at the head office, an old enemy of his father's. I suspect that Mother was urging him to resign. In 1941 he was attached to some company project in Baltimore when their first child, my brother Dale, was born. The Second World War was being fought, still without U.S. participation, and some of the merchant ships they saw in the harbour had huge American flags, two or three hundred feet long, painted on them, so that U-boat commanders in the North Atlantic wouldn't mistake them for British. An old letter I found after her death tells me that when war finally came she was holed up with the three-month-old baby at her parents' farmhouse while her husband continued to travel on assignments. In the letter, Father describes driving eastwards over the Allegheny Mountains late at night and putting up at Cumberland, Maryland. "When I arrived here the folk with whom I room invited me to have a cup of coffee and a piece of cake and we sat and talked and listened to the radio. I wonder if the United States is going to declare war on Japan now after what happened today?" Pearl Harbor.

I can only speculate on what besides his wife's urging made him quit the job. He may have been worried about being drafted, as what he was doing was by no means the sort of essential work for which he might get a deferment. In any event, he finally ignored an order to hurry off to some new assignment and was long gone in another direction before the telegram from his nemesis, telling him he was fired, caught up with him. He went to Martins Ferry where Owen, who had been taken on as a security guard at a machine-tool plant and foundry, suggested that he apply for work at the company's other facility, across the river in Wheeling. The firm had recently retooled for defence contracting and so promised draft exemptions for employees. When my father turned up, a surly personnel manager asked if he was enough of a machinist to make a wristwatch if called on to do so. To this idiotic question he replied yes of course and was soon foreman of a crew of women who assembled anti-aircraft guns for the navy. My brother would say that the ones aboard the ship he served on during the Vietnam War were very likely made there at that time.

Father used to hypothesize that if the war had continued he might have become a success (in spite of himself). As it was, when the troops returned he ceased being a supervisor and lapsed into being a mere machinist and never again had any money beyond what immediate necessities called for. He drove wreck automobiles that were fifteen years old or more, so old that even other workingmen mocked him as he kept them alive season after season by mechanical ability alone. The marriage started to come undone. Reading the letters they exchanged when the times were fat and they were apart, I find no trace of the couple I knew when times were hard and they were together. Whatever flicker of love they might have had in the rapture of convenience faded quickly. It could never reignite, given my mother's steep decline into mental illness, alcoholism and abusive behaviour.

They lived at this time in an apartment on Wheeling Island, within easy sight of the massive cables and deck of the Wheeling Suspension Bridge, which was the longest one in the world when it was built in the 1840s and which throws the same sort of shadow over the Island that its descendant, the Brooklyn Bridge, casts over Brooklyn. Almost every spring, with the Ohio in flood, they would move their possessions to the top floor and sit without heat or electricity as the filthy water climbed the stairs like a heavy policeman and sloshed inside the walls. On one such occasion my father was rowing a punt through the streets helping others, and he picked up a drunk who insisted on standing in the boat. When they struck a submerged stop sign, the passenger fell overboard. Father dived in to save him, which he did without difficulty, but he got separated from the boat and had to make for a ledge on the second storey of a nearby building. When, sometime later, the authorities discovered his empty boat snagged on an obstruction downstream, he was reported missing, and the news found its way onto the radio, to the great anxiety of his friends.

After my brother, there was a second baby, born dead, and I suspect that the marriage already had deteriorated into psychotic combat by the time of the third and no doubt unwanted pregnancy, which resulted in my birth in 1949. The expectation of another child drove them to look for more space, which they found a mile or two outside the city. Their discovery was a homemade four-room structure in Bethlehem, a little village of nondescript houses and even a few old farms, strung along two paved roads that came together in a general store and terminated in tough road-houses at either end. The owner was in difficulty with the law and wanted only $5,000, a sum it took my father about fifteen years to pay off. The lot sloped down to the woods and was flanked by open fields. Along the frontage stood a wide hedge through which speeding cars sometimes crashed en route to one of the notorious road-houses, a place called the Hi-Up. The village constable was an ex-convict who, my brother recalls, used to stop by the local school and let the kids play with his service revolver during recess; later, he changed careers and bought the Hi-Up, where he was beaten to death with a lead pipe.

Like West Virginia as a whole perhaps, Bethlehem combined the worst of the city with the worst of the countryside. The problem was the goddam trees, my mother would say almost nightly. "I look out these windows all day and all I can see is them goddam trees."

One of the most curious aspects of childhood is the ability to accept grotesque surroundings as though they are perfectly normal. Having no basis for comparison, no yardstick of reality, the child believes that whatever's familiar must also therefore be ordinary and proper. Such was the case for me in the early 1950s. My first spurt of growth in other than the purely physical sense was the realization of just how freakish the little world my parents had made for themselves really was. The discovery was both frightening and unbearably sad.

In the late autumn or winter, when the goddam trees

were bare, you could get a wide-angle view of Wheeling from the top of Suicide: Suicide Hill, a mountain road that connected the city to the village. Wheeling was urban. Bethlehem was not, though it was quickly becoming one of Wheeling's bedroom communities. It was popular, for instance, with members of the mob that controlled Wheeling's criminal life, which was one of the city's big attractions to visitors and an important factor in the economy. But ordinary middle-class people were moving in as well, steadily filling up the spaces between the older houses. My mother got on with them even less well than she did with the locals of more or less her own background, who were more inclined to accept her tales of the fabled riches of Columbus. Her hobby was litigation, thanks in part, I believe, to questionable lawyers who took on her suits without a retainer, in the expectation of getting most of the settlement, and she would sometimes threaten action against some of the neighbours with whom, in any event, she feuded for years on end.

Another means of egress, when the soft sandstone cliffs gave way and Suicide was closed by slides, was an unpaved road called the Hollow. It began in a wooded area near our place and ended far below in the grit of 29th Street, Wheeling. Along the way lived families in one- and two-room shacks, supported—like the rusting hulks of cars out front—on four concrete blocks. Dirty-faced kids in torn clothes played in a little stream that carried away sewage, and emaciated, flea-bitten dogs, often with open wounds or terrible growths, were chained to trees and barked maniacally. The other extreme was perhaps no more than half a mile away and included several mysterious residents who were accused of being millionaires, such as Herman Strauss, who owned a junkyard. But even they were easily dominated, as we all were, by the figure of Carl Bachmann, whose large house looked down on the rest of the village from atop a private hill, protected by flood lights and a security network of trees and accessible only by private road. Bachmann was a retired politician, whom Edmund Wilson, writing during the Depression, had called "the caricaturist's ideal of the lower order of congressman… pot-gutted and greasy-looking, with small black pig-like eyes and a long pointed nose." So vast were his holdings in real estate, built up during the thirties, that in conversation he was presumed to be the owner of any land not obviously held by someone else. The village was thus a sort of socio-economic ant farm that any student of abnormality could have studied with profit.

A few houses west was a family I'll call Neuhardt and a few doors to the east of us lived their cousins, who had changed the spelling to Newhart once the head of the household got out of penitentiary. The Newharts had a mentally handicapped son who was left physically handicapped as well, in the polio epidemics of the early 1950s. He was four or five years older than I was but in the same grade at school, and would walk on crutches up and down all Bachmann's sad wooded hills wearing a big sheath knife and carrying a bow and arrow, with his collie playing at his heels. One day he butchered the dog with the knife and strung its intestines from the trees, and we never saw the boy again after that.

The other branch of the family, the unreconstructed Neuhardts, lived in a square insulbrick farmhouse from perhaps the 1870s. The father was a janitor at one of the steel plants and had elected not to accept promotion to another almost equally menial job because, he said, he couldn't deal with the increased responsibility. Then he got laid off and through careful manipulation was able to remain laid off for two years or so. Returning from some tavern late one night, he put his car in the claptrap garage and in closing the overhead door in the dark managed to lodge his thumb in the sash and so suspend himself off the ground. Whether from stoicism or an uncomplicated nature, he refused to call out and was found hours later, unconscious and weak from loss of blood, by his anxious wife. Her name was Dot and she was one of a vast network of inconspicuous women who supported their families making punch-boards for the Wheeling mob, which installed them and other crude gaming devices in every bar and beer-joint. Their daughter married a hillbilly in an elaborate ceremony and moved into a trailer on her new father-in-law's farm, where the bridegroom worked for five dollars a week, his only income.

For a period of several seasons between decades of ill will or silence, my mother had Dot as perhaps her only friend in the village, and it was during this interval that Dot's father-in-law, a recluse who inhabited a cabin-like structure in the woods behind our home, died. For years, Dot had been his only visitor, walking down the ravine along the fetid stream to bring him food. At length she persuaded him to have a telephone, but the calls she made to check up on him were the only occasions the instrument was used, because he didn't know how to dial. It was said that he was a crazy inventor and spent much of his time trying unsuccessfully to obtain patents on various children's games he'd devised. One night I was awakened by the unanimous baying of all the local dogs. Old Man Neuhardt had died and the animals, sensing death, circled the cabin and howled at the moon. Once the body was taken away, Dot, my mother and I went through the fellow's personal effects. They consisted mainly of bent tin cups, cracked dinner plates, the clothes of his long-dead wife, a regimental photograph from the First World War and dusty pieces of kids' games, with moveable squares and boards that were supposed to light up but didn't. Later, the fire department, needing practice, set the house ablaze with kerosene and let it burn to the foundation before trying to extinguish the flames at the last moment, when there was danger of igniting the tall grass and weeds and even the elms and maple poplars, which grew thickly over that part of the country. I can still see the firemen enjoying themselves, their faces distorted through the flames.

I ran away for the first time when I was about three. I had gone only a few hundred yards before being spotted by another of the local characters, a middle-aged woman named Myrtle who spent her days walking up and down the roadside pulling a child's red wagon, always empty. When I reached school age I might have found a more successful type of escape, but didn't. We were far from being one of the poor families—kids from the Hollow would turn up coatless and sockless in winter—but of the others, we were the shabbiest. My mother would often buy us secondhand clothes at the Wheeling Symphony Society Thrift Store; she tended to grab whatever she saw and so I sometimes got girls' tops rather than boys' shirts, with the buttons on the left-hand side, and my brother remembers wearing garments that still had the names of his friends' fathers sewn inside.

The other problem was that I stuttered so badly as to barely speak at all. Asked my name, for instance, I would strain and sputter and turn red, trying to flick the words off the end of my wet tongue until it was sore at the roots. On really bad days, when the veins in my neck were distended as I tried to speak, I'd end up snapping my fingers or even flapping my arms like a big flightless bird, trying to make a rhythm on which I could get started. Most of the teachers were understandably exasperated and, what with their relative lack of training, often questioned whether I was of normal intelligence. One year I was actually kept from moving on to the next grade on the grounds that I was slow, as people said in those days. I withdrew further and further, and there were long spells when I dreaded both going to school and coming home afterwards.

My father got up at 5:30 each morning to leave for the plant and make machines used in making other machines, and he didn't return for twelve hours. He took whatever overtime was offered, to compensate for frequent lay-offs and strikes, and so there were periods when he would work seven days a week. In winter, that meant he wouldn't see daylight for long stretches. Through it all he remained convivial to the point of being jolly, patient to the point of being weak. He would sing "I'm a Ding-dong Daddy from Doomas" and "It Ain't No Sin to Take Off Your Skin (And Dance Around in Your Bones)," songs that scarcely anyone else his own age seemed to remember. The people he worked with all liked him whether or not they respected him, for while his stories of the outside world, told in richly coloured language, were always entertaining, he couldn't help standing slightly apart if for no other reason than that he was more articulate than they were.

Although he was passionate in his desire to see the worker get a square deal, he was ashamed to carry a metal lunch bucket, taking a paper bag instead so that he could dispose of the evidence at the end of each day. Similarly, although he wore old trousers and a type of flannel shirt then associated with labourers, he was always careful that they were spotless and in good repair, not greasy, smudged and torn like the other men's. I remember once being in a shop with him, inspecting some small piece of merchandise, a wristwatch perhaps, when the clerk noticed the rough worn skin of his hands and in condescending fashion guessed that he must work outdoors, as a contractor perhaps. I could see my father was embarrassed and angry, but he said, yes, a contractor, that's right, and we stayed just long enough looking at the watch to make a retreat seem natural. He tried mightily to lose himself in the world his dereliction had made him heir to, but there were always tiny signs of a struggle never to be resolved.

There were a few co-workers whom he saw outside the plant. One was Louie the Welder, who was actually a blacksmith. Another was a man whose shotgun had discharged, taking off his left foot, as he climbed a rail fence during a hunting trip. At the time, his handicap had been useful in keeping him out of the army, but now he was embarrassed by it. So he disguised his limp by always carrying a heavy box of television tubes wherever he went, implying that he was a qualified repairman. Father's closest friend was a large fellow he called Alec who had five or six children who thought he was a drunk and lived across the river, on the Ohio side, in a rickety house that seemed in danger of sliding down the hill in the spring mud and settling in one of the craters left by strip-mining. Father and he would sometimes drink together in a beer-joint where the barmaid was known as Thundergut, owing to a loud intestinal complaint from which she suffered. My mother never shared his affection for such people or for people in general and would become downright venomous if anyone made a claim on his attention.

She would have a head start on the night's drinking by the time he returned from work each day. In addition to knocking off six or eight beers, she would swig from the bottles of bourbon or Canadian whisky kept in the cigarette-burned sideboard. Such prodigious consumption of alcohol did nothing to increase her tolerance for it or improve her outlook. Far from making her maudlin, it activated her bile. By mid-afternoon she would be feeling pretty antagonistic towards the world, though sometimes I would empty out some of the whisky and replace it with water. By the end of the day she was lying in wait, ready to lash out at everyone in sight in the cruellest, most vituperative manner of which her vocabulary was capable. Her eyes would narrow, her face would become contorted and even her voice seemed to change, taking on a guttural unmodulated tone that was made even more otherworldly by the sharpness of her words.

Father would sit down at the kitchen table, under the cheesecake calendar from Levin Auto Parts. She would look peeved. He would ask what the matter was and get no response. Then it would begin.

"Money," she'd say, spitting out the word. "You haven't saved a goddam cent the whole time."

He'd tell her again that he was trying to better himself, working up through the ranks of the union, the only course open to a man without education. He couldn't go on all his life working in a foundry, he would say. "I'm not that young anymore." She'd snort contemptuously. "You don't fool me, running round with them bums!" She was a chain-smoker and had a tendency to chew the end of her unfiltered cigarette, which soon became a sodden mess; wet tobacco would swim out one corner of her mouth as she spoke.

Father would say he was doing it all for her, but he spoke without much conviction. As the fight reached a high pitch, it became increasingly one-sided, with Father staying quiet for the most part, giving the impression of someone who wanted only to lie down.

"What have I done to provoke your wrath?" he would ask.

That choice of words was always enough to send her off in new paroxysms of anger.

By this time, dinner would be under way, something taken from a can and heated or fried in a skillet, though on one occasion I remember vividly an enormous bowl of spaghetti. She raised it over her head and threw it at us, sending noodles everywhere and giving us a coating of tomato sauce that looked like blood. Such violent behaviour was not an occasional thing; it was the daily stuff of life. I remember sobbing spasmodically after being hit. I remember even more clearly how my brother, who by then was taller than she was, simply put up his palms and easily stopped her from hitting him: that really made her mad.

God help me, I'm trying not to recall her in too harsh a light, knowing that her alcoholism masked whatever lay underneath and that, in any event, she was merely exercising the only power she had, the power to make others pay attention to her by raving at them. Yet even now I marvel at the level of destructiveness as well as the crudeness of her emotions. The truth was that her life was drab and meaningless. Giving vent to her hatred seemed the only way she knew to relieve the monotony, though the rage itself became monotonous and could only be alleviated by committing even more emotional vandalism.

By any customary standard of measure, she wasn't a bright woman—just bright enough to know that everyone else seemed smarter, which only heightened her frustration and sense of inferiority. The fact that she wasn't qualified to drive a car played some part in the social claustrophobia she suffered, and she would take or make any opportunity to get away from home for a few hours. For instance, she would drag my father off to funeral homes to view the remains of the most tenuous acquaintances or sometimes, I suspect, those of people she had never met at all. I was expected to be standing at the ready inside the door when they came home, asking "How did he look?" or "How did she look?" with a solemnity I really didn't understand. She would then review the undertaker's handiwork, praising some aspects of it, finding fault with others.

Or she would pretend to have heard a hurricane warning on the radio and insist on being taken to some restaurant in Wheeling, proceeding on the rule, known only to her, that in hurricanes, unlike floods, the low-lying areas are safer than the higher elevations. On rare occasions, this tactic would result in a meal at one of the big round tables at Billy's Spaghetti House, an establishment that Big Bill Lias, the local crime lord, ran in Centre Wheeling (a part of town whose spelling—Centre, not Center—so unusual in America, gives some indication of its age). Most commonly, however, it meant going to Pete & Marie's, a greasy spoon and beer-joint whose front room, where we sat, had display cases full of fishing tackle. These nights out, however, couldn't be depended on to improve her mood, and I came to dread them horribly. At home I could at least hide out of sight if not out of earshot. At Pete & Marie's I was stuck at the same table as my parents as Mother yelled and argued, sometimes attracting attention from the rummies, the welfare families and the occasional hooker who frequented the place. Either because he wanted only peace and quiet or perhaps because he could see her personality deteriorating, Father would seldom speak unkindly *to* her or even *of* her. The harshest comment he would allow himself, and it was used out of her hearing, was a reference to "the Dragon Lady," the name of an Asian virago in the comic strip "Terry and the Pirates."

Another crisis was building in the family at this time. Young as I was, I believe I understood.

When my grandfather Herschel died in 1938, Grandmother Fetherling's finances declined to levels undreamed of even in the Depression. She put the family home on the market. Later I learned that she risked calumny and worse to sell it to a Black family, the first such transaction in what's now almost entirely an African-American area. The money must have gone quickly, for by 1943, judging from the Pittsburgh city directory, she was employed in the laundry of the William Penn Hotel. This can't have been ennobling work for a woman of her background, but she stayed at it throughout her sixties and into her early seventies until in 1954 she came to live with us, over my mother's violent objections.

We rented a small trailer and returned from Pittsburgh in a torrential rain with her belongings. She had lived there in a slum in Carson Street, opposite the Jones & Laughlin steel-mill, whose black and orange discharge covered the neighbourhood with poisonous residue. The mementos of her better days filled every corner of her apartment, and made quite a load. Once Grandmother had settled in with us, Mother was full of derision for these "antiques," a term she imbued with special contempt, and began selling them to dealers who, predictably, she ever afterwards insisted had robbed her blind. Grandmother would sometimes spend time reading books, a practice Mother found infuriating in anyone, particularly her mother-in-law.

They would have long and complicated arguments, or rather, Mother would argue and Grandmother would reply with bewildered moderation, addressing her antagonist as *Dear*.

There were only two bedrooms in the house and Grandmother had to share the smaller one with my brother and me. She slept on a cot placed lengthwise at the bottom of our two beds. There was little privacy. The door to my parents' bedroom was a secondhand one from an old hotel—the number *10* was still visible beneath many layers of paint—but Mother would never allow us to have a door of any sort on ours.

One day I entered the house and heard the two women having the worst one-sided argument yet. Mother was screaming, strutting, banging blindly into furniture. The veins in her forehead were enlarged and pulsating, and I feared the violence might escalate. It was a terrible scene to happen on, like a rape or a battle. The real adversary, of course, was my father, and he lost. Soon Grandmother returned to Pittsburgh and far greater poverty, where as far as I know he contrived to visit her only once or twice, so great being my mother's dislike of her and so worn down had he become by years of his wife's behaviour. I confess that when I succeeded my father I showed no more moral courage than he had displayed in the circumstances. But when, later in the 1960s, Grandmother died in the charity ward of a Pittsburgh hospital, I did argue for saving her from potter's field, and her body was brought to Wheeling where Mother and I sat alone in the funeral home in front of the coffin. Whatever acquaintances she had made in Wheeling during her short stay had predeceased her.

Whatever friends of my father's might otherwise have come stayed away lest they meet my mother. I wanted to have a tombstone put up but Mother wouldn't hear of it.

One of Mother's rhetorical devices was to pinpoint her own shortcomings and attribute them to others. For example, she was more than once banished from a local beer-joint after waddling up to one of the other patrons and drunkenly calling him a lush. In that same spirit she would sometimes accuse Father of being a secret gambler. The charge was laughable, given not only his conservatism about money but also the fact that, for one period of a few years, her own gambling was quite out of control. It led to the only occasion I can recall on which Father took decisive retaliatory action or pretended to.

When I was a small boy she would put on one of her good dresses left over from the Second World War and take me with her to Wheeling Downs, the Island racetrack that Big Bill Lias operated. Lias, who weighed 350 pounds, had started out driving a bread wagon through South Wheeling, a dark labyrinth of narrow brick streets, Polish slums and evanescent factories. It was the last job he ever held free of annoying legal ambiguities. With Prohibition he became a famous bootlegger, then the king of the numbers racket, then proprietor of a string of night-clubs and casinos. He employed a hundred armed men but his payroll was much bigger than that suggests, what with cops, judges, congressmen and the like.

The federal authorities were forever trying to deport him, contending that he'd been born in Greece (his full name was Liakakos), not in South Wheeling. They did manage to convict him of income tax evasion and seize his known assets, including Wheeling Downs. But then, finding themselves with a race-track on their hands, they hired him to run it, an arrangement that broke as a scandal when it was revealed that Big Bill was the third-highest-paid federal employee, close behind the president and the chief justice of the supreme court. I would always be dragged to the Downs somewhat against my will, as I would be dragged other days to the various bookie joints, including one located in the back room of a candy store on Market Street and another whose front was a milliner's shop. Between the bookies and the pari-mutuel window, Mother was losing a hundred dollars a week, which was rather more than my father earned. The hot walker at the track, incidentally, was Charles Manson. Many years later, when lodged in San Quentin for the Tate-LaBianca murders of the 1960s, he would wax nostalgic in the press about his days working for Big Bill at the Downs. He even wrote to the warden of the West Virginia Penitentiary, a few miles from his old haunt, asking if he might be allowed to serve the rest of his life sentences in the same institution where his mother and several other members of his family had done time. The Mansons were excitable people.

It was some while before the worst of Mother's gambling streak ran its course and she relaxed to the point of phoning penny-ante bets to a Centre Wheeling saloonkeeper who made a little book on the side. One day she placed a wager on a rather far-fetched daily double and forgot about it until the late afternoon when she heard the results on the radio and realized that both her long shots had come in. The combination paid several hundred dollars. She immediately called the bookie, who tried to weasel out, saying that he'd forgotten to give it to the runner but would gladly refund her couple of bucks.

She worked herself into an incoherent rage that found its target in my father as soon as he got home from work. After a while he was unable to stand her harangue any longer and went upstairs to a chest-high attic off their bedroom. From its hiding place under the eaves, he extracted the .32 calibre revolver that his father-in-law had carried as a security guard to deter Nazi saboteurs. I must have been eight or nine at the time. I remember that he stuck me in the back seat of the 1949 Ford, which had an elasticised safety rope across the rear of the front seat, which I used as the reins of an imaginary stagecoach and bounced along merrily. It was a summer night shortly after dusk. We drove to a section of run-down Victorian row-houses and decrepit mansions now broken up into furnished rooms. He told me to be quiet, and taking the pistol with him he walked across the street to the saloon-keeper's house.

The buildings in the row were dark except the one my father headed for. Through the open front door, I could see a man's bare feet protruding over the end of a sofa and, some distance away, a square of white light from a television screen. Father looked around him and entered the house. The feet jumped to the floor, making a whole man, wearing an undershirt, come into view. Father closed the door behind him and all I could see was a thin rectangle of light around the edges. There were no shots and I never knew what happened. I'm inclined to believe that Father came away with the money we were owed, but my brother, who's older and therefore knew him longer than I did, feels just the opposite.

Looking back I realize how unhealthy we were. We tended to have bad teeth, for instance, owing to poor care as much as to diet, for the family dentist was an alcoholic. He did little if any work on the patients who came to his office on Market Street and that was just as well. To steady his nerves he found it necessary to disappear frequently into the small adjoining room in which X-rays were developed, emerging with the sickly sweet smell of booze on his breath, his hand no steadier than before. On one occasion he drilled a tooth of mine left-handed. His right, which he normally used, was incapacitated by terrible burns. He had been in an accident with a steam pipe in the laundry of the state mental hospital at Weston in Lewis County.

As for my mother, her vision was poor but she refused to be fitted with proper glasses and instead bought plastic ones at the dime store, thus causing my father to make reference to "the family optician, Dr. Kresge." Of these play-spectacles she had several pair at a time, since in her near-sightedness she was always misplacing them and so required a second pair to locate the first. She wore them suspended from a chain, but would invariably lose that, too, when one of the arms broke off despite the surgical tape and band-aids used to repair it.

When found, the glasses would be filthy with spilt beer and spittle and the loose tobacco from broken cigarettes at the bottom of her handbag. Wiping the specs on her clothes perfunctorily, she would seat herself in front of the television for an evening's entertainment. But she would always find it difficult to concentrate on the plays, as she called all television programmes. "They've just got too many characters in 'em as far as I'm concerned," she'd say. And so it was that she would enlist Father in the nightly visit to 29th Street.

In my *patrie intérieure*, 29th Street is marked indelibly. It was long, wide, low and grey, the line dividing Centre Wheeling from South Wheeling. Centre Wheeling was a strangely comforting place, the site of, for instance, the barber shop my father patronized. The proprietor was a self-ordained minister who would sometimes preach at his customers, snipping and sermonizing interchangeably. He was, I think now, not quite sane, but I liked going there because there were stuffed lizards all over the shop, hanging from the walls and lurking behind the tall glass jars of pale blue disinfectant. Centre Wheeling was a decaying German neighbourhood, much of it built in the 1850s, and it was full of interesting spots such as this. I would sometimes walk through St. Alphonsus parish and see people at dinner safe inside their dirty brick houses and I would envy Roman Catholics their sense of family. Like my secret adolescent longings for the friendship of these family's daughters—all those loving and lovely Anne Maries and Mary Margarets—this was a heresy I kept to myself. South Wheeling was entirely different: menacing and rank. The Angel of Death had a summer place there.

There were elements of both districts in 29th Street where my parents would spend four or five hours each night drinking at a beer-joint called the Top Hat. Occasionally I could persuade them to leave me at home and would sometimes feign illness in order to avoid going. But that meant only that I would worry more as time passed until, finally, their 1951 Mercury (successor to the Ford) pulled up the road. As often as not, though, they would remain seated in the car for perhaps half an hour before entering the house. I could see them through the window, she arguing, gesticulating wildly, while he did nothing in particular. I knew the quarrel that never quite died out had gained new momentum. Soon she'd be stalking through the house, sulking for a bit, then flaring up volcanically amid breaking dishes and general household damage. In the event, it was no better being at home than it was going to the Top Hat.

Mother preferred to enter the Hat by its side door ("Ladies and Escorts"), as though that somehow made the interior better. The place was one enormous room with a low ceiling of pressed tin. A tongue-and-groove partition ran half the length, separating the bar itself from a dark area with wooden tables scattered helter-skelter. At the far end stood a small stage. According to legend, Helen Morgan, the singer of the 1920s, had once performed there in her early days, but no one had used it in years, perhaps decades, and the piano was covered in dust. There was a trap door in the floor, giving access to an underground run where beer-kegs could be cooled if one wasn't afraid of rats. The men's room had a swinging door and the whole place stank of backed-up urinals.

There were spittoons at either end of the bar, behind which, amid the point-of-sale ads for Duquesne, Pabst's Blue Ribbon and Iron City, was the imperturbable figure of Nick, the owner, who dried the drinking glasses on his apron. He was a Pittsburgh boy like my father, a few years younger but close enough so that their nostalgias overlapped. Opposite the bar was a Budweiser ad featuring a print of *Custer's Last Stand* by Cassily Adams, a painting in which Custer's long hair flowed magnificently as he withstood the inevitable slaughter—at the hands of Indians carrying African shields. Below this was a table at which a poker game was always in progress, under an adjustable green-shaded light. One night a man who had joined the game was sitting with his back to someone at the bar with whom he had been having an argument over fifty cents. It was Thursday, pay day at the plants, and a modest spread of cold cuts and pigs' knuckles lay at the far end of the bar. The man not in the game returned from the free lunch with a fork and stuck it in the skull of the poker player, who collapsed bleeding amid cards and chips and was carried off to the toilet by his friends. The attacker finished his beer and left.

In that era it was illegal in West Virginia to sell or consume liquor by the glass, even in hotels and restaurants, but all of the beer-joints freely offered thirty-five-cent shots as the natural antidote to their twenty-cent glasses of beer. Whisky was of course what paid the bills, though it had to be dispensed from bottles kept beneath the bar, in brown paper bags. Even so, a wave of morality would sometimes overtake the authorities, particularly in an election year, and they would raid the beer-joints, confiscating and arresting as they went. The Wheeling police would sometimes be accompanied by county deputies or, if it was necessary to keep the county deputies honest in turn, by state troopers. Every bar in the city got raided a few times except the Hat, because Nick was religious about never missing a payment to Big Bill Lias's agents. Sometimes these field representatives would also force him to accept slot machines (vastly more illegal than whisky). Despite his calm almost somnambulant exterior, Nick always seemed to be looking out the window anxiously, as though expecting rival hoods to appear with sledgehammers. I didn't make the connection at the time, but now, in my presbyopia, I see that this was another fact he had in common with Father. They were both cool on the surface but nervous underneath, like Bing Crosby.

Nor did I realize then what seems blatant to me now as I look back: that the clientele were so obviously the Second World War generation, with the scars to prove it, literally as well as emotionally and economically. One man, who lived in a walk-up apartment directly across the street, always wore long-sleeve shirts with the sleeves rolled down and buttoned, even on the hottest days; his wife once confessed to my mother that after many years of marriage she'd never seen her husband's bare left arm and was told she wouldn't wish to. Another patron was missing a hand. A third, a burly fellow with tight curls of tough blond hair, had been a mercenary pilot in China, one of General Claire Chennault's Flying Tigers, or so he said. I recall them now as sadly disjointed creatures, able to communicate only by grunt or drunken periphrasis.

Two of the regulars, much older than the others, stand out in my memory. The first was a man about seventy, a former boxer, who would sometimes jog by and say, in answer to my father's polite enquiry, "I'm trainin' for the big one, George, trainin' for the big one," as indeed he seemed to believe. The other was Old Louie. He was about the same age and wore baggy blue pin-stripe trousers supported by a pair of braces that stretched up over his massive belly like two mountain highways. He would arrive at the Hat shortly after the first of the month, once he'd cashed his pension cheque. He would drink for maybe three days, until the money ran out and he was senseless. Then, according to ritual, Nick would call a Burns & Church taxi at his own expense and ask several of the other drunks to help Louie into it so he could be returned to his room. Invariably Louie resisted and would have to be trundled into the car against his wishes. As he was being carried off, he would hurl drunken curses at the rest of the patrons. Louie was an urbanite, like Mother, and the worst name he would think to call anyone was farmer. Jammed into the back seat he'd yell, "You farmers you, you agriculturalists!" As the car pulled away, you could hear him screaming, "*Goddam fucking tillers of the soil!*"

I regret to report that many of the ugly scenes at the Top Hat were Mother's doing, and Nick, with the greatest reluctance at losing such loyal customers, would ask Father to keep her the hell away from there, whereupon some other watering hole would be found for a while. There was Manual's, a bit farther down 29th Street, where men from the Schroeder Casket Works came to drink after loading coffins at the rail siding all day. The alternative was more likely to be Katie's, a place on the other side of the street that offered hookers upstairs as well as booze and steaks below, though I'm not certain that Mother ever twigged to the prostitutes. She was not worldly in sexual matters and sometimes used *nudist* as a substitute for the word *reprobate*, which she did not know. A fellow with his belly up to the bar might indeed be surprised to find this fat drunken women suddenly accosting him and accusing him of being a sun-worshipper. She also believed that male homosexuals were all members of a club, literally; at least once I heard her accuse Father of belonging to it: a response to some new sign, I forget what, that the English part of his personality had flashed its presence. In any case, women with red vinyl boots and lots of cheap perfume would have just struck Mother as being classy. She'd hate them for it, mind you, but she'd think they were classy.

One of these periods of exile from the Top Hat lasted a year. I hate to think what she'd done. The punishment, however, seemed to have no effect on her performance.

CHAPTER TWO

NEWSBOY ALLEY

THE PROGRESSIVE MOVEMENT in American politics was torn apart in 1949 with the defeat of Henry Wallace; in January 1950, Alger Hiss was convicted of perjury and President Harry Truman announced the development of a new weapon a thousand times deadlier than those used on Hiroshima and Nagasaki—the H-bomb. The following month, Klaus Fuchs was arrested for espionage, for supposedly passing secrets to the Soviets. And a few days after that (when I was still only one year old) Senator Joe McCarthy, then a rather obscure Wisconsin politician, addressed a local Republican group in the Colonnade Room of the McLure House in Wheeling. There he announced, to the surprise of many people, including himself perhaps, that he had the names of 205 communists in the State Department. A reporter, Frank Desmond of the Wheeling *Intelligencer*, who was covering the rubber chicken beat at the time, grew suddenly sober. He gave the paper the biggest scoop in its history and was showered with glory (which he bequeathed to his widow, with whom I was slightly acquainted in later times). By 1951, American communists were going underground—those not bound for prison.

In seeking to explain the *locus* in which McCarthyism was born, one historian has unearthed a news item from the previous year telling of an uproar over a chewing gum wrapper. It seems that a citizen had purchased a brand of gum whose packaging showed the flags of the world and listed the various capitals. This particular piece featured the Soviet flag and the hated name Moscow. A minor scandal erupted because this was held to be a trick for propagating godless communism among impressionable Wheelingites. Such was the political atmosphere in which I was growing up.

It seems inconceivable to me that there can ever have been, at any point in the festival of credulity that is America, a more patriotic community than Wheeling. It was also, for instance, the birthplace of the American Legion, the front of whose building—Post No. 1—was in my time decorated with the sentiment NO DRAFT DODGERS HERE—100% AMERICAN VETERANS. I felt out of place from an early age, though how early I find it impossible to say; enlightenment was a process, not a series of revelations.

Beginning when I was about twelve, I railed, silently, against having to begin school each day by reciting the Pledge of Allegiance to the Flag, with right hand over heart, if you can imagine such shameless vexillolatry. When I got caught standing there stubbornly not moving my lips, I would substitute my own subversive version of the text, letting the words get lost in the general chanting. Somewhat later I arranged for one of the teachers to be sent a card announcing that he had been given a gift subscription to a John Birch Society periodical. This was my oblique way of commenting on the political content of his English classes. I was suspended. My political impulses included a certain tendency towards social suicide, as though I had nothing to lose. My speech already set me apart, and when it didn't I was sure to isolate myself through glibness. Class differences always made me feel like an alien. School was skewed towards kids from Out the Pike, local parlance for the modern upper-middle-class areas that hugged National Road, the old turnpike of 1818. I was left to cultivate the company of the few other outcasts. At one school, my companion was a fellow who was fated for a sad end. After graduation, it seemed, he took to killing young girls, and so, like the narrator in the Merle Haggard ballad, turned twenty-one in prison doing life without parole.

Once when I was perhaps ten I received a taste of my father's anger, a rare commodity, after I somehow ruined a tool that he had borrowed from his employers. It was a labelling device that embossed letters and numerals on a continuously fed strip of tin. It was designed for making serial-number plates for large pieces of machinery, but I had been using it to identify all the trees by their Latin names. I was a bookish sort of loner, as much at odds with school as school was with me, and I wandered off on my own, plundering libraries and following an unpredictable course, with one book passionately suggesting some other which would lead urgently to a third. Mother feared and detested such activity as much as I craved it. She actually told me once, in one of her extreme moments, that she was strongly opposed to my learning how to read and write. Oh, the obituary column of the Wheeling

News-Register (her own favourite matter) might be all right, or perhaps the headlines on the trashy tabloids. But stupid as she was, she was wise enough to know that even such reading as that, if left unchecked, might lead—well, to books. I set down these words now scarcely able to warrant that idiocy on the scale I'm describing was possible, but it was.

The search for books pushed me to seek out people who might at least have read ones I couldn't find. To this extent, I sometimes left my shell. In this way I located individuals with some taste for learning which they had been forced to paint over if they were to find even a modest place in the oppressive ignorance of darkest America. Once I learned their secret, they were uniformly kind, my youth and dysfluency notwithstanding.

I got to know one of my father's brother machinists who was using the trade to support himself as a kind of independent anthropologist. Through him I met a court stenographer who led a shadow life as an archaeologist and whose field-work had produced an enormous number of scholarly papers. In the back streets of South Wheeling, where it always seemed to be November, there were still a few reminders of a previous epoch, men who wore their hair almost to their shoulders, as they once had done in Serbia or Poland, and aged anarcho-syndicalists and other survivors of the old radical culture that had been destroyed by the Palmer Raids in a great orgy of Americanism after the First World War. One of my best discoveries had once been a reader in one of the stogie factories. Stogies were still made by traditional methods, with the workers sitting at long tables in big airless rooms and paid at piece-rates according to the number of cigars they could roll by the close of each day. In earlier times, such jobs were held by educated people whose foreign birth kept them from more meaningful employment, and it was their custom to select one member of the group to read aloud, with everyone else contributing so many cigars to his or her upkeep. They preferred to hear the classics and general European literature. They had a special affection for Goethe and Schiller of course, but also Stendhal, and from time to time might essay something topical, such as *Die Lage der arbeitenden Klasse in England.* The person I had the most difficulty getting to know was the patriarch of local pawnbrokers. Since arriving in 1908 he had secretly devoted himself to literature, philosophy, music and painting when not hunched over on a high stool, looking at life through a jeweller's loop. His response to decades of anti-Semitism was to emit secretions that formed one hard shell atop another; I was never able to get past the outermost layer but was rewarded for the effort.

The teenager whose crude stirrings I am trying to describe naturally wanted to be a poet, indeed thought he was one already, and even managed to get a few poems published in the type of semi-professional literary magazine often associated with out-of-the-way colleges and universities. For the first and only time in my life, a stranger telephoned to say that she had enjoyed a poem of mine, and in that way I met Mary Tominack, who had the greatest beneficial influence on me of anyone. She was a large lumpy woman who wore the sort of cheap cotton dresses commonly seen in photographs of the Depression. One of the potent events that had informed her life took place in the early 1920s when she was a young girl. The Ku Klux Klan burned a cross in front of her parents' home because they were Poles and Catholics in an anglo and Protestant neighbourhood. Her response was not to cower or even become bitterly defiant but to look for the enzyme that would release humanity into the system. The search brought her heartache as well as gratification. After she was identified as a communist in testimony before the House Un-American Activities Committee, she was literally spit on in the street by such people as didn't avoid her altogether. The *Intelligencer*, by tradition a fearless upholder of the rights of the powerful, had made her existence particularly hard through smears and surveillance. She pushed on.

By the time I met her, she was about fifty and had already exhausted several husbands and still seemed always to have a houseful of children of assorted ages and races. Her entire home, a rotting ramshackle structure on the Island, with the high-water marks of successive floods visible on the side like the growth-rings in a tree, was one enormous office. You wouldn't know it to look at the mess of paper on every flat surface, but her organizational skills were virtually Napoleonic. She was a presence or a force in groups as far apart in their approach as the Congress of Racial Equality and the Sexual Freedom League; the friend, comforter and prodder of agitators, martyrs, refugees, renegades, subversives, outlaws, cranks, dietary reformers and, of course, folk-singers.

How she could afford to do so I can't imagine, but she subscribed to a perplexing array of publications from the most mainstream to the most deliciously obscure and not only devoured them in whatever language they appeared but also clipped them for a housewide filing system which she alone understood but which turned out to be remarkably efficient. She would interrupt the writing of some newsletter, or the completion of a complicated verbal argument, to run her heavy frame up or down flights of stairs, emerging moments later with the incontestable proof that Lyndon Johnson, Richard Nixon and the coffee interests had conspired to kill Kennedy right from the beginning. The information was precisely where it should have been, in the old Quaker Oats carton under the kitchen table on the screened-in summer porch, next to the box where the cats peed. She naturally didn't own any cats but looked after a dozen or so. When the cats' rightful masters and mistresses came to retrieve them, she converted their children to vegetarianism and gave them free piano lessons. She was wonderful.

Her life in the swirl of the present was as vital as her links to the past were strong. In recent years she had marched with Martin Luther King in both Selma and Washington and had often been arrested. But her memories extended back to many figures of the 1930s, including Irving Granich, who as "Mike Gold" became famous for editing the *Liberator*, and Woody Guthrie. Any survivor of that crowd who was going cross country was likely to stop by, while a younger generation used her address as a halfway house and perhaps even as a stop on the underground railroad, as need dictated. She was part of the connective tissue between Old Left and New but also between politics and the arts, by temperament as well as through her wide range of acquaintances. She was a friend, for example, of two generations of the Dunson family in New York: the father, who ran International Publishers, the literary arm of the Communist Party, and the son, Josh, the editor of *Broadside*, the magazine of protest songs whose regular contributing editors included Bob Dylan.

Vietnam was becoming everyone's obsession. The dictator Diem, whom Lyndon Johnson had once called the Winston Churchill of his people, had been overthrown the same way he had been installed originally, with the connivance of Washington, and the build-up of U.S. troops went ticking along as Buddhist monks set fire to themselves in protest. One's tendency was to oppose the war because the government waged it and one's elders condoned it. Under Mary's tutelage I got involved more deeply and learned shame for the killing and destruction that was going on and at times purblind anger over our powerlessness as individuals to do anything at all about it. She naturally knew a couple of brave Christian radicals connected with the local Jesuit college, though they feared censure by their order and rebuke by the Bishop of Wheeling. In a characteristic gesture, for her natural inclination was always towards coalition, she brought them together with everyone else she could convince to take part, and put her cell together with others in places like Pittsburgh and Cleveland as part of what was in those early days a more narrow and more religiously focused movement than it would be even a short time later. I was thus the most junior person in the smallest link in what was still a very fragile chain, but I felt I was growing for once.

I was befriended by one of the Catholic professors in the group, John McIntyre, who possessed the touching faith in human nature that only natural anarchists ever seem to achieve. Through him I moved into an overlapping circle of people associated with the two other small campuses in the area, and in that way met the preposterous figure of Arthur Tarlow. What a pattern of images that old scoundrel's name evokes. Tarlow was a tramp history teacher who on falling into disgrace at some college would land with a thud at an even less distinguished one. By that means, he had worked his way from someplace in the South, whence he originated, through New England and then across the Midwest and back. He wore spectacles in small square frames of thin wire which contributed to the general impression that he might once have been a leprechaun until expelled from the band on grounds of moral turpitude. He sounded a bit like Tennessee Williams, with vowels that went on forever. When he spoke he would roll his ovoid eyes upward as though in disbelief at his own last utterance, which was in fact likely to be one that an earthbound person would find hard to credit. He also shared Williams's sexual orientation and had an ornate and ironic homosexual wit. I don't know how old he was, but he had served in the Second World War. "The Nazis," he said to me once, "had no sense of whimsy."

Tarlow lived at the only place such a person could, the Windsor Hotel, which had seen better days even longer ago than any of its residents, including Tarlow, were able to remember. Its entrance was now on Main though it was built to face Water Street, with a high-columned verandah giving off onto the river. But the steamboats that once tied up at the Wharf, or levee, were generations gone. All you could see through the ragged curtains in Tarlow's apartment was the occasional tug, pushing a load of coal barges upriver through the fog and hooting mournfully as it passed beneath the bridges.

He specifically forbade the hotel maid from ever entering his apartment—I believe he once threatened her with the cord of his well-worn dressing gown, using it as a whip—and so the place was thoroughly disordered, with stacks of books used as tables and the ungraded papers of his students jammed into the cupboards above the hot-plate. One of his principal recreations was trying to put the nash on Bill Forbes, another character who soon became one of my friends. Bill was a young painter, Black, who sometimes worked in construction when necessary, and when truly desperate would extort money from people in bars by impersonating a minister of the Gospel. He had a clerical collar and credentials from some non-existent holy-roller church and gave pretty convincing hell-fire sermons. He would then pass the collection plate. If feeling especially bold, he might also sell the Gideon Bibles he had stolen from various Holiday Inns. He was thoroughly heterosexual, but that didn't seem to keep Tarlow from trying, much to his sorrow. When rebuked yet again, Tarlow would scour the bars in the red-light district in Centre Wheeling, usually with only enough luck to get picked up by the cops. His response to getting busted was always to make sexual advances to the arresting officer or officers, a tactic that seldom did him much good except in that he seemed to enjoy being bloodied. Bill really liked him, as one had to do, and cared about him. And so it went.

The police—we called them the brownshirts, after Hitler's henchmen—were on to Tarlow, were at least more than a little suspicious of Bill, and were aware of me, too, since they routinely staked out Mary's house on the Island. It's difficult to say who led them to whom, but suddenly the heat was on. I got rousted one morning in a laundromat Out the Pike where I suppose I looked as though I didn't belong (I didn't). Bill, being Black, was handled more roughly and sometimes got taken to the station. He would come back with fanciful tales of his incarceration. "I get to the cop-shop, man, and all the brownshirts are watching reruns of *I Love Lucy* on a confiscated TV. One of them is on the floor lying on his stomach with a colouring book. 'Hey Sarge, you got my blue crayola?' and the desk sergeant answers, 'Blow man, I ain't seen it' and the one on the floor says, 'Whaddya you mean you ain't seen it? Howdaya 'spect me to finish my pitcher?' and the Sarge says, 'Hey, so don't draw no skies.' It gave me a warm inner glow to see our tax dollars thus employed."

Bill was forever on the prowl for sex and excitement and I was sometimes able to prevail on him to take me along. There were, however, certain inherent obstacles in such ventures. One was the fact that there were only one or two so-called zebra bars, where Blacks were permitted by reluctant custom to drink with whites. Another was the fact that I was still only about fifteen or sixteen, and looked it, being gangly and with an enormous Adam's apple. Thus we could drink only in places of low resort whose owners weren't interested in observing the legal niceties. For practical purposes this meant a joint on the Island grandiloquently named the Yacht Club. It was in fact a small cement block building with a bar and a rickety walkway over the water leading down to a converted coal barge, and was run by a former acrobat named Walker Dick whose forebears had worked on the river, as steamboat captains and such, for generations. He had been married many times and had once owned a small circus. It was difficult to say which of these vitae the absurd local establishment found more odious. The mere fact that he was ostracized was enough to endear him to us.

Wheeling is one of the few hilly cities in the world where the poor live atop the hills, overlooking the well-off down below. As the east-west streets ran back from the river, they crawled up the steep face of a mountain to a rank slum near the summit. Much to our disgust, the older generation often called this area Niggertown. In those days there was only a single housing project there, of recent origin but already in chaos and decay; otherwise the maze of original frame buildings stood pretty much undisturbed by changes in municipal fashion, with porches rotting away, ceilings sagging, the very houses themselves slanting dangerously as they clung to the precipitous and broken streets. It was an article of faith that the fire department would take its time responding to calls from the area in the hope that the whole place would be burned out. Bill had grown up there, on Charles Street, near what had been the legally segregated Black high school, which was now integrated in name but not in fact. His birthright gave him free access to some curious places around town where I was allowed when I was with him, although he couldn't enter the equivalent white establishments even as a guest.

There was the Beau Brummel Social Club, with its ridiculous suggestion of grandiosity. But the name as well as the music were in the same tradition as the Benjamin Harrison Social Club, the Pittsburgh after-hours joint where Maxine Sullivan (who introduced "Jeepers Creepers" with Louis Armstrong) got her start. And there was a place that sold crawfish out of a bucket down in South Wheeling by the river, where the hobo jungles used to be, the territory described so memorably in some of Davis Grubb's fiction and a couple of James Wright's poems. One night a bunch of us went from there to a hookers' hotel near the old Centre Market. Its only badge of identity was an orange neon sign spelling out HOTEL; it had no other name and so Tarlow began referring to it as the Hotel Hotel and then Le Grand Hotel Hotel, making long-winded and drunken comparisons between it and the Excelsior in Rome. Despite outings with Bill, I never quite succeeded in losing my virginity, such as it was, until both of us became infatuated with a go-go dancer in a bar downtown, the sort of dive that reinvented itself on Fridays, when the busloads of tourists and foreigners came to town for the WWVA Jamboree and the owner put out signs reading NO COVER NO MINIMUM CANADIAN $$$ ACCEPTED AT PAR. I can see this dancer yet. It seemed to us that she was beautiful, though she chewed gum, even while standing in a cage suspended from the ceiling, swinging her arms up over her head, first one and then the other, in approximate time to the music.

To no one else's surprise, but at some cost to my natural romanticism, she turned out to be a hooker on the side. She said she had never done it with a Black guy and Bill very kindly got me included in the one low price as a sort of supercargo, though I still fancied that what she had in mind was a *boff de politesse.* We used Tarlow's apartment, with me first waiting in the corridor, looking stupid, until the two of them had finished. Tarlow, returning at the appointed hour, referred to our activity as "fucking in the biblical sense."

All this while Bill was painting frantically. I never again saw anything like his work until I learned about Beryl Cook's in England years later. He affected membership in the folk tradition and the naiveté was quite believable; one had to be hip to see the hipness from which he drew. He gave me several of his canvases, which I lost one by one in various moves and periods of turmoil over the years, but the example I remember most vividly was one he wouldn't part with. He called it the *Adoration of the Bookies.* It was a Nativity scene that included the faces of various Market Street characters, members of the gaming community. I thought he was a genius and he repaid the compliment in kind. We were young.

Eventually I got out of school, putting an end to the double life I was leading, and tried desperately to find a job. I made lists of twenty businesses each day to call on. The closest I came to employment was when a tree trimmer, under contract to the electric utility, gave me a couple days' work as a high-climbing apprentice. After a week or so I was mightily discouraged. My father suggested I try a friend of his whom he had prevailed on once or twice when he was out on strike. The business was on Water Street, near the Wharf, where it had begun in the early steamboat days selling rope and such to the captains, and it still did a bit of ship chandlery in addition to a wholesale appliance business. But Father's contact had died. With a guitar player I met at Mary's, I launched a plan to make money selling country songs to one of the fly-by-night music publishers commonly found in half-empty office buildings. Our best collaboration was called "I See by Your Leg Irons You're a Prisoner" but though the publisher held out the promise of fifty dollars for the copyright we were never able to collect. Of another of our joint efforts, I recall only one line: "She made a virtue of necessity / and a fool outta me." I spent some time in Pittsburgh looking for groups of writers to be part of, but had little success. Sam Hazo, the Catholic poet and anthologist, dominated the established circle and had no reason to take me seriously, while the underground was led by Ron Caplan, a figure of the day whom I never quite caught up with and who had close links to places like the Coach House Press in Toronto, which had recently opened. I went to Cleveland, too, where Jim Lowell's Asphodel Bookshop in the Arcade was the centre of activity and the leading personality was d.a. levy, who was busted for obscenity at about that time and later shot himself. I hitched to Toronto as well, for Mary had been feeding me clippings and pamphlets about the Vietnam exiles there, and I made some contacts. But I came back to Wheeling, hating the place more than ever. For a while I was ready to take Bill's advice and beg work as a non-union construction labourer, making a good wage for a few days' backbreaking toil here and there. I was resigned to this when I was given the opportunity to pursue a lucrative career in the fast-growing field of commercial dish-washing.

Somebody tipped me off that they needed a dishwasher at Louie's diner, where Short Market Street met Stone's Alley, and the intelligence proved accurate. I would start in the afternoon and work until they closed at night and get twenty dollars a week. The original Louie had been gone for years, but the present owner had inherited his name along with the business. In addition to this Louie, who was the counterman and soda jerk, the only other staff besides myself was the cook. He was a large fellow with a shaven head and a swastika tattooed on the lobe of one ear. Before starting the shift each day, he would give his massive arms and torso a thick coat of glistening oil. Then he would repair to the alley out back and take an almost sexual delight in sharpening all the knives and cleavers on a whetstone. When he failed to show up about my fifth or sixth day, I became the cook as well as the dishwasher. The promotion carried no increase in pay, but then the cooking might consist only of scraping mould off the meat loaf, adding an ice cream scoop of reheated mashed potatoes and covering it all with gelatinous gravy. During the slack periods midway between lunch and dinner and again between dinner and closing, I would read or write for a few moments if I had caught up on my washing. I hadn't been working there more than two weeks when Louie came into the back unexpectedly and caught me writing a poem, an activity that to him seemed as shameful as masturbation on the job. I was fired.

As would happen so often later in life whenever I was fired or fiercely attacked, my emergency generators kicked in and I made instant decisions aimed at defending myself: a legacy, I believe, from having grown up under the constant threat of Mother's explosive temper. In this case I went immediately, almost without thinking, to the Centre Market square where John Palsa, a local hoodlum and former professional fighter who lived in Bethlehem not far from us, had a storefront full of old golf-bags, rusty mufflers and unidentified bits of secondhand plumbing—a not very convincing cover for whatever business he was running out of the back. I knew that he was also engaged in some sort of restaurant. Small-time hoods often ran greasy spoons, for they always needed a legitimate place of business through which to filter cash. I found him wearing a silk shirt and alligator shoes, sitting in his store full of rubbish. He recognized me, thought I was a good kid, and told me that he'd put me to work as a dishwasher at the Academy on Market Street. This was a much grander resolution than I could have wished for, not merely because now I would get twenty-five dollars a week as well as meals, but because the Academy was an important place on the underworld map, the headquarters of Paul Hankish.

"Big Bill Lias was more famous than the president of the United States—whoever that was at the time." That remarkable sentence was uttered by one of Mother's younger sisters, reminiscing about her girlhood in the early 1940s. She could also remember seeing Alma Henderson, Wheeling's grandest and most notorious madam, taking her charges shopping in a red limousine. Alma, who used to send glamorous nude photos of herself to her more important clients, the ones who sat in high leather chairs in the Fort Henry Club clipping their bond coupons, was long gone from the scene when I became aware of such things. Indeed it was vivid evidence of her decline, and the passing of the old order generally, when her son, in the course of robbing a supermarket, shot and killed an acquaintance of my parents. As for Big Bill, he was still around, still had money despite the government seizure of his assets, still had powerful connections. But he was a diminishing force. Speculation about matters like these, and about who had replaced him, and who controlled whoever replaced him, was everyday conversation at the dinner table and the beer-joint.

What seemed clear is that though Lias ran West Virginia and enjoyed a marsupial relationship with one of the state's two U.S. senators, he was himself sometimes indebted to Pennsylvania, at least indirectly, for one of that state's own senators spent his time away from Washington in a suite at the William Penn Hotel in Pittsburgh, giving orders to gangsters through a bank of telephones. The various tax-evasion and deportation proceedings against him made Lias a national figure ("I ain't been no angel," he informed *Life* magazine). That in turn made him still more vulnerable. And then, too, he was growing old and ill. He had always adamantly refused to allow drugs in the city, a restriction his younger rivals thought absurd. "The day I knew Big Bill was finished," a friend of mine said, "was when I walked into the men's room of the Pythian Building and there was a fourteen-year-old kid shooting heroin, trying to look nonchalant." Big Bill's heir apparent or heir presumptive, it wasn't clear which, was the aforesaid Paul Hankish.

Lias had once run his empire from Zellers, a Market Street restaurant and casino where patrons could proceed from one level of illegality to another simply by continuing to climb the stairs. The place was so named because it had once belonged to Dutch Zellers, who had started out as a pickpocket on riverboats in the 1890s but who eventually, following a well-publicized conversion by Billy Sunday, became first a policeman and then an evangelist in his own right. Now, the bar at street level was operated by Hankish. But in the casino above—where in my extreme youth I would visualize tuxedoed millionaires and their seeing-eye mistresses, sipping mock turtle soup and listening to jazz—the windows were boarded up and the leather banquettes mouldering. Still, as far as could be determined, this was a structure in which no legal activity had taken place for forty years or so. That seemed a remarkable record for a building in the private sector, until one considered a certain whorehouse in Centre Wheeling that had been in business uninterruptedly since the red-light district moved there from the Upper Market in about 1905.

The passing of the torch from Lias to Hankish was not entirely smooth, however, for several other organizations had tried to muscle in on the big fellow's set-up. In my childhood these lesser groups were forever smashing one another's pinball machines or blowing the fronts out of one another's warehouses, until finally there was only one serious contender, the Ohio gang, based in Bridgeport, one of the tough little towns on the opposite bank of the river. Tempers flared.

One morning in 1964 (I rely on newspaper clippings for the date), Hankish made the classic mistake of starting his automobile himself. An explosion took off the whole front end of the car and both of his legs above the knee. A person or persons unknown, whom every bookmaker up and down Market Street could name, had wired dynamite to the ignition.

The Academy, where John Palsa, a Hankish lieutenant, kindly put me to work, was across the street from the old Zellers and was Hankish's official address. Hankish was often written about in the papers—"prominent sportsman" was the preferred style for rackets figures, or sometimes "prominent Wheeling gambler"—but he wasn't a public personage the way Lias had been in his prime, not someone adolescents pestered for his autograph, and so I had never actually seen him until I reported for work. At about midnight, the people at the bar suddenly grew quiet. The boys in the backroom laid down the dice and the pool-shooters brought their cues to parade rest. There was Hankish, dark, balding, surprisingly young, walking towards his private office to go over the night's receipts. He strode on artificial legs using aluminum crutches, the sort with hand-grips halfway up, at right angles to the shafts. The Academy had a hard tile floor composed of tiny white octagons. One of his crutches had lost its protective rubber tip, so that when Paul moved he made a metallic *ping-ping* noise. The regulars could hear him coming at a considerable distance, like Marley's Ghost or the crocodile in *Peter Pan*.

The Academy was divided in two, with the bar featuring large expensive mirrors, a billiard room and the Back Room on one side, the restaurant on the other. It was typical of such places that the restaurant was oversupplied with expensive kitchen equipment that was kept in new condition because it was so seldom used, even though there were three cooks and the one on the 11 p.m. to 7 a.m. shift would frequently be called on to make big meals on no notice at some improbable hour.

There was already a dishwasher in place when I arrived but, as Mister Palsa explained, he was a spastic and the task was too much for him. Still, he went on, he wouldn't feel right firing the poor fellow as he had known the boy's father (had probably shot him, I thought). But I could have the job six days a week and the spastic would be the relief man on Mondays. Since the nature of the business and the weight of precedent made the proprietors careful about income tax complications, I would be paid by cheque.

First I would sweep out the place and then haul meat from the walk-in freezer in the basement and take the garbage out to the alley. I was kept busy, though the actual dishwashing was not onerous because so few people came there to eat—that would be like going to the candy store–bookie joint to buy a box of sweets. Tuesdays, following my day off, could be trying, however, since I had to redo the dishes done by the spastic the previous night. He would replace them in the cabinet with pieces of pie and soapsuds still stuck to them, so that a tall stack of saucers could be picked up like a concertina.

I would also cater to the boys in the Back Room, fighting through the cigar smoke to bring them sandwiches and drinks from the bar. Sometimes I would also help out as rack boy in the poolroom or as boardman, writing the odds at the various races on a big slate while standing on a wheeled stepladder from which hung a bucket of water for soaking chalk. The other part of my daily routine was scrubbing the toilets.

I've never known a place where nicknames, which often served as aliases, were more numerous or had such interesting etymologies. There was a fellow called Mouse whose real name was Mauser and another called J.R. simply because he was Somebody Jr., and the people with whom he associated weren't literate enough to know what the abbreviation meant. There was a man called Shooter not because he liked his shooter of whisky nor because he was a gunman (though he may have been, coincidentally). Rather, he was highly excitable and would always enter a crap game yelling, "New shooter! New shooter up!" A patron named Spanish, who looked like a forty-five-year-old version of the comic strip character Henry, was also known as Dos, a misconstruction of Doze or possibly of Dose, as in Overdose, which is perhaps what he had once tried to do. With regard to a person known as Gutter Smith, my researches failed me; I prefer to think the name betrayed his origins and wasn't a corruption of Got Her, but I fear the worst.

The most vivid in my memory is Walleye (after the fish to which he bore a resemblance) but then he loomed the largest at the time. He spoke in the manner of a 1950s jazzman. In summer he wore glossy black shoes with black socks, plaid bermuda shorts and, as in the other seasons, a knit shirt with a little porpoise embroidered on the left breast. The costume was always topped off by a Tyrolean skiing hat complete with a tiny feather. He had begun life as a runner for Bill Lias and was now a small-time fence and freelance bookie, one of a number who used the pay phones at the Academy in exchange for a percentage of the take. He seemed to be in almost telepathic communication with places like Arlington Park and Hialeah, and it was said by way of an advertising claim that he could give you odds that the sun wouldn't rise. It was only by receiving stolen goods that he ever got into legal difficulties and then only when he tried to enter the big time. He had always been the sort of fellow who had access to packs of cigarettes—without tax seals—at twenty cents each, part of some hijacked shipment. Once came a rumour of a room full of air conditioners; another time, a duffle bag of Swiss watch movements. Twenty years after all of this, some newspaper clippings reached me about his recent activity. A large team of heavily armed brownshirts stove in the door of his dismal furnished room and found him lying abed with a fortune in artworks missing since a recent series of burglaries.

One of the cops said in disbelief, considering the surroundings, "Where'd you *get* all this stuff?"

Walleye replied, "Hey, I'm a collector. It's a hedge against inflation."

One day I returned home just before dusk and could hear Mother's nightly temper spilling out into the road, some distance away. When I went inside, however, I learned that I'd been mistaken. It was her laughter, not her arguing, that had reached me through the walls, the sound distorted as it lost its shape in the open air. A trivial incident but one I've remembered because it fell so unexpectedly. It was, after all, six o'clock, when the fighting always began. I was in the habit of steeling myself for the tension that filled the place, tension that ranged from the silent anger of clenched muscles to the violence of protruding eyes and set jaws. Such temporary relief that day was a gift and also a fluke. And so it was, I believe, that the stress finally caught up with Father, aided by cigarettes and alcohol to the extent these represented separate hazards. He had a heart attack. He was forty-nine and was saved only by the quick action of his friend Alec, who scooped him up from the parking lot of the plant and ran with him in his arms to the nursing station. I saw him early that evening in his hospital room. Whether from medication or from fear, a bit of both I suppose, he was in a state that fell between delirium and hysteria. He thought he was dying, and looking at me kept saying "Poor Doug, Poor Doug" in a way that's always touched me with its selflessness but left me to puzzle over his exact meaning.

He was kept in hospital for weeks before being sent home with instructions to avoid stairs, but Mother objected to him sleeping on the sofa on the ground floor and so that arrangement lasted only a short time. Periodically he would see the doctor, who would advise him to get more rest, to which he would reply with a joke. His tinny world of humour became tinnier over the next year, his attempts at jokes cornier and cornier.

He would forget himself and repeat the same ones again and again; his listeners would pretend to smile and he would pretend to laugh. He had lost his excess weight but the change made him look even sicker, his clothes now hung so loosely. He started back at the plant but his co-workers made an agreement among themselves to take all the strenuous jobs. There was no fundamental change at home, however, only the same pattern of ominous lulls and violent abuse. There was only this new twist: that if the argument lasted to 2:00 or 3:00 a.m., he would take a blanket and pad downstairs, though the noise might follow him down for another hour, to just a couple of hours before he had to begin the working day. On still other nights, however, he would wander about in the small hours even though Mother lay sleeping. Restless and sick from something that wasn't revealed in the diagnosis, he would find himself unable to lie down or sit still, and would finally sleep standing up, leaning against the fridge door with his head on his arm.

Just as he kept up working at his job, for he couldn't afford to quit, so too he continued, even increased, his work with the union, an organization that earned Mother's ridicule and jealousy. One day he announced that he would be going out to an important meeting the following night, a strike vote if my memory is correct. Such an absence was rare and he was careful to say that, barring the unexpected, he would return by a certain hour, perhaps ten o'clock. Over the course of the evening, I watched with mounting anxiety as Mother moved with quick little steps from object to object, first straightening things, then unstraightening them and lastly banging them this way and that, a sign that her plunging blood sugar and rising bile had crossed somewhere in the blackness. As ten o'clock neared, she went from room to room and reset whatever timepieces the house had—the ship's clock that had belonged to Grandfather Fetherling, the plastic one on the wall near the kitchen sink, a couple of others embedded in radios, the clock in their bedroom. I was horrified and fascinated to observe her mind at work. The plan, clearly, was to create the illusion that it was later than it actually was, thereby justifying an even louder argument than the normal one that his absence had deprived her of. Except that in her bibulous state she had set all these clocks to different times. When Father returned at ten, the abuse struck him like a blast of oppressive heat as soon as he entered. In a moment, looking at first one clock and then another, he realized what she'd done. It was the only time I ever saw him cry.

Another night, Mother stormed out of the house, pausing only to slam the door more than once; she said that as she was being held prisoner on this damn hilltop she would walk all the way into the city, and started off in the direction of Suicide Hill. Father felt he had no choice but to follow. Fortunately, he reached her before she got to the point beyond which even a healthy person would have huffed and puffed climbing back up again.

One day he had a doctor's appointment immediately after work, and as I was in the city to begin my shift at the Academy, he and I had dinner together alone, for the first time in our lives. We sat in a fast food place near the hospital, overlooking what skyline there was and the river just beyond. He talked about characters he'd known, such as a salesman who always introduced himself as "a traveller in risqué novelties," which indeed he was, or a fellow whose avocation was trying to convince others that the birth of Christ had taken place at a specific moment of a particular day in what would be our July, a claim for which he was never without incomprehensible evidence, crumpled in his pockets. I tried to bring the conversation around to Mother, but he was nervous as usual and in a hurry to reminisce.

Finally I asked bluntly why the two of them didn't separate and get a divorce. I had made the suggestion a couple of times when I was small, when people were surprised that I knew the meaning of the words. This was different. It seemed to me the situation was desperate, though of course I was acting out of concern for my own welfare as well as his. The two of us could get a place to live, I said. It would be the two of us since Dale was overseas now in the navy. I thought I knew of a small apartment. I said there would be enough money to support Mother and still live apart if we played our cards right, not knowing whether the statement was true. But he wouldn't listen. He said that they'd gone to a marriage counsellor once but that she'd kept insulting the man.

"The next time I see the doctor I'll ask him to write her a prescription for some happy pills."

Amphetamines.

And I believe he did so, but of course that was no solution, not even temporarily.

In addition to hoodlums and ward-heelers and their hangers-on, the Academy also attracted a number of newspapermen, including a splenetic columnist on the *News-Register*, who had drunk his way there from the Philadelphia *Inquirer*. There were rumours later, after his death, that he had been on the payroll of the Ohio gang in their war against Big Bill Lias and his successors. I don't know if the stories were true, but anyone could see that he'd shinnied up the local establishment and had a lot of power which he enjoyed exercising.

One evening he appeared, as advertised, to act as celebrity referee in a high-stakes pool game between Don Willis, the eastern states champ, and Wee Willie Nassif, the local favourite. Nassif was a diminutive man, five-feet-two or -three, so short that the sign NO MASSE SHOTS could not possibly have been hung there for his benefit. His pinstripe trousers came up to the middle of his chest and he always wore his hat indoors.

The room looked like a Hogarth engraving of a cock-fight. Spectators were jammed shoulder to shoulder. Those occupying the high seats held fat bouquets of currency in both fists. Of the others, some stood on chairs dragged in from the restaurant and the remainder took their chances with the smoke, which cut the room into thick layers. Wee Willie won the break and ran nineteen or twenty balls at twenty dollars a ball. Then it was Willis's turn. He was still at it after a half-hour or so.

This was a swank cultural event, as important as any first night, and I did a gold-rush business ferrying drinks from the bar. But however preferable that was to some of my lesser duties (for one thing, it brought me gratuities), it wasn't what I hoped to do in life. I thought of myself as a writer. I was gradually pulling together a thick manuscript of poems that I proposed to entitle *Sturdy Cripples.* The phrase came from Coleridge, who praised Donne as "Rhyme's sturdy cripple, fancy's maze and clue;/ Wit's forge and fire-blast, meaning's press and screw." The term seemed to me to have a more forceful application in terms of the lives of people I was familiar with. But I wanted to try every type of writing, not only poetry, so as to be led naturally to whatever form seemed appropriate for the immediate purpose. I needed some place where I could get training, and I had my eye set on one of the newspapers. I had read enough totally obsolete books to know that this was how one proceeded.

Following the match, I debated whether I should approach the columnist. Fearing rejection, I hesitated. It wasn't long afterwards, however, that I overheard part of a conversation between two customers in the restaurant while I was mopping the floor. There was an old fellow (in his forties!) with a faint grey moustache. He was talking to a young guy, obviously a colleague. He was making a point about the relative advantages of working on an AM rather than a PM. I noticed where they went when they left: across Market Street and down Newsboy Alley.

I saw Jimmy Simon, a runner and very small-time bookie, standing where he'd been standing for years, outside Fette's Newsstand, far enough away to pick up on any activity in the street, close enough to hear the ringing of the pay phones inside. I asked him who the guy with the moustache was and he told me. "Bob Terry." I waited days for him to come back in for a cup of coffee when I was on duty. He treated me kindly and told me I should see Haven Thompson at the *Intelligencer.*

Thompson (it's a pleasure to remember him here) was about forty-five, lean, rugged and powerful, suggesting an eagle that had been up all night. I simply stood at his desk until he noticed me and I could fumble out my request. He had no job to give, of course. But as one who was reading the classics among newspapermen's autobiographies, I knew precisely what to do. Every night, as soon as my duties at the Academy would permit, I sneaked back into the newsroom and hovered in his field of peripheral vision, gently reminding him of my existence, waiting to be pressed into service for any purpose, however humble. I was determined to hang about like a stray dog until the proprietors wearied of throwing me out into the street. Certainly it didn't take long to become a familiar object of derision among the staff, a state that delighted me as it proved I was being noticed. In two weeks, my belief in tradition was justified: the editor concluded that my desperation to be on his newspaper was adequate to such a noble ambition. The sports department was short-handed, and I was given a telephone headset and pressed into service taking down box scores from high school athletic events. No job as such was mentioned, no money discussed. Still, I smiled inwardly, knowing that I had won myself a permanent place, though I very nearly spoiled the opportunity.

The next night I came in as usual and was collared by Cliff McWilliams, the red-haired sports editor, who sent me to cover a football game at the Island Stadium.

This was a different matter from typing players' names as they were fed to me over the phone. The simple truth was that I didn't know how football was played, didn't know the rules, didn't know how many innings or periods constituted a game. I doubt that I could retrieve a better proof of how remote I was from the interests of mainstream America, in fact antagonistic to the culture, so called, and it equally so to me. I sat in the press-box, staring anxiously at the printed form on which I was expected to record the manoeuvres of the various players and other vital information. At half-time (a term I knew) a kindly man from a radio station took pity on me when I explained my dilemma and let me copy his information onto my sheet and look over his shoulder for the second half. I never saw him again and have never remembered his name if indeed I ever heard it, but he has always had my gratitude. I've never known whether Cliff McWilliams suspected what had gone on. I imagine that he did and chose to exercise compassion. The decision was ironic since it was he, before Haven Thompson succeeded him as editor of the paper, who had hounded my friend Mary Tominack with a kind of vigilante intensity. He surely would have been hostile if he'd known of my involvement with her. At that time, however, I had yet to become notorious in Wheeling.

Thompson said he had a good report about me from McWilliams and would take me on as a reporter on the night trick. I felt very proud when he sent me to the business office with a letter instructing them to enter me on the payroll as a reporter at eighty dollars a week. A reporter. It sounded wonderful. The money sounded fine as well, a 40 per cent increase over my earnings from the Academy, though after deductions the figure was $67.75. Looking back from even short retrospect, it would amaze me that I should ever have been a reporter, given that I usually couldn't talk on the telephone, was terrified of strangers and had no special interest in the facts—was actually quite hostile to the old-fashioned tyranny of meaningless information devoid of texture, discrimination or style—but then perhaps I was no more unlikely a guest than the *Intelligencer* was a host.

Like the other Wheeling paper and what seemed a majority of those in the state, it had been owned by H.C. Ogden, a queer combination of robber baron and reformer whose initials did not, as his enemies used to insist, stand for Hard Cash. He had died in the 1940s, but his portrait still scrutinized everyone entering the newsroom. His proxy on Earth was his grandson, the publisher, a youthful thirty-one, whom the editorial-page editor, who started in the business in 1911, called the Old Man, for such was the habit of a lifetime.

The structure on Main Street was of about the same vintage as the editorial page editor; it connected through a series of doors to a separate mechanical plant in back. This in turn gave way to a building on Market Street: the publisher's bank—literally, he was the president of it and kept his office upstairs, over the vault. To sentimental cynics, this complex was known as the Ogden School of Journalism. For various reasons, including the fact that it was the headquarters and flagship of the chain, it seemed to attract people on their way up and others on their way down.

Just beyond the reach of my own memory, for instance, was a former diplomat, his foreign service career in yellowed tatters, who insisted on writing his copy in longhand. I do remember another former diplomatist, Malcolm Brice, who had worked on the Montreal *Herald* and the Ottawa *Journal* early in the century and then served in the American embassy in Dublin. Then there was the eccentric business editor who devoted himself to the promotion of what he called the Midland Canal, a scheme that, if ever approved by Washington, would link the Ohio River with the Atlantic and make international ports of Wheeling and Steubenville. Our region editor, it was said, remembered back to the early 1920s when James Thurber was the *Intelligencer's* stringer for Ohio politics, during the period when he was working his way from the Columbus *Dispatch* to the *New Yorker.* This region editor had been on the paper so long, in fact, that he had memorized all the possible signals emitted by the fire-alarm box that went off in the newsroom whenever an alarm was sounded; when the racket began, he would put down his pencil, chew his harelip, and listen for a moment. "Forty-fifth and Wood," he would finally say. "The Christian Steinmetz Cigar Box Factory." He'd then tell the reporter the number of the nearest pay phone to the scene, should it be necessary to elicit a first-hand account from some passerby.

These humans, it seemed to me, were sacred relics of a profane past and older than the furniture, which was decrepit. They went hand in glove with a lot of bright younger people whom Haven Thompson had attracted to the place in his campaign, somewhat over the publisher's dead body, I believe, of attempting to make the paper a model of what one in its circulation class should be. They had found themselves there after coming from points as far apart as Connecticut and Florida. One fellow had gone to Cornell with Richard Fariña, the folksinger who was Joan Baez's brother-in-law, and was rumoured to be the original of Gnossos Popodoupolis, the crazy sixties anti-hero in Fariña's new novel *Been Down So Long It Looks Like Up to Me* (which means that he must have been there at the same time as Thomas Pynchon too).

I wrote hundreds of obituaries, possibly thousands, learning about such matters as the various ways the requiem mass is celebrated in the Roman, Greek and Armenian traditions, and I became well known in mortuary circles. At one time it had been the custom for every white undertaker to appear just before Christmas and leave a bottle of bourbon on the obit desk (for some reason, the Black undertakers were expected to give gin instead). The way this practice had died out was the only evidence of the new spirit of reform that was always said to be rampant in the city. One would still see undertakers in person, however, when the hour was late and the deadline nigh and it was especially important that a deceased, usually a bigwig, make it into the first edition. In one such emergency situation I met Sandra. Her father had a funeral parlour across the river and was also a small-time radio evangelist. Much to her embarrassment, he sent her over one night with some details about a client, and we fell into easy conversation—always a sign with me of a potential friendship.

She worked part-time as a lifeguard at a hotel swimming pool. As the job occupied her only in the afternoons, she wasn't bound to keep regular hours, and was thus free to join me in many of my nocturnal assignments and pursuits. We spent a lot of time together in hospital emergency rooms. There was seldom any trace of the specific news I was sent to such places to fetch, but at least there was a lesson to be had. The lesson was that a knife wound in any place except the heart, serious though it might look, is usually quite survivable, but that a corresponding gunshot wound, however superficial it might seem at first, is always much worse than it appears, given the massive cell damage caused by even the smallest calibre bullet fired from a great distance.

One of my duties on the lobster shift was to make the last check with the police. Around midnight, earlier on Sundays, I would scoot up Newsboy Alley to the cop-shop and ask to see the green sheets detailing recent complaints, accidents and arrests. There was seldom much activity at that hour, and I would often go through the motions of exchanging light banter with Icehouse Hixenbaugh, a portly old desk sergeant, so called because his family had once operated an ice business in South Wheeling. He suffered from a strange condition that I assumed, in my callowness, was proof of stupidity, but now understand was probably a developmental disability akin to dyslexia: he spoke and wrote in redundancies. For example, if there was no one to cover the desk when he needed to nip out for a beer, he would tape a crudely lettered sign to the door, BACK IN FIVE MINUTES OF TIME. Not five minutes of pork chops or five minutes of red-dog slag. I remember one weekend asking him with a cheery voice whether anything was going on. "Not much," he said, flipping through the paperwork on his clipboards, "except that the vice boys have knocked over a whorehouse of ill repute." The phrase has remained with me ever since as a perfect metaphor for journalism. No ordinary whorehouse, mind you, but one of ill repute.

Sandra and I would arrange to steal moments together wherever and whenever we could, depending on her movements and my workload. I remember long talks we had on the wooden bench in the detective bureau, down the hall from the counter where Icehouse stood guard. On one occasion we talked about poetry, but I can't recall what it was I was supposed to be doing at the time. We spent at least one memorable evening necking in a car during a stake-out, waiting for the cops to arrive with their sledgehammers and smash the slot machines at a road-house. The tip was bogus. It wasn't an election year and the brownshirts never showed. Just as well.

Another time she came along when I had to cover a large gathering, a fish fry or an ox roast perhaps, of the local Democratic machine. That was a pleasant assignment to draw because the political science practised there was always a delight for anyone with a sense of the picaresque. One of the men who served as governor in my youth was discovered years later driving a taxi in Chicago; another went to prison with fourteen of his officials and friends on charges of fraud and misuse of funds. The mechanism, with all its peculiarities, always survived such changes. Perhaps it even throve on them. I was too young to have seen it at first hand but heard vivid testimony, for it was all around, of the way John Kennedy had purchased the state in his race for the crucial presidential primary in 1960. At a given signal, his father's men had fanned out to every airfield and train station with bags of cash, lots of it. The cash went to the members of the county sheriffs' association, the same officials who sometimes let their prisoners out to help put up campaign posters. The sheriffs in turn would distribute the loot among those most likely to exercise their franchise in the proper fashion. It was like a paramilitary operation. So indeed was West Virginia politics. Everybody was in the pocket of somebody. It was like a diagram of fishes of all different sizes, such as might be used to illustrate the principle of the food chain. This particular afternoon stands out because Senator Robert Byrd, in his youth a Klan sympathizer and in later years the majority leader of the U.S. Senate, whipped off the jacket of his five-hundred-dollar silk suit, and clambered up onto the flat bed of a truck. There, to attract the crowd for his speech, he put his fiddle to his chin and played "Turkey in the Straw." Played it like a statesman.

One reason for all the sneaking around was that Sandra's father (her mother had died long ago) didn't care for me, despite my respected position as a frequent obituarist. I had my suspicions about him as well, for he was a genuinely creepy character. His nose was covered in blackheads, giving it the look of a fresh strawberry, and his morals were such that they did no credit to the image of funeral directors or evangelists—nor of jewellers, for that matter. In his office in back of the funeral home, he dealt in secondhand rings—Knights of Columbus rings, signet rings, rings with monograms, rings with big stones. He displayed them in stacks of plush-lined trays, the kind in which the rings are protected from theft by a thin bar running down the centre of each row. A nice array of men's and women's watches, also accumulated during decades of stripping the bodies, was more or less a sideline. In an unsuccessful attempt to be nice to each other, I bought a fabulously expensive watch he offered me for only thirty dollars, but later I had to pawn it in New York when I'd run out of blood to sell to the blood bank, and was never in a position to redeem it.

I wasn't at the paper very long before I had an opportunity to play an insignificant part in covering a rather extraordinary story, the Bishop Pike affair. James A. Pike was an Episcopalian bishop or, to be precise, the Resigned Bishop of California. He had previously been the dean of St. John the Divine in New York, the world's largest cathedral (St. Peter's in Rome being technically a church, not a cathedral). But as he rose in the hierarchy, becoming one of the two or three best-known clergymen in the country, his relations with the church establishment grew fractious. The first incident was in the early 1950s when he'd refused to accept an honorary degree from an Episcopal university that didn't admit Blacks. From that point right up to the Vietnam War, he had engaged in a campaign of rebellious liberalism that seemed to be testing the social and in fact the ethical relevancy, not only of Episcopalians, but also of Christian denominations generally. Why only a year before he'd dared to ordain a woman, a known woman, as deacon of his diocese! The bishops assembled in woodsy seclusion at Oglebay Park in Wheeling to try him for heresy. My role was merely to supply some colour to the experienced reporters, but that's enough to allow me to brag of having covered a heresy trial. That's a distinction much rarer than merely to have studied this figure of the

1960s, who's forgotten now but was as important then as, say, Timothy Leary, and who died a few years later in true 1960s (and true biblical) fashion, while wandering in the desert in search of fulfilment.

My only other brush with the mighty was when Walter Reuther, the president of the United Auto Workers union, the architect of the merger of the AFL and the CIO, and the inventor of the sit-down strike, had his bodyguards throw me out of a funeral parlour. His father, Valentine Reuther, an ancient Wheeling radical who had once been a drayman for Schulbach's brewery and often ran for Congress as a socialist, had died. The famous and powerful son was to leave the bargaining table during an impending strike to attend the services, and I was to try to get a comment from him on the progress of the talks. I waited in the parking lot and tried to get his attention as he entered the building. Failing, I had no choice, it seemed, but to approach him in the chapel itself. One of his eyebrows flickered and two thugs in shiny suits put me back in the parking lot again. By luck more than good sense, I managed to reach him by phone later, just as he was leaving town, and got at least some quote, however feeble.

For the most part, though, I was inconspicuous, joyously so, even though I was omnipresent or tried to be. I was able to befriend bail bondsmen and rounders, occasionally stumbling on a feature story that called for a slight literary flair, as when I found an old miner back up in the hills behind the Ferry who had once played in one of the miners' marching bands. "In those days you had your Welshmen's band and your Pollack band and your German band and so on and so forth, and we got four dollars for every miner's funeral we played at and there was enough funerals to keep 'em working all the time."

I was trying to juggle these many different roles, to find my way as a writer while staying alive as a reporter, to remain on acceptable terms with Sergeant Icehouse Hixenbaugh at night while his colleagues trailed me during the day because I was subversive, to keep all my sets of acquaintances apart from one another, and my life compartmentalized. To be productive amid the chaos I had to keep moving all the time, literally day and night. In such a situation, one to which I would find myself reverting for long periods later in my life, I came to value whatever little bits of ritual the whirl of events allowed. One of these was an afternoon meal with some of the old newshounds each Thursday, once we had cashed our cheques at the publisher's bank. The sessions took place at a restaurant near the head of the Alley that hadn't been touched since the 1930s. The cast of diners changed slightly from week to week, but often included Ed Whelan, a man in his early fifties, whose moustache looked as though it had been drawn with a 4B pencil. His worst problem was alcoholism, but he also once had been an inmate of the federal drug addiction facility at Lexington, Kentucky, where he had known several important jazz figures. While the rest of us began to eat, he would put most of his pay into an envelope and send it to his wife in Cincinnati as the weekly instalment on his huge matrimonial debt. Then he would take off his hat—it wasn't a homburg but it had that same air of obsolete solidity. He would look at it and roll the brim up all the way round and then put it squarely back on his head and tell me about his problems.

He had been discharged from more papers than anyone else I've ever known or heard about. He was on his third or so swing through Wheeling and was desperately clinging to his position only through the affection of some older executives who went back to the days of Hard Cash Ogden himself. Whelan drank in long binges, which seemed to be touched off by almost anything. Before capital punishment was abolished, even before the electric chair, when convicts were hanged in the high concrete room in the penitentiary at Moundsville, a few miles downriver, it was the warden's custom to place bottles of good bourbon along the gallery desk so the reporters and legal witnesses could get some refreshment before the gruesome ceremony. Most would require more than a little such preparation. Sober observers said this was what the warden hoped for, so that the press wouldn't notice if the executioner misplaced the noose so that the victim slowly strangled instead of dying of a swift broken neck. After each hanging, I was told, Whelan would disappear for days, maybe weeks, not so much out of horror at the event, which he perhaps had not seen from beneath the table, but because the free bottles had reactivated his need. He would sometimes joke that he was "livin' on Jones Street."

As if that weren't bad enough, he was also an ex-con, and none the better for the experience. Seeing a licence plate was enough to set him off in a wave of harsh nostalgia for the life in the institutions where he'd done time, latterly for taking a pot-shot at a clergyman with whose wife he had been fooling around. His own wife, out of disgust with his drinking as much as from a sense of estrangement due to his absence, had divorced him while he was inside and got custody of their son, who was now grown up and working for one of the wire services. Upon his release Mrs. Whelan had somehow won alimony or support payments retroactive to the start of his sentence.

All in all it was a pretty good joint, he was telling me one day in the restaurant. *Medium security, built for six hundred and with only maybe a thousand guys in it at the time. Everybody got all the beef they wanted and there was plenty of time to walk around on the work details every day. Lockdown every night, of course, four guys in a cell, they were big cells with two pairs of bunks and a head and sink. At first there were only three of us in this one cell, you see, but finally a young fellow transferred in and it came out that he couldn't write, didn't know how, and would I write to his wife for him? Well, this went on for weeks, months. He's telling me what to put in the letters and it's darling this and honey that. Later I find out the guy's in for incest with his twelve-year-old daughter. Here all the time he'd had me writing all this stuff to her. Well, word got out, of course. A con said to him in the rec yard, "I'd never fuck my own daughter, man, unless she was really worth it." Then he stabbed him.*

I was listening but he would have continued even if I hadn't paid attention. That's what he was like when he got caught up in one of his nightmare reveries. He was letting his meal go cold while I ploughed through mine.

Now OP in Columbus, that's a different matter. OP was the Ohio Penitentiary, a literary sort of place. O. Henry had done his time there. So had Chester Himes, the author of *Cotton Comes to Harlem* and other novels, who wrote of seeing two inmates stab each other to death in an argument over whether Paris was the capital of France or France the capital of Paris. *In OP you got forty-six-hundred and they're in the cell all the time except for haircuts every two weeks or the exercise yard or of course in the infirmary. There are people who fell there for nothin' at all, nothin'. I knew one guy, he was in for stealing copper pipe from the place he worked for, for god sake. Being such a student of the mortuary arts, I know you'll appreciate this one: some dumb undertaker put in a fake death certificate for himself so the insurance would pay off a fifteen-hundred-dollar car loan or something. Anyway, all of them seemed to get out eventually on parole or writs. Now the way it was with me was that I was there less than eighteen months and for the first year I got drunk once a week. Julep, they call it. Made from fruit juice, any kind of fruit juice. You make it or you buy it. Nobody's supposed to have more than one dollar at a time but of course everybody does. Lots of things used as a medium of exchange of course. One con paid money for the shit of white boys, so white boys' shit became a kind of money.* I made a face to remind him I was eating. *Sorry, kid. Anyway as I was saying I got out of there, parole, but for two years I wasn't even supposed to go into restaurants where hard stuff was served, not even poolrooms, not to mention that I couldn't leave the country if I'd wanted to. So really, when you come down to it, I figured I wasn't much better off than I was before except that now, outside, I knew that anything you get for free you can keep.*

It was at that point that I looked up and saw Father's friend Alec standing in the doorway, squinting as his eyes adjusted to the darkness. I sensed what the trouble was before the thought was articulated in the brain.

"I've got some bad news for you, son." The softness

in his voice was startling. "Your father's had a sick spell at the plant."

"Is it serious?" The question seemed to be coming from someone else.

"I'm afraid it is."

I was getting my coat from the hook. "He's dead, isn't he?" I asked.

"I'm afraid so, son." Again the gentleness from such a big rough man. "I'm sorry."

Alec had his car out front and we drove to the hospital on 20th Street. It was the hospital where I'd been born and it looked like a crumbling castle. Parts of it hung over the shelf that had been carved out of the hillside. We went down to the cellar. Mother was in the corridor in a state of near hysteria. She kept saying, "They've taken him from me, *they've* taken him from me!" Her sister Ruth motioned me to the morgue and pointed to the body lying on the gurney. We pulled back the sheet. He was wearing a plaid flannel work shirt and his lips were as blue as old denim. His eyelids seemed very thin, almost translucent.

I went back to the paper looking for Haven Thompson. I found him in the back shop, conferring with Winnie Winiesdorffer, one of the compositors, who was working at the stone. I told him what had happened and that I needed some time off. Later that night, after I'd seen the undertaker, I returned to the newsroom and wrote the obituary.

There was much to be done and I did most of it wrong. We notified the Red Cross, which contacted the navy, which granted my brother emergency leave to fly in from California, where he was stationed at the time.

Much to my embarrassment, Father had been a Freemason. This was fine for an English policeman, in my view, but demeaning in a parent, though I see now that he was only looking for companionship and that, once again, Mother ruined everything with her increasingly worrisome behaviour. In any event, Dale and I had both heard him say over the years that he should be buried wearing his Masonic apron, and so we supplied it to the undertaker when we took in his blue serge suit. But the sight of him wearing it there in his casket was a great affront to his fellow Masons, for, as I should have known, the apron is only to be used with official Masonic funerals, which this one wasn't. The screw-up was somehow typical.

Mother carried on wildly and those who came to pay their respects were for the most part chary of talking to her. In her first few days as a widow, she sold all her husband's tools and began throwing out photos of his parents. A year or so later, long after I had left, she had a tombstone put up over his grave. It bore the inscription

Step softly please
Here lies my soul mate
His constant and tender love
Shall forever light my way

which frankly I thought was a bit much in the circumstances. But I saw it for the first time more than ten years after the fact.

By then, Wheeling seemed to have disappeared almost totally. With the collapse of the American steel industry, the city lost at least half its population and virtually all of its claim on urban-ness. The city I remember was a late-modernist miniature, complete in every detail, with a financial district, say, and a jewellery district and a wholesale produce district. It was a big city shrunk in scale. When I saw it next, downtown was largely vacant, and arsonists who had nothing better to do worked to make it seem even worse than it was.

Ironically, both Bethlehem and 29th Street were destroyed in one swoop, by construction of one of the last links in the nationwide system of Interstate highways, which President Eisenhower had initiated as a means of evacuating the people during a communist attack from the air. Even the mob had called it quits, and eventually the authorities would finally succeed in putting poor Paul Hankish, by then a seriously ill diabetic, away for life.

The city was returning to the frontier whence it came. Deer started wandering down from the hills. They quickly lost their fear and their numbers grew. Wild turkey were next. The wilderness was getting its health back perhaps. Vines were poised to start climbing up the monuments.

I could recognize a few buildings here and there. There were even a few people still around I remembered, but they hated me for my political apostasy. I felt that my personal past had vanished, been used up, been consumed in a fire-storm, and I soon came to feel that this was probably just as well.

But I've allowed myself to run ahead of the narrative.

I was in New York now, living under the name A.J. Hand, trying to come to terms with recent events.

Father hadn't left any money, but in his last few months he had paid off the mortgage on the hate-filled little house in Bethlehem, and I got the impression that there were some unexpected windfall sums, small insurance policies from his employer and his union, perhaps even from the Freemasons. I wasn't certain Mother was capable of maximizing whatever resources there were. I proposed that together we make a full accounting, so we would know what our position was. We fell to arguing when she refused to share any information whatever. The quarrel was of course only a shorthand reference to her lifelong anger and also to my newfound sense, which I've needed years of thought and therapy to put behind me, that she was culpable in his death—the death of the only person who I never doubted for a moment loved me. I told her I would stay for twelve months, pay the bills from my newspaper salary (they consumed it) and help her in whatever other way I could. By the end of the given period, I figured, the money from the estate would either be gone or it wouldn't: whichever way would be a clear sign of the true situation. I never determined how much of her mourning was guilt or what portion of her grief was loneliness. I could see only that, without her foil, her temper deteriorated even further. I was hard put to avoid the gaping pit, and finally had to move out of the house.

I checked into the YMCA on 20th Street where a friend of mine lived who was talking about launching a little magazine (as with so many little magazines, one would need only the premiere issue in order to have a complete run). There was barely space in his room for the iron bed and the chest of drawers with cigarette burns all round the edge, much less for the portrait busts he'd been making. I found the Y a loudly congenial place, as it was about to go off, pending the day when methadone users would outnumber Methodists. At twenty-one dollars a week, however, the rent was more than I could afford. When one of the reporters at the *Intell* left town, I was able to assume her spot in a communal apartment in the old flat-iron building at Main and South Streets, between the newsroom and the cavernous railway freight sheds by the river. Five of us lived there for what one or two persons might have expected to pay for other accommodations of equivalent squalour. A determining factor in the price was the way that one could reach the place only by passing through the premises of the business that occupied the ground floor. The establishment was called the Stark Artificial Limb Company. We had latchkeys and at night would grope our way across the showroom in the dark, bumping into wooden legs and other such prostheses.

I marvel now at how busy I was and to so little purpose. No doubt it was partly to put emotional distance between Mother and myself that I ran everywhere and took part in everything, though beneath the desperation, I believe, was a real sense of joy at being able to indulge an appetite for experience. The war dominated the news and reaction to it was becoming the central element in the arts, whether boldly stated or not, and I entered into a stage, lasting perhaps a dozen years, when I felt completely attuned to the rhythms of the popular culture even though I was not a direct consumer of its goods. All through that period, for example, I never had a stereo or even a radio but knew all the new music intimately, as though some generational organ inside me had sucked it in from the atmosphere and drawn it through my pores. Looking back, I seem to have been balanced on the moment, living in past and present alike, nocturnally and in daylight. I was sick, frightened and disgusted most of the time, but strangely I was never more open to experience.

Through Mary Tominack I got to know Don West, a famous folk poet, the author of *Anger in the Land* and other chapbooks in the obsolete conventions: the son of a southern sharecropper, he was a far more important person than he was a writer. After studying in Sweden, he returned to America to open a racially integrated school designed to coax abilities out of students from throughout the Appalachians. Later, he defied death threats to help unionize the miners in Kentucky and the textile workers in North Carolina, and subsequently taught in Atlanta, where the state government fired him for his anti-segregationist views and the Ku Klux Klan burned his house. Later still, the McCarthy witch-hunters went after him. (How often I heard of those being attacked by the Klan also being pursued by the House Un-American Activities Committee, a convenient coincidence in the same manner as the Chicago mafia and the CIA working together to harass Castro.) Through Don in turn I met his daughter Hedy West, the folk-singer and songwriter who lived in England; from her exile she put me in touch with various people there, particularly after I promoted and did the advance work on a series of concerts she gave in the Wheeling area to benefit one arm of the Movement or the other. Working nights allowed me pretty free access to the newspaper's cameras and darkroom, which led me to photography, and I got to the point where some friends in the Movement put on an exhibit of my slumscapes at the Jesuit college. That in turn encouraged me to make small personal films. The first was small indeed, though Bill Forbes and Arthur Tarlow appeared in it, along with a girlfriend of the day, whose devoir was to run along the top of a retaining wall with her long hair trailing behind her as required by the script, which I made up as we went. Tarlow kept insisting that the film be called *Prometheus in Bondage.* The second one, I decided, should be more ambitious, and I began scrounging equipment and personnel. Among the volunteers I met Jasmine Erskine, who was two or three years older than I was.

I find it difficult to describe her without using the word *very.* She was very attractive, with a sort of butterscotch complexion, and very smart and very funny, very rebellious towards authority, and very committed to politics, being the child of wealthy liberal parents who, though divorced, were united in seeing opposition to the war as part of a continuum that also included the New Deal. It wasn't long after volunteering her services that she pronounced my filmmaking silly and drew me into her own world of personal expression, a plexus of painting, found sculpture and assemblage. One day at an abandoned building I happened on a wonderful wooden sign, as weathered as some old hobo's face. Large red letters had once said POSITIVELY NO TRESPASSING but only the first word still remained. I carried it around with me for months as all-purpose statement, as a pet almost, finding it an adjoining seat in restaurants and at the theatre. Nothing further needed to be said.

Jasmine's father was a physician who, in addition to his medical practice, operated a clinic where well-heeled alcoholics could dry out in a bucolic setting. Over the years the business had made him as wealthy as any of his patients, and Jasmine had been reared in an up-to-date kind of opulence that left me, in my first brush with prosperity, ill at ease. She was quick to put down my obvious discomfort and just as quick to trivialize her advantages, but that did little to improve my situation and had the effect, I believe, of increasing the attraction I felt, which was dangerously unrequited even when she was at her most passionate. Dr. Erskine was perplexed by all this, as he must have been by all her male friends, whom he tended to mistake for one another. He was a big man with a bald bullet-shaped head and no neck, somewhat in the manner of Erich von Stroheim. Silver-framed spectacles only added to the general air of metallurgy that contradicted his expansive cordiality in most matters except his daughter's moral welfare. He was extremely proud of his richly panelled den, where by pressing buttons he could make a complete bar appear from behind one wall. "Come on in here, boy," he would say, grabbing my shoulder. "I want to introduce you to a couple friends of mine. Jack Daniels and Johnny Walker." Her mother had remarried and lived in New York and Jasmine, it was understood, would join her there next autumn when she started NYU. An odd choice, that, for her father, I'm fairly certain, had gone to Columbia and she had the money and the grades to study wherever she pleased, but typical of her also. Until then she was putting in her time at Bethany College, a local private school, where she somehow got me a meal ticket to the cafeteria so that I could keep up my caloric intake.

The doctor always seemed to be at home, and I had a growing number of roommates who came and went at all hours. These facts went together to force Jasmine and me to make love at unusual times and in even stranger places, though this was very much her preference. She enjoyed a thin blade of danger to heighten the excitement. The need may have been a family trait, as her father, it seemed to me, liked to see how close he could come to alcoholism without erasing the line that separated him from his clientele. On one occasion, she and I undressed each other within sight of him, or what would have been in sight of him had he not fallen asleep in a deep leather chair with a crystal decanter at his elbow. That time, I believe, we risked homicide, for he was especially protective of his remarkable daughter, particularly given the guilt he felt at the divorce.

Her eroticism was so extreme and yet so offhand: that's half of what made her irresistible. It was as though she were possessed of wonderful arcane knowledge that it is given only a few people to have—alchemy, perhaps, or a mastery of some delicate surgical procedure—that bored her to tears except at the precise moment it was being put at the service of a memorable cause. She reserved much of her intensity for art, about which she was in fact downright profligate in her love (that was the other part of the attraction). I've never forgotten a day we spent walking through the Carnegie International at Pittsburgh where her brilliant impromptu comments drew a small crowd. The people followed us around the gallery from room to room, huddling just within earshot, and all the while Jasmine remained oblivious to them, showing a combination of scrutiny and myopia that was altogether characteristic. I suppose that like those eavesdroppers I was always courting condescension to associate with persons who were smarter than I was. Only by that method could I create an environment in which I felt I was developing whatever talent or ideas might have got trapped inside me somehow.

I was determined to save myself from the vacuousness that was all around me as well as from the hatred and violence. I wasn't proficient at articulating my ideas even to myself, and that's always a much easier proposition than transmitting them; but I did know in so many words what the larger difficulty appeared to be. The problem was not the war, the problem was America. For some time I had been nurturing a plan. Now with Jasmine I had an escape route as well.

The stated period during which I had promised Mother that I would remain close to her side was drawing to an end. As the deadline approached, she became more imaginative in her denunciations, daring me to leave as she damned me to hell. One night I went into her room and found her sitting up in bed scowling. I've come to say goodbye, I said. She was distant but not actually hostile.

I left.

Jasmine's mother, a stylish and well-coiffed woman, lived with her second husband in a spacious apartment at Fifty-eighth and Lex that was full of expensive art and heavy ornaments. She seemed to feel that Jasmine's interest in me could be explained only in terms of my being a collectible. She had extra bedrooms galore and insisted that Jasmine live there with her and her stepfather while going to university. It did make economic sense. I knew what the housing problem was like, for I was sharing a place on Avenue A near Tompkins Square, where each morning the discarded syringes lay thick as walnuts on the ground. The ancient rooms were high but narrow, with mould forming on the outside walls, and the corners were full of stuff that lay unclaimed since the time whoever owned it had died or been sent to Riker's Island. But Jasmine and I were together every day when she came down to Washington Square for classes.

In those days Greenwich Village was still a flourishing enterprise, though it had taken a rough turn. Walking up and down, huddled inside a reefer-coat from the army surplus store, you got somewhat the same feeling you get in England, that history lies in layers beneath your feet. The past was almost tactile but it wasn't real. What set it apart was its improbable innocence. Whether you looked at the residue of the First World War generation of writers or the atmosphere that Dylan had bequeathed to his folk-singing friends in 1963 or so, you couldn't help being brought up short by the lightness and optimism that had vanished somehow, been killed off by the new realities. One of these was the occupation of the East Village. It didn't have the same artistic history—until relatively recently it had been part of the Lower East Side of Italian and Jewish immigrants—and there was nothing to give it the hard centre of cultural humanism so apparent in the other, which people were beginning to call the West Village. The New Wave was under way there. You could see it in the rejection of gentleness and in the violence that informed the happenings, the light shows and most of all the street life.

I had a routine because I had a mission. Each morning, before the lack of sleep disabled me, I would ascend Fifth Avenue to the main public library at Forty-second Street and study the Canadiana there. It wasn't all in one place but it amounted to an extraordinary collection. Since the day Mary Tominack first put the notion of Canada in my head, I had been subscribing to Canadian periodicals and through Jasmine's example monitoring the CBC. In time I got to the point of maintaining a correspondence with a few Canadian writers. Now, sitting in the library, sometimes taking pills to help me stay awake in the impossibly overheated reading room, I deepened my commitment to learning Canadian politics, economics, culture—the works. The abiding tradition of anti-Americanism, always present deep down in the lay public if not always pursued by cowardly governments, was one I found especially attractive, though I was careful not to let my own enthusiasms shape my curriculum. For the only time in my life, I was a serious pupil in addition to being a good student.

Jasmine's commuting schedule, from uptown to downtown, from downtown to uptown, allowed her to get lost along the way by the simple expedient of disappearing at the bottom of the loop. At the end of the day, when I had returned bleary-eyed from the library, she would vanish conveniently from Washington Square to reposition herself in the area around St. Mark's Place. W.H. Auden lived somewhere along that street, but we never saw him; he would have been incongruous to say the least among the poets who did hang out there, such as Ray Bremser, with his famous mumble, or Ted Berrigan, or Joel Oppenheimer, the leading figure of that day and place.

It was not easy to forget that there was a war on. The city was polarized, and our group certainly, and perhaps the opposing one as well, sought safety in numbers. Yet there was no community as such, the way there surely had been in the West Village for so long. People cultivated a secondhand appearance and lived a secondhand aesthetic but without any reference to what had gone before (in clear contrast to the style that the Beatles were setting at the time). There was a metallic edge to people's lives that prevented intimacy with either past or present. To be high all the time was the ideal, but it seemed to me to be based on the recognition of despair, not the search for joy or peace or even excitement. New York had lost touch with the vernacular in itself. Living there, at least in circumstances such as ours, was like subsisting everyday on soup that tasted only of chemicals. The feeling wasn't remotely so strong with Jasmine as it was with me, however.

The centre of disrespectable literary life was the Peace Eye Bookstore on East 10th Street between B and C. Hebrew letters on the window, left over from the days when a butcher shop had occupied the premises, attested to the fact that the establishment was kosher, which it most certainly no longer was even in a metaphorical sense. In the front room the proprietor, Ed Sanders, a fiercely intelligent drug-culture poet with a degree in Egyptology, had arranged unusual paperbacks under thematic headings of his own devising, such as *glop* and *slupe.* Mementos lined the walls. A photograph reminds me that he had the famous sandwich board that Allen Ginsberg, now an East 10th Street neighbour, had worn at a seminal demonstration in 1964: the one with the words POT IS FUN in huge black letters. Sanders also sold genuine Allen Ginsberg pubic hairs, packaged individually in the type of glassine envelopes used by philatelists. In the back room sat the mimeograph machine on which Sanders produced his literary journal, *fuck you / a magazine of the arts.* I found him a cynical and distant figure, quite the opposite of his collaborator, Tuli Kupferberg.

Tuli, who has always looked younger than his years though he's perpetually haggard, had been around the Village for long enough to have known Max Bodenheim (murdered in 1954) and other hold-overs from the twenties. He was and has continued to be a poet of singular originality, publishing most of his material himself (in those days, as Birth Press, an imprint he used on mimeographed books which he then gave away). I once saw him react to some unwittingly surrealistic utterance by a child of perhaps two, in such a way that his whole body and spirit seemed to give in to laughter. He and Sanders, along with a third man, Ken Weaver, a drummer, a round and silent presence whose long straight hair was like the inversion of his enormous beard, had teamed up as a group called the Fugs, originally the

Village Fugs—*fug* being the word that Norman Mailer's publisher had forced him to use in *The Naked and the Dead* in place of *fuck*. The band was one of the important protest instruments of the sixties. Tuli, who was capable of writing a beautiful art song as well as, more typically, "Johnny Piss-Off Meets the Red Baron," provided most of their material (the rest was adapted from Blake). I learned only years later that Tuli was the person Ginsberg described in *Howl* who "jumped off the Brooklyn Bridge this actually happened and walked away unknown and forgotten into the ghostly daze of Chinatown soup alleys & firetrucks not even one free beer." Except that it wasn't the Brooklyn Bridge but the Manhattan Bridge (Allen's memory was often loose with such details). I once had the honour of performing with the Fugs on stage. While Tuli and Ed sang one of their standards, I paraded about with a placard bearing the slogan FUCK FOR PEACE or some other platitude of the day.

For a time I took up with a street-theatre group called Teatro de Tripas, the gut theatre. We practised a primitive form of performance art, such as when we stood at busy intersections dressed in old tuxedos and gave public readings from *TV Guide* in English and Spanish while smashing television sets with a stolen fire axe. I hid out in my Canadian studies during the day but was drawn at night into an ever more bizarre world of jagged nerves and wino cafeterias. I was sick much of the time with bronchitis that in my ignorance I thought was congenital but that turned out to be more sartorial: I didn't have a coat that buttoned up to the neck and lacked the means of getting one.

Jasmine and I were growing apart as we learned more about each other. She didn't believe that the nihilist mood was at base concerned with the absence of humanity all around us, and I suppose I was contemptuous of the comfortable position from which she in her own way protested the war, a way different from mine though of course just as valid. In any case, the war was the proper metaphor for our relationship as it was for everything. I got in deeper and feared what withdrawal might do to me and so could only become even more involved than before. As I did so, I grew even to dislike her and was repaid in kind. Yet we stayed together, with mutual morbid fascination slowly taking the place of shared affection. It was the Vietnam of love affairs all right. It took time, though, before I could admit to myself what I had been forced to conclude: that beneath it all, she was an American, she was infected with the great American virus, that love was just as impossible there as any other worthwhile impulse, state or endeavour, all of them rendered unworkable by the institutionalized violence, the purblind worship of stupidity and all the rest. I felt I could never again have a serious intimate relationship with an American, and I have not.

These matters seemed like the great revelations of my young life up to that time, yet I find it difficult to express them with the intensity of that moment, now that I have lived with them so long. What did America feel like then, what did it seem to be?

In 1966 I thought that Americans were the salt of the earth: and so wherever they walked, nothing would ever grow again. What was most astounding was their hard shell of ignorance that seemed to preclude any acknowledgement of guilt. And they had so much to be guilty for. The business of America, Calvin Coolidge's remark to the contrary, was not just business, it was everybody else's business, an attitude that inevitably led to violence. There were clear historical reasons for it. The whole notion of the frontier in its boundlessness combined with the calvinist heritage to create a religion of conscious destruction. The people had no connectedness to say the least, and they took their chaos with them wherever they went. It produced a kind of evil. Murder was how these folks showed affection. I wouldn't have been surprised if Death actually turned out to be an American. "Mr. William T. (Bill) Death Jr. at your service," he'd say in some flat, nasal accent. "Death's the name and death's the game."

"Is there good money in that?" you would be expected to ask, shaking his bony hand.

"Well, I'm comfortable."

America with all its apocalyptic furniture! The point wasn't simply that every night was Hallowe'en for real. It was that everyone was on moral disability. LAND OF MUTANTS should have been the motto on the licence plates. Since 1820, when fairly accurate records started to be kept, about fifty-two million people had immigrated to the U.S. As far as I was concerned, they were all wrong to have come. It's all a big mistake, I would have said to them. Go back and face the czar or the desiccated potatoes. It's one big joke, the oldest and cruellest joke in the world—if you buy the premise, you buy the punchline. The great experiment, they called it. But the experiment failed, nothing good was proved, the laboratory exploded and the stench of rotten eggs and sulphur pervaded everything. Emerson said that being an American was not a nationality as such but a moral condition. He was close. It is an immoral condition. The line between genealogy and criminology got mighty blurry sometimes.

No one was contending that one government was necessarily any better than another in its potential for good or disposition towards evil (by this time I'd discovered George Woodcock). Some are simply worse, more vicious, more stupid, wholly owned subsidiaries of the devil, because they mirror the culture, in the broadest sense, that supports them. Yet, perversely and triumphantly, it's only in their culture that one society sometimes expresses qualities that transcend their governments and their businessmen and so help compensate for them. What was the real reason all those men in the Top Hat had fought the Nazis?, I wanted to ask. Surely not revulsion at malevolence and worse, more a question of rivalry, of hating the Germans' education and wanting to destroy Britain economically. As forever unfathomable as the Holocaust seemed, it was, to us, equally incomprehensible that a deed so evil could have escaped somehow being America's fault, at least in part. Everything was calculated violence and spontaneous greed. There was no moral commitment because there was no civilization worth the name, and no civilization because there was no education, no humaneness, no sense of the necessity of ongoing improvement, except in a few brave and isolated people, saintly really, whose lives showed what culture really was. It was always shocking to discover such a person since the majority stated the problem so convincingly and with such apparent unanimity. You could see Americans returning to their roots, with their pop culture superstitions and their television cabbala. It was only a question of time until grave goods came back into fashion and the dead would be buried with their credit cards and small appliances, sitting upright in Fords and Chevs, facing east, towards Wall Street and the Pentagon.

I found it a constant struggle to keep out the terror and let the stimulation enter. It proved impossible, in fact. Some days the history would rise in the gorge like vomit, then go down slowly with my thoughts of escape. One had to remove oneself to avoid being contaminated. One had to resign. My only ambition now was to be a last-generation American and a first-generation Canadian.

"Did you grow up in the States?" somebody would be sure to ask.

"No one in the States grows up. That's the problem."

Under the Canadian Immigration Act in force at the time, you had to be eighteen in order to enter Canada permanently. I had turned eighteen now.

"Why did you come to Canada?" people might enquire.

"Privacy," I would tell them.

But all the while I was saying something quite different to myself. First the border formalities loomed and then, after a short time, they receded. *Fuck you America*, I was screaming silently. *Have a nice day.*

CHAPTER THREE

FINE ICONIC BOOKS AND DEEP COMBATIVE EGOS

A FEW MONTHS before I took up permanent residence in Toronto in 1967, two young English professors met to establish a small publishing house, an event that would have great significance for the Canadian book world and coincidentally for me as well. Legend, which was soon to encrust the people and happenings I am about to describe, once insisted that the founding took place over beer at the Bay-Bloor Tavern of blessed memory. In any event, the principals were David Godfrey and Dennis Lee, figures with quite different sensibilities who soon came to be the separate halves of an enterprise that was better known and more complex than its individual components. It was called House of Anansi Press, or at least that was the style for all but the first printing of the first book, Dennis's collection of poetry, *Kingdom of Absence*, whose title page spelled the name Ananse. Both renderings were acceptable for the spider-god and trickster found in African and Caribbean folklore. As far as I'm aware, however, neither had any special relevance to the little basement publishing firm except that Dave Godfrey, like so many other young liberals, had been in CUSO, or Canadian University Service Overseas, doing volunteer labour in the Third World. In his case that meant teaching school in West Africa (while also, it was said, playing trumpet in a group called the Gold Coast Jazz and High Life Band). So stated the oral equivalent of his curriculum vitae and hence the African name.

Dave, who was twenty-nine when I first met him, was bamboo-slender with a prognathous chin and a great deal of brown hair that was at once both straight and unruly. He moved everywhere in a bright haze of nervous energy, as though surrounded by some strange electromagnetic field. This condition allowed him to work simultaneously on an extraordinary number of projects and causes, at least for short periods. It also contributed to his mystery, which was already considerable. He was a Winnipeger by birth but got all his education, undergraduate and otherwise, in the States. He was one of those students whose literary promise had always impressed people, or so Wallace Stegner, who had been one of his instructors at Stanford, told me years later. Now he was teaching English at Trinity College and pursuing a variety of nationalistic missions and keeping up a prodigious output of writing, including proto-postmodernist short stories with outdoor settings. These were appearing in *Saturday Night* disguised as a sports column, with the helpful connivance of the magazine's managing editor, Kildare Dobbs (with whom Dave would soon sever relations and attack in Picquefort's Column, a pseudonymous department he conducted in the *Canadian Forum*).

While at Stanford, Dave had met his wife, Ellen, whom rumour made the daughter of an important Illinois industrialist—accurately so, I believe. She seemed friendly but most proper and reserved, and so I was surprised one day when she told me that she had once dated Neal Cassady, the mythic wild man after whom Jack Kerouac had patterned Dean Moriarty in *On the Road*. The Godfreys were living at 671 Spadina Avenue, in an impressive Edwardian house they rented from the university, which counted a few such gems among all the slum properties that otherwise made up its extensive real-estate portfolio. I had exchanged a letter or two with Dennis Lee and so knew about Anansi, but I hadn't actually met him and was slow to make contact after arriving in town during a crystalline blizzard. Perhaps a couple of weeks passed before I telephoned one day and spoke to Dave, who invited me over.

He gave me the tour. It started in the garret, which he rented to a student from Ghana whom he introduced as Kwame John. It concluded in the cellar, one end of which had been converted to an office while another area, a furnace room set off by partitions, was shelved for the inventory of Anansi books.

At this point Anansi had published only a few titles in addition to *Kingdom of Absence*, the long meditative poem that Dennis had written in England five years earlier and whose failure to find a publisher, they said, was what prompted the two of them to go into business for themselves. There were also poetry chapbooks by Barry Charles and Janis Rapoport, two extremely young writers who prefigured Dennis's interest in people at the first stage of their careers (after which he often lost interest in them). The press had just received its first Canada Council grant to pursue a more professional programme, which included a new edition of *Absence* as well as three other books. Two were poetry: *The Absolute Smile* by George Jonas, the urbane Hungarian emigré, and *The Circle Game* by Margaret Atwood, who was more or less unknown, though the Contact Press edition of the book had won the Governor General's Award after its 250 copies had sold out. The other book was *Death Goes Better with Coca-Cola*, the collection of Dave's wonderfully anti-American short fiction from *Saturday Night* and elsewhere.

"This is it," Dave said with impatient pride.

I said it was an attractive set-up, or words to that effect.

Some bustling was evident upstairs on the ground floor, with heavy suitcases being bounced down the steps one at a time.

"Ellen and I have to go to Chicago for a couple of weeks. Do you have any place to stay?" I confessed that I hadn't. "You can stay here until we get back if you'll look after filling the orders as they come in." He showed me the system for invoicing, which I forgot almost immediately, and then they were off, whisked away in the middle of a commotion, the sort that always seemed to attend Dave's movements.

Dennis Lee never turned up. In fact, we didn't meet until some while later, once Dave had returned and hired me as Anansi's first full-time employee—for thirty-five dollars a week, fifteen of which I then kicked back to him in rent for the attic room I was to share with Kwame John.

It seemed just a little incongruous that Dave was teaching at Trinity. As far as anybody knew, he was not an Anglican—word was that he had converted to Judaism or was about to—but more importantly he was not what might be called an Anglican type. He was an entrepreneur. An entrepreneur of ideas at the moment but, in theory, of anything, as later events would prove. His nationalistic hatred of America was based on disillusionment and ultimately repulsion during his own experiences there. Dennis, when I finally got to know him, was quite different. His cultural compass had pointed across the Atlantic before the needle swung about to show him the way back home. He taught at Vic, which seemed perfect, for he was the heir to a staunch kind of middle-class suburban Methodism, most of whose adherents no doubt considered him an apostate because he had grown up to be an intellectual. He was secretly drawn to the Quakers as well as to the other extreme, though I suspect he feared that High Church people were looking down on him. One never knew for certain, for it was impossible to penetrate his wry cordiality without striking condescension. That is to say, he had the congenial manner of someone to whom the quality did not come naturally but had been made a habit though constant vigilance until it finally became permanent.

He was twenty-eight, with an enormous domed forehead stuffed with English literature and social conscience. He sported a little blond goatee and usually wore *djiskais*; he chain-smoked small cigars with plastic mouthpieces and gave the impression of fighting hard against the constriction and shrinkage that a certain type of WASP likes to write novels of rebellion about. He had yet to publish any of the children's verse that he had begun writing for his own kids, but it was certainly clear even then that the high culture in which he was schooled was always warring inside him with the popular culture from which he felt cut off. You can see the tension in the diction of his serious poetry and other work and hear it in the way he talked, with great precision and joy in language, but also with a gentle mockery that was a kind of reaching out. He was trying to teach himself quantum mechanics at night, and he played the piano, loudly and in the key of C. He spoke of Martin Heidegger and Al Purdy volubly and with almost equal reverence. I quickly made myself a disciple, or tried to; there were few places available and a great many applicants.

George Woodcock was right when he wrote in a letter to Dennis that "something unprecedented happened to Canadian publishing and even to Canadian writing when Anansi came on the scene." And indeed whenever I hold them in my hands today in secondhand book shops, I'm reminded how fresh and sophisticated, how powerful and, yes, how revolutionary the old Anansi titles seemed. As examples of bookmaking, they may also have been incredibly amateurish and naive, but in turning the obsolete pages, I always find preserved some suggestion of what the period was like. During the Centennial and for a couple of years afterwards, Anansi was at the forefront of a movement that it both helped to create and then gave voice to. There were many other little presses, of course, most of them personal vehicles for their editors, transient and homeopathic, but with some genuine place in the long equation of literature. Anansi was different. It was out to change writing by displacing the old generation with the new: the same implied function that the Hogarth Press or Boni and Liveright had voiced in their own day, with the same cocky self-assurance. In the process, though, Anansi actually wanted to change publishing as well, and to that end it was more successful.

Barring only Jack McClelland, who once gave Anansi a prognosis of six months, Canadian publishers were insufficiently interested in the new writers who were turning up in large numbers, driven, so it seemed at the time, by some great consensual imperative. Macmillian and Ryerson and Clarke, Irwin and Oxford and the University of Toronto Press all brought out Canadian books, but they seemed to Dennis to be unadventurous affairs, the inevitable result, so Dave, I believe, must have imagined, of the cautious corporatism or institutional restraint with which houses like that were burdened. McClelland was a separate case. He was a corporate showman, using his talent for ballyhoo to make a few select authors into public personalities, a process that included career-long commitments to promoting them and their works, both current and backlist. To Dave, who saw publishing as a political act, and Dennis, to whom it was a moral one, such behaviour, though fascinating, was abhorrent. In any event, it was often said that McClelland's skill as a talent scout had deteriorated. The youngest of his stars (of the ones whose shine persisted) was Leonard Cohen, who was past thirty-five and had defected to the States. Dennis once publicly compared Cohen's work more or less unfavourably with that of Bliss Carman.

Anansi was small in sales volume but big in its goals. Its main ambition, as seemed obvious even then, was to publish its own people, the ones engaged in the expression of a new Canadian reality, urban, politically savvy and "freewheeling" (Dennis's favourite word at the moment), and propel them into the mainstream. The place seemed haphazardly run, with erratic schedules, inconsistent design, almost non-existent promotion. Yet we were the new attractions at the zoo, drawing large crowds, and the media had to pay close attention even though they had never seen such animals before. Incredible though this may sound today, the big newspapers rushed to do full-page stories on us.

A few other small presses on the scene were engaged in interesting publishing too. Talonbooks was in the process of emerging from *Talon*, the little magazine, and there was another Vancouver press of some importance: Very Stone House, which the poets Patrick Lane and Seymour Mayne had started in 1966. But Very Stone House tapered off after a while, as Pat roamed restlessly around the country, haunted in some measure, I think, by the tragically early death of his elder brother, the poet Red Lane. Towards the end, their publications were chapbooks or folded broadsides under the imprint Very Stone House in Transit, put out from wherever Pat happened to be—logging in B.C. somewhere or hunting in the Rockies.

The most important underground press prior to Anansi had started in 1965 when Stan Bevington and a number of others had opened Coach House Press in Toronto, on Bathurst Street below Dundas, in a perfectly nice slum, which an overly officious city government later razed for a park. One approached the eponymous coach house by navigating a muddy little alley running beside a deserted building that had once been a locksmith's shop. Bevington, a printer, had red hair and wore a big beard, and was friendly in a slow-moving non-specific way—and equally so to everyone, in a style then associated with the young generation of British Columbians. His interest was in handsetting type and keeping his old Linotype in operating condition. The Coach House logo, then and later, was a cast-iron platen press with an enormous fly-wheel, and in those days they actually printed on the press from which the image had been made. Later, in the 1970s, Bevington made a complete volte-face, suddenly abandoning the traditions of the craft for the vanguard of computer-generated graphic arts. The switch was probably coincidental to the emergence of Coach House as one of the primary institutions of what would later be the prevailing orthodoxy, but the two events were parallel in time.

Bevington was a craftsman and designer, not a literary person, and had always looked to a variety of writers to work out among themselves what he should be printing. One of the earliest was bp Nichol, whose *Journeying & the Returns,* which I remember being excited about when it came out in 1967, was among the most imaginative of their works: a box containing a chapbook, an envelope of poems on individual cards, a flipbook that one fanned with one's thumb: all sorts of different work forms, including a plastic phonograph record of the author chanting. At one point, some of the Coach House poetry books were designed deliberately to make the poetry almost unreadable on the page—silver type on purple paper, that kind of thing. For some years, as a hallmark of their quality, the books all carried the motto "Printed in Canada by Mindless Acid FreaKs."

That's when Coach House was on the outside, knocking to be let in. Later (in retrospect, rather quickly) it became one of the most important pieces of infrastructure in the all-important Vancouver-Toronto axis that had sprung out of the old journal *Tish* and the Vancouver Poetry Conference of 1963: the Canadian members of the Black Mountain school as they were then thought of, later known as the language poets, the postmodernists. They were a cliquish bunch, a complete and almost closed society of theorists as well as prose writers and poets who, by the deadly serious late 1970s, had come to the top of Canadian literature. This was because they controlled much of the critical machinery, with *Open Letter* and many other journals, and what they wrote eventually became the dominant mode in English departments, particularly in those west of the Quebec-Ontario border.

But back in 1967, small press books sold hundreds of copies, not thousands; they didn't get reviewed in the *Globe and Mail* or stocked by Coles or the independent shops or the all-important department stores. And no writer ever made a proper career in small presses without graduating to more commercial ones. Anansi is important partly because it changed all that, at least for a time.

My grandfather, Herschel Fetherling: engineer, entrepreneur, amateur orientalist and collector of murder weapons. His financial ruin in the 1929 stock market crash brought about the family's expulsion from the upper middle class.

My English grandmother, Ethel Fetherling, fresh out of a European finishing school. She would come to a bad end in America, working as a hotel laundress well into her seventies and only narrowly escaping a grave in potter's field.

LEFT: "Remarkable for his Welshness," my maternal grandfather, Owen Jones, far younger—and more cheerful—than I can remember him. He was by turns a boxer, steel-worker, farmer, beer-salesman and saloon-keeper. "Like Aldous Huxley, of whom he most assuredly never heard, he died on the day that President Kennedy was shot and was thus shortchanged in the amount of space the news of his passing was accorded in the papers."

BELOW: My parents, George and Mary Emma Fetherling, nightclubbing in 1941. He was 26, more than halfway through his short unhappy life; she was 30 and beginning to show signs of the mental and emotional instability that would damage everyone around her.

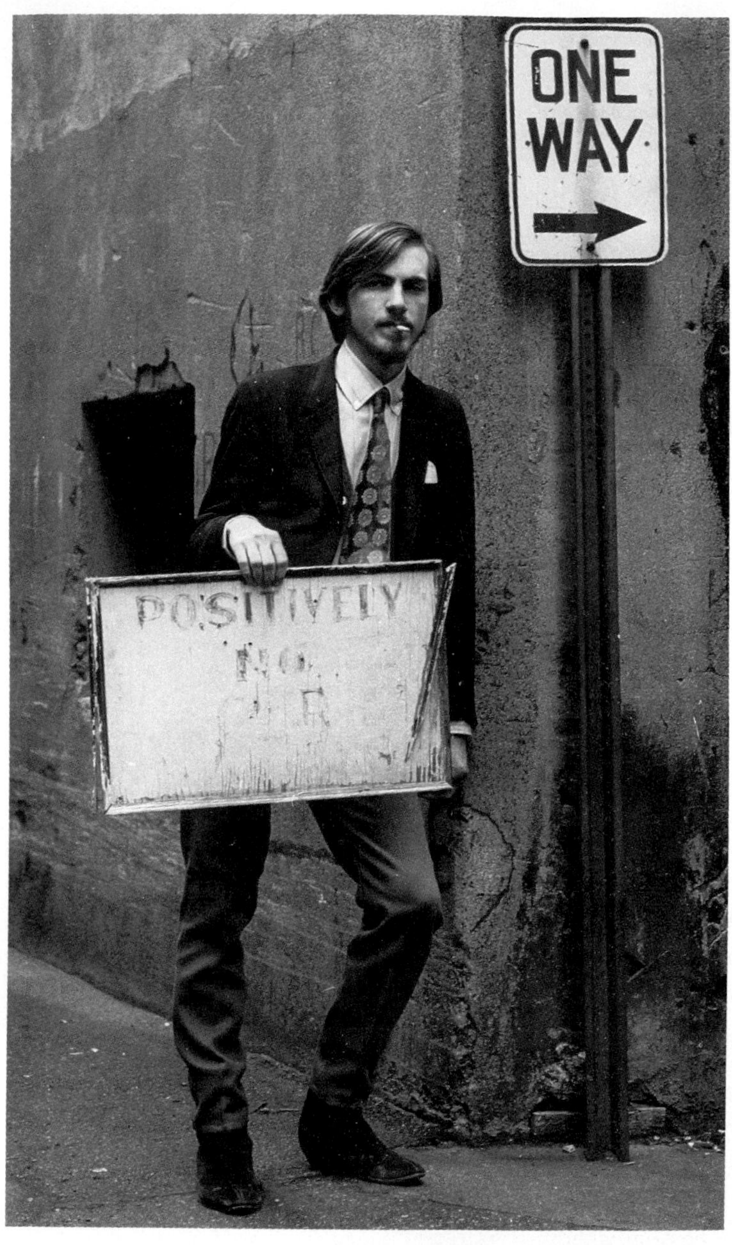

The author, holding a piece of found sculpture, at the entrance to Newsboy Alley in 1966. The photograph was taken by the redoubtable Jasmine Erskine.

The original home of House of Anansi Press as it looked in 1968, the year after the revolutionary publishing firm was founded by David Godfrey and Dennis Lee, with the author as its first full-time employee. *(Photo by Stan Bevington)*

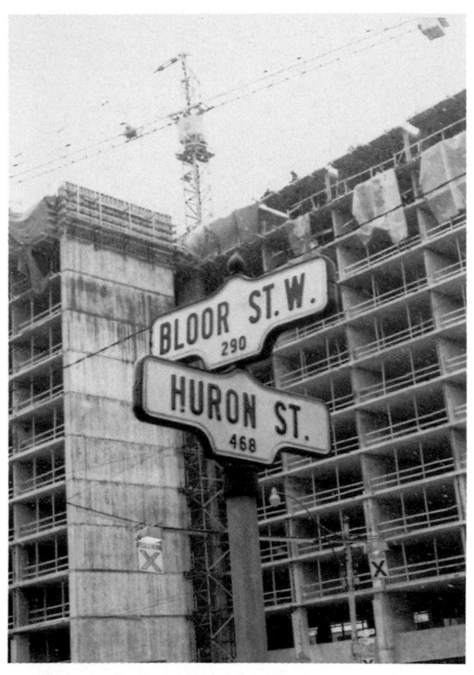

LEFT: Rochdale College, the 18-storey educational experiment (and internationally infamous drug supermarket) under construction not far from Anansi. "I would chart the progress as I walked along Bloor Street every day." A photo by the author, taken in February 1968.

BELOW: The author and Allen Ginsberg in Toronto, 1968.

Gwendolyn MacEwen at the Royal Ontario Museum in 1968.
(Photo by Mac Reynolds)

Bill Kimber, looking every inch the sixties artist and illustrator. The place I shared with him and Elizabeth Woods on Church Street turned into a salon that became famous in Toronto underground circles: part literary drop-in centre, part intellectual after-hours joint. *(Photo courtesy of Bill Kimber)*

On a number of occasions, Anansi may have published some Coach House writers such as George Bowering, but the two presses were fundamentally different. There was no unspoken Anansi manifesto, beyond a kind of vague literary liberalism that was more of a sensibility than a philosophy (and in any case didn't necessarily even seem liberal some of the time). Anansi writers tended to be tortured by some enemy whose name they couldn't agree on. Dennis Lee spoke of *absence* as the fact of cosmology brought home to daily living. George Grant (one of Dennis's mentors) cited *technological empire* as the problem. Charles Taylor, the former China correspondent (and a Grant protégé by way of Dennis), wrote of *radical Toryism* as the solution, while Margaret Atwood, for her part, was characteristically the most forthright and unambiguous in locating the villain somewhere between patriarchy as a social system and maleness considered as a pathological condition. In fact, it seemed to me with certainty then, and still seems to me even now, that they were all, at some fundamental level, against more or less the same thing: Americanism, with its republican brutality and hatred of culture. I wasn't an important writer but I found a great sense of discovery in locating a group of people who hated the same enemy I did (even if, because I had been born there, they sometimes found it necessary to hate me in the bargain).

Such was my private interpretation. But there was no Anansi school in any sort of literary sense whatever. There weren't even many authors who stayed with Anansi for book after book. Dennis had a few generic enthusiasms like anybody else—he was always a sucker for a certain kind of ironic diction that was just on the verge of going bad in the fridge and turning into curdled surrealism—but he was remarkably broad-minded and catholic. This, I believe, was his true strength as an editor, rather than his ability as a talent-scout of unpublished writers, a gift much vaunted in what's written about him but which time has not necessarily confirmed.

In any case, Coach House was originally about craft and then about taking over the Can lit agenda and making what was previously unappreciated the standard curriculum. In that way, it must forever be a more important press than Anansi, which never had much sense of the book arts and led to developments in publishing more than to developments in literature as such. What it did manage to do, however, was to put a lot of new writers into the hands of the existing readership that didn't know about them. Often this was because no one else knew of them either (Anansi published an extraordinary number of first books, including my own). Sometimes, though, it was a matter of Anansi, with its flair for publicity, propelling a writer's career by pushing the *second* book, making the person a figure of public discussion. This was the case with, for example, Marian Engel. Her first book was *No Clouds of Glory* (a poor choice of title, I always thought—like a romance novel's—but forced on her by Longmans, a mainstream branch-plant house of the day). Anansi published her next one, *The Honeyman Festival*, which I still find the most satisfying and most whole of her works (though admittedly it was not so ambitious as some that followed); it was also the one that started to give her a place as a feminist writer. No one knew it at the time, but the most important intellectual figure whose first book bore the Anansi name was Michael Ignatieff. The book, which he co-edited, was a collection of papers on religion. Sounds terribly dull, but it derived from the first annual "international teach-in" held at the U of T and betrays Dennis's interest in educational reform, a subject that, in a way, would help shape Anansi's rise.

To say the least, Anansi had low overhead. In these early days especially, it sold a great deal through direct mail and by phone, though this was the result of fumbling, not mastery of any marketing techniques; and the house benefited from tremendous word-of-mouth and other automatic publicity. Because it was small and swift, it didn't need much infrastructure, and this seemed baffling to the Canadian trade publishers of those days, who, typically, had large staffs and published modest Canadian lists from the profits of the agency agreements under which they represented foreign publishers' lines in Canada. If Coach House was first about craft and printing the work of a few friends and later about technology and controlling the academic agenda, then Anansi was only ever about one thing: publishing. That was its genius really, and the soul of its expedient amateurism—something which career publishers found perplexing. Marsh Jeanneret of the University of Toronto Press once said to Dennis: "You mean to say that you people publish these *paperback books* [the italics were like tongs for picking up a disgusting object] with dirty words in them and they're reviewed in the *Globe and Mail* and sold at Britnell's?" He was genuinely mystified. We were thrilled.

We were also exhausted most of the time, and not infrequently on edge. I remember typing some letters for Dave one afternoon. One was to Charles Wright, the *New Yorker* poet with whom he had become friendly at one or another of his U.S. campuses—the University of Iowa, I believe. With publication of *The Dream Animal* in 1968, Wright became Anansi's token resident American on the list (until I acquired a manuscript for us from Allen Ginsberg), and Dave later published another of Wright's collections once he moved on to his next publishing venture. Anyway, Dave was telling him by mail what was happening to Anansi, how ten books had become twenty and then forty, and how more people were coming to work there all the time, how some days the place appeared to be operating twenty-four hours—and how, Dave wrote with a note of desperation, *all this is going on in the basement of my house!* In this case, the italics were those of disbelief.

As our books started to take hold and Anansi became famous as the apotheosis of underground, a steady procession of would-be authors, antagonists, job-seekers and potential hangers-on began knocking on the front door of No. 671, ignoring the printed notice urging them not to do so, and sometimes giving poor Ellen Godfrey reason to doubt our sanity or at least our moral probity. They would be instructed to go around the corner to Sussex Avenue, down a laneway and through the old walled garden full of weeds and children's toys. There they found a low doorway that gave onto a laundry room. Beyond that was the pathetic little hooch that I had made for myself after vacating the attic and leaving Kwame John in peace. It was a space about the size of a generous prison cell, which I shared with the furnace and the furnace pipes. My only piece of furniture was an old cot; I would unfold it at night and shake off the soot that floated down from the ceiling whenever the Spadina bus hissed to a stop out front. Only after passing that spectacle did the visitor encounter the office itself. The fact that such camouflage did nothing to diminish the traffic was all to the good, for to a remarkable degree Anansi depended on volunteer labourers, though for such a tiny company it offered a variety of employment options.

People with diverse backgrounds would soon go on to equally divergent futures. For example, the woman who designed the stylized spider that was Anansi's logo sold candy in one of the sleazy all-night cinemas on Yonge Street; I would sometimes see her there when I went to experience some camp Audie Murphy film at four in the morning. When asked why the spider she created had only six legs, she would always remark demurely, "The other two are up its ass." One of the sales people was an ex-soldier who lived above the Brunswick House tavern, another was a wavering divinity student, and there were poets in sullen profusion, so young and yet so misunderstood. The redoubtable Arden Cohen, the ex-wife of Matt Cohen, an early Anansi author, had found her way to Anansi because she was one of several U of T students (she was taking Chinese) who rented rooms in Dennis Lee's house. She started as production manager but soon became the conscience of the whole place and later, as Arden Ford, moved on to other trade houses and then to a career in scholarly publishing. Shirley Gibson appeared one day to put up posters for her husband Graeme Gibson's novel *Five Legs*, one of Dennis's epochal discoveries; she eventually wound up the president of the company.

There were usually one or two people from Dave's or Dennis's classes helping out as well. One of these lived in a commune on Brunswick Avenue that I soon began using as my other residence. This commune didn't have a religious or political underpinning; it existed merely to let a lot of people live inexpensively and make mischief. Among the communards there was, however, a freelance holy man named Kim, who had the authentic smell of the guru on him though I always suspected he came from the suburbs. For a time he was rather prominent in secret mystical circles.

"I keep hearing about his power," Dennis said one day. "Perhaps there's a book there."

"He can't write," I said. "I mean he doesn't. He's much too spiritual for that."

I once stayed up most of the night hunched in the corner of his bare room while he and a female co-suburbanist, who had not yet shed the outward manifestations of that lifestyle, worked their way through a truly extraordinary inventory of sexual positions, illuminated only by the candles on the floor and a transcendental inner glow.

Another resident was an ex-Nazi named Otto who lived there for economic reasons. He was a waiter by profession but his alcoholism kept pushing him to jobs in restaurants of less and less consequence. He told us once that he began to fear for his own life after a distant member of his family, a cousin if I remember correctly, was garrotted with piano wire after being implicated in the July 1944 attempt to assassinate Hitler. Drunk or sober, and he was usually the former, Otto never failed to polish his shoes each evening and align them with precision by his door. He aroused only pity rather than hatred or resentment, even from another resident who called himself the Rabbi for professional reasons. The Rabbi's profession was dope dealing.

Across the hall from the Rabbi lived an American deserter of immense charm who had escaped from a military prison and then a civilian one and had come north following a slow zig-zag course, working a few days at jobs that did not require sophisticated proof of his identity. The only such employment he could find in Chicago during Christmas 1966 was as a seasonal mail sorter in the federal building in the Loop. Each day an unsmiling special agent would descend from the FBI office upstairs to collect the mail. Each time he counted out the envelopes, wondering if one of them contained his own wanted poster. Now, in Toronto, he tried to support himself in various ways while studying criminology part-time. When the Drug Addiction Research Foundation began paying five dollars for true accounts of certain types of drug experiences, he approached those in charge with a proposition: three for twelve-fifty.

His girlfriend, a sweet, gentle person, much befuddled by the pressures of the day, had once tried to kill herself, leaving a note pleading self-defence. After she had undergone a long series of treatments, someone at 999 Queen, the provincial psychiatric hospital, issued her a document attesting to her sanity. It was intended to help in finding a job, but she would flash it whenever she experienced one of her devastating psychotic episodes. Once some of us had to restrain her. One person had grabbed her around the waist from behind and was trying to get her onto the bed, but she was flailing at us with her fists and waving this paper. "The government doesn't think I'm crazy," she screamed. Tears rolled down her cheeks. "*I have documentary proof!*" Forensically, of course, she did have the rest of us at a disadvantage.

Many's the night I left the basement cot at Anansi that severe winter and trudged through the deep snow to the Brunswick Avenue house, usually staying over, sleeping in my clothes in places ranging from some temporarily unoccupied sofa to the glassed-in summer porch, which was unheated. A couple of times I must have gained warmth through the rapidly shifting sexual alliances around that place. In 1983, when Katherine Govier published her short story collection *Fables of Brunswick Avenue*, I, and I imagine an unaccountably large number of other people our age, smiled in recollection at the name, though my fables, and theirs, may be different from the ones Katherine spins under that perfect piece of title-making.

Before coming to Toronto, I had had some correspondence and phone communication with Allen Ginsberg. I have a hazy memory of calling him about something on his birthday. I reached him at the home of his elderly father, Louis Ginsberg, in New Jersey. The senior Ginsberg was the traditional rhyming poet, a widower now, after many trying and destructive years with his sad psychotic wife, Naomi, as Allen described in *Kaddish* with such unforgettable power. In any case, I had got myself in the black phone book that Allen Ginsberg carried around, one of the most important practical documents of the sixties, for Allen would whip it out and put people in San Francisco in touch with ones in Tangier or Ahmadabad: it was a kind of secret bulletin board of the Movement, huge and highly efficient. So it was, somehow, that I knew he would be coming to Toronto to read at Hart House and that I was to be his handler.

My recollection of the immense Great Hall is that hippies and near-hippies took up every possible bit of space on the floor and along the wainscotting and may even have begun to hang from the mock-medieval beams, so to as make its benefactor, Vincent Massey, who had died only months earlier, perform at least one revolution in the family mausoleum.

Allen was the most compelling reader I had ever heard. Not a bombastic declaimer like Irving Layton, not a charmer and intensifier by turns, like Earle Birney. Certainly not the kind of defiant minimalist that Margaret Atwood, because of her platform monotone, sometimes appeared to be. He was funny and dirty, and he made punctuation with his fingers. The right forefinger and middle finger placed over his moustache and beard, with a space free for the mouth, was a sure sign of some impending emotional revelation, deeply felt and pried from the bottom of the consciousness only after years of other people's therapy and his own self-medicative techniques. The same position but accompanied with a gentle stroking of the beard while he talked was often the signal for descriptive narrative—Allen at his most Whitmanesque. Conversely, the forefinger suddenly raised straight up in the air as though to illustrate a point was always the signal for one of those Beat urban ironies of his, the sentences delivered without much in the way of definite or indefinite articles. They were a sign of hope amid the chaos of the world. Chalk one up for the human spirit, they said. At these, his voice would rise, taking on a sweet tone, and his face assume a dear if not downright beatific expression. With his finger-cymbals and his little wooden harmonium, he wavered between poetry and song, and took the listeners on a midway ride of word-music, and rhythms and images—with the word-music, I would say, always having the strongest claim on the emotions, as music does. Later—I believe it must have been at McMaster University, before an audience of, by comparison, rather straight university kids—he sucked nerves and jacked off people's emotions all night, performing those of his works most popular at that moment. When he read his long anti-Vietnam War poem "Wichita Vortex Sutra" and inserted the variant lines "Language, language, there is no language left save the ageless one of cocksuckers," the house broke down in tears.

I had been trying to get moments here and there to evangelize Allen about the work we were trying to do with Anansi. I remember attempting this once when we were rushing to a television taping in the back of a limo, accompanied by a TV publicist named Lexy. Allen interrupted, wanting to know what that black skyscraper was down by Lake Erie (unlike Whitman, he always got Lakes Erie and Ontario confused, even in his poetry). I told him it was the first phase of the T-D Centre. Toronto was early not late modernist in those days: no other big glass towers yet imposed themselves on the skyline. Now finally, after the Hart House reading, we were alone in one of the Massey College guest rooms by the porter's lodge, and he pumped me for more information. He also made a pass at me, but this was pro forma for Allen, and after being caught off guard just a second, I accepted the undeserved compliment with good humour, as there was no suggestion I was anybody special. After all, I knew this man's whole biography. How he had experienced a vision of Blake in the New York tenement in 1948. How he had been crowned Queen of the May in Czechoslovakia before being deported. How he had been similarly thrown out of Cuba, supposedly for saying that Fidel Castro's brother Raul was "cute" (an utterance that, if true, just goes to prove the old adage that one's man meat is, well, another man's meat). I knew that Allen would sometimes explain to people how Whitman had slept with one of his disciples, the poet and philosopher Edward Carpenter, who was supposed to have slept in turn with Gavin Arthur, an astrologer who was the grandson of President Chester A. Arthur. The younger Arthur is then said to have had an affair with Ellen Godfrey's friend Neal Cassady—whom Ginsberg, and of course Kerouac too, had been in and out of love with for years, requitedly so. Ergo, Allen would summarize, I have slept with Whitman.

Ginsberg's poetry as printed in books was almost always what he had taken from his notebooks, in which he scribbled more or less spontaneously as he ricochetted around the U.S. and the world in his role as alternative culture leader. Spontaneity was certainly the poetry's strength. The unrelieved nature of the spontaneity, however, was also its greatest defect, particularly when read on the page. In any case, he let me see his current poetry notebook at Massey that evening, and we copied out enough new poems to make a booklet for Anansi. This was typical of his dealings with various widely scattered small presses—anyone below the girth of City Lights, his primary imprint, presided over by his old friend Lawrence Ferlinghetti from above the City Lights bookshop in North Beach, San Francisco.

We talked much of the night. When I left, I walked the streets for a couple of hours and then had breakfast at a wonderful pure unreconstructed 1959 drugstore, the kind with magazine racks and a soda fountain, which stood on Hoskin Avenue (but not for too much longer—it was soon razed for the Robarts Library). Then I went back to 671 Spadina full of enthusiasm for the book that was about to be hatched. Allen had called the manuscript *Airplane Epiphanies.* Dennis later got him to change the title to *Airplane Dreams: Compositions from Journals.*

Simply being part of that address book of Allen's made one a member of an international secret order whose only obligations, as far as one could tell, were to put up (and put up with) those whom Allen sent your way. One afternoon a tall cadaverous fellow carrying a guitar case gave Ellen Godfrey a terrible start at the front door. She reported that he said, "Allen told me I could crash." She also picked up some additional message along the lines of "They're after me again." I apologized for the disturbance (I think she sighed) and hustled my charge downstairs. His name was Jerry Benjamin, though he wrote as "Jeremiah," and his guitar case turned out to hold, not a musical instrument, but most of his worldly effects—poetry and play manuscripts, which others had not found very publishable, and one great prize indeed, a dramatized version of Ginsberg's *Kaddish*, which Allen had given him permission to have produced in Toronto if possible. This was typical of Allen, who was as generous with his work and reputation as with his money, which he was forever giving away to other poets.

During the Beat ascendancy, I learned, Benjamin had been a considerable figure in certain theatrical circles in New York. He directed the first productions of *Arise, Arise* by Louis Zukofsky and *Ankle Sox and Jive Shoelaces* by John Weiners, as well as those of a pair of plays, *The Baptism* and *The Toilet*, by LeRoi Jones (later Imamu Amiri Baraka). His role in these last two events was duly acknowledged in the playscripts published by Grove Press. Some other amazing old evidence of his glory would also surface from the wodge of papers in his guitar case (a gift from Allen, he said). One was a decaying *New York Times* clipping from 1959 showing a photograph of two avant-garde filmmakers at work, Andy Warhol and Jerry Benjamin, both of whom were virtually unknown at the time. Jeremiah would always remain so. He looked much different now than in the yellowing half-tone, because at some subsequent point he had had his teeth extracted.

Dave was uneasy having this character crashing, however briefly, in his basement and so threw him out or rather ordered me to do it. Jeremiah took it quite well, as I got him on one of those days when he projected the artificial gentleness then associated with acid heads. After that he would come and go, never staying long in the city but never long out of it either. I think of him as one of the hundreds of bizarre characters attracted to the place in those days when chaos reigned only a short distance to the south. The situation, I imagine, must have been very similar to the one that obtained in Toronto and Montreal during the American Civil War a hundred years earlier, when, as contemporary accounts suggest, Canada was full of exiles and spies—that is, those who cared too much and were sad and those who cared too little and were angry.

I think Benjamin must have been in Buffalo when he wasn't hanging around Anansi and the other stops on his Toronto rounds, for he seems to have had links to some of the writers there, such as a wild former merchant seaman who wrote long poems about Che Guevera, or maybe even to Allen De Loach, the poetry czar of Buffalo. In any case, one night I was walking in Chinatown and ran into him carrying his guitar case, and he told me he had just got into town at the bus station at Bay and Edward. We began to talk and stroll, stroll and talk, heading generally in a westerly direction towards a vast area of undifferentiated streets where immigrant women sometimes let rooms. Now in those days, a diligent transient might—just might—find a room for ten dollars a week. I watched with amazement as Benjamin, using some mysterious primal sense or instinct, located without direct enquiry of any kind, what was surely Toronto's or North America's only *five-dollar* room. It was just big enough to allow one chair and a bed, and the chair had to be moved out of the way when one opened the door.

He paid the landlady two weeks' rent and when she left started to unpack his guitar case and change his clothes. He was wearing bellbottoms and a bright floral shirt that hung loosely on his skinny frame.

"Allen's always telling me to do what he does and buy durable cheap clothes in the Army and Navy," he said. He gave a look to indicate that he had tried but was a natural-born slave to fashion, what he could he do?

When he took off his pants, I saw that he had a belt of marijuana wrapped around his waist. He removed it carefully and tucked it under the pillow.

I was amazed. "Aren't you afraid to cross the border like that?"

"Not at all. In the theatre you learn how to make yourself the master of other people's impressions of you."

On a certain crude level, he was right. I remember once standing with Dennis at the traffic roundabout at St. George and Hoskin when Benjamin came up behind us and we went somewhere for coffee. Dennis was always unkind about Benjamin's writing (it was indeed drivel) but never to his face, and by comparison to Dave at least, was always somewhat partial to him, though perhaps reluctantly. Dennis asked him what progress he was making on the *Kaddish* project.

"I have begun the first round of auditions," Benjamin replied. "So many attractive young people. I encourage them all to disrobe completely. I find it creates a good working atmosphere."

Dennis said nothing but looked surprised. Benjamin explained that, well, some people get upset and leave and those are the ones without a future in the theatre.

Like so many figures of the time, Jerry Benjamin simply disappeared one day, creating an absence that would be noticed only in long nostalgic retrospect. I last heard of him in the late 1970s when the catalogue of an American antiquarian bookseller listed some relatively recent poetry chapbook of his. I remember that it had a California imprint. That must be where he went. Years later, in 1981, there was, finally, a Toronto production of a play based on *Kaddish*, but not one that Jerry Benjamin had anything to do with as far as research can reveal. He would be in his sixties now, I guess.

In the 1970s, after they had forced the provincial government to stop the Spadina Expressway, which would have cut across the heart of the city, destroying the whole by ruining the constituent neighbourhoods, everybody in Toronto aspired to be some kind of urban affairs expert. Unsupervised gangs of self-taught city planners and land-use critics were permitted to roam the streets freely, writing essays and being aggressively earnest. Later, many of them actually took over the municipal government from the property developers and other rogues who traditionally controlled it. This gave Toronto, if not a *belle époque*, then a little civic respite, such as it enjoyed once before—in the 1890s when a reform movement overthrew what one historian calls the "usual band of thieves and horse traders who occupied City Hall." But in the late 1960s nobody in Toronto yet wanted to be an urbanist. In those days the people I was acquainted with all wished to be educational reformers.

Personally, I found it hard to be more than just generally sympathetic with their views. I had concluded that education, which I wanted badly, was one of those things that if one wished done right one had better do oneself. That was the very essence of what I saw myself becoming in the world: a kind of radical whig autodidact. To reject the Tory idea that one was given a job description at birth was essential to also rejecting the idea that one was signed up at birth for a particular ideology, as though it was an exclusive private school with a waiting list a generation long. I wanted to educate myself, make myself into a humane person. I also wanted to show that anti-Americanism could be a grid for responding to the world, that one could at least privately use it as a full-blown economic, moral and philosophical *ism*, as Marxism or Christianity were or feminism would soon become. Of America, I thought, one could spend one's existence trying to attain, in an almost Buddhist way, an ever higher and more perfect form of rejection. I couldn't truly connect with these nice kids who were excitedly reading Jerry Farber's much-reprinted essay "The Student As Nigger" and demonstrating because their classes at the University of Toronto were too crowded. Their destructive energy had originated on campuses below the border, so I could applaud when at least part of what they did here had the effect of returning the missiles on a long arc.

But I couldn't muster anything like empathy. The campus, where I often had cause to go, selling Anansi titles into the U of T Book Room on the quad, gave me a chilly feeling that found expression in a haiku I wrote years later:

> *Art flourishes in strange precincts*
> *life drawing offered at the morgue*
> *books written at the university.*

But Dennis was of another view completely. As first a student and then a teacher there, he had come to rail against the impersonal not to say dehumanizing nature of a place as large and bureaucratic as the U of T. The composition of the institution was such that it seemed to him to render the mission—the infusing of liberal education—impossible. With many others, such as a John Stuart Mill scholar and frequent Anansi contributor named John Robson (who lived around the corner from the press), he came to speak and write of the horrors of the multiversity (a California coinage). In fact, he was coming to fundamentally rethink the process of education at all levels. This led, ultimately and improbably, to the erection of an eighteen-storey high-rise at Bloor and Huron, a block from Anansi. It was called Rochdale College, and was by far the biggest drug supermarket that Canada and maybe the eastern half of North America had ever seen. More importantly, it was a closed dystopian society of the most rigid kind, an authoritarian nightmare of a place where biker gangs, hired as security forces, set up checkpoints in the lobby and patrolled the corridors with vicious dogs: precisely the opposite of what poor Dennis had envisioned.

The story is this. Dennis was one of those rare people whose love of education couldn't be separated from his genuine love of children, his own and other people's (a quality made public later when he stumbled into a remarkably lucrative career as a writer of verse for kids). Just as repulsion with the multiversity was a reaction that he and the others frankly admitted they had taken from conditions at Berkeley, so Rochdale was tied in with Everdale, an alternative free school some people in Toronto were running, modelled on A.E. Neill's Summerhill in England. The Everdale group integrated crafts and unstructured tutoring. They even had a printing press. Dennis's *Kingdom of Absence* had been printed on it (before Dave put Anansi on a more businesslike footing, with the year's list contracted out to a large commercial printing house paid for by a line of credit at a bank in faraway Mississauaga, where Dave, after some diligent searching, had located that rarest of all creatures, a branch manager who liked publishing). The Everdale people published a stubby, self-involved journal of their ideas called *This Magazine Is about Schools* (which, under different guidance, evolved in time into *This Magazine*, the periodical of general political comment). It had offices in one of the Huron Street houses of Campus Co-op, the well-established organization that fixed up big old places all round the edge of the campus as a means of providing decent student accommodation at low cost.

Campus Co-op had long been as modest as its aims, but recently it had taken off, expanding in all directions.

This frenzy of non-profit enterprise was instigated by Howard Adelman, a contemporary of Dennis's, now teaching philosophy at York University. The two of them, but with Dennis, I think, the theorist of the pair, founded Rochdale as a college within the university where students would live and work independently of the normal university structure, running the place by purely democratic means, forming into seminars as organic need suggested, breaking away for solitary work when that appeared the better course instead: no faculty, no grades, none of the oppressive infrastructure of the old way: what Dennis would call "Rochdale's doctrinaire unwillingness to prescribe or proscribe any activity whatever as educational for the person carrying it on." The quotation is from his essay "Getting to Rochdale," a confession of his disillusionment with the university and of his search for alternatives. It was a piece that exerted a tremendous pull on people's thought at the time but would soon come to seem rather innocent.

In the essay he went on to knock off several possible criticisms of what he was doing. "The issue which Rochdale raised was this: were we not recreating a more libertarian version of [the liberal education of old] with our attempt to allow people to do what they pleased? If I can write poems and you can write poems and John Jordan can read Greek, and nobody will ever say us nay, are we not going even further toward making a specious virtue out of our own poverty in the face of that root question, 'What is it good to know?'" What caught my eye was the use of *libertarian.* As far as I know, Dennis was not familiar with, or even much interested in, the vast literature on intentional communities nor with any sort of anarchist theory of decentralization except as it applied *ad hoc* in this one particular situation. Maybe this is what made the experiment so interesting. Maybe this is what made it such a disaster.

Adelman I never knew well, but looking back now I can't help but wonder whether he was another Dave Godfrey in Dennis's life: another scholar-entrepreneur who made Dennis feel inadequate at being only, supremely, the thing before the hyphen and not, by skill or temperament, the thing that followed it. Anyway, with Adelman turned a kind of anti-development developer, in command of the fund-raising, Rochdale moved from the six Co-op houses to the high-rise, financed with a mortgage from the federal government. I would chart the progress as I walked along Bloor every day, and remember the moment when the cranes and the hoardings came down and the finishing work began. The essential and immutable problem, of course, is that Rochdale was to be two things to two sets of people: an immensely valuable piece of co-op real estate to some, a laboratory for further educational experiments to others. The educationalists thought it great that their people should study and live in the same space, which they would administer themselves in totally egalitarian fashion, but that convenient dual function was hardly essential to their idea of what they meant by *community*. For their part, the real-estate types didn't need the educators or particularly care about them.

Dennis was to be one of two "resource persons" at Rochdale when the new temple to unstructured education was complete. In his essay he tells of first being concerned with the size and location of their offices there, when someone from the crowd of rabble asked who he imagined he was to think in those terms. His first response was defensiveness, "because I thought somebody was sniping at me. After a bit, though, we realized that he was perfectly right. Why should two members of the college have offices to themselves when we are crying for space? And, more important, wouldn't that institutionalize everything we were trying to get beyond both in other people's responses and in ourselves?" This reminds me of an essay by that equally good and great soul, Paul Goodman, about the proper democratic way for people to arrange the chairs when meeting in solemn session to change the world. We think of the 1960s as a time when bureaucracy was suppressed for a while. In fact, it merely assumed an alias.

Dennis said that he often recalled the scriptural passage in which Christ advises the lads to be as crafty as serpents and as innocent as doves. Dear Dennis was always a model of dove-like behaviour but in this instance fell sadly short in the snake department. Once the Rochdale high-rise was completed (amid dark rumours about who might have benefited from its construction), everything utopian about it started to come to a halt. It did attract some important developments in art (all of them collective or corporate, not individual), as when General Idea and Theatre Passe Muraille were hatched or for that matter when Stan Bevington relocated Coach House Press to another coach house, almost identical to the one on Bathurst Street, in an alley to the rear. But these developments also had to do with the cheap rent and availability of sex and other necessities of life as they were then understood. What the place was most famous for, and justly, was its violence and drugs and disorder.

Right from the start Rochdale was a media circus, as reporters tried to respond to every fresh rumour of some LSD-induced suicide from the roof or a drug-related murder. Three levels of police were constantly trying to infiltrate the place when not actually raiding it, partly no doubt because of the way Rochdale became a magnet for thrill-seekers from all over the continent and even Europe. What happened at Haight-Ashbury in San Francisco in 1967 on a broad horizontal plane was repeated at Rochdale in Toronto the following year, and the year after that and the year after that, in a tall vertical space that could be made fairly secure against unwanted intrusion. This only increased the paranoia of the authorities without, which in turn did the same for the paranoia of those within. It became the most Americanized place in Toronto, not excluding the U.S. Consulate on University Avenue: a kind of tower of urban decay and social chaos, reaching to the sky above the Annex. At one point, Rochdale was home to a group of satanists that exerted an influence on the thinking of Charles Manson, according to the Manson book by Ed Sanders, my old Fug-leader.

I never contradict the people I meet these days who reminisce warmly of the time they lived at Rochdale (where some of them purchased the phoney college degrees the Rochdalers were always peddling—the ultimate insult to Dennis, I suppose). They were usually away from home for the first time and speak now with easy nostalgia, surrounded by the middle-class comforts to which they've long since returned. For myself, at the time, I couldn't always avoid Rochdale. To be sure, I had a few friends there. A likeable Dutch fellow named Bernie Bomers was the Rochdale business manager (a title full of pyrotechnic irony); later he was a teller at the Bank of Nova Scotia across from the Victory Burlesk on Spadina, where he got to know all the strippers as they came to cash their cheques; he and I and two young women from Saskatoon once drove frantically, 'non-stop, to Quebec City, on a sort of urgent mission of joy whose meaning escapes me completely now. But Rochdale struck me as a place to bypass when possible. Too much armed posturing, too much publicity. Certainly there was nobody there learning anything, as far as I could tell, even studying anything, or even reading much.

When it all started to turn sour so poisonously, which was almost at once, Dennis resigned, and the other idealists were soon given the sack. I think Rochdale must have been a great pain in Dennis's heart for years afterwards. I bring up the subject here because it also had a profound effect on Anansi.

One of Dave Godfrey's causes was finding a cheap means of feeding the hungry in Africa. To this end he had invented a product called Makka. The name, he said, was composed of syllables that were common to all the world's languages. Makka was a powdered substance which when mixed with water was supposed to provide one adult with a drink containing all the nutrients and vitamins necessary for a single day's healthy existence. It came in foil pouches and tasted terrible, just terrible. For though Makka never got into production, there were many cartons of the prototype batch lying round the Anansi office, and I had to dip into them from time to time to supplement my own Third World diet.

Another of Dave's causes, at least briefly, was SUPA, the Student Union for Peace Action, which Dennis was involved with for a while too. SUPA occupied a little green building at 658 Spadina which over the years, until finally razed in the 1980s, would house a startling succession of political groups, not excluding the Trotskyites. One of SUPA's many projects, started as early as 1965, was helping American draft resisters settle in Canada as a means of avoiding or protesting the Vietnam War. They published a pamphlet entitled *Escape from Freedom* (I always wondered whether the title was supposed to echo Erich Fromm). As the SUPA initiative led eventually to the much more professional body called the Toronto Anti-Draft Programme, so did the pamphlet lead to a book, notorious and helpful in its day, the *Manual for Draft-Age Immigrants to Canada*, which, through Dave's brokerage, was published jointly by the TADP and Anansi. Both the *Manual* and *The University Game*, the essay collection edited by Howard Adelman and Dennis and containing "Getting to Rochdale," appeared in January 1968. They were both runaway successes, garnering an enormous amount of attention, most of it positive, and going quickly into second and third printings. At this remove, they seem to me to represent the dimorphic and perhaps therefore unworkable nature of Anansi as it was at that stage.

The *Manual* was a product of Dave's entrepreneurial social activism, so ahead of its time. The title-page bore the name of Mark Satin, the publicity-conscious head of TADP (who I once heard say, "Anonymity would kill me"); he later moved back home and was among the first to popularize the term New Age. In fact, though, the *Manual* was a packaged sort of book, rather than one that had been written or even edited (in the sense that an anthology would be). It was clever, being designed to look as much as possible like a Government of Canada publication you would find at the Queen's Printer on Yonge Street. And it was controversial. Anansi immediately became the object of government surveillance. A couple of years later, a Bell Canada lineman doing some routine work took aside a friend of mine who was staying at the old Anansi place and showed him how clumsily the Mounties or the Metro Police intelligence unit had tapped the phones. "Look at this," the repairman said in resignation and disgust, pointing to some crude wiring. "They're always using this crap." The fact that Dave very soon afterwards did an about-face on the whole question of U.S. draft evaders, seeing them as agents of the great contamination, doesn't detract from my picture of the book as a perfect expression of his genius. Rather, it enhances it.

Like so many other Canadian couples, Dennis and Donna Lee were counselling draft dodgers one evening a week. They would form little groups in their living room up at the other end of Brunswick Avenue, close to Dupont. They too became disillusioned with what they were doing. But their gradual turning away was not the same as Dave's abrupt rejection, any more than *The*

University Game, with its earnest dove-like mission of enquiry, resembled Dave's *Manual*, which seemed to seek useful subversion in the marriage of politics and commerce. Compared to Dennis and most other people, Dave was always extreme in his politics, which meant that he was more prone to swings as well. Dennis was a standard liberal humanist and poet who just chanced, by some genetic happenstance, to be brilliant. Which is not the same thing as being worldly—the commoner quality by a factor of millions, but also one, it seemed to me, Dennis sometimes appeared to know he lacked. Dennis was one of those writers, far more numerous now than then, who struggled anxiously to write seriously without disdaining or rejecting the popular culture. For me, the best illustration was the libretto he wrote for a John Beckwith cantata about Toronto. Dennis worked in the street cries of the news butchers selling the *Star* and the *Telegram*. So now, striving to do something about Dave's implicit put-downs, he drew his politics more and more from the civic side of his general nature, where the pop cult stuff resided with his strange personal mix of art and Christianity.

No coincidence, then, that his next Anansi publication was *Civil Elegies*. I speak of the first edition, a simply designed, squarish book in blue and grey wrappers. It is textually much different from the edition of 1972 and also much more difficult to locate in decent condition, as most of the run was ruined by water damage after being stored in what was originally the coal bin of the Anansi house. The book came out in April 1968, at just about the time that I was upstairs one evening talking to Dave about the day's book orders when Ellen flew in the front door in an agitated state to say that Martin Luther King had been killed. We wouldn't know it for a long time, but the assassin, James Earl Ray, had slipped out of the U.S. and into Toronto, with the help of accomplices in whom the authorities would never take much interest. He would soon be hanging around the Silver Dollar Room, a tavern just down Spadina, at College, past the Crescent.

That was an astonishing year, an *annus mirabilis*, one of those watershed times that just pop up in history every now and then, like 1848 or 1939. For those of us wrapped up in the unfolding horror of the war, it was the year of the Tet Offensive, which began at the end of January. In a coordinated series of surprises, the Vietcong and North Vietnamese regulars swept into Danang and other seaports where the Americans had important bases. They captured a hundred cities and towns in the Delta and made similar inroads in the highlands and up in the mountains. In Saigon, which was not only the capital but America's impregnable jukebox hometown-in-exile, VC attacked the airport, the radio station and the presidential palace. In a particularly lovely bit of symbolism, they blasted their way inside the U.S. Embassy compound—then left. Within a few months they'd let the Americans reclaim it all, to remind them just how overextended the empire had become. In later years U.S. revisionists, writing for those coming along afterwards, would pooh-pooh the importance of the Tet. But anybody looking at the events at the time could see clearly enough what had happened. General Giap had served notice that though the Vietnamese were weak in everything but stamina they would still win, by chasing the woolly mammoth until it dropped. It took another seven years for the Americans, so very much stronger than their enemy yet so badly out-soldiered, to pack up. Seven years seem scarcely to have made a dent in Vietnamese resolve.

Dave and Dennis were having open spats now as their two personalities, and two visions of publishing and life and Canada, came into conflict. I can remember Dave sweeping in one morning and saying offhandedly to everyone who happened to be there, "Don't be alarmed, but it looks like we may have to publish a book by John Robert Colombo." Dennis could see he wasn't kidding, that Dave must have committed to some scheme as a trade-off against part of some other scheme, neither of which he (Dennis) knew anything about. He looked wounded and perturbed. (The book, whatever it was, never materialized.) On another occasion, Dave said to me, "You'd think somebody with the brains to get a Ph.D. could figure out how to run a small business." In fact, Dennis, unlike Dave, didn't have his doctorate, but that was beside the point. At one stage I saw some books on elementary finance and commercial practice lying on Dennis's desk. Faced with a problem, he must have been doing what I always do: seek out the phrase books and grammars and see how to teach myself enough to get out of trouble. Dave, I imagine, found such a response risible. In May, with the spring term at Trinity over, Dave and his family decamped for France, where he would write his long-awaited African novel, *The New Ancestors.*

None of the parties involved could have foreseen

this, but the Godfreys' departure brought me a great gift which has enriched me down through the years. Dave sublet the house to a young couple, Daniel and Judy Williman and their three small daughters. Dan was a politically active expat American but not a draft resister. He had once been immune from service as a Catholic seminarian; later, his records were among those destroyed by the famous renegade priests, Ted and Daniel Berrigan, in their raid on the draft board at Catonsville, Maryland. He was teaching a course at York (commuting there by bicycle because he was so poor) while doing advanced study at the Pontifical Institute of Mediaeval Studies. He was a fourteenth-century man, moving towards his licentiate or Vatican Ph.D., with a huge multi-volume work on the manuscripts collected by the Avignon popes through the papal right of spoil. This effort would go on for years, in time, I believe, becoming one of the first original applications of computer technology to medieval studies. This was characteristic of Dan, who soon became a close friend. He had great technical and mechanical gifts which reminded me of my father's. As a matter of course, he made the family furniture and taught himself trades as complicated as printing. Later, when they had a couple of acres of space, he grew their food, including wheat, which he'd flail by hand. I'm proud to say that I once helped him (not very successfully, it's true, as I inherited none of Father's manual skill) with a house he was building on the Bruce Peninsula, for he was a decent self-taught architect as well.

Another trait I liked in Dan was that he saw teaching and learning as inseparable functions. He knew so much—in history, in law, in research disciplines like paleography—that I couldn't help but learn from him, though he never slipped into a pedagogic diction; giving and taking knowledge, it was all part of a natural flow. He knew the importance of ceremony—he was, like me, a person in search of a continuum to climb aboard—but strove to live simply and enjoy his fellow creatures and their best handiwork. He read voraciously in all fields, all areas, listened to all the music old and new, looked at all art and cinema, searching for the highest quality goods so that he could offer himself totally on the altar of complete soul-cleansing enjoyment. He and Judy practised charity as well. I remember how, the first time they received a windfall—an academic prize or a tiny inheritance, I can't remember which—they promptly sent cheques to all the people they knew who were less materially well off than they were. That was typical of them. Judy, for instance, was convinced I was heading for a physical collapse, sleeping in the cold basement, living on caffeine and goddam Makka, and never warmly enough dressed, so she seconded me for their family breakfasts each morning.

Dan threw himself into the life and culture of whatever community he was in (a quality I always find easy to admire as I recognize it in myself), but he was also that rarest of birds, the totally cosmopolitan American, relaxed and authentic in his moveable comforts. He could go almost anywhere in the English-speaking world at almost any level of society with only the most minor vowel adjustments. He moved pretty freely among the French and the Italians also (and when I first got to know him was successfully teaching himself German from the cheapest titles available at a little German bookshop down Spadina). Like the rest of us, he had his blockages and inherited obstacles to freedom. In his case they came from a strong father, an acquiescent mother, and the all-powerful culture of the Catholic Church, whose shadow was getting shorter but blacker the whole time he was growing up. We've followed each other through years of *problemas sentimentales* as well as *problemas economicos.* In one of his letters I find him speaking of his "divorce car" with the explanation: "The Latin *divortium* primarily signifies the branching of a road, while *repudium* was used to mean the dissolution of a marriage contract; once again, an aging culture returns to verify the poetry of an earlier age, as the typical marriage dissolution now requires the purchase of a separate vehicle."

I've learned a lot (but not as much as I wish I could learn) from his example. About, for instance, seeking the perfect Tolstoyean balance of mind work and body work, of being respectful of the past as a tool of the present, of going at each new day like a rescued castaway tasting ice cream again for the first time.

As I've said, Anansi had at least collateral connections to both Rochdale and the anti-war movement. Of these I was more interested in the latter, which in fact came to touch me directly.

Fed by images in movies, younger people now believe that it was the U.S. military itself that was selecting who would be drafted and who not. Such a national scheme under direct military control would have carried its own problems with it, but by its very bureaucratic facelessness it would have been fairer than the one that was actually in place. The Selective Service Act empowered local committees in each large and small community to do the necessary selecting and rejecting, according to various quotas. To keep paperwork from going astray as it flew back and forth across the country, one's fate was always determined by the district one resided in the instant one turned eighteen. An eighteen-year-old living in Boston or Greenwich Village could thus pretty much be assured of liberal treatment, an eighteen-year-old in some hotbed of illiberalism (why single out one or two from the thousands available for naming?) was likely to "serve." These local boards might be made up of a used-car dealer, an undertaker, a lawyer, a football coach, all of them political appointees with the power of life and death. In addition to making regional inequities inevitable, they also made worse the class and racial biases already built into the national guidelines for exceptions and deferments based on educational status.

Of the many hundreds of thousands who protested by doing more than simply staying on in college or university, the biggest category, it seems to me, were those primarily protesting the unfairness of the draft, as I think it was perfectly legitimate and necessary to do. Next came a smaller but more solid group who were earnestly protesting the war and were often committed pacifists. Finally there was a third category, which didn't preclude membership in the other two: those such as myself (I met very few others) who simply didn't want to be Americans any more ever again and would spend the rest of their lives trying to deal with the moral guilt of having had the misfortune to be born in the United States. I've never found *draft dodger* a useful term unless used precisely. The draft dodgers were of two types: the ones who stopped coming to Canada after the Selective Service introduced a lottery system which at least gave non-fighters a fighting chance, and the ones who, if they were in Canada before the lottery, went back home after the limited amnesty of President Gerald Ford or the universal one of his successor, Jimmy Carter. Of course, many who might have returned if still young and single, chose to remain because they had started careers or families that they couldn't or wouldn't uproot.

My own situation was typically surreal. When I duly registered, shortly before leaving the country, I was routinely classed I-A, ready for shipment to the paddies. I said: No, no, there's been a mistake. While my brother is in the navy, I'm contributing to the support of my widowed mother whose condition (they assumed physical, based on some misleading evidence; I meant mental) left her unfit for work. I was reclassified IV-A, a hardship case. I never got called up for physical, psychological or patriotic tests, none of which I would have passed if the game wasn't rigged too badly. Even with the dealer using marked cards, I couldn't have passed them all. Believe it or not, stuttering was one of the disqualifying handicaps; I had a therapeutic history going back to 1955 and on a bad day couldn't utter a complete sentence. And my patriotic health was even then a matter of public concern, FBI file and all. Personally, I thought I deserved, as a reward for long residence on the edge, the coveted I-Y, or psychiatric deferment. In any case, memory tells me that when I settled in Canada I even gave the board my change of address, as the law required. Whereupon the local burghers in Wheeling decided to draft me on the basis of the postmark. They kept sending me orders to report to various places for induction, which I naturally threw in the rubbish with an oath appropriate to each.

Down by King and Bathurst in those days there was a storefront bookshop, almost never open, filled with books from Dick Higgins's Something Else Press in New York and Ferlinghetti's City Lights Books in San Francisco, two lines for which the proprietor of the shop, a strange individual named Harry Fine, had somehow obtained Canadian distribution rights. Harry was a recovering businessman—an accountant, I believe—who had, as people said in those days, turned on, tuned in and dropped out. Sort of. Eventually he would devote himself totally to consciousness expansion and related pursuits. At the moment, though, he was in an uncertain middle stage between Bay Street and Nirvana, analogous, I suppose, to the awkward position in which a pre-op transsexual finds him/herself. The way one knew of Harry's predicament was that he still wore his expensive three-piece suits but with a turban at one end and what looked like Vietcong sandals at the other.

He lived on the second floor, above the seldom-opened bookshop, where he supposedly published an underground newspaper and certain works of erotica.

Leaks in the ceiling dripped brown water onto the new electric typewriters and expensive typesetting equipment. For staff, he had a few hangers-on, one of them a bear-like biker dressed in khaki (you could still read his rank and outfit in the silhouettes of thread where the flashes had been sewn on). He was stoned all the time—on what, I'm not sure—and he kept saluting people, as a kind of involuntary action. Whenever he saluted in his perpetually goofed-up state, he would giggle. There's something mildly stressogenic about a 240-pound biker giggling. Another of the people who hung about Fine's shop and, who knows?, may even have been paid for his obvious work, was James Ellis. This acquaintance of mine was a pioneer in Vietnam draft evasion, having come to Canada in late 1964. The notorious dungeon at Marion, Illinois, had not yet opened in 1964, and Alcatraz, which had been built originally to house two categories of prisoners—A) those too spirited for the rest of the federal prison system, and B) pacifists—had only recently been shut down. But the authorities still took a stern view of what they judged Jim to be guilty of. Although there was a twenty-year statute of limitations on draft offences, it didn't include any time spent outside the U.S., and the sentence if you were caught on their side of the border could be five years in federal prison. The danger had been brought home forcefully once, a couple of years before I met him, when Jim was flying on the newly named Air Canada from Vancouver to Toronto to get married. Because of severe snow storms, the pilot announced he was putting down in Cleveland. Jim thought of cutting up his ID and ditching it in the toilet. He thought of trying to switch ID with someone else. He even thought of refusing to deplane and seeing what the law said about an Air Canada plane providing legal or at least moral sanctuary. Instead, after a panicky half-hour or so, he decided to bluff his way through, which worked fine. He was lucky.

Now the marriage had collapsed and, growing weary of the pharmaceutically induced gridlock on King Street, Jim decided to return to Vancouver. On the third and topmost floor of King Street lived a sexual philanthropist named Ruth, who during much of this whole period was sharing her place with a five-member rock band of some local acclaim. The band was breaking up, regrouping, mutating, metamorphosing, as rock groups were forever doing, and Jim was able to acquire their VW van, which was covered, front, top, sides and back, with carefully revised graffiti, in which the band members took the same pride a Regency dandy would have taken in his epigrams. In lieu of his unpaid wages from Harry Fine, which were undeniably long in arrears and nowhere in sight, Jim appropriated the stock of City Lights books, which filled the back of the van, and so, in that condition, set off. He was sending cards urging me to join him and open a bookshop in Kitsilano.

Growing up in the atmosphere I did left me a dread of ultimatums and most other types of personal confrontation. To this day I can't bear television programmes on which people talk too loud. By now the undercurrent of hostility at Anansi was growing more powerful, and I begged an unpaid vacation to hitchhike west. Jim, when I found him, was living in a chaotic environment in one of those old frame houses with the wide porches (nearly every one of them gone now) that used to be the standard domestic architecture in much of the West End. The place was decorated mostly with Moroccan chimes and a few sticks of broken furniture which others had intended for the dump. He had traded or sold the books for food, and the famous van had somehow become a matched set of 1953 Austins, acquired from someone who was going to prison. He kindly gave me one for my trouble, but one day when I wasn't paying attention, I forgot to notice where I'd parked it. No doubt it was impounded by the police eventually. I had no intention of enquiring.

In those days, when the health department was more relaxed in such matters, there were three rather famous hole-in-the-wall restaurants in an unmarked Chinatown alley between Pender and Hastings. They had no names so far as English-speakers could determine but were known by the colours of their doors—Green, Orange, and Red, I think—and were always spoken of collectively as the Doors. Each was one small square room, half below the level of the laneway. At two of them you could get a bowl of steamed rice for five cents, and at one of the three, I forget which, a respectable enough portion of barbecued pork for a quarter. Thus you could keep yourself going for a base rate of only thirty cents per diem. The police were troublesome in Vancouver in those days, but the city was, then and forever, crawling with writers, and the livin' was generally easy. Not for the last time in my life, I made the mistake of not staying there permanently.

When I got back to Anansi, there was a business card of an RCMP officer in my pigeonhole with a note that I call him immediately. The message was weeks old. I phoned and went to meet him above the post office on St. Clair Avenue East. He informed me that the FBI had enquired after my whereabouts and happiness and asked what my intentions were. He then pulled the oldest trick in the book, I couldn't believe it. He produced a fat manila file labelled FETHERLING, put it on top of his desk, then excused himself for a few moments to attend to some other matter in another room. I didn't bite. He returned and we parted cordially, he in the knowledge that I was staying where I was, I with a fresh understanding that matters were picking up speed in Wheeling.

What was happening there, it turned out, was that I was indicted *in absentia* and a bench warrant was sworn out for me as a fugitive. A deputy United States marshall went to my mother's house in a vain attempt to serve me with it and instead ended up becoming Mother's boyfriend. He was very near retirement even then. He came from a town called Cameron, one county distant, and from a family that had made a little money in the Sistersville oil boom of the 1920s. As he had no relatives left, save one nephew, the money stuck to him. He was a stern, authoritarian man who, paradoxically, looked the image of Henry Miller. Mother would sometimes telephone me to report gleefully that through his influence she was going to work for the FBI. This was an assertion that not even the low regard in which I held my loyal antagonist J. Edgar Hoover could make me believe. A shameful admission, but she wasn't smart enough to work for the FBI, or almost anyone else, and indeed had held no regular employment since 1938. What she was doing, I eventually learned when I subpoenaed some of my files years later, was simply volunteering information about me to the draft authorities. Mother being Mother, she got almost all of it wrong.

She called this new man of hers Mac, and once he hung up his side arm and handcuffs, they spent almost every evening together for the next twenty years, drinking and playing bingo. Mother treated him horribly behind his back and sometimes not much better to his face, but he was as pathetically lonely as she was, and he suffered more and more as time went on from an astounding list of serious illnesses and diseases, including emphysema so severe he could walk only a few yards at a time. Mother was determined she was going to outlive him and get the money. The race was going to be a close one. By the end of the 1980s she had recovered from one operation for bowel cancer and was ambulatory while his emphysema worsened and he became permanently bedfast. The finish appeared to be in sight but no one could call it. Her cancer showed signs of a recurrence, though this was matched by Mac's heart, which was deteriorating rapidly.

One night she telephoned me out of the blue to inform me that I was a disgrace to her, to her family, to my dead father's memory, to the United States and to the entire white race. I could feel only varying degrees of contempt for the rest of her list, but her inclusion of number three hurt me deeply. She ended by slamming down the receiver, as usual. A few months later, while watching the television she could never quite understand, she dropped dead of a heart attack, her first, which no one had been expecting. She was seventy-eight. Mac died not long afterwards. The nephew got the money.

There was an enormous party at Anansi; I believe the only publishing party Anansi ever threw in that wonderful old house on Spadina. My memory places the event in the late summer of 1969. From cellar to garret, the place was jammed with people, elbow to elbow. As far as the outside world knew, the press was in its glory. In remarkably short order it had put together a small backlist that contained a few titles, *The Circle Game* for instance, that would go on selling forever. At the same time, it was pushing ahead with all sorts of innovations. Until this point, Anansi had been known more for its poetry than for its fiction, but this was about to change, signalling, I think, the rise of a whole generation who would monopolize attention for years to come, including the novelists who a few years later would be instrumental in setting up the Writers' Union.

Dennis was now getting more interested in finding the young fiction writers (fiction was Dave's old turf), and he conceived a series of short, cheaply produced works called Spiderline Editions. They were uniform in their simplicity and their role in launching careers. Matt Cohen's first book was a Spiderline, *Korsoniloff*, which began a steady production of ever more sophisticated books to come from him in the decades ahead. Another first book was the Spiderline *Fallout* by Peter Such, a figure who would be quite important through the 1970s as a novelist with an interest in aboriginal peoples, archaeology, Canadian composers: an interesting fellow. Like some Anansi initiatives of a later era—for example, the Lost Works series edited by Margaret Atwood—the Spiderline idea was shortlived, with only five books in all. The others were *Eating Out* by John Sandman, *The Telephone Pole* by Russell Marois, and *A Perte de Temps* by Pierre Gravel.

Marois, a Quebecois who wrote in English, I got to know better than the others because, having no other place to work on *The Telephone Pole*, he would come into the Anansi basement late at night. He was a thin, blond, intense fellow, always chain-smoking. We would talk and talk, and in a while I would stretch out on my cot as he carved away at his tight surrealistic book about Montreal street life, writing in longhand on canary copy paper. It would be his only published work. In 1971, when returning to Toronto from his native Sherbrooke, he lay down on the railway tracks at Port Hope and was killed by a CN train. He was twenty-six.

Almost exactly two years later, Harold Sonny Ladoo, another of the writers in whose future Anansi had such faith, was found murdered in a ditch in Trinidad, where he'd returned on some family business. He had published one book, *No Pain Like This Body*, and left another, *Yesterdays*, which would come out posthumously; he would also inspire Dennis to one of his most powerful poems, "The Death of Harold Ladoo." I believe I met Ladoo only once, when he was leaving the office of some editor as I was entering. He was twenty-eight. Later, another death shook Anansi's bones. John Thompson, a mysterious poet (who I always thought looked in photographs as Grey Owl would have looked without his aboriginal drag) also killed himself. Rumour linked his death to an Anansi love affair gone sour. But this was in 1976, long after my time, and I had no way of knowing what had happened.

Purely as a publishing idea, the most interesting of the Spiderlines was *A Perte de Temps*, because Anansi published it in French, untranslated, but with generous vocabulary notes and other helpful bits of encouragement for English readers, who Dennis felt, or hoped, would struggle through, reclaiming their old high school French as they went and emerging all the better for it. I'm not sure that the experiment as such was altogether successful. A flurry of translating between Quebec and English Canada had begun about 1960, but throughout the 1970s seemed to be interrupted by each new surge of separatist feeling. It wasn't really until the 1980s that writers from the two cultures began translating, publishing and reading each other on a limited scale out of a love of what they shared. Which, in the cases to which I refer—a group that includes Nicole Brossard, France Theoret and Louise Cotnoir in French, Daphne Marlatt, Sharon Thesen and Erin Mouré in English—was a specific interest in feminist poetics. But I think that *A Perte de Temps* did lead Anansi to commission translations, most notably from Sheila Fischman, of a lot of Quebec writing. The author who benefited most was Roch Carrier, whose first book with the press, *La Guerre, Yes Sir!*, was another of Anansi's hardy perennials and the start of Carrier's enduring popularity in English Canada.

La Guerre had not yet appeared at the time of the

Anansi party, but contact had been made, offers were in the offing, because one of my most vivid memories of the evening is of Dennis, upstairs at the end of the first-floor bannister, telling a very long and highly complicated joke. When I joined in, he was telling it, in French, to Roch and, in German, to some German-speaking person whose identity I never learned, all the while switching from French to German to English, without losing anyone's comprehension or missing a beat. The other reason the party is memorable to me is that I met a young English woman who was a university student and wrote poetry. She seemed to me quite wonderful, largely because I inferred she thought I might have possibilities as well. Her name was Sarah.

In France, Dave had met up with two other Canadian writers, the novelist Jim Bacque, ruggedly handsome and socially prominent, and the sometime poet and sometime fiction writer Roy MacSkimming, a very accessible fellow whom I'd met when he was an editor at Clarke, Irwin (and who would fill every conceivable type of job in the book industry down through the years). Together, the three of them had resolved to start a new press, which they would call new press, lower case. Dave was definitely finished with Anansi. He'd leave all that to Dennis and pursue a less literary but, considered as publishing, rather more imaginative list. And new press, located a short distance along Sussex Avenue on the other side of Spadina, near enough for the address to be a taunt, would do some very interesting trade publishing while it lasted. In a few years Maclean Hunter invested in the company, later increasing its holdings but finally disposing of the business to the General Publishing group, run by Jack Stoddart Sr. By that time Dave had already founded a third publishing company, Press Porcépic, which he later moved to Victoria when he went there to teach. Porcépic would change its name to Beach Holme after first spawning a hugely successful software company.

The Godfreys' return from France coincided with the Willimans' departure for Italy (Dan had got a grant from the Canada Council to work in the Vatican Archives), and suddenly I was told I couldn't sleep in the basement anymore: I had to find some other place to live. I didn't have to go far. I took a furnished room atop the Williams Funeral Home, right next door. Later I would joke about this with Bob Flanagan, another of the Anansi poets. He lived not atop but beneath a former undertaker's on Dupont, in what had been its embalming room. The floor was on a slant and there was a large drain in the centre.

Looking back on it now, I can see clearly how Anansi went through all the stages I have since seen repeated in other presses. How initial success caused the company to over-expand. How, in order to utilise its new capacity efficiently, it briefly took on distribution of other people's books (those of Coach House, in this instance) only to find that efficiency, as such, was the last result that should ever have been expected. Mostly what I see, however, was the growing uneasiness all round. Self-absorbed as I was, I couldn't help but sense acutely that we were all going through our respective sticky patches. Dennis captures the mood of exhaustion perfectly in his poem "Sibelius Park," which he had printed as a broadside at Coach House. The title came from the green space and playground across from his house on upper Brunswick. He wrote of himself in the third person hauling his body towards home every night with a feeling of desolation.

> *Rochdale Anansi how many*
> *routine wipeouts has he performed since he was born?*

I can't read it even now without recapturing the sense of fatigue everybody felt—he most of all, no doubt—at putting so much energy into making and selling "fine iconic books" in such piteously small numbers while the important human issues seemed to slip away in the lethal fog of the events in Vietnam. His mood, I believe, was made even bleaker by fissures in his marriage, though there was certainly no mistaking that politics was corroding all the surfaces of life for people with literary or artistic personalities. The poem speaks of "the grim dungeon with friends—men with/ deep combative egos, ridden men, they cannot sit still, they go on brooding..." I always assumed that he intended me to feel included in this reference—though not a me I'd honestly recognize now, with all my combativeness long since gone.

Anansi had a system for paperwork (I don't know whose invention it was—probably Dave's) which I've used ever since in whatever office I've had. There were three trays marked TODAY, TOMORROW and PROBLEMS. Some of the problems could be thorny—lost shipments, angry authors, production nightmares—and everyone had a quota of them to tackle. The biggest problem of all turned out to be Allen Ginsberg's *Airplane Dreams*. This was 1969, the year before the United Church sold the Ryerson Press to McGraw-Hill and set in train a series of political responses that would echo for almost twenty years. But thanks in no small part to Anansi, publishing Canadian books, and building a permanent audience for them, was already a defiant act, and a certain political infrastructure had begun to assume shape. One of the red flags for Canadian publishers was the so-called Manufacturing Clause of the American copyright law. This was a measure aimed at protecting U.S. book printers from foreign competition. It held that the copyright on books by American citizens printed outside the United States would be lost if more than 3,000 copies were imported for sale into the U.S.

Dennis took complete charge of the Ginsberg once I brought in the manuscript; except for arranging for the author's cover photo to be taken and a few other small chores, I had nothing to do with the project, as my duties had always been of a more general office character, with some fulfilment and promotion thrown in. What's more, the book materialized during the period when Dave and Dennis were splitting up. Which is to say, at the point when Dennis was at some pains to show himself and others that he had keen commercial instincts or at least a certain familiarity with the practical end of life. He decided to print 6,000 copies of the book—a bigger print order than other Anansi books by a factor of six. True, Ginsberg's *Howl* had sold far more than 100,000 copies at that stage, but it was his major work, which *Airplane Dreams* hardly was, and in any case had sold them over a thirteen-year period. (When Coach House published Ginsberg's *Iron Horse* in 1973, it brought out its normal and prudent 500 copies, later going back to press for another 500.) I wasn't encouraged to voice an opinion. The reason the Anansi run was so large is that Dennis had made Anansi's first foreign distribution agreement, or thought he had. Flexing his entrepreneurial muscles, he had cut a deal with Ferlinghetti at City Lights to take most of the run.

Airplane Dreams needed one of Anansi's "sheepish errata," as Dennis would call them in "Sibelius Park." It took the form of a bookmark, and on the other side of it Dennis took it on himself to denounce the Manufacturing Clause, proclaiming that 5,000 copies of this work were being shipped across the border in defiance of the offensive American law. I'm not sure whether Ferlinghetti really understood the dangers or whether the author did either, though Dennis's little manifesto on the bookmark said the challenge was being made "with Allen Ginsberg's permission." In any case, the inevitable happened. The shipment was seized by U.S. Customs. Dennis was summoned to offer his defence and argue why the books should not be destroyed as contraband. He had no defence, so they were.

Poor Ferlinghetti, already chary of Canadians over non-payment of all the books sent up to Harry Fine on credit, vowed never again to do serious business with Canadian publishers, as I believe he has not, though he and Dennis worked out a joint-imprint edition of *Airplane Dreams* the following year to save face and assuage the author.

Shortly after this, Dennis asked me to come have a coffee with him at the Varsity Restaurant up on Bloor Street, an Anansi hang-out a few doors down from Meyer's Cigar Store where he bought his cigarillos every day. He promptly amazed me by saying I was fired. He didn't phrase it that way, explaining instead that he was bringing about a major reorganization and expansion of the press in which he didn't feel he could keep me on. In fact, he did just what executives are always taught never to do; he told half a dozen other people that he was firing me and gave all of them different reasons. I knew from the moment he finished the fatal pronouncement that I was the scapegoat for all the money lost on the Ginsberg fiasco. I felt as though all the air had been suddenly vacuumed out of my chest cavity, *swoosh*. But I recovered, as I always did. True, I had no money and wondered how I was going to feed myself. But then again I was twenty and it was time to turn the page and do something that would give me more opportunity to get on with my own writing. I've never harboured the least resentment against Dennis as I've followed his career appreciatively down through the years from a short distance away (for though we both moved any number of times we still seem to wind up in the same old neighbourhood). My regret is only that, after the Anansi days as during them, I was never able to communicate with him as effectively as I would have wished. I'm careful not to say that *we* can't communicate well, for it's my transmitter and not his receiver that's faulty somewhere. It saddens me.

As for Anansi, the story can be wrapped up quickly. Dennis was not a successful or happy manager, and the press was soon under the presidency of Shirley Gibson, who had been involved with the theatre and was the estranged wife of Graeme Gibson. One of the books she published was her own, a first collection of poetry. Then Margaret Atwood, who had commenced her loving partnership with Graeme Gibson, became more heavily involved in the press. Another of those interested was Ann Wall, who later bought out all the minority shareholders, including the ones like me with only a few shares. She had come to Canada long ago with a draft-aged husband, who had been an early Anansi volunteer. Peggy Atwood's former husband, Jim Polk, a talented and pleasant man with advanced degrees in both English and music, then became the editor of the press, which by this time had long since left Spadina, first for a house near the CBC on Jarvis and later for a co-operative publishers' building on Britain Street, a little spit of a street around Sherbourne and Queen.

The Anansi books in this later period, through the 1970s and well into the 1980s, were much better chosen, better edited and better designed than the early ones—mostly thanks to Polk, I believe. The range continued to be broad, and the trend, already apparent, of showing more verve in fiction than in verse was exacerbated. And there were a few more bestsellers, such as Atwood's *Survival*, though of course bestsellers were never really the point. Social comment, the third force on its list, had always been a ragged, haphazard affair under the original team. Now, under Gibson, Wall, Atwood and Polk (later reduced to Wall and Polk), it took on a fresh sense of purpose: more realistic in its causes, more practical, more consistent. But for all that, Anansi books never again seemed so important.

This is not a trick of perspective from my own vantage point, but the fact that the publishing landscape, thanks partly to Anansi's efforts but to a lot of other people's as well, had changed fundamentally—and for the better, so far as Canadian books were concerned. There were now Canadian publishers galore who were more or less small and to some degree commercial or non-exclusionary. As a result, Anansi's books were no longer big events. They didn't get into so many stores or get so many reviews. Even people like me who paid strict attention to these matters could discover some interesting Anansi book by chance, years after its publication. In growing up, Anansi was somehow diminished. In 1989 Ann Wall sold the imprint to Jack Stoddart Jr., son of the man who had bought out new press. There were no sad obituaries.

The general feuding of Anansi's vital if immature years dragged on in people's memories, of course. When the Godfreys were settled permanently in Victoria, Ellen, to some people's surprise, I think, began to write mysteries and true-crime books. Her first detective story was set in a small publishing house where a young bearded poet lived in the basement. The fictional murderer bore a strong resemblance to Dennis Lee.

CHAPTER FOUR

CHILD-OF-LETTERS

SARAH LIVED in Rosedale. Her place was at the south end of Glen Road, close to the ravine and the Sherbourne Street Bridge. It was in a former mansion that had been broken up into a dozen or more bed-sitting rooms, all occupied by young women of quality. On that, her landlady insisted. Sarah was studying creative writing at York University, and in her own time read Victorian novels. When I knew her, for instance, she was pushing her way through the oeuvre of Harrison Ainsworth, the low-grade Sir Walter Scott whose romances, like *Old St Paul's* and *Tower of London*, focused on individual buildings. For a dollar or so each, she had picked up odd volumes of these, bound in quarter-leather and with red marbled end-papers, at Old Favourites, the big secondhand bookstore on University Avenue. The books always lay scattered on her mantle-shelf. She was the kind of person to whom having a mantle-shelf seemed right. As such, she was certainly living in the perfect house.

I found the coziness, the human comfort and the bookishness a narcotic combination, especially during dark or rainy days, when we would stay in bed together, reading for hours. Sometimes she would read aloud—she had a beautifully modulated middle-class English voice, not too plummy and never arch. Sometimes we would even exchange books back and forth between us. I can still remember many of the titles we consumed together there. In fact, despite decades of moves and other traumas, I can still put my hands on some of the actual copies.

We had a slight problem with her landlady, Mrs. Kemeny, who frowned on male visitors. Once, after a particularly literary evening, we awoke in the morning to noises in the corridor. The other residents, wearing their dressing gowns, were shuffling up and down the carpet runners, queuing at the bathrooms with toothbrushes in their hands. Soon there was the shrill Hungarian voice of Mrs. Kemeny, getting nearer. Sarah went out to mingle with the others while I activated the emergency plan we had devised long before. I left by the window. From the nearly horizontal portion of the downspout that ran along the side of Sarah's room, it was only a short drop to the ground.

I had a problem with my own accommodations as well: I couldn't very well go on living at the funeral home next door to Anansi. So I began a campaign to convince Sarah that we should find a place of our own and move in together. Depending on the mood, I presented this as a plan that was either ruggedly practical or a romantic inevitability. She was reluctant to give up her cocoon-like space, reluctant even more to commit to me, but she promised to give the thing a try. As we didn't have much money even after pooling our resources, yet wanted something large and airy, the search proved tiresome. At one point we were lucky and almost had an apartment in one of those 1920s buildings up the Avenue Road hill towards St. Clair, all light brown brick and leaded windows, but the landlord who was showing us the place overheard some remark Sarah made to me that betrayed my place of birth, and he suddenly grew hostile, saying he didn't rent to Yankees.

In the end we were rescued by Sarah's younger sister, Holly. She lived with a dope dealer on St. Nicholas Street, a strange combination of warehouses and residential buildings that ran north/south between Yonge and Bay, from Wellesley all the way to Charles. Or rather she had been living with him for a while but they were now breaking up. Anyway, she knew the two-bedroom across the hall was coming on the market. It was only $110, utilities included. So what if the plumbing didn't usually work? Sarah was sceptical—because, I thought, she didn't approve of her kid sister's paramour. In fact, I was pressuring her into an arrangement she wasn't ready for or didn't totally believe in.

One day while Sarah was at school, I moved all my stuff over from Spadina, using the subway. This took much of the morning and the whole afternoon. By the time of the last trip I was carrying only my bed, which was a big five-inch-thick slab of foam from the army surplus store. It was getting on towards rush hour now, and I had the foam doubled over in my aching arms, like a dancing partner. Inevitably, other passengers pushed, the subway pitched and yawed, and the damn thing got away from me, striking a fat lady in the ass and knocking her across the aisle, shades of Groucho, Harpo and Chico.

But that night, when I offered to help Sarah start moving her stuff as well, I found out that she hadn't actually begun to pack. In fact, she hadn't even given her notice to the loud Mrs. Kemeny. We had what felt like long talks—one endless discontinuous talk, it seemed to me—the result of which was Sarah's conclusion that I couldn't communicate, and she didn't mean my speech impediment. I wouldn't admit it then, but of course I came to see that she was right—like to think that I knew it even then but was suppressing what I didn't wish to recognize. Anyway, she moved a few, a very few, of her things to St. Nicholas Street. Still, I could never get her to stay the night there with me. She would come almost every day and see Holly to comfort her during her travails, and even put aside her disdain of the dope dealer long enough to help Holly pack. I tried to lend a hand but was told I wasn't needed. I knew I'd never see Sarah again once she had helped her sister move to some place she had found for her out the Danforth.

All of us, I believe, have rooms that we re-inhabit only in our dreams, where the layout and atmosphere are so totally familiar to us that we find nocturnal comfort there. For me, that space is 52 St. Nicholas Street, corner of Inkerman. Some imposter of a building now occupies this site, but in my time there was a four-storey H-shaped structure with bow windows in front, put up before the First World War. It was here I decided to stay on alone and try to make my way solely by writing, though the rent was more than I could afford. There is an exact twin of No. 52, doubtless the work of the same builder, elsewhere in the city, and I always make a point of going out of my way to pass by. Whenever I do, I smile.

I was on the second floor. Immediately below me were two nursing students whose real interests were making sculptures out of old surgical devices. Their place was filled with them, and some hung in the window, causing passersby to wonder. As for Holly's former boyfriend across the hall from me, he kept his apartment dark with what I imagined might be blackout curtains from the Second World War, using only candles for illumination. Sitar music played constantly, and the stale air, thick with incense, would sometimes be enlivened by the tinkling of chimes, which hung suspended from all the doorways and window-frames—a crude security system, I guessed. His cover was that he worked a couple of nights a week as a teacher of English to new immigrants. This was ironical, as he himself was only recently arrived from Merseyside and spoke the thickest, most incomprehensible Scouse I had ever heard: a matter not of accent alone but of a vocabulary understood only within a certain section of Liverpool. The speech of John Lennon, when he was off-stage and tired, tended in this same direction, as I found out when I interviewed him around this time during one of his Toronto visits, but was not impenetrable to remotely the same degree. Several months into my life there, I noticed, as who could not?, that the building was suddenly being staked out. Some nights two male caucasians with beefy shoulders and little hats would spend hours across the street in an unmarked four-door sedan with a whip antenna and no dealer's decal. As they took no pains to be subtle, I assumed their presence was intended to rattle someone out into the open. To my surprise, they proved not to be after my neighbour but a young guy I'd never actually seen who lived holed up on the ground floor, in a little room far at the back, in what I suppose must once have been the custodian's quarters. It seems he was a fellow fugitive, wanted in the States for I forget what violent crime. The In the Courts column of the *Tely* had all the details.

Visitors were always coming and going at St. Nicholas, and one day Michael Ondaatje stopped by with a camera round his neck. He was in one of those periods, which his many friendly critics have tended to downplay, of wanting to be a photographer, a playwright and a filmmaker, or at least of wanting to mix any or all of those callings with his poetry and fiction (as he would in fact do with such success). He took some shots of me inside the apartment. But I never saw them and now he says they're undoubtedly lost.

Like most every poet for the preceding couple of generations, I made one of my first periodical appearances in the *Canadian Forum*, then being edited by Milton Wilson, and kept adding, one by one, the credits of such little magazines as would have me. I also had an early patron in Bob Weaver, a kindly anecdotal sort of man who ran the literary department of CBC Radio and was also editor of the *Tamarack Review*, the quarterly with in those days the widest and deepest moat (though this began to change not long afterwards). Bob's preferred method of doing CBC business was an annual coffee at the Four Seasons Hotel, across Jarvis Street from the Radio Building. There he would clean and re-clean his pipe and tell you his latest warm and affectionate story about Morley Callaghan or Margaret Laurence and behave in a generally circumlocutory way until the end of the meeting. Then, sometimes while rising to find his coat, he would let drop that he would buy such and such a batch of poems or this or that short story for broadcast.

I was not averse to picking up small jobs from book publishers either. In the basement of a building on Inkerman Street, a few doors away from my apartment, was Peter Martin Associates, one of the earliest of the generation of small presses which later, when Anansi came along to give definition and train a pool of transient talent, came to be seen as the Anansi generation. PMA, as it was called, was run by the husband-and-wife team of Peter and Carol Martin, then in their early thirties, I suppose, who put out a big list of general-interest books. Their publishing sprang originally from their book club, the only one for Canadian titles exclusively, which they had started in 1959 and were still pursuing, along with *Canadian Reader*, a magazine for the members. Their books had a small-l liberal and sometimes even a civil libertarian slant to them, which I liked, but dealing with Peter was difficult. Carol was invariably kind, solicitous, knowledgeable, friendly and efficient—qualities she later carried with her, following their divorce, to her roles as a Canada Council arts officer and then as a publishing consultant. Peter had neither her taste in Canadian writing nor her likable personality. What's more, he was impractical in business matters. He kept an enormous staff, largely, I think, because it made him feel successful, but too few of the books he published ever found their way into enough stores to support the kind of place he ran. He was also, like many alcoholics, a bully. Whenever he and I talked, he would manage to work into the conversation the fact that he had attended all the best private schools and I had not. My retort, which I always managed to keep from saying out loud, was to ask why if, as he claimed, he'd gone to all these places, he hadn't been taught proper manners. So I tried to deal mostly with Carol, and as such edited a poetry anthology for them and wrote prefaces to a few of their other books.

I tried never to turn away hack work if it had some connection to books and the arts, and while I never invested such jobs with more seriousness than they deserved, I never looked down on them either. I offer two examples to stand for the many. At *Maclean's*, which was then still a general-interest magazine and not yet a news weekly, the end of the budgetary year coincided with the approach of spring, and the editor, Peter Newman, was to some extent reduced to living off his inventory, like a householder using up all the leftovers in the fridge in the last week before payday. Throughout the year, the magazine had been sending top-notch photographers like John De Visser back and forth across the country on assignment; the result was now a lot of expensive transparencies which, though already paid for, had never, for one reason or another, been used. Staff members at light-tables in the art department kept arranging and re-arranging them in different combinations, trying to find a common theme. There were Atlantic fishermen working their nets. There were Ontario farmers preparing the ground for ploughing. There were extreme close-ups of dew drops on the leaves of weeds somewhere on the Prairies. So it was decided to run these all together as a tribute to spring in Canada. There was room for a certain precise amount of text—say, 2,435 words—to run like a serpent around the various images, and for some reason it was decided to have me interview Marshall McLuhan about the place of spring in the Canadian psyche. They could hardly have come up with a celebrity less obviously interested in the role of spring, or anything else, as it applied to the Canadian psyche.

I tracked down the famous reeve of the Global Village, the great guru of mass media, at the special institute bearing his name at the University of Toronto. With mounting embarrassment, I explained the premise. He remained silent for what seemed the longest time, and I thought certain our interview had ended before it had got under way. Then suddenly he said words to the effect of "OK, kid, take this down." Whereupon he switched on his fountain of wonderful nonsense and out came a stream of something very much like prose, all quite fresh-sounding and superficially deep, exactly 2,435 words' worth of it. He then bade me good morning. The money pains at the magazine turned out to be nothing more serious than gas, so I was paid off and the piece never ran.

At this time I had some friends at the madhouse called McClelland & Stewart, and I was not too proud to take unsolicited manuscripts from the slush pile to be read and reported on for as little as ten dollars each. The relationship led to one of my more bizarre bits of editorial troubleshooting. Peter Taylor, a former novelist on the M&S list who had become the company's marketing manager, phoned me in a panic to say that the bright young person they had taken on as a copywriter and of whom they had entertained high hopes had let them down by having a nervous breakdown or some such. Anyway, could I write all the copy for the autumn catalogue by Monday morning? I pointed out that this was Friday and that I hadn't read any of the books. No problem, Peter replied cheerily; in many cases, there were rough notes from some of the editors saying what the works seemed to be about. And anyway, he went on, we'll pay you—and he named what sounded to me an impossibly large sum of money.

By simply working through the night for two nights running, I had the job done by Sunday. I was ready to defy anyone, even the poor authors, to recognize that in most cases I didn't have the foggiest idea what I was talking about. I grew so cocky, in fact, that I used Sunday to write a satire on the process of writing fall catalogue copy. One of the autumn titles, I remember, was a sumptuous book on Alfred Pellan's art. The real copy began something like this: "No expense has been spared in the fidelity of the reproductions of these seventy-five works by the master of Quebec surrealist painting between the wars…" My translation into truth would have begun like this: "Jack McClelland was in Harry's Bar in Venice and he met this Italian printer…" I completed these rival versions for all the books in the catalogue, and on Monday morning called a courier to take the two sets off to M&S in a single package. I then waited for weeks with anxiety bordering on panic to see whether, in their haste, the company might have printed the wrong ones. Stranger things happened at

McClelland & Stewart in those days, much stranger.

When, in a celebrated political event around this time, the provincial government bailed the company out by guaranteeing some major bank loans, the politicians naturally imposed a stipulation on the deal: the right to appoint the M&S chief financial officer. My friends were terrified that the person from Clarkson Gordon would arrive in his three-piece suit and instantly eliminate all the fun and freedom that made their work there bearable, even enjoyable. Some months later I happened to be at the offices, and was expecting to see all my buddies with short hair and suits. Instead I saw the dreaded person in question. He was wearing a string of beads. This was the first sign that instead of Clarksongordonizing McClelland & Stewart, he himself had been McClellandized.

Most of the book publishers were still downtown in those days, having not yet fled to Don Mills, Richmond Hill or Markham (as they would do in the mid-1970s, only to return a decade later, at least their editorial and publicity departments). McClelland & Stewart may have been divided, with its main shop on Hollinger Road in East York and most of its editorial and design people downtown, at King and Simcoe Streets, above a place called Speedy Auto Glass. But the others were fully integrated at their individual locations. For example, according to one of my feeble witticisms of the time, Macmillan was *in* Bond Street while Doubleday was *on* Bond Street. Most of the magazines, too, were located in what, until the Great Fire of 1904, had been the printing and commercial arts district whose main thoroughfares were Adelaide, Richmond and Wellington Streets, an area that still retained traces of that heritage—primarily because the rents were cheap.

I had quite a ways to go before the big magazines would accept me as a regular, but every week I made my rounds. Checking the trap-line, as a friend calls it. My stops included two editorial offices a block from each other on Adelaide Street: that of *artscanada*, then a kind of thematic extravaganza, often surprising and usually late in appearing, and that of *Toronto Life*, which had commenced only in 1966 and was already on its third editor, a legendary character who wore moccasins in the office and carried a bullwhip. The owner of *Toronto Life* at the time was Michael Sifton, an Ontario member of the western newspaper-owning family, and the magazine seemed to reflect what a series of editors thought a wealthy amateur publisher would wish for. As a result, Sifton, who owned an indoor polo field and was an avid equestrian, had the pleasure of seeing the horsey set displayed in his magazine every month. That is to say, the magazine's sometimes embarrassing journalistic adolescence was bound up partly with trying to make the periodical reflect some veneer of sophistication that the city did not in fact then possess. *Toronto Life* had a society editor: an effervescent, prematurely blonde woman who emitted some faint suggestion of perhaps once having been a Hungarian. She and one of the magazine's photographers would show up at parties and openings, taking down names and snapping pictures. I cherish the memory of the cutline beneath a photograph of a certain cultural figure of my acquaintance. The caption ran, in its entirety: "Here's perky Sandra, hosting a visiting Peruvian!"

By now, I was well underway on my lifelong policy of trying to continue my education through book-reviewing. They didn't know it, but I used literary sections of papers and magazines to subsidize my studies while earning myself a pittance in the bargain (a kind of student loan, doled out fifty or seventy-five dollars a throw, which never had to be paid back). As time went on, I grew more not less ambitious in reviews, until I thought nothing of reading four or five other books if necessary to deal adequately with the one at hand, and I came to dislike reviews that attempted to slide by on a reviewer's subjective opinion—book good, me like; book bad, me no like—without always comparing every possible facet to that of some other book or writer and without trying to deal with ideas. No reviews without ideas, this almost became a battle cry. A few people tolerated the kind of reviewing I was interested in developing, but seldom for very long. I found a thousand ways to disguise serious intent, as a baby's parents learn to hide green vegetables in other foods they know won't be spit out.

The three daily newspapers were important stops on my trap-line: the *Star* at the famous address 80 King Street West, where I would sometimes pause in the Stoodleigh Restaurant downstairs to gather my will or have a shoe shine at the barber shop next door to make myself less unprepossessing; the *Globe and Mail*, a bit farther along King, at the corner of York; and the *Telegram*, down on Front, just west of Spadina, its new building, which the *Globe* would later get for itself like a hermit crab taking over another's vacated shell. I was happiest at the *Star*, whose liberal politics were then still pretty firmly intact, and several people were particularly nice to me, including Nathan Cohen, the famous drama critic and mythomane, though his severe countenance scared me to death. But the *Globe* was more receptive to the kind of reviewing I wanted to do, and could give me almost as many books as I could ingest. It was a strange place, however, with odd sensitivities—and sometimes very limited space. When the autobiography of the White Russian novelist Nina Berberova was first published in English, in 1969, I wrote a short and, in retrospect, stupid notice of it. Within days, the author had dispatched a reproving personal letter to Dic Doyle, the *Globe*'s editor. Bill French, the editor of the books section, warned me that Doyle was rumoured to be impressed with the letter's logic. For the next several weeks I came and went by the *Globe*'s back door in Pearl Street and wrote under imaginative yet opaque pseudonyms. In those days I often had to use pseudonyms to survive. Custom said that one couldn't review for both the *Globe* and the *Star*, for example. But while writing in the *Globe* as Fetherling, I also, with the connivance of French's rival, Kildare Dobbs, wrote in the *Star* as Ronald Upjohn. No one was any the wiser until Upjohn launched a scathing attack on Fetherling one week. In any case, I was delighted when, twenty-two years later, Phillipe Radley's translation of the Berberova memoirs was republished, and I was able to write a long and better-considered piece on it.

As for the *Telegram*, the organ of an older Toronto, with roots in the Conservative Party and a WASP identity that few had seemed to question until well after the Second World War, one might have expected that its book coverage would be similar to that of, say, the Montreal *Star*, where John Richmond, the influential literary editor, could be counted on to review any books about the royal family and related concerns. But in fact, the *Tely* had a thoughtful and cosmopolitan book page presided over by Barry Callaghan, whose father, Morley, was the city's senior literary figure. The joke was always that if John Bassett, the proprietor, learned that he had a book page, he would have been cross. I never broke into the page at the *Tely* but hung about all the same, as I did at the other two papers, hoping for whatever crumbs of other writing might be going begging; but my links with the *Telegram*'s culture and aesthetic, so to call them, were never sympathetic, as with the *Globe*'s, nor organic, as with the *Star*'s. I met John Bassett only once, for example, and was impressed by the fact that his jaw-line was a perfect right angle, making him look as though he had been drawn by Milton Caniff (whose comic strip "Steve Canyon" appeared in the *Star*). Also, I couldn't help but observe that, though it was only four in the afternoon, he was wearing a tuxedo.

Even more so than later, publishers took an I-shot-an-arrow-into-the-air approach to publicity by sending out scores of review copies and hoping for the best. The review slips always gave Saturday release dates because Saturdays the newspapers' review pages appeared (there being no Sunday papers then). Such dates were broken at one's peril. Consequently, there was considerable competition to review new books on time, rather as new plays are reviewed, and just as in the theatre, there were parties to mark the occasion. Macmillan often threw sedate little parties with sherry, M&S sometimes lavish ones at exotic locations, such as the floor of the stock exchange or some rich person's roof garden. In September and October there might be several soirées a week, allowing a young reviewer, trying to get by in a world he never made, to exist almost entirely on gin and canapés. The saving in groceries, combined with the couple of dollars the review copies fetched in the secondhand bookstores, might permit him a badly needed scuttleful of coal.

Of those parties at which I was conscious, the one that sticks in my mind was a terribly posh affair thrown by Doubleday for their dreary money-spinner Arthur Hailey. It was at the old Granite Club on St. Clair Avenue and no doubt cost $40,000 or so in today's money. A poor commissionaire, stationed at the entrance, questioned the identity of two of the arriving guests, who turned out to be the all-powerful industrialist E.P. Taylor and his wife; the commissionaire was never heard from again. I remember meeting at that function a person who was already one of my favourite perennial fellow guests. He was a second- or third-string Toronto *Star* reviewer and entertainment writer who as a child had lived in the Ritz in London where his father had been head pastry chef and where one of his father's apprentices, drawn from the foreign-student quarter, was the young Ho Chi Minh. The war in Vietnam was still on the lips and in the lungs when the scene I describe took place, and hearing my *Star* friend let drop this autobiographical gem (which he did at every such occasion), a number of people gathered about him, pumping his hand with real emotion and pressing him for whatever memories of the great man, however small, he might possess. His response was to grab another fistful of crab puffs from the next waiter who floated by. "Not like Uncle Ho's," he would say. "His crusts were, well, *superb.*"

As a salesman of myself, I left almost everything to be desired. One old editor confided to me recently that when I first called on him in those days, his secretary tried to discourage him from seeing me, but he remembered a boy in his class at Upper Canada College who had stuttered and so decided to risk it. Yet I persisted. When I think back to this time in my life, it is always to grey days in winter, when the afternoon is shrinking into dusk and I'm getting more and more depressed as I bang on doors and have endless cups of coffee and make my case for myself and then go home in the dark to begin the little bits of work I've managed to secure. Sometimes I would be out from early in the morning and not return until after six, so I wouldn't know until the evening what had arrived in that day's post. Once I can remember coming home with a bag of Chinese food for dinner and pausing at the mail-box in the lobby to find a $250 cheque which I hadn't been expecting. Anyone who thinks this too trivial an anecdote to include has never been a freelance writer—or an independent writer, as I preferred to think of myself. Thus did I sidestep a term I disliked, one I associated with people of base purpose (who, parenthetically, were also much more successful at it than I was—a connection I couldn't quite see). If one can't be independently wealthy, I seemed to be saying to myself, at least one can be independently poor, but in any event, bloody independent. By being an independent or non-aligned writer, I meant more or less what a small freeholder means who tells you that mixed farming is best and wants no truck with agribusiness. It was a moral choice, if maybe also a moral choice one had forced on oneself as by some quirk of personality.

November 1987, almost twenty years later, early in the afternoon. I was packing to leave Toronto, trying to decide what I should take to Kingston, where I was to spend most of each week writing a books-and-ideas column for the *Whig-Standard.* Suddenly there was a savage banging at the door. Ruben Zellermayer was a sculptor who lived and worked in the basement of the adjoining house where I would sometimes see my old friend Gwendolyn MacEwen. He was in a state approaching shock.

"Gwen's dead," he blurted out. As he told me of finding the body at her apartment, he was actually rubbing his head back and forth in his hands, as though to erase the image from his mind. The first person he thought to tell was Joyce Marshall, one of Gwen's writer friends who lived close by. Then he came to me.

He was so distraught that I didn't know how to handle him, so I walked him round the corner to my wife Janet's bookshop on Bathurst Street. She's much better at emergencies than I am, emotional ones in particular.

That night, of course, and frequently thereafter in the coming months, I fell to thinking about poor Gwen, not the one whose photograph Ruben hung at the entrance to his studio, but the vibrant, mysterious and not in the least crazy Gwen I'd first met at Anansi and got to know back in the St. Nicholas Street days. She was only forty-six when she died, so she had to have been twenty-seven when I met her in 1968. Our first conversation was about the fact that I had been using the name Gwendolyn in some of my poems—until then, I'd never actually met a Gwendolyn; I simply thought it was a lovely combination of syllables. She looked exactly as she did on the dust-jacket of her most recent poetry collection, *A Breakfast for Barbarians.* She was petite, as people then said, and had large sad eyes under striking black brows, and wore her hair in a flip. The clothes she was partial to were first of all simple. She once admitted a liking for a particular type of lisle stockings which, she said, could only be bought at some virtually clandestine shop which catered to Roman Catholic nuns. But her clothes were dramatic as well, with flowing sleeves and silk here, brocade there. Of her appearance, I should say that she was totally up-to-the-minute by virtue of being indebted, in some vague but absolutely unmistakable way, to a much earlier time. All this made her inadvertently stylish, as she knew but wouldn't deign to acknowledge.

Like the work of Northrop Frye, Jay Macpherson and so many others, Gwen's was often concerned with the intersection of myth and life (and in her case particularly, with magic and anthropology). But she stood apart from the others, in large part because she wasn't an academic. She was in fact an autodidact (maybe that's why she and I got along so well) who, despite scholarship offers, had dropped out of school at eighteen in order to write. At twenty, she was an important figure in the little Toronto bohemia whose centre was Gerrard Street Village, the one whose feeling, I think, is best evoked in the text Harold Town did some years later for a book on Albert Franck's painting. Gwen published two poetry chapbooks, *Selah* and *The Drunken Clock.* When she was twenty-two, Eli Wilentz of the 8th Street Bookshop in New York brought out her first novel, *Julian the Magician.* This represented quite an undertaking for his press, Corinth Books, which until then had published only short works by most of the major Beats, nothing ambitious and nothing far afield. That is to say, Gwen became an early literary star. But unlike many people who find their talents are fashionable when they're quite young, she didn't disappear from the scene later on, as soon as the fickle media found someone else.

She had *noticed* the attention all right, but I don't think she was fazed by it. There was probably no one else in Canada then writing poetry made of the same materials as hers—the deep sense of magic and its relation to personal history, for example—yet she touched many different groups and circles in ways you would expect only a more public sort of writer to do. Michael Ondaatje told me once how terribly important it was to the community of poets studying and teaching in Kingston in 1965 when she agreed to come to Queen's to read. And of course a lot of feminist writers would look back to Gwen as a kind of pioneer. They saw her, I believe, as someone who got her start just barely before their own time and wrote from some of the same concerns, though not necessarily in the same diction as themselves (it hadn't been coined) nor even from the same stance (not yet rediscovered). Margaret Atwood, for example, would be a loyal champion of Gwen and her work until the end—and beyond.

I can only speculate what it meant for Gwen to live out her life in the city that was the scene of her unpleasant childhood. She wasn't the sort of person to reminisce, but one gathered that her upbringing had been somehow desolate. She never mentioned her father, an alcoholic Scot, whom her psychotic mother had left in the early 1950s—that is, not until her final book, *Afterworlds*, published eight months before she died, in which she used a photograph "by the author's father, Alick MacEwen A.R.P.S. (1904–1960)." But her mother, Elsie, a Cockney, was around Toronto during the years I refer to, living for a time in what was then the Elmwood Hotel for Women. I went there once with Gwen. It smelled of impending death and was decorated here and there with potted palms that resembled pathological specimens. The Elmwood was the sort of place where English women who had left decent homes to come out to Canada between the wars ended up in a state of impoverished widowhood, wondering how life went wrong. It also housed recovering psychiatric patients. Years later, the building was taken over by one of the granddaughters of the first Lord Thomson, who redid it as an exclusive dining club and spa for executive women with too much money.

Gwen's closest relative was her sister, Carol, who lived near Eglinton and Weston Road in the Borough of York. For years, particularly when she was working intensely on complicated projects like *King of Egypt, King of Dreams*, her novel about the pharaoh Akhenaton, she would use her sister's place as an accommodation address, meeting acquaintances, if she had to meet them at all, at a nearby drugstore soda fountain, which appeared not to have changed in thirty years.

She had amazing talents, some of which the public saw and others they didn't. She had genuine psychic ability, for example. Once I was sitting silently, trying to remember the title of a movie I had seen based on an H.P. Lovecraft story. (Even now, I have to go look it up: *The Shuttered Room.*) I hadn't spoken aloud about this, not so much as a word, when Gwen came into the room and said matter-of-factly, "The name on the mailbox is Tierney." I nearly fell off my chair, for this was a line of dialogue on which the horror plot turned. Better known was her gift for languages, which served her well both as a literary translator and as a traveller. It was typical of her, though, that her knack extended beyond the romance languages or any one family of languages. For example, she taught herself enough Arabic to translate some Arabic writers (though the only fruits of this study to be published was a collection of folk tales for children, *The Honey Drum*).

As a young girl she had been a violin prodigy. So once when we went to a party together and she wandered off to a serious corner, she picked up a guitar that happened to be lying there and started trying to figure out how to transpose what she knew to this foreign instrument. When she started, she was holding it across her lap like a dulcimer and using her long nails to strike the strings. By the time we were ready to go, she was holding, fretting and fingering it in the conventional manner, and playing quite freely. This wasn't the sort of thing she'd ever mention again; it was just done to pass the time. I had known her reasonably well before I discovered by chance that she'd recently taken up painting, had done a roomful of interesting work, and then stopped—for good. Literature was her calling.

She wrote single-mindedly, as a writer must, and was never much tempted by material comforts, as most people are as they get older. When she needed extra money, she wrote plays—I remember many radio plays, richly evocative but never in the least romantic, for Bob Weaver at the CBC, and a new translation of *The Trojan Women* for one of the middle-class subscription theatres. She also gave splendid poetry readings, wearing a frock and the perfect eccentric earrings, performing faultlessly for a half-hour or an hour without consulting her book, which she held unopened in her hand—a mere prop—and sometimes dispensed with entirely. Much later, she would do a term here or there as writer-in-residence, but she was never a careerist, and she never stopped writing poetry—and never stopped always trying to write much different poetry—even after she began publishing short stories, a travel narrative, all sorts of things. People would never associate her with the tradition, because she eschewed all its cant and self-importance, but she was in fact a genuine *femme des lettres.*

"Can I ask you a personal question?" I said to her once.

She laughed. "If not now, I don't know when." We were in bed at St. Nicholas Street at the time. It was somewhere between winter and spring. I remember there was a big storm kicking up outside.

"What's the story on you and Milt?"

Everyone who had been around the Toronto writing scene at the time seemed to have tales about the incongruous and, I gathered, disastrous marriage of Gwen and Milton Acorn, the foul-smelling poet and self-proclaimed proletarian. People had told me of their days together on Wards Island, of how the two of them danced naked in their garden like William and Catherine Blake. I was incredulous. I mean, this had been only about six years earlier. It seemed unthinkable that she could ever have been mated up with Acorn if he was anything like the Acorn of 1968 and later: a red-nosed, red-necked wreck of a fellow who wandered the streets talking to himself, shouting out insults, threatening people with injury or even death.

"It was a mistake," she said. "The mistake of my life. I was a teenager." In fact, she had been twenty-one or twenty-two, and he thirty-nine or forty. "It didn't even last a year. Later, we got divorced." She talked a little more about it, making it sound like a whim that turned into tragedy. The tragedy was mostly that Acorn, having somehow had the astounding good fortune to find a woman like Gwen in love with him, never recovered from the rebuke when it turned out that she wasn't. First he went into self-imposed exile on the West Coast. One often heard stories of his life there. An antiquarian bookseller in Vancouver once showed me the carbon copy of one of the strangest literary projects I could imagine: a collaborative poetry collection, never published of course, by Acorn and bill bissett. Anyway, Acorn had returned to Toronto only in the past couple of years, and at this stage was living in a cheap rooming house on Spadina Road. Soon he would find a permanent home at the Waverley Hotel, where men without work waited each day for the Fred Victor Mission to open and where people in the beverage room drank beer to see if they could forget who they were. All the while he nursed an incredible hatred towards Gwen, but it was, I think, a hatred he could never quite bring himself to believe, and he heaped calumny on her friends, probably including Bob Mallory, an artist who had hung around the Gerrard Street Village (and who later, for no apparent reason, insisted on being called Leo—and then, after another rebirth of some kind, Leo Revised). One of Acorn's poems read:

For a woman to get published in the Tamarack Review
If she has a good husband, she must leave him;
Write sad existential letters about he was so
goddam noble
She couldn't stand it, whilst laying the dirtiest
bastard in town;
Then send poems to the Tamarack Review
More explicit than a marriage manual but not so
passionate.

Then, just as today, Acorn had his loyalists. Some of the tolerance he engendered in people was because of—as well as despite—his politics, which were those of a 1930s cartoon in the *New Masses*, crudely drawn and without much relevance to present agonies. But mostly of course the people who put up with him did so for the sake of his poetry. For it was a curious fact that unlike the other similar figures one could name in literary history—from Dr. Johnson's friend Richard

Savage to Maxwell Bodenheim to Julian Maclaren-Ross—Acorn in fact had a big talent (the sample quoted above notwithstanding). Not, I think, one supplemented by much intellect or one much improved on down through the years, but an original voice all the same, and it was a calling he was faithful to. Maybe at base it was that focus and commitment that Gwen and he had in common. Maybe she saw the very real danger of her talent (if not his too) being trampled by the realities of living with a crazy man. At least that was what I picked up between the lines as she talked.

Years later, after both of them were dead, Al Purdy told me the part of the story she left out, even between the lines. Al had always looked up to, and looked after, Milton, one of the heroes of their shared literary youth. People said Milton had been hurt in the war, that he had a plate in his head and drew a disability pension. I never knew the extent of the truth, except that he used to be a carpenter before he downed tools to write about the working man instead of being one. The Purdy house on Roblin Lake at Ameliasburg, the setting of many a poem by Al and any number of others, started out as a simple A-frame that Al and Milton had built together with their own hands, using secondhand lumber, in 1954. Al, in short, was Acorn's closest and oldest friend, which is to say, his most tolerant and forgiving one. It was to him, Al told me, that Gwen came, asking if he would give evidence as the co-respondent in the divorce case if called on. Al said he felt he had no choice but to agree. He also said he was certain that Acorn never found out about her request.

In some ways, Gwen was English Canada's Marie-

Claire Blais, if for no other reason than a shared precocity and range. The two were certainly friends, so that when Blais won the Governor General's Award for fiction for *Les manuscrits de Pauline Archange*, she invited Gwen and me to be her guests at the ceremony in Ottawa. We decided to make Rideau Hall the site of situational theatre and mock the occasion by dressing in a high Victorian manner appropriate to the general air of pomposity. Gwen more or less chickened out, but I wore a frock coat and also a top hat, which I delighted to hand to an attendant as we entered. Prime Minister Trudeau came to the reception afterwards, giving evidence of knowing who all the writers were if not perhaps having read the books, and he was very attentive to Gwen, with that dry-ice charm of his. The year was also memorable not so much because Hubert Aquin refused the award, as francophone writers were forever doing, but because Leonard Cohen declined as well, for his *Selected Poems*, or rather first declined, then accepted, then declined again, disdaining to attend any of the celebratory parties but showing up at one of them anyway.

About this time, Al Purdy put together a substantial collection of Acorn's new and old poetry, *I've Tasted My Blood*, and was trying to persuade the Ryerson Press to publish it. It duly appeared, and many of Acorn's sentimental or political boosters hoped it would win the Governor General's for works published during 1969. When the awards were made known, however, the prize for poetry in English was shared, by George Bowering, for *Rocky Mountain Foot* and *The Gangs of Kosmos*—and Gwendolyn MacEwen, for *The Shadow-Maker*. Personally, I thought *Rocky Mountain Foot* easily the most important of the three. In any event, anyone could have foreseen what Acorn's reaction would be. He had long taken delight in writing and saying vile things about Gwen—in that respect, nothing changed. From this point forward, however, he seemed to exist at ever greater odds with reality.

The whole matter of Acorn's book became a cause, and a contingent of his friends proposed to organize a public ceremony, a kind of anti-Governor General's Award, at which Milt would be fêted, toasted and presented with a medallion proclaiming him the People's Poet. The event—I remember it well—was held at Grossman's Tavern on Spadina. The room was jammed with poets and readers and hangers-on and a surprisingly large delegation of the media. Eli Mandel, a poet of Acorn's age but an irredeemably conventional middle-class academic one who taught at York, was the master of ceremonies. Mandel was one of those profs who managed, in a way that was not in the least paradoxical to writers of that time, to turn out both dry academic criticism and elegies for dead rock stars. On the day in question he was using his populist voice, though he had forgotten to change from his academic's clothes—an expensive turtle-neck and slacks. When the TV cameras rolled and the medal was slung around Acorn's neck, Eli grabbed the microphone, raised a clenched fist in the air and shouted, "All power to the people!" There were no *people* present, not in the sense he was using the word. If by some miracle, a faction similar to the Red Guards had chosen that moment to rise up, however, they would of course have had Acorn and Eli and the whole lot sent off to re-education camps immediately. But no, I'm being much too harsh on Eli, who was merely letting himself look foolish in what he thought was a good cause.

Many of the folks involved in this *affaire* were caught up in its anxieties, including George Bowering, whom the Acorn troops began attacking quite fiercely. In a letter to George at about this time, I made a weak jest, in an awkward and totally misguided attempt to lighten the mood. Under stress, as anyone would be in that situation, he easily misread this inarticulate expression of sympathy and, much to my very genuine sorrow, reacted badly. Emotions were running high anyway, because by this time the United Church had made its decision to sell Ryerson Press, for generations the hearthstone of Can lit, to McGraw-Hill, of all people. I remember being part of at least one mass meeting, but the protests took many forms, including a decision by a small number of Ryerson authors to abrogate their contracts. There was a fashion at this time among certain writers to declare that "copyright is obsolete," that creative work should be treated like an element of life, not like a commodity. Victor Coleman, for example, went through a period of pointedly declaring his published work outside the artificial construct of the Copyright Act. Acorn now joined in and went so far as to inform McGraw-Hill Ryerson, as the Canadian branch plant was rechristened, that he would refuse to accept any tainted McGraw-Hill money that might come due him from *I've Tasted My Blood.* The McGraw-Hill types, an untutored lot of business people, unsophisticated in literary matters, stupidly took him at his word and pocketed some reprint fees that came in for him. Al Purdy had to act as intermediary and get poor Acorn his money.

Gwen would enjoy another green period, different from her first bout of literary fame, and lasting the better part of a decade. She married again, to a singer, Nikos Tsingos, and they operated a Greek coffee house out on the Danforth that always seemed to be full of food and music and old friends. Except that it was noisy, it was a kind of salon, and she was in her element—the perfect backdrop for the antiquarian side of her personality. She naturally acquired an easy fluency in Greek, spoken and written, and began translating Greek writers and making trips to Greece, including the ones recounted in *Mermaids and Ikons*, a travel narrative Anansi later published, a book whose prose I've long admired for its beauty and control. Gwen had always been attracted to the Near East—a rare quality in Canadian writers up to that time, who had generally preferred Africa or Latin America; attracted not only in a romantic way, as reflected in her poems about T.E. Lawrence (spurred, I think, by an interest in the Turks), but visually and linguistically as well, and to Israel and Egypt alike. Greek culture, as well as being a new source of joy in itself, seemed to give her the imaginative boost she needed to bring together her various long-standing interests—mythology, illusion, harmony, richness of textures, magic (or should I say magick?). Her writing only improved still more as she got older, though the devils began to snap at her ankles.

I don't know how else to phrase it. I certainly don't know how to explain it. Sure, the marriage to Nikos ended eventually, and I'm certain she was lonely. To dwell on those facts would be simplistic, yet I can offer no better insight, only observations from ever more infrequent meetings. She grew puffy from drink and could be sharp and sour on occasion. Twice she telephoned and monologized for half or three-quarters of an hour, full of almost incoherent complaints about neighbours and others. At these times, she would express theories about their behaviour that seemed to me to border on the paranoid (though I use the term only as a layperson does). I think her circle generally grew much smaller and less rewarding, and one heard that she would take up with questionable characters (perhaps trying to relive something—that's as far as I would care to go in the direction of analysis).

I didn't know until quite recently how much her death affected me. I feel the pang strongly when I read certain of her books again and I'm warmed by the memory of the brief time we were in communication. I'm quick to add that I claim no special privilege of recollection. Many others knew her much better than I did and over a longer period. Yet she was always, I believe, the sort of person to keep her acquaintances in separate compartments—we spotted that in each other right away. There was, however, one friend we had in common, and in the first few days after Ruben brought the horrible news, I wrote a letter to Vera Frenkel, the video artist. She had been acquainted with Gwen at intervals since the early 1960s and had recently come to form a friendship with her. She was away in England at this time, as artist-in-residence at the Slade School, so I sat down to give her the facts as I'd learned them. I told her how Ruben

> hadn't talked with Gwen since Saturday and, fearful that something might have happened, went to

her place on Major Street and let himself in with the hidden latchkey. He quickly sensed tragedy and found her body in the bedroom where she'd died sometime in the previous 24 hours....

Janet had telephoned Gwen about a week earlier but had got her during a bad spell (the DTs or verging on the DTs). Ruben says that for the last little while she had been experiencing small stroke-like episodes. It was apparently a larger version of the same that killed her. She was dressed and had her feet on the floor but her torso across the bed, as though she had fallen while passing through the room. She had been eating an apple. Certainly there was no note or other evidence of suicide nor any sign of foul play, though the cops apparently believe somebody may have been in the apartment before Ruben and left without notifying anyone. Ruben reported that they were looking for a drinking buddy, a construction worker who'd been staying there a couple days.

What a bloody awful waste. As I say, I hate to be the one to tell you but I'm certain you're not seeing the *Globe* there (and the copies at Canada House are always three weeks old in any case) and I thought you'd want to know.

In the last days before Sarah left me, or thought better of me, she and I went to a party in a coach-house apartment in the Annex. The hosts were an actress friend of hers I didn't know and her housemate, a square-jawed young journalist named Bill Cameron. In later years Bill would be one of the faces of the national news on CBC Television, but in those days he had two far less significant jobs, writing a column for the *Star Weekly*, then being edited by Peter Gzowski, and hosting, only temporarily as it turned out, a Sunday morning magazine show on CBC Radio. The column was called "Bohemia by Bill Cameron" and dealt with such matters as House of Anansi and the thousands of suburban kids and rubberneckers who thronged Yorkville every Friday and Saturday night, hoping to sight some hippies and smell an illegal fragrance. The radio show was called *Sunday Supplement* and was produced by Howard Engel, whom Bill introduced me to that evening. Howard was a gentle and urbane man in his late thirties who had recently come back to Toronto after freelancing for the Corporation in France and on Cyprus. He was an intensely literary fellow, interested mostly in the classic modernists but with broad tastes. He was married to Marian Engel, who had just then published her first novel, *No Clouds of Glory*.

When Sarah went out of my life, I was overcome, slowly but steadily and with worsening effects, by a state of depression. Not for the first time in my life nor the last, I felt like an old hard-hat deep-sea diver, moving along the ocean bottom in leaden boots. Both my own writing and my bread-work fell off, and I realized that if I were going to keep the place on St. Nicholas, with its luxury of the second bedroom to be used as an office, I had better get some sort of small base income that I could depend on every month to help with the rent. In quest of such an arrangement, I went up and down my trap-line, and importuned my contacts. Finally I was thrown back on making entirely new acquaintances for this purpose. It was in this spirit that I went to the CBC Radio Building one day and called on the poet Phyllis Webb, who was producing *Ideas*, the talks series she had originated a few years earlier. I was an admirer of her work, particularly the collection *Naked Poems*, and we chatted about poetry for a while before I explained my dilemma. While promising to consider me for freelance work in the future, she sent me over to see Howard (whom I think she also might have telephoned the instant I left her office). As luck would have it, Howard had just been down talking to Marty Ahvenus, proprietor of the Village Book Store in the old Gerrard Street Village, asking what was new and hot, and Marty had pressed on him a copy of my Anansi book. Never had timing worked more in my favour. It was clear I couldn't be a broadcaster (though in time I did manage to do a few bits of on-air work—they always involved long hours at the Ampex, painstakingly eliminating my strained pauses and repetitions with a single-edge razor blade). But there was a lot of miscellaneous writing and story-vetting to be done on a ninety-minute weekly magazine programme, and Howard gave me a short contract. That soon expired and was extended with another one, this time at a gross of $125 a week—more money than I had ever earned.

Thus, Howard Engel, a genial friend of writers and a frustrated writer himself (until, many years later, following his divorce and remarriage, he parted from the CBC acrimoniously and to support himself stepped up production of the mystery stories he had started to create, employing the durable character of Benny Cooperman). Howard made few demands and was quick to praise, and actually seemed to enjoy watching me build a kind of literary career partly on office time while making sure that I had a chance to meet or work with some of the figures in broadcasting history who were still around—people like Andrew Allan, the dapper little drama producer, and J. Frank Willis, the veteran news correspondent associated with the 1936 Moose River Mine Disaster and so many other big stories of the past. And Howard understood completely when, after I'd saved enough money from the munificent salary, I bid him adieu and moved to Vancouver for a time, while still keeping my place in Toronto—indeed, while still trying to maintain the illusion that I hadn't really left. This action would inevitably provoke some contradictory sightings by other people, but I found that I was following an impulse that has always been with me, to maintain places in more than one city, or at least to have post office boxes elsewhere and cash and clothes and supplies stashed in other venues where I could get to them quickly, always plotting silently how to escape the momentary pressures of the one for the fleeting pleasures of another: a sort of geographical bigamy without sex or intimacy, but only a certain amount of comfort of a different and solitary kind. I became a type of mental-health hypochondriac, you see, always fearful that I might be showing the first signs of slipping into my mother's psychosis. My vigilance was constant. So, starting later, I resolved instead to let Father's personality rise to dominance, especially in my dealings with what was proving the rough, knockabout world of writing, publishing and journalism. I was determined to treat others better than they treated me. My selfish reward, which was years even decades in taking effect, would be greater calm and a little self-assurance (but not necessarily an enhanced immunity to other people's stings). It was to heal myself that I hitchhiked to Vancouver on that occasion, and when I felt I was better I returned. I then pursued all the publishers and magazines and even the CBC with renewed dedication.

As I couldn't really sell myself—that is, my slick presentation of self, for I had none, but only the kind of awkwardness of manner that the naive often mistake for sincerity—I had to become a dealer in ideas instead, at both the wholesale and retail levels. I regularly gave or sold book and article ideas to writers or publishers, and I managed to make myself modestly useful as an outside assessor of ones generated by others. For this was a time, like all times, when a lot of flabby nonsense was in the air, masquerading as thought. I'm remembering a visit to Toronto by John Wilcock, the putative father of the underground press movement, and it was in that sense, I suppose, that Seymour Krim once wrote of him as one of the most important American journalists of his time. John was an Englishman, then in his mid-forties, who had worked in Toronto years earlier, first at British United Press and then at Jack Kent Cooke's Consolidated Press, which published *Saturday Night* and *Liberty* and a number of trade magazines, trying to rival Maclean Hunter. Then he went to New York where he founded the *Village Voice* with Norman Mailer and Daniel Wolf (his part always ignored or downplayed in historical retellings). Later he had a hand in starting the two most important American hippie papers as well, the *East Village Other* and the *Los Angeles Free Press.* He was an insatiable traveller now (and the anonymous author of Arthur Frommer's original *Mexico on $5 a Day*), and for years he'd been bumming about Europe, putting out a little alternative press digest called *Other Scenes.* Bundles of it would arrive from time to time, postmarked New York or Amsterdam, and stuffed as well with what the CIA called pocket litter—lewd matchbook covers, subversive political buttons, unintentionally hilarious foreign advertisements written in English by non-native speakers. One day he was back in Toronto and we were having a conversation in the CBC canteen when we bumped into Tuli Kupferberg. I sat back amazed as these two gentle souls fell to bickering, then loudly arguing, in rancorous earnest, about whether or not appearing on the *Tonight Show* with Johnny Carson was in and of itself, *ipso facto*, a counter-revolutionary act. This was a particular and rather hypothetical controversy I confess I hadn't heard before, though in later years I've seen references to the anguish it caused at the time among people like Neil Young.

Anyway, I was an idea-pedlar, but the best idea I had never saw the light of day. I remained full of fervour against the war in Vietnam, which still threatened to go on forever, but I was in the ironic position of finding it impossible to deal with other people who had fled the States for Canada. They didn't care about Canada, it appeared to me, and indeed a large portion of them returned "home" once they could. What's more, they seemed too full of rugged American individualism to be able to work collectively. These resisters were losing the publicity war in the States and lately in Canada, too, just as surely as the Americans were losing the fighting war in Vietnam. At this time, Islamic fundamentalism had not yet become the main source of anti-American agitation in the rest of the world. The role was performed instead by a variety of socialist states, particularly Cuba and Algeria, which harboured America's political refugees, people such as the brilliant prison-essayist Eldridge Cleaver, and otherwise supported those working inside and outside America against Washington's interests.

My idea was to hit up the Cubans and Algerians for a couple hundred thousand dollars—we could have done it, too; this was pocket change for them—to establish a media counter-offensive. The plan was to name a U.S. government-in-exile temporarily housed in Canada until the undemocratic war could be brought to a halt and free and fair elections held—in the States. We would find articulate and well-scrubbed young draft exiles from Oberlin College and other expensive schools to stand for election among their peers as president and vice-president. This would have been irresistible—irresistibly irritating and provocative—to the U.S. networks, the newsmagazines, the wire services and the big newspapers. My estimation was that the novelty would have worn off in a few months, but until then our leaders-in-waiting would be absolutely ubiquitous, giving the Movement an entirely new way of communicating the anti-war message—and probably generating enough donations not only to make the scheme self-supporting, but also to set up a relatively sophisticated propaganda campaign that would be aggressively proactive rather than merely passive and situational. The biggest obstacle, it seemed to me, was how to determine in advance whether the newly elected Trudeau government, so generally sympathetic to anti-American initiatives, would close down the operation under some quibbling provision of the neutrality statutes, or whatever other law the solicitor-general could find. I located reliable, well-placed people who made ever so discreet advance enquiries, and no word came back that in such a hypothetical situation the government would be cross enough to do anything rash. The problem then became one of getting the U.S.-born portion of the Movement to act in an organized way. Working with them was like trying to keep a large litter of puppies cradled in your arms without dropping any or letting any get away. "No, no," I can still remember saying to someone, "*I* can't be the president of the United States! I'm the wrong type for Christ's sake and anyway I don't have *time* to be president of the United States! *You* be the president!" It was hopeless.

My sentiments against the war grew stronger but they grew more intensely private as well. In retrospect I wonder to what extent this was a self-protective device. Here we were, eighteen or twenty years old, being misquoted in *Time*: there was a danger in anti-war celebrity. I remember the sad end of Phil Ochs, the American protest singer, once spoken of in the same sentences with Dylan. He was often in Toronto ("entertaining the troops," he'd say), and wrote at least one of his best-known songs in the tiny dressing room of Bernie Fiedler's Riverboat, one of the dozen or so coffee houses along Yorkville, Cumberland and Avenue Road. We became acquainted. He was a funny, cynical, sharp and gentle man, with an unmistakable voice but a level of musicianship that wasn't thought adequate at the time (but which I heard praised a generation later by a student at one of the best music schools in the United States who was too young to have any interest in the lyrics). I was terribly upset when Ochs hanged himself in his sister's bathroom in New Jersey in 1976, a few months after the war ended. He was troubled by drink and politics, politics and drink: it was difficult to say what the exact relationship was. But surely the timing was not coincidental.

CHAPTER FIVE

LIFE WITHOUT INSTRUCTION

ELIZABETH WOODS was about ten years older than I was, tall and slender with a strong face and straight dark hair that hung down to her waist. She had been, briefly, one of the volunteers who flitted in and out of the Anansi basement, hoping, I suppose, to have her writing discovered by Dennis Lee. I saw her there only a couple of times and only a few more thereafter, until we bumped into each other at some point early in 1969. She invited me to her small apartment upstairs over a shop on the east side of Church Street between Wellesley and Maitland (almost the entire west side being vacant land in those days, used for overflow parking when the Leafs were performing at Maple Leaf Gardens). This area was not then the centre of gay and lesbian Toronto, as it became some years later, but just a shabby neighbourhood of small 1920s apartment blocks and older run-down houses.

One announced oneself at the apartment—two small bedrooms, a tiny living room, and a kitchen with a dangerously slanting floor—by pulling a string that dangled down from the unenclosed summer porch, activating a small cowbell that hung on a nail upstairs. By rights, the place belonged to an artist named Bill Kimber. He had been sharing it with Eleanor Beattie, an actress, but Liz had grabbed the second bedroom when Eleanor moved on. It had been, I believe, Liz's destiny since adolescence in Prince George, B.C., to preside over some sort of salon, and she had quickly made 489 Church (a different building stands there now) into a sort of all-night drop-in centre for poets and performers and a number of others who approached bohemia from one direction or another without penetrating beyond its raffish fringe. I started spending evenings there myself as part of the crowd, but some of the faces I remember most vividly were those of people who visited only on occasion.

One was Patrick Lane, who had known Liz in high school, and would come by whenever he was in Toronto on poetry business and regale us with stories of logging and hunting and working on fire crews. And it was at 489 Church that I first became aware that Juan Butler, whom I'd known already through the publishers Carol and Peter Martin, was in fact slipping into madness.

Butler, a wildly good-looking guy of mixed Spanish and Irish heritage, had written a short epistolary novel called *Cabbagetown Diary*. It wasn't very important, certainly not worth all the praise it would receive, but it was an accurate forecast of two other far more substantial and more experimental books to come during his all too short career, particularly the anarchist novel *The Garbageman*.

> Question: Tell me, in the anarchist society that you envisage, where all men will be free, where no one will ever be in a position to impose his will upon his fellow man, where "doing your own thing" will be the norm rather than the exception, where creative leisure—as opposed to material success—will be the aspired-for work goal, where all political authority will disappear and economic controls will exist on a purely voluntary basis, who will pick up the garbage?
>
> Answer: The garbageman.

I read the manuscript of *Cabbagetown Diary* for Carol and Peter Martin and agreed that they should publish it. At that time, Juan, who was fluent in Spanish, was working as a bartender in some Hispanic restaurant on College Street, and Peter had the idea of throwing a party there to launch the book. As he imagined the scene, all the bigwig reviewers would be there, the Fulfords and the Frenches and so on, being served drinks by this young man in a starched white jacket as they speculated among themselves who—and where—this new genius could be. Just before the suspense became orgasmic, Juan was supposed to leap over the bar, whip off his waiter's tunic and reveal himself as the Author.

Like most of Peter's plans, this one didn't quite work. Invitations were issued, but Juan got fired the day before the event was scheduled to be held. Like me, Juan was forever getting fired, I suppose. Another of his jobs, I remember, was clerking in a bookstore on Yonge Street run by a well-known old Toronto communist.

The proprietor had quit the Party, or at least begun to feel his faith waver, after a doctrinal argument at the communist printing house, during which he had thrown a lead ingot at his antagonist. Now, years later, he was running this bookstore with a full range of hard-to-find political literature of all stripes. He hobbled about on crutches because, it was said, a legal case was still pending that stemmed from an incident in which his ex-wife's bodyguard was alleged to have shot him in the foot. The crutches were necessary, it seemed, because although the wound had healed, the court docket was still very crowded. I would stop in there occasionally, sometimes in the company of Jim Christy (who put out the anarchist paper *Guerrilla* from his tiny apartment over an ultra-expensive jewellery shop on Bloor). The two of us would connive with Juan to ask the proprietor if he had any of the works of, say, Errico Malatesta. We knew what would happen. After first scrutinizing the store and looking up and down Yonge Street to make sure no private investigators were about, he would put down his crutches and, in an almost balletic leap, jump up and grab what we wanted from the very topmost shelf.

Juan, who also wrote some iconoclastic art criticism, lived at this time in a Chinese-run rooming house on Dundonald Street, not far away. In the foyer was a crudely lettered sign imploring the residents in broken English to please flush the communal toilet. When one visited Juan there of an evening to talk about writing, the conversation would be punctuated by an horrendously loud *thwack!* coming from the room immediately above, followed by a light shower of plaster dust from Juan's ceiling. The space overhead was occupied by a man who enjoyed lying abed while trying to kill cockroaches on the opposite wall with a ten-foot bullwhip.

The sad story of Juan Butler is that as his fiction got better and better, his mental state got worse and worse. Such were his vibrations that I once saw a normally quite pacific little dog begin to tear about in irrational circles, crying, barking, cowering, all at the same time, when this human it didn't know approached up the street from a fair distance away. Unlike a number of other people of the sixties, he did manage to make it through the seventies, though barely and with increasing difficulty. One day he appeared with his face tattooed, with *LOVE* spelled backwards under one eye and another word—impossible to make out and probably misspelled—under the other. In 1981, while in psychiatric custody, he hanged himself. He was thirty-seven. Judith Fitzgerald, who I think met him later but knew him much better than I did, published a book of poetry about him.

A much more regular attendant at the Church Street goings-on was Joe Nickell, a slight, good-looking blond chap from Kentucky. He had served in VISTA, the domestic Peace Corps, and had worked on one of the best underground papers, the *Great Speckled Bird* in Atlanta, before fleeing to Canada in his VW van. He was a poet of some talent and sophistication, a former disciple of Wendell Berry, though nothing at all like Berry on the page. Once settled in Toronto, he continued to read and publish poetry and otherwise take his calling seriously. (In my recollection, which is sometimes imperfect, he once broke a fellow's jaw in an argument about Baudelaire.) Yet he also developed, as no one else I've ever known has done, a well-thought-out agenda for the rest of his life. As a civil servant might say, he established a failure-standard. That is, he would consider his life a failure unless he became in turn a professional stage magician, a croupier in a casino, a stuntman in the movies, a Pinkerton detective—I forget what some of the other goals were. He accomplished them all. He was also an expert on forgery, especially as it concerned the chemical properties of various inks and papers.

But in many ways the most appealing character around Church Street was Bill Kimber, the actual lessee and a person of immense likability. He was of Ontario rural stock and had come to the city from St. Catharines, where he had taken an English degree as part of the first-ever graduating class at Brock. He had a large and unusual talent as a visual artist which he was developing quickly, finding his own style, but he had a rough go making his way without an art-school background. He was short, quick-witted, hip, verbally playful, always smiling, always flirting with whoever he met: a person impossible to dislike, a real mensch. But he had such low self-esteem that he had nicknamed himself the Gnome. His drawings were of the sort that people always at a loss when confronted with originality tended to call Beardsleyesque (for Beardsley was big then). Gnomes and other such mythical creatures appeared in them constantly, along with an endless cast of strong or well-born ladies, ladies of leisure and refinement, all symbols of the unobtainable. He said he found the Pre-Raphaelites pretty corny, but liked the spirit in which they were composed. So he had no hesitation about working in figures as seemingly unfashionable as one he called "Irate dumpy wife paying the surprise visit to *la belle dame sans merci* who's stolen her husband's affections." The drawings were obviously a map to what he figured to be his place in the scheme of life. Not for that reason, but because these drawings truly represented an entire imaginative society, they slowly found a loyal audience.

Church Street had only the two bedrooms, but it had a third bed—a narrow camp-bed in one corner of the living room, next to the brick-and-board bookcase—and often at the end of a long evening's wine and conversation I'd simply stay over there, though it was only a few blocks from St. Nicholas. In some past moment of exuberance, someone had jumped on the bed, splintering both of its bottom legs, so that it now more properly resembled a slant-board. I didn't mind. In fact, I liked the people so much that I was considering moving in, as Liz, whose novel was her full-time job, and Bill, who worked with another artist a few nights a week sorting documents at a brokerage house on Bay Street, were having trouble making the rent each month. I had always been happy at St. Nicholas Street, because it had felt like my first real home and the place where I set up shop as a writer. But I was lonely there as well, haunted by what happiness I might have had with Sarah if she hadn't decided, after such long and sometimes painful deliberation, that I fell short of her requirements.

I was talking all this over with Howard Engel one day at the CBC Radio Building, and he pointed out that if I left the loneliness of St. Nicholas Street for the twenty-four-hour bohemian scene on Church Street, I'd have no quiet place to write. So saying, he gave me the key to his office and told me I was free to come in after normal business hours and use it all night if need be, so long as I was gone before the staff started arriving in the morning. I tried to thank him, but he wouldn't let me, telling me instead how Harry Boyle, his own old CBC boss and later a novelist of sorts, once did the same for him, when Howard was just back from Europe, feeling broke and stateless. As space for possessions at Church Street was severely limited, I relived the always painful experience of selling my books to the secondhand bookdealers and moved into what soon proved an even livelier milieu than I had imagined. A somewhat notorious one as well.

Howard was right about the CBC. So long as I was careful not to leave fingerprints that could be found in the morning, I had a splendidly quiet and well-equipped place in which to write, with only a few checks on my concentration. One of these was a Métis named R.R. Sands, a freelance of a kind, who seemed to have copies of *everyone's* keys and who actually *lived* at the CBC. He was a bit of a legend actually. During the day he'd do research (or sleep) in the public library and make the cursory rounds of the *Star Weekly* and the other publications that sometimes bought little squibs of this and that. Other days, he'd put his feet up and watch four old movies in a row at the Biltmore Theatre on Yonge Street. Come nightfall, he would make dinner of the leftovers in the CBC canteen and jiggle the vending machines that sold candy and snacks. He might watch television for a few hours or play music from the immense record library downstairs on one of the office turntables. He kept his changes of clothes, such as they were, in the desk of one of his friends, a producer in the Religion department, who was suspected of being CBC Radio's in-house drug supplier. When necessary, Sands would wash out a few delicate items in the men's loo and have them dry on the radiator before morning. He had staked out the locations of all the sofas in the offices of the more important executives where he might take his well-deserved rest. He even knew that the TV Building across the parking lot had a couple of shower stalls as a convenience for on-air personalities.

Sands was from Olds, Alberta, but seemed rooted in a small bohemian group in Edmonton centred on a few institutions like the club called the Yardbird Suite. I rather liked him, though I found he was uncritically sentimental and almost wept at country music. I used to sometimes get Dan Williman, once his daughters were safely abed, to accompany us to a place in Chinatown where all the hookers and cabbies hung out (it stayed open until five). But Sands always regarded his stays in Toronto as raiding parties on the great fortified city where all the freelance budgets were kept under guard. When he made a strike by selling some article or (more likely) an idea for a radio programme, he would celebrate wildly. I was with him once when he virtually scaled the face of the parliament buildings at Queen's Park (it was 3:00 a.m. or so) to cut down a huge Maple Leaf flag that he wanted to wear, cloak-like, as a symbol of his victory. When he had enough of a grubstake together, he would return to Edmonton with all his goods in his pack, a Trapper Nelson No. 9, longing for the girlfriend of whom he often spoke (and whose picture he kept in a special pocket sewn into one of his cowboy boots).

Church Street life was unstructured. There were no rules, only the bell on the long cord. The pattern, however, was that anyone could stop by of an evening to read or listen to poetry or argue violently about dialectics, art, whatever. People held their positions tenaciously. Some Marxists from Rochdale were by one night and gave the first long discussions about the women's movement in the city that I remember hearing. More typical, though, were blues jam sessions in the wee hours, often involving excellent musicians. Some guests took enormous liberties, and enormous risks, in bringing their own drugs, not simply marijuana and acid and mescaline (a staple commodity at that time) but worse stuff. What's more, this was at a time when the U.S. Consulate on University Avenue had its hands full making life difficult for dangerous pacifists, and as a number of people who patronized 489 Church were actively in flight from America, this may have helped to bring the place to official notice. The fact that the Church Street scene was freely biracial was probably another sore point with the authorities in a time when Toronto had relatively few people of African descent compared to only a short time later. At least once one of the intelligence-gathering or police agencies made a rather clumsy attempt at infiltration, sending in someone who didn't fit in at all, mainly because he looked as though he had the word *cop* stencilled all over him, from his short-back-and-sides haircut to his shiny shoes. He claimed to be a deserter from Seattle but under gentle questioning could not produce a credible past, including the name of either Seattle newspaper or the call letters of any of its radio stations. One time later, a lone cop in an unmarked car parked for the night in the lot directly across the street, staring intently into our upper porch and occasionally taking notes. Some people were afraid to leave, others no doubt afraid to enter. Once this had gone on for four or five hours, Liz telephoned the Metro cops, playing the distressed woman of the house, explaining how some strange man, probably a rapist or burglar, was watching her apartment. No. 52 Division sent a patrol car. From behind the curtains we could see the pantomime of two cops in low-key professional discourse for a few moments before the Metro one motioned the other (whoever he was) to follow, and they both disappeared. They never tried that particular ploy again.

By June of 1969 it was getting pretty warm on Church Street, unseasonably so, and Liz decided this would be a good time to visit her mother in Vancouver. By diligent application to my clandestine writing on CBC property, I found myself perhaps a thousand dollars ahead of the game. For his part, Bill had sold some drawings, while Liz continued somehow always to exist outside the world of specie. So the three of us decided to slow the metabolism of the apartment and sublet it for the summer. Separately but sometimes together, Bill and I would make our way to the Coast and the three of us would meet at a certain place on a particular day.

Bill was under the mistaken impression that I still had a valid driver's license. I thought he knew that I didn't, as people would sometimes chide me about this, just as they would chide me for not using drugs. Bill found a drive-away agency that would pay him a modest fee to deliver a van to Winnipeg, and he was grumpy the whole time at not having anyone to spell him off on the long trip round the Lakehead. There had been some talk of my doing a poetry reading with Gwen at Winnipeg, but she and I missed each other or the offer was withdrawn, so I decided to push on alone for a time while Bill lingered, seeing artist friends. I hitched rides to Edmonton to see Sands and his strange entourage, which included poets and actors who lived communally in a large old house on the west side. The morning I arrived, they were scattered about from a party the night before, the occasion for which was the arrival of a package from Morocco. It was a fairly straight neighbourhood for such a house, and within the next day or two R.R. and I were refused service at the greasy spoon around the corner because we had long hair (this was a common occurrence in those days, though not usually at obscure greasy spoons). As it happens, a reporter for the Edmonton *Journal* (short-haired) was having a coffee there, saw what happened, interviewed us both, and wrote a story about the city's mistreatment of honest literary fellows.

In a few days Bill turned up, found another free van, this one bound for Vancouver via Calgary. My old Vancouver friends like James Ellis seemed to have vanished in the rain, and so Bill and I started making the rounds of the poets I knew, hoping for someone to put us up overnight. We first called on Seymour Mayne, the poet who had been Pat Lane's partner in publishing the Very Stone House books (an unlikely pairing, I always thought), but he seemed preoccupied, so we went over to bill bissett's place in Kitsilano—a green frame building once occupied by Acorn, I believe, and by a whole exaltation of other poets, stretching back to the dawn of the decade. This was during one of the periods when bill was being shamelessly harassed by the local authorities and may even have been one of the occasions when he was facing some jail time. Certainly he wasn't home, so we entered through a rear window that seemed to invite such egress to the ground floor, a former garage that bill was using as a studio. It was chilly and dank and full of his shamanistic paintings stacked everywhere, warping and mildewing. Our defenestration was as polite and unobtrusive as our entry had been.

Weary now, we began walking round trying to find a room in the West End and finally got something ridiculously cheap in a house on Bute Street, in the first block or so down the hill from Robson. In those days, the characteristic domestic architecture of downtown Vancouver was the wonderful large frame houses with green roof and green trim, of which no more than a handful, I suppose, survived the rush to high-rise apartments and condos that accelerated disgustingly all through the seventies. With his habit of making friends effortlessly (how I envied him his personality), Bill spent half the first night in Vancouver talking with a sixty-year-old merchant sailor who lived across the hall and liked to drink a lot and misquote Shelley, which he did proudly and from memory. When someone banged on the door the following morning, I naturally feared that the seafarin' man was back. To my surprise, the caller was John Newlove, one of the poets I and everybody else, it seemed, most admired. Such was the speed of the bush telegraph that he knew of our arrival almost before we'd unpacked. He'd changed greatly since I'd seen him last in Toronto, where he worked at McClelland & Stewart. Some bladder ailment had made his him swell up alarmingly, and he'd gone completely grey.

I spent the summer running into poets and writers I knew and meeting other ones for the first time. Through a reading, I got to know Stanley Cooperman, who had written an interesting study of the American novel in the First World War and created a poetic alter ego for himself in a character named Cappelbaum, who, like Cooperman, seemed to toss off poems with an easy fluency bordering on glibness. Cooperman had taught at Indiana and a number of other American universities. For a while, he had even taught in Iran, during the heyday of the Pahlavi dynasty; as a sideline, he wrote for the English-language paper, doing a nightclub column headed "Teheran after Dark."

He was a man who worked hard at being unusual. One example was his obsession with owls. Owls riddled his books, such as his selected poems, *The Owl behind the Door*, and he and Jennifer's house in North Van was infested with stuffed owls, paintings of owls, plastic owls, wooden owls—hundreds of owl images in all. Cooperman was disliked at Simon Fraser and beyond, because he was part of the vast in-migration of American academics that took over English departments across the country during this time. He never seemed to fit into Canada very well, but I mean this as a compliment as well as a criticism, for neither did he seem to fit in within the army of occupation of which he was part.

He was a profoundly unhappy man, I thought, with a strong vein of displaced irony. He killed himself in his Simon Fraser office not long afterwards, in 1974, and was almost instantly forgotten as a poet. One prominent and perpetually angry figure on the Vancouver scene wrote that Cooperman was "an unattractive man who is remembered only by those who didn't like him." It's to contradict that statement and protest that kind of brutality that I write of him here.

One day when I was out with Bill I bumped into Avo Erisleau (one of the original contributors to *Tish*, though no longer called to mind as such); he had been working at the Ryerson Press in Toronto before its controversial closure, and was now off to Tanzania as a CUSO volunteer. The last Bill and I saw of him was this thin blond Scandinavian figure using his copy of *Teach Yourself Swahili* to wave goodbye to us from the window of the train. Jim Brown of Talonbooks took me round to see Warren Tallman (the only time I've ever met him); we sat in his back garden while the Tallman family dog raced round and round a tree without stopping, and I met up again with Phyllis Webb, who had quit the CBC and returned to her native province: we had a picnic on the beach.

Earle Birney was especially attentive and friendly and kept inviting me to call on him at his high-rise apartment on Barclay Street near English Bay (which high-rises in too great abundance had not then obscured from view). He was still trying to edit a complete annotated edition of the poetry of his late friend Malcolm Lowry in partnership with Lowry's widow, Marjorie, and the collaboration was proving difficult (the book, as such, never got published). To raise his spirits, Earle was composing poems on Japanese paper, which he would make into elaborate kites and release over the beach, hoping the air currents might actually carry one to some culture beyond our own. He was already of retirement age but was still aggressively in pursuit of, not the past (which he avoided talking about), but youth. He kept rewriting and rewriting his poems, and republishing and republishing them, making them younger and younger looking on the page, while his new work at this time was an enthusiastic embrace (never quite successful, I thought) of the op, the pop and the concrete. He was still living with his first wife, Esther, who would sometimes appear in the apartment when I was there, once saying out loud, and with total lack of conviction, how lucky she felt to be living among books and manuscripts.

One July day, Earle was showing me something while the television blared in the corner of the living room. It was the live transmission of the first human landing on the Moon.

"This is a historic occasion," I said. "A milestone in the life of imperial America. A generation from now, people will remember where they were and what they were doing."

"Don't be an ass," Earle said. "This is hype, nothing more, engineered by the Americans for public-relations purposes and of no lasting interest whatever to anybody else."

We were both right.

Bill was slightly peeved when I got back.

"You left at six in the morning saying you were making a phone call and then I didn't see you all evening. You're always doing that."

But we fell quite naturally into a rhythm that summer that was highly productive for us both and, given the cramped quarters, this was no mean achievement.

He would rise early and hit the beach, inspired to work by the lithe bodies all around him, or else, if it were raining, go body-hunting through the West End. At City Hall one day he met Vancouver's official town fool, Joachim Foikis, and came back rhapsodizing about his beauty of movement, his jester suit and his beatific face. Bill was working alternately in his dreamworld mode and in another more darkly surreal vein.

"The universe is perverse," he would say on these latter occasions. "Therefore I would like to illustrate it with sacred normalcies."

When the light waned, he would trudge back to Bute Street where I would often still not be awake and so would sometimes be his sleeping model unwittingly. "You're an interesting sleeper," he said to me once as I woke to find him with the chair drawn up next to the bed, scratching away in his sketch book. "You slept in several new positions today. For comic relief, I liked the one where you wrapped yourself up in the sheets like a cocoon and sort of wore the pillow on your head like a turban."

We'd cook our rude meal together (once stinking up the whole house so badly with tainted fish that we had to evacuate for twenty-four hours). Or else we would eat for a buck or two at the Doors in Chinatown and kick round down in skid row way out East Hastings, where there was a Yonge Street type of movie house we liked—the Lux. Then it would be Bill's turn to assume the single bed. I'd mould my long legs into the spring-busted easy chair with the 1940s upholstery and begin my night's writing. Sometimes he'd snore all night long, which I found restful. At one time, a sound-truck would slowly crawl up and down the streets of the rooming house district, broadcasting its never-changing message: "Fifty lovely girls who wanna meet you tonight down at the Marco Polo. Yessir, fifty lovely girls."

Towards the end of the summer, Sands decided to hitch over the mountains to join the three of us (for Liz had turned up by then and was briefly sharing a hotel room her mother was paying for). But finances were running low. As I had the most, I lingered the longest, I guess, and finally hitched back to Toronto in two great arcs—Vancouver to Winnipeg non-stop and Winnipeg to Toronto. Bill had a theory that hitchhiking eastward was always easier than hitching westward, an experience that notoriously becalmed people for days in places like Wawa.

"It's the trade winds," he would say.

I've known no other artist who sketched as constantly as Bill did. There was never a moment, such as when Liz was in the bathtub reading Peter Beagle, one of her favourite writers, when he wasn't likely to appear with a Rapidograph and one of his sketch-books bound in black pebbled cloth. I think he was around too many writers and musicians and not enough other visual artists. Mind you, I think he found these associations useful in a number of ways. Once I brought Margaret Atwood over to see his stuff, which, with her love of the Gothic, she liked at once, as I knew she would. She bought a number of drawings, sent Bill off to the studio of her friend Charlie Pachter and, most importantly of all, got him to do the famous tarot card cover design for her collection *Power Politics* a couple of years later. There was a lot of technique freely exchanged in those days. Joe Nickell, who in one of his careers had been a travelling sign-painter and in another a political cartoonist, introduced Bill to coloured inks. Bill in turn first got Pat Lane interested in drawing, which has remained a part of his poetry, and even gave him one of his Rapidographs. Writers were Bill's fans and his patrons. One year I paid him to design book plates for me and some of my book collecting friends, and this led to other small commissions from outside the circle. Paul Martin, the Liberal senator, saw one of them and extended a commission of his own. At this time Bill was also managing to sell some spot drawings to *Quarry*, the *Fiddlehead* and other literary magazines, and some cover illustrations for small presses. His finest job as a book artist was one he hated, doing six large illustrations for *Black Azure*, a book of poetry by Walter (Bud) Osborn in an edition of 250 copies. The author was one of the numberless young writers who passed in and out of 489. I can recall nothing of him except that he was always seen in the company of a fellow called Shelley who seldom spoke or bathed.

Bill was playing with juxtaposing visual references in these drawings, using both Rapidograph and a brush, pulling back a lot on his symbolist vocabulary in favour of something more like the brand of German expressionism that surfaced, transmuted, in the U.S. during the 1920s, in people like Wallace Smith. The six *Black Azure* illustrations were all figures, ones that resembled the artist. The most impressive was a drawing of a couple locked in coital embrace. The man, on top, with his back and bum to the viewer, had Bill's body, while the woman on the bottom, looking up from the centre of a great sunburst of hair, had Bill's face.

So while these writerly connections were good for him, I felt he suffered from want of contact with other visual artists. His one artist-friend was Michael Behnan who was often part of the crowd along with his wife, Sue, and there were sketching sessions and general shop talk. (Behnan later went in a very different direction artistically, towards a kind of folk art, and had a meteoric vogue in the commercial galleries and with important critics; he died of cancer in the 1980s when he was only thirty-five.)

Bill only began to participate in a visual art scene when he got laid off from his menial part-time job in the Bay Street counting house. He was always sorely pressed for money (unlike Liz, who had no money but never seemed to let it bother her). Student loans lay heavily on his conscience, and now he would be locked in a long combat with the unemployment insurance authorities as well. He decided he should throw himself into being a life model at different art schools around the city. No one ever applied himself to the task with more dedication, both in learning to be a good model in the way that each situation demanded and in beating on doors to drum up work; he would come home moaning, "A rough day in the naked business." Eventually, he was working variously at the U of T, York, the Artists' Studio, the New School, the public school system, even at a seniors' home. He often modelled for classes instructed by people as established as—to take three very different examples—Dennis Burton, known for his grossly erotic paintings of women in garter belts; Telford Fenton, known for his portraits and theatrical scenes; and Kenneth Lochheed, one of the original Regina Five, who must have been some sort of visiting teacher in Toronto round this time. At length, Bill became one of the most trusted models, with the skill and discipline to form a specialty in what was called Life without Instruction: classes with a model but no teacher to give orders or criticize. In time Bill even acquired some private clients, including one man who had him travel to his suburban home to be photographed as Nude Christ in Chains.

What strikes me as most curious now as I look back is how people managed to get their creative work done given the fact that there were wild parties in those days—wild. A note survives in my memory about someone called Electric Martha, who would always offer acid to whoever wanted some, in contradistinction to those people whose drug of choice was a compound called MDA. The drug stuff always made me uneasy. Big Bill Lias was right in that respect: it was nothing but trouble. What made the parties so unusual, though, was their extreme breadth. A lot of people of the older generation would turn up, as when Al Purdy or someone like that would be in Toronto giving a reading and would stop by and stay all hours, as a party sort of welled up around him. The same almost happened once with Allen Ginsberg, I remember, who was reading in the area, but I couldn't get him to follow me back to Church Street.

Sometimes things got a little rowdy. Peter Martin, the perpetually struggling publisher, a drink in one hand, made some extravagant claim with the other, putting his arm through the glass in the kitchen window and cutting himself up to the elbow. Another time I fell—tumbled actually, in an inebriated ball—down the flight of thirty or so stairs leading to the street, and it pains me to remember that I once poured a beer on the head of Paddy Hynan, an expatriate Irish fellow who did literary documentaries for CBC Radio. He was one of Liz's many male friends. I forget what obnoxious thing he had said, but it must have been more obnoxious than my response. Once a six-piece band arrived and announced they would play all night. They were still at it at three, at four, at five. Poor Bill would sometimes return from a modelling job at night to find his bed occupied by multiple strangers. Or else he would have a few hours to recuperate between the end of a party and the beginning of a tiring commute to a life-drawing class at some remote outpost of culture such as the Scarborough campus of the U of T or even Sheridan College. Other mornings, though, he would be free, and there was always something invigorating, after being up all night, about walking with him down Yonge Street just after dawn when the air was still clean and crisp in our lungs and we were still young enough to be proud of how we could abuse our bodies with delayed retribution we mistook for impunity.

The parties, the talk, the drink, the smoke, the marathon work sessions, the essentially manic nature of everything we did was, I think now, consistent with a lot of young people who somehow resented the youth which they were supposed to relish, and were eager to accrue experience at far faster than the normal human rate. In doing so, we sacrificed a lot of intimacy for the sake of sex and missed a lot of chances at friendship in the welter of acquaintance. We were a noisy community of strangers.

Looking at my work from those days, and at Bill's, I know that he saw this more clearly than I did.

"I did a drawing today of a monk gazing out his cell window," he said once over breakfast at the Devon, a nearby Chinese restaurant we frequented.

"Sounds William Morrisy."

He paid no attention.

"There's an unfinished illuminated manuscript on the writing table. I'm feeling very monkish lately. I really think I understand their way of life."

He was serious.

"In Anglo-Saxon days monks were often lonely men who entered the monastery because it was the only place that would accept strangers. They'd often been strangers or outcasts from the small family-kingdoms. Strangers were unwelcome: once you separated from your family, you were *really* alone. I feel like that sometimes. Forced to accept a solitary life, separated from the good times and the women. Living through others and through the imagination...." He trailed off, taking the Chinese teacup in both hands. "The detail work," he said.

Men were always calling on Liz, in what seemed to me an almost old-fashioned kind of way. I don't mean without lustful intent when appropriate but in some manner that befit her role as the penniless patroness who ran a salon whose fame, or notoriety, was spreading. One night she had dinner with Stephen Vizinczey, whom I believe she met through George Jonas, his compatriot in the Hungarian Revolution. She mentioned at dinner that Bill had been doing some erotic drawings—that is to say, drawings whose eroticism was more in the open than customary. There was one in particular which Bill described as "masseuse deciding to give an evil client a hand job." Vizinczey was most eager to see the portfolio. Bill should be "discovered," he said. He promised to use his influence with an important critic in England (who was it? Edward Lucie-Smith perhaps? I forget) to have a book of his erotic work published there. People were always saying such things to him. In time, he learned not to get his hopes up.

Another of Liz's friends was Don Cullen. In fact, Don was everyone's friend. He was an actor and comedian who back in the late 1950s had founded a coffee house called the Bohemian Embassy, a famous establishment while it lasted. I used to pass its boarded-up entrance every day on my way from the bottom of St. Nicholas Street heading north. The young Dylan had played there, the young Peggy Atwood had given her first reading there. Gwen, too, had been a regular, and there were close and intricate ties between it and the Gerrard Street Village. Don was forever looking for some opportunity to reopen the place in a new location, and eventually did so, first at Rochdale and then, years later, on Queen Street. It was the literary reading series he launched at the Rochdale venue that eventually grew into the Harbourfront readings and literary festivals that became so much a part of Toronto's cultural life in the 1980s and 1990s.

Don was a fine fellow with good taste (he later married Janet Inksetter, who later married me and then set herself up as an antiquarian bookseller), but I think he failed to see that the coffee house era, developed round acoustic music, was pretty much gone. There were still some dreary poetry readings at the Penny Farthing on Yorkville and acts still played at the Riverboat down the street, the other survivor from the old era, but already, in just eighteen months or so, Yorkville had changed radically, with expensive boutiques forcing out the coffee bars and head shops. But all Don's talk about the Embassy, I believe, had put it in Liz's head to open a sort of small updated version of the coffee house ideal, as an extension of the scene at Church Street, or perhaps as a way to impose some order on it. An inspiration of a different kind may have been John Robert Colombo. In those days, before retreating from the literary scene for a career in pop trivia and research into the paranormal, John liked to be at the centre of things, in perhaps what he fancied was the manner of some ersatz European *littérateur*, and he started a series of fortnightly get-togethers, where book-industry people and artsy folks would mill about, drinking and talking. John was ill-advised enough to christen this enterprise the Family Compact: not everyone was certain that he intended the name ironically. The most interesting aspect of these soirées was the location. They were held in the cellar of the

Temple Building, the wonderful Romanesque skyscraper which Oronhyatekha, the wealthy Mohawk businessman, had erected in the 1890s on the southwest corner of Queen and Bay, kitty-corner to the Old City Hall, whose style it complemented. The building was callously pulled down shortly thereafter to make way for the ugly world headquarters of Thomson Newspapers, and Colombo's band never regrouped.

So it was, in any event, that Liz and a core of perhaps a dozen Church Streeters operated a place called the Soft Cell in a third floor industrial space down on King between Church and Yonge, and on regularly prescribed evenings would organize readings and performances there, and made plans for an accompanying magazine, to be called *Bread*, taking its name from the elusive substance sought by all.

The other extension of Church Street was a farm in Renfrew County, in eastern Ontario, which had come into the possession of Al and Eurithe Purdy through inheritance from Eurithe's side of the family. It was not much of a farm—twenty-five acres of more or less untillable land with the usual old frame farmhouse that the wind whistled through—and yet it was lovely, set on the face of a small hill with woods behind and an enormous barn that Bill instantly dismissed as Wyethesque. Al and Eurithe were getting no use out of it and so kindly offered to lease it to me for only $600 a year, which I figured I could just barely afford. I planned to use the place to get away to from time to time when I had to make headway on some more substantial piece of writing. In fact, the others, perhaps as many as a dozen at a time, used it more than I did. Joe Nickell, the poet and polymath cursed with ownership of a van, was charged with transporting everyone and enough supplies for all. The size of the load combined with the condition of the van meant that the trip sometimes took six hours though the distance was only about 150 miles. One day, when all was peaceful, Eurithe stopped by to visit, bringing Margaret Laurence, who lived near Peterborough. I was glad they didn't see the place at its more typical. There was also a lot of sexual activity taking place—ménages divisible by factors of two and three. Some people seemed to sign on for weekends in that expectation—with Liz and Joe benefiting the most, if envy has not clouded my recollection. Also, those who dropped acid did so regularly there, and either lay down for long reposes or else cavorted merrily through the woods and across the meadow and round the pond that was home to two beavers. My private view was that this was much safer than their tripping-out in the city, especially if the buddy system were strictly enforced.

I was in the habit of spending Thursday evenings in the back room of the Village Book Store on Gerrard Street West. This was the establishment of Marty Ahvenus, the person who by talking me up to Howard Engel had helped me land my job at the CBC. Marty is a wonderful man to whom I was first introduced by Raymond Souster, the poet who spent his weekdays in the securities department in the cellar of the Canadian Imperial Bank of Commerce's main branch. Marty was the friend of all writers and artists and small-press publishers. He had grown up in Toronto's now totally forgotten Finnish community whose centre of gravity was near Dundas and Beverley Streets, and being blessed with a likeable manner and a taste for conversation he had first been a travelling salesman and had also worked the front desk in hotels. But he knew he wanted to be a bookseller—he was already a part-time book scout—and so he threw over secure employment and took a lease on the tiny two-storey building on Gerrard, formerly a Chinese fraternal lodge. He lived upstairs, sold books out of the front part of the ground floor, and on Thursday evenings convened these parties in the smaller room behind.

These were opportunities for Marty to reminisce. Sometimes he would tell us about the great meals he had had at the most out-of-the-way little places in his days on the road. Though many years had gone by, he could still rhapsodize about the pecan pie at a diner outside Saskatoon, for example. But mostly the talk was about books and the book trade. Marty himself had marked but unusual tastes in his personal reading. He was particularly fond of Jack Kerouac's *Dr. Sax*, giving away dozens of copies in an attempt to make converts, and when Kerouac died in October 1969, he draped the shop window and made a little memorial display of Kerouac's works. He also liked cookery books, books about the hotel business and the writings of the Czech fantasist Karel Čapek (who coined the term *robot*). The other regulars at Marty's Thursdays included an Irish playwright, a former clergyman turned dealer in Canadian art and assorted other booksellers and collectors—and one librarian, our friend Richard Landon, of the U of T rare books department. From time to time Marty would gather those still ambulatory after these sessions and take us out for a substantial meal.

It was while returning worse for the wear from one of these that I first met, and heard, Jim Byrnes, "Missouri Jim" as he tried to call himself for a while. There was no deception involved. A ruggedly handsome guy with thick straight black hair and an unbeatably diabolical smile, Jim was a blues singer of transcendent talent (his version of "Guns and Roses" was a magnificent affair) and was in fact a native Missourian. He was also, at that moment, on the lam from the U.S. Army at Fort Leavenworth, Kansas, after a bizarre series of incidents, adventures and hair's-breadth escapes which he retold to entertain those who chose to listen only to their narrative surface. Bill characterized him at once as a "priceless madman." Liz and I were instantly drawn to him, too, each in our different way, but then everybody liked Jim. He had a voice with a bit of whisky in it and was linguistically very playful while, at the same time, projecting a faint suggestion of danger, perhaps somewhat as Byron is said to have done. One day Mike Behnan was cutting Bill's hair in the kitchen and I overheard the two of them discussing how individuals like Jim seemed to have bigger adrenalin glands than other people.

"I wonder what I'd be like if I ever actually snapped?" Bill said.

"You'd be catatonic," Mike replied. "I'd be violent."

"No, I'd rather be violent. I mean, isn't the whole point to suddenly wig out and become totally unlike your old self?"

In any event, no one of us had any doubt in our minds that Jim was destined for musical stardom. Certainly it took him no time whatever to be the biggest draw in every non-union room in downtown Toronto. At some point quite early on, he went from being a single to being part of a duo. His partner, escaping not the military but America and God knows what else, was an almost equally memorable musician, though without the same stage magic.

This was because he was frequently incoherent from heroin: here was a drug problem on a level I didn't much care to contemplate. I'll call him Phillip, though I suspect that he's been beyond hearing for some years now, dead or in prison.

In January 1970 Liz would be turning thirty—it seemed impossible, she looked so young—and we, the standing committee of disconsolate bohemians who were her friends, decided to throw her a party. No, a wake, to mourn the death of her youth. After a good deal of nagging, we had persuaded the landlord of the building, who ran a pizza joint on Yonge Street, to enclose the long verandah or rather to give us enough extra-heavy PVC to do so ourselves. (He did, but he also hiked the rent, to $181 a month, and our relations with him were never the same after that.) This extra space wasn't heated but could be warmed by cramming enough bodies into it. We would invite everyone any of us knew and announce it as a masquerade. It was going to be a strange affair.

By this time a couple of the people who routinely spent the pre-dawn hours at Church Street had found themselves renting accommodations across town at the lower end of Beverley Street, where there was a once-magnificent terrace of white 1880s houses with mansard roofs: places now preserved with pride but then in a poor state of repair indeed and subject to rumours about their demolition. Some of the planning took place there as well, which drew other people in the process. Some of these were transvestite friends of friends, who set about helping with costumes in a few cases. For example, they made Bill a pierrot costume. "For some reason," he said earnestly, "it makes me look like an East Indian drag queen in desert boots, none of which I am." Later, he found he had to wear it with silk pajama bottoms to really make it work for him.

It was only at this point that male homosexuals (the word *gay* was just beginning to become current in this context, struggling against the neologism *homophile*, which soon lost out) were becoming conspicuous in the arts world in Toronto. Liz and Bill and many others would always make a production of Hallowe'en when the transvestites left the safety of the St. Charles Tavern, a converted Victorian fire hall on Yonge Street with a decaying clock-tower, and took to parading up and down outside—the one night of the year they could do so without the threat of police harassment, according to an unwritten code. Later, thinking back on my friend Bill, I wonder what his private thoughts were. Foolish of me, but I never knew; it was an area we never touched on. Anyway, looking at his work, and enjoying his personality, you could see that while he was the farthest thing imaginable from a misogynist he nonetheless always positioned himself in the role of someone whom the women he knew and drew would always reject. This was not an anthropological phenomenon, like something out of *The White Goddess.* Here was a person we cared about deeply, and often shared a platonic bed with, beginning to enter some great period of doubt and torment that you couldn't help but recognize in his work but that we, I, couldn't see clearly enough in his life to help with in any way that would matter. "I've done a drawing of a drunken gnome in heat, pestering party-ladies," he said in anticipation of the forthcoming masque. "I guess I have a rather sickeningly good-natured view of my own absurdity." He laughed.

I must say it was a memorable wake. The press thought so and so, I believe, did the police. The place was thronged with an incredibly wide cross-section of people. Some, such as Stephen Mezei, were quite imaginative in their get-ups. He was another of those urbane Hungarians who had fled first the Nazis and then the communists. Now he was the editor of *Performing Arts in Canada*, the sort of perpetually penniless magazine for which we, Liz and I, both wrote, and Bill drew. Stephen came as a mad Turk, with pantaloons, a brocade waistcoat covering his hairy chest, and a red tarboosh. His wife, Rosa, whose English was less perfect than his, wore an antique gold-threaded cape and told everyone she was supposed to be an imp.

On climbing the long narrow stairs, the guests were overpowered by the smell of funeral incense, only to be met by me, the usher, in my frock coat, who showed them (*ushered* them, I suppose I should say) to the verandah. There lay Liz, stretched out in a black coffin. It had been built by one of the hangers-on, Ken

Williams, and painted by Liz herself, who had lined it in white satin. Ruthie Nickell, Joe's wife (for only a short time longer), struck a series of convincingly grief-stricken poses and wailed like the best-paid mourner imaginable, except that she was doing so for free. The crowd was belly-to-belly and hip-to-hip and included, I remember, one young man in what looked like his grandmother's see-through flapper dress. He was a friend of Sandy Stagg, a person most of us met that night for the first time, who would turn out to be the animating force in what lay ahead for Toronto bohemia and one of the important characters in the social history of the city. In the morning, the bodies of those who couldn't make it home lay scattered throughout the apartment in undignified postures of slumber. Bill's mattress was soaking wet, we couldn't tell why. There was broken glass and bits of food everywhere, and extraneous bits of costumes that had come loose or been jettisoned during the festivities.

I had scarcely started working for Anansi when I became acquainted with Peggy Atwood. One side of her family had long, thick roots in Nova Scotia, and though not reared there herself, she had a bit of the Maritimes twang in her voice. It was a remarkable voice, once heard never forgotten, full of unexpected inflections, but one which tended towards a monotone when she read poetry in public. That's what she was doing when I first encountered her. We were in Victoria College. She was standing behind a lectern that was too tall for her, reading *The Circle Game* and some of her forthcoming work, *The Animals in That Country*, into a superfluous microphone. I sat at the back of the room, ready to sell copies of the former text from a folding card table.

Sometimes it seemed she had been at the University of Toronto with about half of the individuals I was coming into contact with in my professional dealings: the magazine editors, publishing people and other writers who were all starting to get their first really important jobs now that they were in their early thirties. Peggy was loyal to all of them and they to her. She had many impressive qualities, including a level of justified self-confidence I had never encountered before (her parents must have loved her from the instant of birth), but I think loyalty was the most attractive of her many attributes. It was the rarest and the one people would most like having themselves. When Peggy was your friend, she was your friend for life (and what's more, in a world of impractical poets and artists, she was worldly-wise in the extreme). With people who didn't quite qualify as contemporaries, she had a special kind of almost sisterly relationship, and that certainly applied to some of the folks at Church Street, particularly Bill, whose work she continued to buy while trying to find others who would do the same. She was really good that way.

Because her reputation and talent made her the senior person in any group in which I could claim even probationary status, I was always fascinated to see not only her easily jocular relationship with her contemporaries like Dennis Lee, but also how she acted with those of the older generation whose work or pioneering accomplishments she admired. There was some note of uneasy deference in her long (but never particularly intense) acquaintanceship with Earle Birney or Al Purdy (but definitely not Irving Layton, whose braggadocio and ballyhoo could only irritate her). It was in this connection that I recall a trip to Montreal a couple of weeks after Liz's wake.

Some congress of poets was taking place—possibly under the auspices of the new League of Canadian Poets, I'm not certain—and the Montreal locals such as Louis Dudek, Frank Scott and the now almost forgotten Ron Everson were the hosts of one or another of a string of small parties. I admired Dudek as a humanist but found him dour as a personality, not to say sour, while I fear he must have seen me as a speechless barbarian. Certainly he gave me the impression of someone who, having risen from the stigma of an immigrant neighbourhood to study at Columbia, befriend Pound and return to McGill in a triumph of respectability, could not now help but look down on an immigrant who had done none of those things. As for Scott, he was a lesser poet (and, as events during the October Crisis a few months distant were about to prove, a great lifelong champion of civil liberties except when they were most in danger). But he was a certified Great Canadian. It was my privilege during this period to meet a number of that breed. They always gave me a satisfying chill of historical recognition, the same feeling I had the time John Diefenbaker threatened to sue me (a rather common distinction but one I cherish). Scott, an impressive figure with kind eyes and a profile befitting the notarial class, told the story of a 1964 canoe trip with Pierre

Trudeau and a number of other male friends in the Northwest Territories. Scott had been taking 8mm film of the trip and had captured Trudeau clowning in the nude after a ritual morning swim in the river. The instant Trudeau became prime minister, Scott said, Mounties appeared at his door and confiscated the film. (Scott later revised the story to the form given in Sandra Dwja's biography of him, in which Scott does the gentlemanly thing, calling the Mounties' attention to the existence of the film and voluntarily submitting it for destruction lest it fall into the wrong hands.)

Peggy said that she wanted me to meet a friend of hers, John Glassco, known as Buffy. Domestically, his standing as a poet, a rather conventional type of poet, was in recession at that point, while his international reputation as a pornographer had yet to become widely known here. I knew the name mainly because I had just finished reading a wonderful excerpt from his forthcoming book, *Memoirs of Montparnasse*, in the *Tamarack Review*. It told of his being bounced out of a party at the studio of Gertrude Stein ("a large rhomboidal woman"). Later, of course, it became known that *Memoirs of Montparnasse* was not what it claimed to be, a work begun on the spot in Paris in 1928 and finished back in Canada in 1931, but a work mostly of the 1960s—and largely of the imagination. He did not, for example, know the old roué Frank Harris, as he would claim.

Glassco had come from a modestly wealthy family, but had spent much of his adult life separated from them, living simply in the Eastern Townships, writing poetry and delivering the Royal Mail for a livelihood.

These days he was keeping a place in Montreal, a basement apartment on the west side of Mountain Street, if I recall correctly. This seemed perfect: it was as inexpensively as one could live and still be round the corner from the Ritz.

Peggy had made an appointment for us to see him at ten in the morning. When we arrived, he affected not to be expecting us, but he was wearing a silk smoking-jacket and a cravat and was having his breakfast champagne. Perhaps because he had heard that I took a liking to them (chameleons are the most polite of creatures), he made a point of playing up the colonial aristo, posing, with perhaps a bit more enthusiasm than strict accuracy allowed, as a sort of dissolute and bohemian Vincent Massey. I told him how much I had enjoyed the chapter in the *Tamarack* and asked when the book itself might appear and (obvious question) whether he had known the other famous expats of 1920s Paris—Joyce or the Fitzgeralds perhaps or Hemingway? "Ah, Hemingway," he replied. "Big, rambunctious American sort of chap, you know. Always eating bacon and eggs, as I remember him. Most curious." He furrowed his brow in distaste at the recollection.

Peggy's admiration for Buffy as a mischief-maker as well as an artist was palpable and obvious, respectively. Later, when we had joined him in champagne and strawberries, he took an ornate little lock from the pocket of his smoking-jacket and opened the front of an antique *cloisonné* secretary to retrieve a book.

"Douglas, perhaps you might be interested in seeing my latest work."

It was called *The Temple of Pederasty* and purported

to be the translation, by a modern Japanese, of an ancient Japanese text by one Ihara Saikaku. But of course this was an honourable and expedient tradition, born of long years of persecution, thinly disguising the fact that the entire text was a John Glassco production from first to last. Later, he took down a copy of the Grove Press edition of Aubrey Beardsley's unfinished pornographic novel *Under the Hill* and pointed out the exact spot where the original manuscript ended and he, Buffy, had picked up the thread and finished the story in faultless imitation of Bearsdley's style.

But it was *The Temple of Pederasty* that was on his mind. Later that night he and Peggy and I and George and Angela Bowering had dinner together at some unprepossessing Chinese restaurant in the East End that was supposed to be renowned for its fish. Buffy fantasized that public demand would soon make a second printing of *The Temple* necessary and that, to satisfy this eventuality, we should all compose jacket blurbs. He passed a pen and blank sheet of paper round the table. George wrote in praise of the subject matter, saying that if his mother had taken him to a pederast when he was a boy he wouldn't have bad feet today. When the paper came to me I wrote, "John Glassco's *The Temple of Pederasty* is a book that leaves nothing to be desired." But Peggy produced a splendidly subtle squib, a thing so expert that only physical examination could have detected the tip of her tongue in her cheek.

When I got back to Toronto quite late the next evening, Bill told me that the plans for a bunch of people to go to the farm had taken an unexpected turn. Someone (not Joe Nickell but a new recruit) was going to drive them there "but he seems to be in a bit of a predicament. He's gone mad. No, really. He's having wild, interesting adventures which could lead to his arrest and deportation." Certainly they were enough to postpone the trip and leave the living room, hallway, perhaps even the kitchen of No. 489, studded with sleeping bodies. On my own broken-down bed, no wider than a seaman's bunk, there were two poets who hated each other when awake. Not for the first time, I accepted Bill's invitation to share his room for the night. As always, he was a perfect gentleman, because he had not yet come to terms with being otherwise. What's more, it was so cold all through the house that everyone could only sleep wearing multiple layers of clothing, including sweaters. Even then, we shivered.

There were troubles in Bohemia. Phillip, the other blues guitarist who worked with Jim Byrnes, was squeezing a friend of Liz's named Mary-Anne Carpentier, a Franco-ontarien from Sudbury or Timmins who had moved south to study art conservation. Phillip had come to expect that she would help satisfy his heroin habit.

She claimed that when she failed or refused to do so, he beat her. This was starting to feel like being back in A———. I didn't like using the word anymore, or hearing it.

The positive note was Sandy Stagg, the very smart blonde Cockney who, second only to the corpse of honour, had been the big hit of Liz's wake. Originally, she had come to Canada attached to a thoroughly anglicized, Canadian-born male journalist who eventually returned to England without her. This was London's loss. Sandy was a vibrant spirit who made lots of creative activity happen by working at it or simply by standing still and letting others spin off from her own enthusiasm. Her disciplines were all decorative ones, her talent was a talent for making shifts in taste. At the moment she had found an empty theatre somewhere down by Soho Street and saw it as a great umbrella for various groups. She dragged Liz and others along to see it, thinking that the Soft Cell might move there. The energy had been leaking out of the Cell pretty fast, particularly since the night a freak blizzard kept everyone at home and the person who was supposed to be reading—Dennis Lee—was in bed with the 'flu. Sandy thought the Cell could revitalize itself as one of the client elements of this old theatre, which she also visualized as harbouring everyone from renegade fashion designers to erotic conceptual artists.

After protracted dreaming and negotiations, nothing came of that particular idea, but a lot more was to come from Sandy. She was one of the people somehow connected to the start of the Open Studio. At the time the Studio was pretty much the only alternative business of any sort on Queen Street West, which was then a run-down section of the city, with the usual greasy restaurants, beer parlours and specialized industrial-supply shops. It was a working-class streetscape, with the windows of all the crumbling Victorian buildings blacked out on the second and third storeys and with the tan-and-purple streetcars rattling along out front, picking up dreary people here and depositing other dreary people there. Later, after the period covered in these notes, she took over one of the old restaurants, the Peter Pan, and made it the focal point of the reinvention of Queen Street as the main drag of artistic Toronto. At least one other restaurant followed, and an antique-clothing business that caught people's fancy at just the right time. She was one of the great visionaries of Toronto culture, one of the main custodians of the city's artistic self. You never knew what she was working on. One day she stopped by struggling under the weight of two enormous parcels, the one of pork chops, the other of artificial fur. Whatever she started was soon copied by dozens of other people, and some area was brought back to life, a different kind of life. Later she worked her magic in London, where she had to return regularly to supply her shops, and in New York. She threw terrific parties, much better than ours: more original, certainly more colourful. By April there was talk of Sandy moving into a larger house down near Queen where more people could be accommodated. This was followed by talk of our giving up Church Street so as to be sufficiently near by that the two scenes could really merge. The tectonic plates under Bohemia were shifting.

Jim and Phillip were playing everywhere together and never to less than enthusiastic if not always coherent audiences. Their biggest venue was the Global Village at 17 St. Nicholas, a combination espresso place and theatre, with red, green and black lights and seating on various levels, where the wildness might just be getting started at 1:00 a.m. or so. Mary-Anne had got out of her abusive relationship with Phillip, thank God, but he was cutting a swath through the rest of the population and also, we suspected, feeding his habit by other means—namely, threatening and robbing terrified Korean immigrant families who ran milk stores. We had no direct proof of this. But it got so that his haunts, including ours, were being watched again, and once, when two of our acquaintances were crossing the border at Fort Erie, they were stopped and interrogated for a couple of hours about Phillip, his movements, his aliases, his whereabouts, the other people he knew. Suffice it to say his reputation had begun to precede him wherever he went. But I can't remember to what extent, if at all, this was a factor in the three of us deciding to give notice to the landlord and move somewhere closer to Sandy down by Queen. It seemed to me that Phillip's friends, if not Phillip himself, were bringing the hard stuff into the apartment. I decided to do what I always did when a cooling-off period was needed: go to Vancouver.

A strange opportunity had opened up along these lines. One of the regulars at Church Street the past year or so was a red-headed, bright-eyed and very eager young poet named Bill Howell (later a radio producer). To say the least, he didn't share the same aesthetic as the others in the group. He was down-home and folksy to a degree that most of us could scarcely warrant. He had an identical twin brother back in Nova Scotia and was forever going on about the wonderfully strange effects of being in that situation. He chattered constantly of the love of family and other concerns not all of us were familiar with in the same degree. I write of him here sheepishly, for after his first collection of poetry was published a few years later I was unconscionably rude to him in print (particularly, I seem to recall, because he had included a poem entitled "I Can't Wait to Get Home for Christmas and Be Hugged by Mom") and have been hoping to run into him ever since so that I might apologize.

Anyway, Howell had somehow come to know the concert artist Anton Kuerti, who had a special VW van remodelled to accommodate his favourite grand piano, so that he could take it with him wherever he performed. The vehicle had a kind of demi-lune-shaped dorsal fin on top; one tipped the instrument on its side and slid it on a track until it fit snugly between heavily padded bulkheads. Kuerti was playing in Vancouver, and would pay Bill and a companion to travel ahead with the rig, so that he could arrive later, by plane. Bill drove and got a few hundred dollars plus expenses, I rode shotgun and shared in the free food and lodging. An ideal arrangement except that I grew more frustrated with his almost criminal naiveté, as it then seemed to me to be, in those days when I wasn't exactly Vietnamese in my patience. It got so we couldn't stand the sound of each other's voices. As a result, I jumped out at Calgary, leaving him to negotiate the mountains by himself, and made my own way to Vancouver, where I knew how to get lost and wring the most benefit out of an urban monastic silence.

When I returned, Sandy Stagg had found Liz and Bill and the rest of us the perfect place to live, 52 Beverley Street, one of the Victorian terrace houses, steps from Queen. The rent (there was no lease) was $250, which was more than we were accustomed to paying, but then it was a big old place. Pat Lane had come back to town and he and Joe Rosenblatt, the dour but mocking poet and artist, author of *The LSD Leacock* and other contemporary classics, had helped the residents move in. People drew lots for rooms. I got one *in absentia*, and when I saw it for the first time, found it being slept in by Jim and Phillip and Jim's Swedish girlfriend, Annica, with traces of previous occupation by Erling Friis-Bastaad, another poet of that place and time (who subsequently moved to the Yukon). Bill took over the attic of the house and made it into a studio: the first he'd ever enjoyed.

With Sandy round the corner, it was now as if the two households were joined, though they were not precisely interchangeable. Sandy's chaos was different from ours. For the people at Beverley Street tended to be poets and musicians, particularly the musicians who played at the Global Village when, to take an example, there was a great benefit in aid of the *Harbinger*, an underground newspaper that had been busted. Our people also tended to be more politically active, demonstrating at the U.S. Consulate, for example. Sandy's place, by contrast, was theatrically inclined. It included a number of drag queens (one, named Murray, kept doing Sandy's hair in ever more outrageous ways) and many people who were involved with the Electric Circus on Queen Street East rather than with the Global Village. In fact, the entire resident dance company of the Circus lived at Sandy's for a while.

The actors in Sandy's circle made up some of the cast when the Global Village put on *Children of the Night*, whose *dramatis personae* was listed as a Queen, a

Straight Guy, the Bull Dyke, the Dirty Old Man, and the Junkie. The last of these was supposed to be deaf-and-dumb, which made it the perfect role for Yuri, another member of Sandy's ménage, who spoke very little English and understood far less and was in real life the sometimes boyfriend of the fellow playing the Queen, for whom the part was not a stretch. The point is that there was a new theatrical dimension to all our lives, if only by association. Two doors away lived Marcel Horne, a professional fire-eater. He was a muscle-bound fellow from Leamington, Ontario, whom Jim Christy, the anarchist and adventurer, befriended. Christy encouraged Marcel in the writing of his crude autobiography, which he was then able to persuade Peter Martin Associates to publish. *Annals of a Fire-breather* was not always easy to take literally. It told of Horne first running afoul of the law at seventeen, of how he followed that course for a while (including one arrest for bootlegging) and did nine months in solitary before turning to the carnival for a livelihood. In time, the account continued, he learned the physical and mental skills of fire-eating from a gypsy in the New Mexico desert. At one point, using the name Diablo, he managed his own sideshow troupe, until his knife-thrower missed and the blade slid into Marcel's chest. Marcel enjoyed joint Swiss/Canadian citizenship—I've forgotten how—and had more than one passport. At one point, not too long before the Beverley Street days, there was some story of his being jailed in Casablanca with a homosexual leper but making good his escape to Canada via Paris after the frontiers had been closed. One never knew how much of this was true and will never know now. He died a few years later in a car crash. Christy's friends tended to be of this order. Another of his heroes was a junkie and minor jazz musician named Charlie Leeds, whom he also encouraged to write—and got PMA to publish. A sad character. "Three days before his death," Christy would inform me later, "he had been down in Florida, trying to get a job as a caddy and reading Chaucer and Maupassant."

All this while there was anxious talk about finding Jim Byrnes and Phillip job offers so that they could become legal immigrants. Such offers were procured, but later, for reasons which time is obscuring from me now, they needed to find Canadian citizens to marry them. Liz had been romantically linked with Phillip, but I think it's fair to say that she was actually in pretty deep emotionally with Jim, as perhaps everyone but Jim himself could see. One night in March, the situation was made far stickier, and more dangerous, when Phillip turned up at Sandy's with the news that Jim and a young woman friend of Liz's had been busted for marijuana possession when the cops stopped Jim's car on Spadina Avenue. His companion was released on her own recognizance, I think, but Jim was being held pending bail. A collection was quickly taken up at the Global Village, and Liz and the others got the money together to spring him from the cells at 52 Division.

At that point, Phillip, whose stuff it probably was anyway, withdrew discreetly across the border but returned a week later to be a witness, along with Bill, when Liz and Jim were married in a Unitarian church, using a service I had written for the occasion (of which I now cannot recall a single word). By a nice coincidence, the nuptials were scheduled for the same day as the next episode in the marijuana case. The morning of the ceremony, Jim's co-defendant phoned Bill in a panic to say that matters had taken an unexpected turn for the worse in court. Instead of remanding the case, as the lawyer advised would be the usual procedure, the judge, noting Jim's record as a deserter, raised his bail to $1,000 and had him thrown into the Don Jail. Now Liz, Joe Nickell, any of us with a few dollars, had to cough it up. The wedding had to be postponed until the unfashionable hour of 5:30 p.m. The bridegroom wore a denim jacket he had stolen from the Don, with the name of the institution stencilled on the front and back. Phillip wore a purple bandanna and a full-length black cape. "It's difficult to say which freaked out the minister more," said Bill.

Jim and his co-defendant were in court again about ten days later, and it went smoothly: no more bail, and a remand. But a palpable fear hung over the proceedings. An Ontario judge wouldn't burden the taxpayer with the expense of sending Jim to jail for a long stretch. If convicted, Jim would be simply be deported back into the arms of the American military. Having escaped once, Lord knows when he might see light a second time.

The parties till 3:00 and 4:00, even 5:00 a.m., were still going on, yet people managed to get their work done somehow—I by making the now much longer trip to the CBC each night, Bill by retreating up to his studio, which he had decorated with a huge mural. But some people, the ones actually interested in new means of community, were becoming tired and sick.

"Some of the acid folk were still in various stages of high when I dragged my ass home this afternoon after a modelling job," Bill confided in me one day. "They all seem to want to keep up the drug thing. I'm soon going to be *very* paranoid." One night there were five uninvited all-night guests at our place alone, all very loud, and this was not a rare occurrence. The kitchen always overflowed with people. There was so much music it became just noise. You never knew who would be in which bed when you returned from a social outing, such as any performance by the Peoples' Revolutionary Band (a favourite group of the household's, with much more innovative musicianship than the name would suggest) or the Be-In held on the little lawn in front of Rochdale or, the following month, a demonstration at the U.S. Consulate with forty-seven arrested (a good turn-out). Bill wondered if he should try to play the role of tough cop (he wasn't sure if anyone would listen) or if he should just silently slip away and find another home (what a shame to leave his studio). In the end Liz was the one who assumed the tone of parental authority and gave notice to Jim (her legal husband), Annica (her legal husband's actual girlfriend), Phillip and his girlfriend, and a couple of others, literary people from the West, whose presence was actually my doing. Some begged extensions, some were miffed for a time, but generally the transition was handled effectively. This created room for a few more legitimate communards. Among these was the choreographer who gave dance lessons at the Global Village and to whom Bill had always been secretly attracted, in that gnomish way of his: too shy to talk without trying to be funny and self-deprecating, and so confining his lusts and thoughts to endless series of drawings.

The old decade had been over for months. It seemed as though something new should happen. There were a series of happy endings and some that were not so happy. Bill and the choreographer began living together and were a couple for five years, but Bill finally discovered to his certainty that he was intended to be happy with men, not women, and so moved in that direction, finding, I think, a lasting and rewarding relationship with a fine fellow. Because of the change he was eager to avoid his old friends, but after years of wearing him down with invitations, copies of new books and other gentle indications that he should look elsewhere for prejudice, that he was still my friend as I hoped I was still his, he came round, and we see each other frequently.

When the marijuana case finally came to trial, it proved anti-climactic. In a plea bargain the charges against Jim were dismissed and his co-defendant was fined only $200 on conviction. Phillip had simply disappeared back down the rabbit hole of America, and soon afterwards Jim relocated to the West Coast. One day not long after that, his old car ran out of gas on Vancouver Island. While Jim was pushing it up a mountain road, another driver, not seeing him round a curve, struck him a terrible blow. Both Jim's legs were amputated above the knee. Liz helped to nurse him back to health and to teach him to walk again. This was a great expression of love on Liz's part, but the two of them never lived together as husband and wife. Instead, Jim settled down to a stable home life with someone else, in Vancouver, and made his musical career all over again there, with the same rapturous success he'd had in Toronto. In the 1980s he became one of the stars of a U.S. television series, playing a handicapped character.

As for me, I was looking for roots which, in my innermost imagination, had already been planted for me long ago, for facts that had to do with my father and how I never really had the chance to benefit long enough from the love I knew he had for me. Our rents were due on the thirtieth of each month. After hearing the final outcome of Jim's court case on the eighteenth, I moved out of the house so as to avoid running into the next rent period and was determined to go to Montreal as soon as I could and there take ship for England.

I'd already missed the last CP liner, so I had to wait a few days until I could get a night train that would connect with a Russian ship bound for London. One of the people who had flitted in and out of first Church Street and then Beverley from the beginning had the small top floor of a house on the east side of Kendal Avenue in the Annex, a few steps from the Sibelius Park of Dennis Lee's wonderful poem. She offered to put me up for free until it was time for me to get to Union Station with my one Edwardian suit, my bag of essential books and a silver case of engraved calling cards. The arrangement was purely platonic. Indeed, I kept having to vacate the bed at odd hours so that she could frolic with a flutist named Claude (who later married the woman convicted in the marijuana case). But Bill didn't know this, nor did I know that he had secretly—in some of his most secret drawings—been lusting after her. As a result, he harboured needless jealousy of me, in his self-assigned role as the poor distant observer of all this activity of which he found himself in the middle. This too may have contributed to our being out of touch for a period later on.

Life was going to be much more productive and harmonious once I could get away for long enough to prepare myself properly to return. I had turned twenty-one, you see, and time was passing me by.

Clones and clones.

DATE			

W9-BZC-552

CLONES and CLONES

also by Martha C. Nussbaum

The Fragility of Goodness
Love's Knowledge
Cultivating Humanity

also by Cass R. Sunstein

Free Markets and Social Justice
Legal Reasoning and Political Conflict
Democracy and the Problem of Free Speech

CLONES and CLONES

Facts and Fantasies About Human Cloning

edited by

Martha C. Nussbaum

and

Cass R. Sunstein

W · W · Norton & Company

New York London

Printed in the United States of America
First Edition

For information about permission to reproduce selections from this book, write to Permissions, W. W. Norton & Company, Inc. 500 Fifth Avenue, New York, NY 10110.

The text of this book is composed in 12/14 Perpetua
with the display set in Bodega Serif Medium and Light
Composition and manufacturing by The Haddon Craftsmen, Inc.
Book design by Margaret M. Wagner

Library of Congress Cataloging-in-Publication Data
Clones and clones : facts and fantasies about human cloning / edited
by Martha C. Nussbaum and Cass R. Sunstein.
p. cm.
Includes bibliographical references.
ISBN 0-393-04648-6
1. Cloning—Social aspects. 2. Cloning—Moral and ethical
aspects. 3. Human reproductive technology—Social aspects.
4. Human reproductive technology—Moral and ethical aspects.
5. Human genetics—Social aspects. 6. Human genetics—Moral and
ethical aspects. I. Nussbaum, Martha Craven, 1947– .
II. Sunstein, Cass R.
QH442.2.C55 1998
174'.25—dc21 97-51781
CIP

W. W. Norton & Company, Inc., 500 Fifth Avenue, New York, N.Y. 10110
http://www.wwnorton.com

W. W. Norton & Company Ltd., 10 Coptic Street, London WC1A 1PU

1 2 3 4 5 6 7 8 9 0

In memory of

Martha Goodrich Sunstein,

1917–1997

Contents

PART III ETHICS AND RELIGION

PART IV LAW AND PUBLIC POLICY

PART V FICTION AND FANTASY

Introduction

When Ian Wilmut and his colleagues at the Roslin Institute announced the successful cloning of a sheep from the mammary cells of an adult female, the world reacted with intense emotion. Experiments in cloning had been going on for at least forty years. But the arrival of Dolly made it clear that human beings would soon have to face the possibility of human cloning—and it has been this idea, far more than the reality of animal cloning, that has caused public anxiety. To many if not most of us, cloning represents a possible turning point in the history of humanity. Some view the prospect with alarm; some with disgust; some with joy; some with grief for the life we used to have, and will shortly have no longer. Some, too, are calm and matter-of-fact about the entire affair, urging us to let science take its course before we conclude that dreadful things are at hand. But almost everyone is asking questions.

What is all the emotion about? Human beings have always been afraid of their own creative power, and the idea of man-made life was scary long before science was in any position to think of procedures that might make it reality. The Greek god Hephaistos, god of artifice and metalworking, cleverly stocked his workshop with robots, making anthropomorphic metal creatures to be his slaves and lighten his burden. He fashioned tripods that could move of their own accord, rolling off to the assembly of the gods and back again, "a wonder to behold." Stranger still, he also created young

women out of gold, "just like living girls," with "intellect" and "voice" and even "strength," to help him in his labors.[1] These agile workers were human bodies without regular human souls, children without parents, neither human nor bestial nor even divine. To the Greeks already, then, the idea that there was a "natural" way of reproducing, and that creatures who bypassed that route were a little peculiar, came quite easily, without science to back it up. Not that the gods and heroes were without their own peculiarities, choosing such strange means of birth as being released from the forehead with a hammer (Athena), being sewn up in one's father's thigh (Dionysus),[2] getting children out of some decayed old dragon teeth that happened to fall into the fertile earth of Thebes (the Theban "sown men"),[3] and even, with a simple economy of means, masturbating into the fertile earth of Athens to create a nation of male clones without bothersome mothers. (The Athenians were thus, in their own civic mythology, a nation descended from male clones, very proud to have no jot of the female in their makeup.)[4] The gods, in short, were clearly not convinced that nature had ordained just one way for human beings to be born, and they tirelessly experimented with new technologies. But gods and heroes are free from many constraints that they impose on mere mortals. Prometheus got his liver eaten out by an eagle for giving us fire, thence metalworking and other creative arts; and the idea that new arts are all new transgressions, each bringing divine punishment in its train, is a very old idea in Western thought about what it is to be human.

The scientific advances of modernity, however, gave these anxieties new intensity and specificity. The idea of a life-form made in a laboratory that would ultimately destroy its creator underlies the horror of *Frankenstein,* a tale made profound by the monster's noble simplicity and its victimization by the "normal" among us. The idea that we might make a human being without a soul was a source of horror; equally horrible, however, was the thought that we might make a being who *did* have a soul, but who, by virtue of its strange

origin, would be doomed to live without love. More recently, the immensely popular film *Invasion of the Body Snatchers* associated abnormal man-made life with the soulless automata that Americans saw when they imagined a life under Communism. The people who came out of the pods were, in effect, clones of the people whose lives they took over. They looked like us, and kind of talked like us. But they didn't like jazz, they never got angry or frightened, and when you kissed one of them, then you really knew what fear was. Sex, freedom, anger, being American, and music were thus lined up on one side; abnormal origins, totalitarianism, soulless passivity, being foreign, and nonmusic were carefully arrayed on the other. What's to choose? We have to stop them, before they stop us.

These are some of the nightmares and fantasies that underlie the intense outpouring of negative emotion in response to Dolly's life. We want to know what human cloning would mean for the children born in this way. Would they really be creatures without souls, not fully human? Even if they weren't, would we treat them this way? What would cloning do to the parent-child relationship? What kind of lives could, or would, clones have? If we could choose the genetic makeup of a child, would unconditional love for children become rarer than it is now? And what would the option of cloning do to us more generally? Would we stop wanting to have sex? Want sex only for superficial self-gratification? Or would we go on wanting to express love and friendship through sex? Would people's sense of partnership even lead them to prefer natural children to clones, since they would be the mingling of the genetic equipment of both parents? What is the relationship between cloning and our various religious traditions?

Who would choose cloning—the infertile, the narcissistic, people with a loss they want to make good, people with a grudge against humanity, people who hate chance? Whom would they choose to clone? Themselves? Their favorite basketball star? Hitler? Gandhi? Mozart? And what would become of our world, with dozens of Hitlers running around, opposed by hundreds of Gan-

dhis? Could we make it better? Wouldn't it almost surely be made worse? And what about basketball and music—surely they wouldn't remain the same either. It's comforting to think of dozens of Mozarts and Beethovens, since music seems to be one of those goods that expands without limit, and admits of no diminution through excess. But what about a National Basketball Association filled with teams of Michael Jordans (with a Scottie Pippen and a Dennis Rodman on each, we may hope, or fear, and a Phil Jackson coaching everyone)? Would that still be the same game? Or wouldn't the limits of the human body against which talented athletes strive lose their meaning when we could just make another Michael Jordan any time we wanted to?

These questions can be posed by science, and science can give us the real facts, telling us that many of the possibilities we envisage are very unrealistic. We attempt to outline the basic facts about cloning here, and in a way that will be easily intelligible to non-specialists. Thus, the distinguished scientists in this volume remind us that clones occur already in nature: identical twins. They also remind us that nature's form of cloning hasn't yet produced horror movie scenarios, except in horror movies. Science can also shed a great deal of light on a much-discussed issue, the interaction of genetic endowment with environment, and scientists may remind us—as do several writers in our first section here—that a clone is probably going to end up very far indeed from being the same person, even farther than are identical twins with separate upbringings, given that clones will also be born into different generations. In these many ways science can set us straight about what questions we should really be asking.

Science, however, doesn't give us the answers to the ethical, political, social, and religious questions raised by cloning. These answers need to be worked out, ultimately, in the course of public debate. But the humanities and the social sciences can help us lay out the options in a clear way, and give us some good arguments to ponder. Our second section brings together a group of commen-

tators from a variety of social perspectives. They think about the relationship of cloning to the psychological development of children; to our most basic feelings about our bodies and their products; to feminism and to homosexuality; to myths of the dangerous or useful double.

Our third section turns to normative argument in ethics and religion. The authors analyze the major ethical arguments that bear on the decision whether human cloning should be permitted and ask what insights several major religious traditions offer us about the strange future we may face.

In our fourth section we turn to issues of law and public policy, as specialists in economics, sociology, and law think about whether governments should allow human beings to be cloned. They also discuss the implications of cloning, and any bans on cloning, for children and actual or prospective parents; for the freedom of scientific inquiry; for constitutional debates about privacy and equality; for the position of existing citizens who challenge current social attitudes about sexuality; for the fertility of the species; and for other ethical issues concerning the family. Some of the arguments of this and the previous section played a role in the controversial report of the National Bioethics Advisory Commission, whose recommendations we reprint here.

But cloning, so far, is still in our future. Like the Greeks, therefore, we also feel the need for fiction and fantasy, to map out some alternative futures for us with the imagination's flexibility and precision. We therefore end with a poem and three short stories—one by a writer of science fiction and two by fiction-writing philosophers. Deliberative, elegiac, horrifying, and happy, these pieces map the trajectory of our sentiments about cloning, even as they ponder its possibilities.

M.C.N.
C.R.S.
Chicago, October 1997

Endnotes

1. For the tripods, see *Iliad* 18.375; for the young women, 18.417–20.
2. For the double birth of Dionysus (once from his mother, Semele, once from Zeus's thigh), see Eruipides, *Bacchae,* 88–98. Zeus pinned the young infant up in his thigh, creating an artificial womb, to hide him from Hera, who was angry at his adultery.
3. This story of the "sown men" is central to the plot of Aeschylus's *Seven Against Thebes,* and is retold in Plato's *Republic* as a crucial part of Socrates's "noble lie" about the origins of the citizens of the ideal city.
4. On myths of misogyny connected with the idea that Athenian males were created without sexual reproduction as a result of Erechtheus's masturbation, see Nicole Loraux, *The Children of Athena: Athenian Ideas About Citizenship and the Division Between the Sexes* (Princeton: Princeton University Press, 1993; originally published in French, Paris 1981).

Acknowledgments

We are very grateful to our secretaries, Shirley Evans and Marlene Vellinga, for excellent work in organizing a somewhat unruly editorial process. We are also grateful to our outstanding editor, Alane Mason, who provided overall guidance and wisdom and who offered superb suggestions throughout.

Cass Sunstein's mother, Marian Goodrich Sunstein, became ill and died as this book was nearing completion. She knew about the project and found it a particular source of fascination and delight; perhaps her son may be forgiven for saying that it was a great gift to be able to discuss it with her in her final months.

M.C.N.
C.R.S
December 1, 1997

PART I
Science

Viable Offspring Derived from Fetal and Adult Mammalian Cells

I. Wilmut, A. E. Schnieke, J. McWhir, A. J. Kind, and K. H. S. Campbell

Fertilization of mammalian eggs is followed by successive cell divisions and progressive differentiation, first into the early embryo and subsequently into all of the cell types that make up the adult animal. Transfer of a single nucleus at a specific stage of development, to an enucleated unfertilized egg, provided an opportunity to investigate whether cellular differentiation to that stage involved irreversible genetic modification. The first offspring to develop from a differentiated cell were born after nuclear transfer from an embryo-derived cell line that had been induced to become quiescent.[1] Using the same procedure, we now report the birth of live lambs from three new cell populations established from adult mammary gland, fetus and embryo. The fact that a lamb was derived from an adult cell confirms that differentiation of that cell did not involve the irreversible modification of genetic material required for development to term. The birth of lambs from differentiated fetal and adult cells also reinforces previous speculation[1,2] that by inducing donor cells to become quiescent it will be possible to obtain normal development from a wide variety of differentiated cells.

It has long been known that in amphibians, nuclei transferred from adult keratinocytes established in culture support development to the juvenile, tadpole stage.[3] Although this involves differentiation into complex tissues and organs, no development to the

adult stage was reported, leaving open the question of whether a differnetiated adult nucleus can be fully reprogrammed. Previously we reported the birth of live lambs after nuclear transfer from cultured embryonic cells that had been induced into quiescence. We suggested that inducing the donor cell to exit the growth phase causes changes in chromatin structure that facilitate reprogramming of gene expression and that development would be normal if nuclei are used from a variety of differentiated donor cells in similar regimes. Here we investigate whether normal development to term is possible when donor cells derived from fetal or adult tissue are induced to exit the growth cycle and enter the G0 phase of the cell cycle before nuclear transfer.

Three new populations of cells were derived from (1) a day-9 embryo, (2) a day-26 fetus and (3) mammary gland of a 6-year-old ewe in the last trimester of pregnancy. Morphology of the embryo-derived cells is unlike both mouse embryonic stem (ES) cells and the embryo-derived cells used in our previous study. Nuclear transfer was carried out according to one of our established protocols[1] and reconstructed embryos transferred into recipient ewes. Ultrasound scanning detected 21 single fetuses on day 50–60 after oestrus. On subsequent scanning at ~ 14-day intervals, fewer fetuses were observed, suggesting either misdiagnosis or fetal loss. In total, 62% of fetuses were lost, a significantly greater proportion than the estimate of 6% after natural mating.[4] Increased prenatal loss has been reported after embryo manipulation or culture of unreconstructed embryos.[5] At about day 110 of pregnancy, four fetuses were dead, all from embryo-derived cells, and post-mortem analysis was possible after killing the ewes. Two fetuses had abnormal liver development, but no other abnormalities were detected and there was no evidence of infection.

Eight ewes gave birth to live lambs. All three cell populations were represented. One weak lamb, derived from the fetal fibroblasts, weighed 3.1 kg and died within a few minutes of birth, although post-mortem analysis failed to find any abnormality or

infection. At 12.5%, perinatal loss was not dissimilar to that occurring in a large study of commercial sheep, when 8% of lambs died within 24 h of birth.[6] In all cases the lambs displayed the morphological characteristics of the breed used to derive the nucleus donors and not that of the oocyte donor. This alone indicates that the lambs could not have been born after inadvertent mating of either the oocyte donor or recipient ewes. In addition, DNA microsatellite analysis of the cell populations and the lambs at four polymorphic loci confirmed that each lamb was derived from the cell population used as nuclear donor. Duration of gestation is determined by fetal genotype,[7] and in all cases gestation was longer than the breed mean. By contrast, birth weight is influenced by both maternal and fetal genotype.[8] The birth weight of all lambs was within the range for single lambs born to Blackface ewes on our farm (up to 6.6 kg) and in most cases was within the range for the breed of the nuclear donor. There are no strict control observations for birth weight after embryo transfer between breeds, but the range in weight of lambs born to their own breed on our farms is 1.2–5.0 kg, 2–4.9 kg and 3–9 kg for the Finn Dorset, Welsh Mountain and Poll Dorset genotypes, respectively. The attainment of sexual maturity in the lambs is being monitored.

Development of embryos produced by nuclear transfer depends upon the maintenance of normal ploidy and creating the conditions for developmental regulation of gene expression. These responses are both influenced by the cell-cycle stage of donor and recipient cells and the interaction between them (reviewed in ref. 9). A comparison of development of mouse and cattle embryos produced by nuclear transfer to oocytes[10,11] or enucleated zygotes[12,13] suggests that a greater proportion develop if the recipient is an oocyte. This may be because factors that bring about reprogramming of gene expression in a transferred nucleus are required for early development and are taken up by the pronuclei during development of the zygote.

If the recipient cytoplasm is prepared by enucleation of an

oocyte at metaphase II, it is only possible to avoid chromosomal damage and maintain normal ploidy by transfer of diploid nuclei,[14,15] but further experiments are required to define the optimum cell-cycle stage. Our studies with cultured cells suggest that there is an advantage if cells are quiescent (ref. 1, and this work). In earlier studies, donor cells were embryonic blastomeres that had not been induced into quiescence. Comparisons of the phases of the growth cycle showed that development was greater if donor cells were in mitosis[16] or in the G1 (ref. 10) phase of the cycle, rather than in S or G2 phases. Increased development using donor cells in G0, G1 or mitosis may reflect greater access for reprogramming factors present in the oocyte cycoplasm, but a direct comparison of these phases in the same cell population is required for a clearer understanding of the underlying mechanisms.

Together these results indicate that nuclei from a wide range of cell types should prove to be totipotent after enhancing opportunities for reprogramming by using appropriate combinations of these cell-cycle stages. In turn, the dissemination of the genetic improvement obtained within elite selection herds will be enhanced by limited replication of animals with proven performance by nuclear transfer from cells derived from adult animals. In addition, gene targeting in livestock should now be feasible by nuclear transfer from modified cell populations and will offer new opportunities in biotechnology. The techniques described also offer an opportunity to study the possible persistence and impact of epigenetic changes, such as imprinting and telomere shortening, which are known to occur in somatic cells during development and senescence, respectively.

The lamb born after nuclear transfer from a mammary gland cell is, to our knowledge, the first mammal to develop from a cell derived from an adult tissue. The phenotype of the donor cell is unknown. The primary culture contains mainly mammary epithelial (over 90%) as well as other differentiated cell types, including my-

oepithelial cells and fibroblasts. We cannot exclude the possibility that there is a small proportion of relatively undifferentiated stem cells able to support regeneration of the mammary gland during pregnancy. Birth of the lamb shows that during the development of that mammary cell there was no irreversible modification of genetic information required for development to term. This is consistent with the generally accepted view that mammalian differentiation is almost all achieved by systematic, sequential changes in gene expression brought about by interactions between the nucleus and the changing cytoplasmic environment.[17]

Methods

Embryo-derived cells were obtained from embryonic disc of a day-9 embryo from a Poll Dorset ewe cultured as described,[1] with the following modifications. Stem-cell medium was supplemented with bovine DIA/LIF. After 8 days, the explanted disc was disaggregated by enzymatic digestion and cells replated onto fresh feeders. After a further 7 days, a single colony of large flattened cells was isolated and grown further in the absence of feeder cells. At passage 8, the modal chromosome number was 54. These cells were used as nuclear donors at passages 7–9. Fetal-derived cells were obtained from an eviscerated Black Welsh Mountain fetus recovered at autopsy on day 26 of pregnancy. The head was removed before tissues were cut into small pieces and the cells dispersed by exposure to trypsin. Culture was in BHK 21 (Glasgow MEM; Gibco Life Sciences) supplemented with L-glutamine (2 mM), sodium pyruvate (1 mM) and 10% fetal calf serum. At 90% confluency, the cells were passaged with a 1:2 division. At passage 4, these fibroblast-like cells had modal chromosome number of 54. Fetal cells were used as nuclear donors at passages 4–6. Cells from mammary gland were obtained from a 6-year-old Finn Dorset ewe in the last

trimester of pregnancy.[18] At passages 3 and 6, the modal chromosome number was 54 and these cells were used as nuclear donors at passage numbers 3–6.

Nuclear transfer was done according to a previous protocol.[1] Oocytes were recovered from Scottish Blackface ewes between 28 and 33 h after injection of gonadotropin-releasing hormone (GnRH), and enucleated as soon as possible. They were recovered in calcium- and magnesium-free PBS containing 1% FCS and transferred to calcium-free M2 medium[19] containing 10% FCS at 37°C. Quiescent, diploid donor cells were produced by reducing the concentration of serum in the medium from 10 to 0.5% for 5 days, causing the cells to exit the growth cycle and arrest in G0. Confirmation that cells had left the cycle was obtained by staining with antiPCNA/cyclin antibody (Immuno Concepts), revealed by a second antibody conjugated with rhodamine (Dakopatts).

Fusion of the donor cell to the enucleated oocyte and activation of the oocyte were induced by the same electrical pulses, between 34 and 36 h after GnRH injection to donor ewes. The majority of reconstructed embryos were cultured in ligated oviducts of sheep as before, but some embryos produced by transfer from embryo-derived cells or fetal fibroblasts were cultured in a chemically defined medium.[20] Most embryos that developed to morula or blastocyst after 6 days of culture were transferred to recipients and allowed to develop to term. One, two or three embryos were transferred to each ewe depending upon the availability of embryos. The effect of cell type upon fusion and development to morula or blastocyst was analysed using the marginal model of Breslow and Clayton.[21] No comparison was possible of development to term as it was not practicable to transfer all embryos developing to a suitable stage for transfer. When too many embryos were available, those having better morphology were selected.

Ultrasound scan was used for pregnancy diagnosis at around day 60 after oestrus and to monitor fetal development thereafter at 2-week intervals. Pregnant recipient ewes were monitored for nu-

tritional status, body condition and signs of EAE, Q fever, border disease, louping ill and toxoplasmosis. As lambing approached, they were under constant observation and a veterinary surgeon called at the onset of parturition. Microsatellite analysis was carried out on DNA from the lambs and recipient ewes using four polymorphic ovine markers.[22]

References

1. Campbell, K. H. S., McWhir, J., Ritchie, W. A. & Wilmut, I. "Sheep cloned by nuclear transfer from a cultured cell line." *Nature* **380,** 64–66 (1996).
2. Solter, D. "Lambing by nuclear transfer." *Nature* **380,** 24–25 (1996).
3. Gurdon, J. B., Laskey, R. A. & Reeves, O. R. "The developmental capacity of nuclei transplanted from keratinized skin cells of adult frogs." *J. Embryol. Exp. Morph.* **34,** 93–112 (1975).
4. Quinlivan, T. D., Martin, C. A., Taylor, W. B. & Cairney, I. M. "Pre- and perinatal mortality in those ewes that conceived to one service." *J. Reprod. Fertil.* **11,** 379–390 (1966).
5. Walker, S. K., Heard, T. M. & Seamark, R. F. "*In vitro* culture of sheep embryos without co-culture: successes and perspectives." *Therio* **37,** 111–126 (1992).
6. Nash, M. L., Hungerford, L. L., Nash, T. G. & Zinn, G. M. "Risk factors for perinatal and postnatal mortality in lambs." *Vet. Rec.* **139,** 64–67 (1996).
7. Bradford, G. E., Hart, R., Quirke, J. F. & Land, R. B. "Genetic control of the duration of gestation in sheep." *J. Reprod. Fertil.* **30,** 459–463 (1972).
8. Walton, A. & Hammond, J. "The maternal effects on growth and conformation in Shire horse–Shetland pony crosses." *Proc. R. Soc. B* **125,** 311–335 (1938).
9. Campbell, K. H. S., Loi, P., Otaegui, P. J. & Wilmut, I. "Cell cycle co-ordination in embryo cloning by nuclear transfer." *Rev. Reprod.* **1,** 40–46 (1996).
10. Cheong, H.-T., Takahashi, Y. & Kanagawa, H. "Birth of mice after transplantation of early-cell-cycle-stage embryonic nuclei into enucleated oocytes." *Biol. Reprod.* **48,** 958–963 (1993).
11. Prather, R. S. *et al.* "Nuclear transplantation in the bovine embryo. Assessment of donor nuclei and recipient oocyte." *Biol. Reprod.* **37,** 859–866 (1987).
12. McGrath, J. & Solter, D. "Inability of mouse blastomere nuclei transferred to enucleated zygotes to support development *in vitro.*" *Science* **226,** 1317–1318 (1984).
13. Robl, J. M. *et al.* "Nuclear transplantation in bovine embryos." *J. Anim. Sci.* **64,** 642–647 (1987).

14. Campbell, K. H. S., Ritchie, W. A. & Wilmut, I. "Nuclear-cytoplasmic interactions during the first cell cycle of nuclear transfer reconstructed bovine embryos: Implications for deoxyribonucleic acid replication and development." Biol. Reprod. 49, 933–942 (1993).

15. Barnes, F. L. *et al.* "Influence of recipient oocyte cell cycle stage on DNA synthesis, nuclear envelope breakdown, chromosome constitution, and development in nuclear transplant bovine embryos." *Mol. Reprod. Dev.* **36,** 33–41 (1993).

16. Kwon, O. Y. & Kono, T. "Production of identical sextuplet mice by transferring metaphase nuclei from 4-cell embryos." *J. Reprod. Fertil.* Abst. Ser. **17,** 30 (1996).

17. Gurdon, J. B. *The Control of Gene Expression in Animal Development* (Oxford University Press, Oxford, 1974).

18. Finch, L. M. B. *et al.* "Primary culture of ovine mammary epithelial cells." *Biochem. Soc. Trans.* **24,** 369S (1996).

19. Whitten, W. K. & Biggers, J. D. "Complete development *in vitro* of the preimplantation stages of the mouse in a simple chemically defined medium." *J. Reprod. Fertil.* **17,** 399–401 (1968).

20. Gardner, D. K., Lane, M., Spitzer, A. & Batt, P. A. "Enhanced rates of cleavage and development for sheep zygotes cultured to the blastocyst stage in vitro in the absence of serum and somatic cells. Amino acids, vitamins, and culturing embryos in groups stimulate development." *Biol. Reprod.* **50,** 390–400 (1994).

21. Breslow, N. E. & Clayton, D. G. "Approximate inference in generalized linear mixed models." *J. Am. Stat. Assoc.* **88,** 9–25 (1993).

22. Buchanan, F. C., Littlejohn, R. P., Galloway, S. M. & Crawford, A. L. "Microsatellites and associated repetitive elements in the sheep genome." *Mammal. Gen.* **4,** 258–264 (1993).

We thank A. Colman for his involvement throughout this experiment and for guidance during the preparation of this manuscript; C. Wilde for mammary-derived cells; M. Ritchie, J. Bracken, M. Malcolm-Smith, W. A. Ritchie, P. Ferrier and K. Mycock for technical assistance; D. Waddington for statistical analysis; and H. Bowran and his colleagues for care of the animals. This research was supported in part by the Ministry of Agriculture, Fisheries and Food. The experiments were conducted under the Animals (Scientific Procedures) Act 1986 and with the approval of the Roslin Institute Animal Welfare and Experiments Committee.

This article first appeared in *Nature,* volume 385, February 27, 1997, pages 810–813. The figures and tables originally accompanying the article can be found there; they have been deleted for this book.

The Science and Application of Cloning

National Bioethics Advisory Commission

What Is Cloning?

The word *clone* is used in many different contexts in biological research but in its most simple and strict sense, it refers to a precise genetic copy of a molecule, cell, plant, animal, or human being. In some of these contexts, *cloning* refers to established technologies that have been part of agricultural practice for a very long time and currently form an important part of the foundations of modern biological research.

Indeed, genetically identical copies of whole organisms are commonplace in the plant breeding world and are commonly referred to as *varieties* rather than *clones.* Many valuable horticultural or agricultural strains are maintained solely by vegetative propagation from an original plant, reflecting the ease with which it is possible to regenerate a complete plant from a small cutting. The developmental process in animals does not usually permit cloning as easily as in plants. Many simpler invertebrate species, however, such as certain kinds of worms, are capable of regenerating a whole organism from a small piece, even though this is not necessarily their usual mode of reproduction. Vertebrates have lost this ability entirely, although regeneration of certain limbs, organs, or tissues can occur to varying degrees in some animals.

Although a single adult vertebrate cannot generate another whole organism, cloning of vertebrates does occur in nature, in a limited way, through multiple births, primarily with the formation of identical twins. However, twins occur by chance in humans and other mammals, with the separation of a single embryo into halves at an early stage of development. The resulting offspring are genetically identical, having been derived from one zygote, which resulted from the fertilization of one egg by one sperm.

At the molecular and cellular level, scientists have been cloning human and animal cells and genes for several decades. The scientific justification for such cloning is that it provides greater quantities of identical cells or genes for study; each cell or molecule is identical to the others.

At the simplest level, molecular biologists routinely make clones of deoxyribonucleic acid (DNA), the molecular basis of genes. DNA fragments containing genes are copied and amplified in a host cell, usually a bacterium. The availability of large quantities of identical DNA makes possible many scientific experiments. This process, often called *molecular cloning,* is the mainstay of recombinant DNA technology and has led to the production of such important medicines as insulin to treat diabetes, tissue plasminogen activator (tPA) to dissolve clots after a heart attack, and erythropoietin (EPO) to treat anemia associated with dialysis for kidney disease.

Another type of cloning is conducted at the cellular level. In *cellular cloning* copies are made of cells derived from the soma, or body, by growing these cells in culture in a laboratory. The genetic makeup of the resulting cloned cells, called a *cell line,* is identical to that of the original cell. This, too, is a highly reliable procedure, which is also used to test and sometimes to produce new medicines such as those listed above. Since molecular and cellular cloning of this sort does not involve germ cells (eggs or sperm), the cloned cells are not capable of developing into a baby.

In the early 1980s, a more sophisticated form of cloning animals was developed, known as *nuclear transplantation cloning.* The nucleus of somatic cells is diploid—that is, it contains two sets of genes, one from the mother and one from the father. Germ cells, however, contain a haploid nucleus, with only the maternal or paternal genes. In nuclear transplantation cloning, the nucleus is removed from an egg and replaced with the diploid nucleus of a somatic cell. In such nuclear transplantation cloning there is a single genetic "parent," unlike sexual reproduction where a new organism is formed when the genetic material of the egg and sperm fuse. The first experiments of this type were successful only when the donor cell was derived from an early embryo. In theory, large numbers of genetically identical animals could be produced through such nuclear transplantation cloning. In practice, the nuclei from embryos which have developed beyond a certain number of cells seem to lose their totipotency, limiting the number of animals that can be produced in a given period of time from a single, originating embryo.

The new development in the experiments that Wilmut and colleagues carried out to produce Dolly was the use of much more developed somatic cells isolated from adult sheep as the source of the donor nuclei. This achievement of gestation and live birth of a sheep using an adult cell donor nucleus was stunning evidence that cell differentiation and specialization are reversible. Given the fact that cells develop and divide after fertilization and differentiate into specific tissue (e.g., muscle, bone, neurons), the development of a viable adult sheep from a differentiated adult cell nucleus provided surprising evidence that the pattern of gene expression can be reprogrammed. Until this experiment many biologists believed that reactivation of the genetic material of mammalian somatic cells would not be complete enough to allow for the production of a viable adult mammal from nuclear transfer cloning.

Remaining Scientific Uncertainties

Several important questions remain unanswered about the feasibility in mammals of nuclear transfer cloning using adult cells as the source of nuclei:

First, can the procedure that produced Dolly be carried out successfully in other cases? Only one animal has been produced to date. Thus, it is not clear that this technique is reproducible even in sheep.

The successful generation of an adult sheep from a somatic cell nucleus suggests that the imprint can be stable, but it is possible that some instability of the imprint, particularly in cells in culture, could limit the efficiency of nuclear transfer from somatic cells. It is known that disturbances in imprinting lead to growth abnormalities in mice and are associated with cancer and rare genetic conditions in children.

[W]ill the mutations that accumulate in somatic cells affect nuclear transfer efficiency and lead to cancer and other diseases in the offspring? As cells divide and organisms age, mistakes and alterations (mutations) in the DNA will inevitably occur and will accumulate with time. If these mistakes occur in the sperm or the egg, the mutation will be inherited in the offspring. Normally mutations that occur in somatic cells affect only that cell and its descendants which are ultimately dispensable. Nevertheless, such mutations are not necessarily harmless. Sporadic somatic mutations in a variety of genes can predispose a cell to become cancerous. Transfer of a nucleus from a somatic cell carrying such a mutation into an egg would transform a sporadic somatic mutation into a germline mutation that is transmitted to all of the cells of the body. If this mutation were present in all cells it may lead to a genetic disease or cancer. The risks of such events occurring following nuclear transfer are difficult to estimate.

Why Pursue Animal Cloning Research?

Research on nuclear transfer cloning in animals may provide information that will be useful in biotechnology, medicine, and basic science. Some of the immediate goals of this research are:

- to generate groups of genetically identical animals for research purposes
- to rapidly propagate desirable animal stocks
- to improve the efficiency of generating and propagating transgenic livestock
- to produce targeted genetic alterations in domestic animals
- to pursue basic knowledge about cell differentiation

CLONING ANIMALS FOR RESEARCH PURPOSES

Inbred strains of mice have been a mainstay of biological research for years because they are essentially genetically identical and homozygous (i.e., both copies of each gene inherited from the mother and father are identical). Experimental analysis is simplified because differences in genetic background that often lead to experimental variation are eliminated. Generating such homozygous inbred lines in larger animals is difficult and time-consuming because of the long gestation times and small numbers of offspring.

Repeated cycles of nuclear transfer can expand the number of individual animals derived from one donor nucleus, allowing more identical animals to be generated. The first nuclear transfer embryo is allowed to divide to early blastomere stages and then those cells are used as donor nuclei for another series of transfers. This process can be carried on indefinitely, in theory, although practice suggests that successful fusion rates decline with each cycle of transfer. One experiment in cows, for example, produced 54 early embryos after

three cycles of transfer from a single blastomere nucleus from one initial embryo (Stice and Keefer, 1993). Viable calves were produced from all three cycles of nuclear transfer.

This approach is likely to be limited in its usefulness, however. A group of cloned animals derived from nuclear transfer from an individual animal is self-limited. Unless they are derived from an inbred stock initially, each clone derived from one individual will differ genetically from a clone derived from another individual. Once a cloned animal is mated to produce offspring, the offspring will no longer be identical due to the natural processes which shuffle or recombine genes during development of eggs and sperm. Thus, each member of a clone has to be made for each experiment by nuclear transfer, and generation of a large enough number of cloned animals to be useful as experimental groups is likely to be prohibitively expensive in most animals.

ADVANTAGES OF NUCLEAR TRANSFER CLONING FOR BREEDING LIVESTOCK

Nuclear transfer cloning, especially from somatic cell nuclei, could provide an additional means of expanding the number of chosen livestock. The ability to make identical copies of adult prize cows, sheep, and pigs is a feature unique to nuclear transfer technologies, and may well be used in livestock production, if the efficiencies of adult nuclear transfer can be improved. The net effect of multiplying chosen animals by cloning will be to reduce the overall genetic diversity in a given livestock line, likely with severe adverse long-term consequences. If this technique became widespread, efforts would have to be made to ensure a pool of genetically diverse animals for future livestock maintenance.

IMPROVED GENERATION AND PROPAGATION OF TRANSGENIC LIVESTOCK

There is considerable interest in being able to genetically alter farm animals by introduction and expression of genes from other

species, such as humans. So-called "transgenic animals" were first developed using mice, by microinjection of DNA into the nucleus of the egg. This ability to add genes to an organism has been a major research tool for understanding gene regulation and for using the mouse as a model in studies of certain human diseases. It has also been applied to other species including livestock.

Currently, the major activity in livestock transgenesis is focused on pharmaceutical and medical applications. The milk of livestock animals can be modified to contain large amounts of pharmaceutically important proteins such as insulin or factor VIII for treatment of human disease by expressing human genes in the mammary gland (Houdebine, 1994). In sheep greater than 50 percent of the proteins in milk can be the product of a human genes (Colman, 1996).

Another major area of interest is the use of transgenic animals for organ transplantation into humans. Pig organs, in many cases, are similar enough to humans to be potentially useful in organ transplants, if problems of rejection could be overcome.

Foreign DNA, such as a human gene, could be introduced into cell lines in culture and cells expressing the transgene could be characterized and used as a source of donor nuclei for cloning, and all offspring would likely express the human gene. This, in fact, was the motivation behind the experiments that led to the production of Dolly. If a human gene such as that for insulin could be expressed in the mammary gland, the milk of the sheep would be an excellent source of insulin to treat diabetes.

GENERATING TARGETED GENE ALTERATIONS

The most powerful technology for gene replacement in mammals was developed in mice. This technique adds manipulated or foreign DNA to cells in culture to replace the DNA present in the genome of the cells. Thus, mutations or other alterations that would be useful in medical research can be introduced into an animal in a di-

rected and controlled manner and their effects studied, a process called *gene targeting* (Capecchi, 1989).

This use of gene replacement has been responsible for the explosion in the generation of "knock-out" mice, in which specific genes have been deleted from the genome. These mice have been invaluable in current studies to understand normal gene function and to allow the generation of accurate models of human genetic disease. Gene targeting approaches can also be used to ensure correct tissue-specific expression of foreign genes and to suppress the expression of genes in inappropriate tissues. If applied to domestic animals, this technology could increase the efficiency of the expression of foreign genes by targeting the introduced genes to appropriate regions of the chromosome. It could also be used to directly alter the normal genes of the organism, which could influence animal health and productivity or to help develop transgenic organs that are less likely to be rejected upon transplantation.

BASIC RESEARCH ON CELL DIFFERENTIATION

The basic cellular processes that allowed the birth of Dolly by nuclear transfer using the nucleus from an adult somatic donor cell are not well understood. If indeed the donor cell was a fully differentiated cell and not a rare, less differentiated stem cell that resulted in this cloned sheep, there will be many questions to ask about how this process occurred. How the specialized cell from the mammary gland was reprogrammed to allow the expression of a complete developmental program will be a fascinating area of study. Developmental biologists will want to know which genes are reprogrammed, when they are expressed, and in what order. This might shed light on the still poorly understood process of sequential specialization that must occur during development of all organisms.

Basic research into these fundamental processes may also lead to

the development of new therapies to treat human disease. It is not possible to predict from where the essential new discoveries will come. However, already the birth of Dolly has sparked ideas about potential benefits that might be realized. To explore the possibility of these new therapies, extensive basic research is needed.

Potential Therapeutic Applications of Nuclear Transfer Cloning

The demonstration that, in mammals as in frogs, the nucleus of a somatic cell can be reprogrammed by the egg environment provides further impetus to studies on how to reactivate embryonic programs of development in adult cells. These studies have exciting prospects for regeneration and repair of diseased or damaged human tissues and organs, and may provide clues as to how to reprogram adult differentiated cells directly without the need for oocyte fusion. In addition, the use of nuclear transfer has potential application in the field of assisted reproduction.

POTENTIAL APPLICATIONS IN ORGAN AND TISSUE TRANSPLANTATION

Many human diseases, when they are severe enough, are treated effectively by organ or tissue transplantation, including some leukemias, liver failure, heart and kidney disease. In some instances the organ required is non-vital, that is, it can be taken from the donor without great risk (e.g., bone marrow, blood, kidney). In other cases, the organ is obviously vital and required for the survival of the individual, such as the heart. All transplantation is imperfect, with the exception of that which occurs between identical twins, because transplantation of organs between individuals requires genetic compatibility.

In principle, the application of nuclear transfer cloning to humans could provide a potential source of organs or tissues of a pre-

determined genetic background. The notion of using human cloning to produce individuals for use solely as organ donors is repugnant, almost unimaginable, and morally unacceptable. A morally more acceptable and potentially feasible approach is to direct differentiation along a specific path to produce specific tissues (e.g., muscle or nerve) for therapeutic transplantation rather than to produce an entire individual. Given current uncertainties about the feasibility of this, however, much research would be needed in animal systems before it would be scientifically sound, and therefore potentially morally acceptable, to go forward with this approach.

POTENTIAL APPLICATIONS IN CELL-BASED THERAPIES

Another possibility raised by cloning is transplantation of cells or tissues not from an individual donor but from an early embryo or embryonic stem cells, the primitive, undifferentiated cells from the embryo that are still totipotent. This potential application would not require the generation and birth of a cloned individual.

ASSISTED REPRODUCTION

Another area of medicine where the knowledge gained from animal work has potential application is in the area of assisted reproduction. Assisted reproduction technologies are already widely used and encompass a variety of parental and biological situations, that is, donor and recipient relationships. In most cases, an infertile couple seeks remedy through either artificial insemination or in vitro fertilization using sperm from either the male or an anonymous donor, an egg from the woman or a donor, and in some cases surrogacy. In those instances where both individuals of a couple are infertile or the prospective father has nonfunctional sperm, one might envision using cloning of one member of the couple's nuclei to produce a child.

Cloning and Genetic Determinism

The announcement of Dolly sparked widespread speculation about a human child being created using somatic cell nuclear transfer. Much of the perceived fear that greeted this announcement centered around the misperception that a child or many children could be produced who would be identical to an already existing person.

This fear reflects an erroneous belief that a person's genes bear a simple relationship to the physical and psychological traits that compose that individual. This belief, that genes alone determine all aspects of an individual, is called *genetic determinism*. Although genes play an essential role in the formation of physical and behavioral characteristics, each individual is, in fact, the result of a complex interaction between his or her genes and the environment within which they develop, beginning at the time of fertilization and continuing throughout life. As social and biological beings we are creatures of our biological, physical, social, political, historical, and psychological environments. Indeed, the great lesson of modern molecular genetics is the profound complexity of both gene-gene interactions and gene-environment interactions in the determination of whether a specific trait or characteristic is expressed. In other words, there will never be another you.

Thus, the idea that one could make through somatic cell nuclear transfer a team of Michael Jordans, a physics department of Albert Einsteins, or an opera chorus of Pavarottis, is simply false. Knowing the complete genetic makeup of an individual would not tell you what kind of person that individual would become. Even identical twins who grow up together and thus share the same genes and a similar home environment have different likes and dislikes, and can have very different talents. The increasingly sophisticated studies coming out of human genetics research are showing that the better we understand gene function, the less likely it is we

will ever be able to produce at will a person with any given complex trait.

References

Capecchi, M. R., "The new mouse genetics: altering the genome by gene targeting," *Trends in Genetics* 5:70–76, 1989.

Colman, A., "Production of proteins in the milk of transgenic livestock: Problems, solutions, and successes," *American Journal of Clinical Nutrition* 63:639S–645S, 1996.

Houdebine, L. M., "Production of pharmaceutical proteins from transgenic animals," *Journal of Biotechnology* 34:269–287, 1994.

Stice, S. L., and C. L. Keefer, "Multiple generational bovine embryo cloning," *Biology of Reproduction* 48:715–719, 1993.

This is an abridged version of chapter 2 of the NBAC report on human cloning (June 1997). Much of the material in the original version is derived from two commissioned papers provided by Janet Rossant, Samuel Lunenfeld Research Institute, Mount Sinai Hospital, Toronto; and by Stuart Orkin, Children's Hospital and Dana Farber Cancer Institute, Boston.

Dolly's Fashion and Louis's Passion

Stephen Jay Gould

Nothing can be more fleeting or capricious than fashion. What, then, can a scientist, committed to objective description and analysis, do with such a haphazardly moving target? In a classic approach, analogous to standard advice for preventing the spread of an evil agent ("kill it before it multiplies"), a scientist might say, "Quantify it before it disappears."

Francis Galton, Charles Darwin's charmingly eccentric and brilliant cousin, and a founder of the science of statistics, surely took this prescription to heart. He once decided to measure the geographic patterning of female beauty. He attached a piece of paper to a small wooden cross that he could carry, unobserved, in his pocket. He held the cross at one end in the palm of his hand and, with a needle secured between thumb and forefinger, made pinpricks on the three remaining projections (the two ends of the cross bar and the top). He would rank every young woman he passed on the street into one of three categories, as beautiful, average, or substandard (by his admittedly subjective preferences)—and he would then place a pinprick for each woman into the designated domain of his cross. After a hard day's work, he tabulated the relative percentages by counting pinpricks. He concluded, to the dismay of Scotland, that beauty followed a simple trend from north to south, with the highest proportion of uglies in Aberdeen, and the greatest frequency of lovelies in London.

Some fashions (tongue piercings, perhaps?) flower once and then disappear, hopefully forever. Others swing in and out of style, as if fastened to the end of a pendulum. Two foibles of human life strongly promote this oscillatory mode. First, our need to create order in a complex world begets our worst mental habit: dichotomy, or our tendency to reduce a truly intricate set of subtle shadings to a choice between two diametrically opposed alternatives (each with moral weight and therefore ripe for bombast and pontification, if not outright warfare): religion *vs.* science, liberal *vs.* conservative, plain *vs.* fancy, "Roll Over Beethoven" *vs.* the *Moonlight* Sonata. Second, many deep questions about our loves and livelihoods, and the fates of nations, truly have no answers—so we cycle the presumed alternatives of our dichotomies, one after the other, always hoping that, this time, we will find the nonexistent key.

Among oscillating fashions governed primarily by the swing of our social pendulum, no issue could be more prominent for an evolutionary biologist, or more central to a broad range of political questions, than genetic *vs.* environmental sources of human abilities and behaviors. This issue has been falsely dichotomized for so many centuries that English even features a mellifluous linguistic contrast for the supposed alternatives: nature *vs.* nurture.

As any thoughtful person understands, the framing of this question as an either-or dichotomy verges on the nonsensical. Both inheritance and upbringing matter in crucial ways. Moreover, an adult human being, built by interaction of these (and other) factors, cannot be disaggregated into separate components with attached percentages. It behooves us all to grasp why such common claims as "intelligence is 30 percent genetic and 70 percent environmental" have no sensible meaning at all, and represent the same kind of error as the contention that all overt properties of water may be revealed by noting an underlying construction as two parts of one gas mixed with one part of another.

Nonetheless, a preference for either nature or nurture swings back and forth into fashion as political winds blow, and as scientific

breakthroughs grant transient prominence to one or another feature in a spectrum of vital influences. For example, a combination of political and scientific factors favored an emphasis upon environment in the years just following World War II: an understanding that Hitlerian horrors had been rationalized by claptrap genetic theories about inferior races; the heyday of behaviorism in psychology. Today, genetic explanations are all the rage, fostered by a similar mixture of social and scientific influences: for example, the rightward shift of the political pendulum (and the cynical availability of "you can't change them, they're made that way" as a bogus argument for reducing government expenditures on social programs); an overextension to all behavioral variation of genuinely exciting results in identifying the genetic basis of specific diseases, both physical and mental.

Unfortunately, in the heat of immediate enthusiasm, we often mistake transient fashion for permanent enlightenment. Thus, many people assume that the current popularity of genetic determinism represents a final truth wrested from the clutches of benighted environmentalists of previous generations. But the lessons of history suggest that the worm will soon turn again. Since both nature and nurture can teach us so much—and since the fullness of our behavior and mentality represents such a complex and unbreakable combination of these and other factors—a current emphasis on nature will no doubt yield to a future fascination with nurture as we move towards better understanding by lurching upward from one side to another in our quest to fulfill the Socratic injunction: know thyself.

In my Galtonian desire to measure the extent of current fascination with genetic explanations (before the pendulum swings once again and my opportunity evaporates), I hasten to invoke two highly newsworthy items of recent months. The subjects may seem quite unrelated—Dolly the cloned sheep, and Frank Sulloway's book on the effects of birth order upon human behavior—but both stories share a curious common feature offering striking insight into the

current extent of genetic preferences. In short, both stories have been reported almost entirely in genetic terms, but both cry out (at least to me) for a reading as proof of strong environmental influences. Yet no one seems to be drawing (or even mentioning) this glaringly obvious inference. I cannot imagine that anything beyond current fashion for genetic arguments can explain this puzzling silence. I am convinced that exactly the same information, if presented twenty years ago in a climate favoring explanations based on nurture, would have been read primarily in this opposite light. Our world, beset by ignorance and human nastiness, contains quite enough background darkness. Should we not let both beacons shine all the time?

Creating Sheep

Dolly must be the most famous sheep since John the Baptist designated Jesus in metaphor as "lamb of God, which taketh away the sins of the world" (John 1:29). She has certainly edged past the pope, the president, Madonna, and Michael Jordan as the best-known mammal of the moment. And all this for a carbon copy, a Xerox! I don't mean to drop cold water on this little lamb, cloned from a mammary cell of her adult mother, but I remain unsure that she's worth all the fuss and fear generated by her unconventional birth.

When one reads the technical article describing Dolly's manufacture (see previous essay, by Wilmut *et al.*), rather than the fumings and hyperbolae of so much public commentary, one can't help feeling a bit underwhelmed, and left wondering whether Dolly's story tells less than meets the eye.

I don't mean to discount or underplay the ethical issues raised by Dolly's birth (and I shall return to this subject in a moment), but we are not about to face an army of Hitlers or even a Kentucky Derby run entirely by genetically identical contestants (a true test

for the skills of jockeys and trainers)! First, Dolly breaks no theoretical ground in biology, for we have known how to clone in principle for at least two decades, but had developed no techniques for reviving the full genetic potential of differentiated adult cells. (Still, I admit that a technological solution can pack as much practical and ethical punch as a theoretical breakthrough. I suppose one could argue that the first atomic bomb only realized a known possibility.)

Second, my colleagues have been able to clone animals from embryonic cells lines for several years, so Dolly is not the first mammalian clone, but only the first clone from an adult cell. Wilmut and colleagues also cloned sheep from cells of a 9-day embryo and a 26-day fetus—and had much greater success. They achieved 15 pregnancies (though not all proceeded to term) in 32 "recipients" (that is, surrogate mothers for transplanted cells) of the embryonic cell-line, 5 pregnancies in 16 recipients of the fetal cell-line, but only Dolly (1 pregnancy in 13 tries) for the adult cell-line. This experiment cries out for confirming repetition. (Still, I allow that current difficulties will surely be overcome, and cloning from adult cells, if doable at all, will no doubt be achieved more routinely as techniques and familiarity improve.)

Third, and more seriously, I remain unconvinced that we should regard Dolly's starting cell as adult in the usual sense of the term. Dolly grew from a cell taken from the "mammary gland of a 6-year-old ewe in the last trimester of pregnancy" (to quote the technical article of Wilmut *et al.*). Since the breasts of pregnant mammals enlarge substantially in late stages of pregnancy, some mammary cells, though technically adult, may remain unusually labile or even "embryo like," and thus able to proliferate rapidly to produce new breast tissue at an appropriate stage of pregnancy. Consequently, we may only be able to clone from unusual adult cells with effectively embryonic potential, and not from any stray cheek cell, hair follicle, or drop of blood that happens to fall into the clutches of a mad xeroxer. Wilmut and colleagues admit this possibility in a sentence

written with all the obtuseness of conventional scientific prose, and therefore almost universally missed by journalists: "We cannot exclude the possibility that there is a small proportion of relatively undifferentiated stem cells able to support regeneration of the mammary gland during pregnancy."

But if I remain relatively unimpressed by achievements thus far, I do not discount the monumental ethical issues raised by the possibility of cloning from adult cells. Yes, we have cloned fruit trees for decades by the ordinary process of grafting—and without raising any moral alarms. Yes, we may not face the evolutionary dangers of genetic uniformity in crop plants and livestock, for I trust that plant and animal breeders will not be stupid enough to eliminate all but one genotype from a species, and will always maintain (as plant breeders do now) an active pool of genetic diversity in reserve. (But then, I suppose we should never underestimate the potential extent of human stupidity—and localized reserves could be destroyed by a catastrophe, while genetic diversity spread throughout a species guarantees maximal evolutionary robustness.)

Nonetheless, while I regard many widely expressed fears as exaggerated, I do worry deeply about potential abuses of human cloning, and I do urge a most open and thorough debate on these issues. Each of us can devise a personal worst-case scenario. Somehow, I do not focus upon the spectre of a future Hitler making an army of 10 million identical robotic killers—for if our society ever reaches a state where such an outcome might be realized, we are probably already lost. My thoughts run to localized moral quagmires that we might actually have to face in the next few years—for example, the biotech equivalent of ambulance-chasing slimeballs among lawyers: a husting little firm that scans the orbits for reports of children who died young, and then goes to grieving parents with the following offer: "So sorry for your loss; but did you save a hair sample? We can make you another for a mere 50 thou."

However, and still on the subject of ethical conundrums, but

now moving to my main point about current underplaying of environmental sources for human behaviors, I do think that the most potent scenarios of fear, and the most fretful ethical discussions on late-night television, have focused on a nonexistent problem that all human societies solved millennia ago. We ask: Is a clone an individual? Would a clone have a soul? Would a clone made from my cell negate my unique personhood?

May I suggest that these endless questions—all variations on the theme that clones threaten our traditional concept of individuality—have already been answered empirically, even though public discussion of Dolly seems blithely oblivious to this evident fact. We have known human clones from the dawn of our consciousness. We call them identical twins—and they are far better clones than Dolly and her mother. Dolly only shares nuclear DNA with her mother's mammary cell—for the nucleus of this cell was inserted into an embryonic stem-cell (whose own nucleus had been removed) of a surrogate female. Dolly then grew in the womb of this surrogate.

Identical twins share at least four additional (and important) attributes that differ between Dolly and her mother. First, identical twins also house the same mitochondrial genes. (Mitochondria, the "energy factories" of cells, contain a small number of genes. We get our mitochondria from the cytoplasm of the egg cell that made us, not from the nucleus formed by the union of sperm and egg. Dolly received her nucleus from her mother, but her egg cytoplasm, and hence her mitochondria, from her surrogate.) Second, identical twins share the same set of maternal gene products in the egg. Genes don't grow embryos all by themselves. Egg cells contain protein products of maternal genes that play a major role in directing the early development of the embryo. Dolly has her mother's nuclear genes, but her surrogate's gene products in the cytoplasm of her founding cell.

Third—and now we come to explicitly environmental factors—identical twins share the same womb. Dolly and her mother ges-

tated in different places. Fourth, identical twins share the same time and culture (even if they fall into the rare category, so cherished by researchers, of siblings separated at birth and raised, unbeknownst to each other, in distant families of different social classes). The clone of an adult cell matures in a different world. Does anyone seriously believe that a clone of Beethoven would sit down one day to write a tenth symphony in the style of his early-nineteenth-century forebear?

So identical twins are truly eerie clones— ever so much more alike on all counts, than Dolly and her mother. We do know that identical twins share massive similarities, not only of appearance, but also in broad propensities and detailed quirks of personality. Nonetheless, have we ever doubted the personhood of each member in a pair of identical twins? Of course not. We know that identical twins are distinct individuals, albeit with peculiar and extensive similarities. We give them different names. They encounter divergent experiences and fates. Their lives wander along disparate paths of the world's complex vagaries. They grow up as distinctive and undoubted individuals, yet they stand forth as far better clones than Dolly and her mother.

Why have we overlooked this central principle in our fears about Dolly? Identical twins provide sturdy proof that inevitable differences of nurture guarantee the individuality and personhood of each human clone. And since any future human Dolly must differ far more from her progenitor (in both the nature of mitochondria and maternal gene products, and the nurture of different wombs and surrounding cultures) than any identical twin diverges from her sibling clone, why ask if Dolly has a soul or an independent life when we have never doubted the personhood or individuality of far more similar identical twins?

Literature has always recognized this principle. The Nazi loyalists who cloned Hitler in *The Boys from Brazil* also understood that they had to maximize similarities of nurture as well. So they fostered their little Hitler babies in families maximally like Adolph's

own dysfunctional clan—and not one of them grew up anything like history's quintessential monster. Life has always verified this principle as well. Eng and Chang, the original Siamese twins and the closest clones of all, developed distinct and divergent personalities. One became a morose alcoholic, the other remained a benign and cheerful man. We may not think much of the individuality of sheep in general (for they do set our icon of blind following and identical form as they jump over fences in the mental schemes of insomniacs), but Dolly will grow up to be as unique and as ornery as any sheep can be.

Killing Kings

My friend Frank Sulloway recently published a book that he had fretted over, nurtured, massaged, and lovingly shepherded towards publication for more than two decades. Frank and I have been discussing his thesis ever since he began his studies. I thought (and suggested) that he should have published his results twenty years ago. I still hold this opinion—for, while I greatly admire his book, and do recognize that such a long gestation allowed Frank to strengthen his case by gathering and refining his data, I also believe that he became too committed to his central thesis, and tried to extend his explanatory umbrella over too wide a range, with arguments that sometimes smack of special pleading and tortured logic.

Born to Rebel documents a crucial effect of birth order in shaping human personalities and styles of thinking. Firstborns, as sole recipients of parental attention until the arrival of later children, and as more powerful (by virtue of age and size) than their subsequent siblings, tend to cast their lot with parental authority and with the advantages of incumbent strength. They tend to grow up competent and confident, but also conservative and unlikely to favor quirkiness or innovation. Why threaten an existing structure that has always offered you clear advantages over siblings? Later

children, however, are (as Sulloway's title proclaims) born to rebel. They must compete against odds for parental attention long focused primarily elsewhere. They must scrap and struggle, and learn to make do for themselves. Laterborns therefore tend to be flexible, innovative and open to change. The business and political leaders of stable nations may be overwhelmingly firstborns, but the revolutionaries who have discombobulated our cultures and restructured our scientific knowledge tend to be laterborns.

Sulloway defends his thesis with statistical data on the relationship of birth order and professional achievement in modern societies, and by interpreting historical patterns as strongly influenced by characteristic differences in behaviors of firstborns and laterborns. I found some of his historical arguments fascinating and persuasive when applied to large samples (but often uncomfortably overinterpreted in attempts to explain the intricate details of individual lives, for example, the effect of birth order on the differential success of Henry VIII's various wives in overcoming his capricious cruelties).

In a fascinating case, Sulloway chronicles a consistent shift in relative percentages of firstborns among successive groups in power during the French Revolution. The moderates initially in charge tended to be firstborns. As the revolution became more radical, but still idealistic and open to innovation and free discussion, laterborns strongly predominated. But when control then passed to the uncompromising hardliners who promulgated the Reign of Terror, firstborns again ruled the roost. In a brilliant stroke, Sulloway tabulates the birth orders for several hundred delegates who decided the fate of Louis XVI in the National Convention. Among hardliners who voted for the guillotine, 73 percent were firstborns; but 62 percent of the delegates who opted for the compromise of conviction with pardon were laterborns. Since Louis lost his head by a margin of one vote, an ever so slightly different mix of birth orders among delegates might have altered the course of history.

Since Frank is a good friend, and since I have been at least a minor midwife to this project over two decades, I took an unusually strong interest in the delayed birth of *Born to Rebel*. I read the text and all the prominent reviews that appeared in many newspapers and journals. And I have been puzzled—stunned would not be too strong a word—by the total absence from all commentary of the simplest and most evident inference from Frank's data, the one glaringly obvious point that everyone should have stressed, given the long history of issues raised by such information.

Sulloway focuses nearly all his interpretation on an extended analogy (broadly valid in my judgement, but overextended as an exclusive device) between birth order in families and ecological status in a world of Darwinian competition. Children vie for limited parental resources, just as individuals struggle for existence (and ultimately for reproductive success) in nature. Birth orders place children in different "niches," requiring disparate modes of competition for maximal success. While firstborns shore up incumbent advantages, laterborns must grope and grub by all clever means at their disposal—leading to the divergent personalities of stalwart and rebel. Alan Wolfe, in my favorite negative review from the *New Republic* (December 23, 1996; Jared Diamond stresses the same themes in my favorite positive review from the *New York Review of Books,* November 14, 1996), writes: "Since firstborns already occupy their own niches, laterborns, if they are to be noticed, have to find unoccupied niches. If they do so successfully, they will be rewarded with parental investment."

As I said, I am willing to go with this program up to a point. But I must also note that the restriction of commentary to this Darwinian metaphor has diverted attention from the foremost conclusion revealed by a large effect of birth order upon human behavior. The Darwinian metaphor smacks of biology; we also erroneously think of biological explanations as intrinsically genetic (an analysis of this common fallacy could fill an essay or an entire book). I suppose that this chain of argument leads us to stress what-

ever we think that Sulloway's thesis might be teaching us about "nature" (our preference, in any case, during this age of transient fashion for genetic causes) under our erroneous tendency to treat the explanation of human behavior as a debate between nature and nurture.

But consider the meaning of birth-order effects for environmental influences, however unfashionable at the moment. Siblings differ genetically of course, but no aspect of this genetic variation correlates in any systematic way with birth order. Firstborns and laterborns receive the same genetic shake within a family. Systematic differences in behavior between firstborns and laterborns cannot be ascribed to genetics. (Other biological effects may correlate with birth order—if, for example, the environment of the womb changes systematically with numbers of pregnancies—but such putative influences have no basis in genetic differences among siblings.) Sulloway's substantial birth-order effects therefore provide our best and ultimate documentation of nurture's power. If birth order looms so large in setting the paths of history and the allocation of people to professions, then nurture cannot be denied a powerfully formative role in our intellectual and behavioral variation and in setting the paths of human history as well. To be sure, we often fail to see what stares us in the face; but how can the winds of fashion blow away such an obvious point, one so relevant to our deepest and most persistent questions about ourselves?

In this case, I am especially struck by the irony of fashion's veil. As noted before, I urged Sulloway to publish his data twenty years ago—when (in my judgement) he could have presented an even better case because he had already documented the strong and general influence of birth order upon personality, but had not yet ventured upon the slippery path of trying to explain too many details with forced arguments that sometimes lapse into self-parody. If Sulloway had published in the mid 1970s, when nurture rode the pendulum of fashion in a politically more liberal age (probably dominated by laterborns!), I am confident that this obvious point

about birth-order effects as proof of nurture's power would have won primary attention, rather than consignment to a limbo of invisibility.

Hardly anything in intellectual life can be more salutatory than the separation of fashion from fact. Always suspect fashion (especially when the moment's custom matches your personal predilection); always cherish fact (while remembering that an apparent "fact" may only record a transient fashion). I have discussed two subjects that couldn't be "hotter," but cannot be adequately understood because a veil of genetic fashion now conceals the richness of full explanation by relegating a preeminent environmental theme to invisibility. Thus, we worry whether the first cloned sheep represents a genuine individual at all, while we forget that we have never doubted the distinct personhood guaranteed by differences in nurture to clones far more similar by nature than Dolly and her mother—identical twins. And we try to explain the strong effects of birth order only by invoking a Darwinian analogy between family place and ecological niche, while forgetting that these systematic effects cannot have a genetic basis, and therefore prove the predictable power of nurture. So, sorry Louis. You lost your head to the power of family environments upon head children. And hello Dolly. May we forever restrict your mode of manufacture, at least for humans. But may genetic custom never stale the infinite variety guaranteed by a lifetime of nurture in the intricate complexity of nature—this vale of tears, joy and endless wonder.

This essay first appeared in *Natural History,* vol. 106, no. 5, June 1997, pages 18–23, 76.

What's Wrong with Cloning?

Richard Dawkins

Science and logic cannot tell us what is right and what is wrong (Dawkins, 1998). You cannot, as I was once challenged to do by a belligerent radio interviewer, prove logically from scientific evidence that murder is wrong. But you can deploy logical reasoning, and even scientific facts, in demonstrating to dogmatists that their convictions are mutually contradictory. You can prove that their passionate denunciation of X is incompatible with their equally passionate advocacy of Y, because X and Y, though they had not realized it before, are the same thing (Glover, 1984). Science can show us a new way of thinking about an issue, perhaps open our imaginations in unexpected ways, with the consequence that we see our personal Xs and Ys in different ways and our values change. Sometimes we can be shown a way of seeing that makes us feel more favorably disposed to something that had been distasteful or frightening. But we can also be alerted to menacing implications of something that we had previously thought harmless or frivolously amusing. Cloning provides a case study in the power of scientific thinking to change our minds, in both directions.

Public responses to Dolly the sheep varied but, from President Clinton down, there was almost universal agreement that such a thing must never be allowed to happen to humans. Even those arguing for the medical benefits of cloning human tissues in culture were careful to establish their decent credentials, in the most vig-

orous terms, by denouncing the very thought that adult humans might be cloned to make babies, like Dolly.

But is it so obviously repugnant that we shouldn't even think about it? Mightn't even you, in your heart of hearts, quite like to be cloned? As Darwin said in another context, it is like confessing a murder, but I think I would. The motivation need have nothing to do with vanity, with thinking that the world would be a better place if there was another one of you living on after you are dead. I have no such illusions. My feeling is founded on pure curiosity. I know how I turned out, having been born in the 1940s, schooled in the 1950s, come of age in the 1960s, and so on. I find it a personally riveting thought that I could watch a small copy of myself, fifty years younger and wearing a baseball hat instead of a British Empire pith helmet, nurtured through the early decades of the twenty-first century. Mightn't it feel almost like turning back your personal clock fifty years? And mightn't it be wonderful to advise your junior copy on where you went wrong, and how to do it better? Isn't this, in (sometimes sadly) watered-down form, one of the motives that drives people to breed children in the ordinary way, by sexual reproduction?

If I have succeeded in my aim, you may be feeling warmer towards the idea of human cloning than before. But now think about the following. Who is most likely to get themselves cloned? A nice person like you? Or someone with power and influence like Saddam Hussein? A hero we'd all like to see more of, like David Attenborough? Or someone who can pay, like Rupert Murdoch? Worse, the technology might not be limited to single copies of the cloned individual. The imagination presents the all-too plausible spectre of *multiple* clones, regiments of identical individuals marching by the thousand, in lockstep to a Brave New Millennium. Phalanxes of identical little Hitlers goose-stepping to the same genetic drum—here is a vision so horrifying as to overshadow any lingering curiosity we might have over the final solution to the "nature or nurture" problem (for multiple cloning, to switch to the positive

again, would certainly provide an elegant approach to that ancient conundrum). Science can open our eyes in both directions, towards negative as well as positive possibilities. It cannot tell us which way to turn, but it can help us to see what lies along the alternative paths.

Human cloning already happens by accident—not particularly often but often enough that we all know examples. Identical twins are true clones of each other, with the same genes. Hell's foundations don't quiver every time a pair of identical twins is born. Nobody has ever suggested that identical twins are zombies without individuality or personality. Of those who think anybody has a soul, none has ever suggested that identical twins lack one. So, the new discoveries announced from Edinburgh can't be *all* that radical in their moral and ethical implications.

Nevertheless, the possibility that adult humans might be cloned as babies has potential implications that society would do well to ponder before the reality catches up with us. Even if we could find a legal way of limiting the privilege to universally admired paragons, wouldn't a new Einstein, say, suffer terrible psychological problems? Wouldn't he be teased at school, tormented by unreasonable expectations of genius? But he might turn out even better than the paragon. Old Einstein, however outstanding his genes, had an ordinary education and had to waste his time earning a living in the patent office. Young Einstein could be given an education to match his genes and an inside track to make the best use of his talents from the start.

Turning back to the objections, wouldn't the first cloned child feel a bit of a freak? It would have a birth mother who was no relation, an identical brother or sister who might be old enough to be a great grandparent, and genetic parents perhaps long dead. On the other hand, the stigma of uniqueness is not a new problem, and it is not beyond our wit to solve it. Something like it arose for the first in vitro fertilized babies, yet now they are no longer called "test tube babies" and we hardly know who is one and who is not.

Cloning is said to be unnatural. It is of more academic than ethical interest, but there is a sense in which, to an evolutionary biologist, cloning is more natural than the sexual alternative. I speak of the famous paradox of sex, often called the twofold cost of sex, the cost of meiosis, or the cost of producing sons. I'll explain this, but briefly because it is quite well known. The selfish gene theorem, which treats an animal as a machine programmed to maximize the survival of copies of its genes, has become a favored way of expressing modern Darwinism (see, for example, Mark Ridley, 1996; Matt Ridley, 1996). The rationale, in one tautological sentence, is that all animals are descended from an unbroken line of ancestors who succeeded in passing on those very genes. From this point of view, at least when naively interpreted, sex is paradoxical because a mutant female who spontaneously switched to clonal reproduction would immediately be twice as successful as her sexual rivals. She would produce female offspring, each of whom would bear all her genes, not just half of them. Her grandchildren and more remote descendants, too, would be females containing 100 percent of her genes rather than one quarter, one eighth, and so on.

Our hypothetical mutant must be female rather than male, for an interesting reason which fundamentally amounts to economics. We assume that the number of offspring reared is limited by the economic resources poured into them, and that two nurturing parents can therefore rear twice as many as one single parent. The option of going it alone without a sexual partner is not open to males because single males are not geared up to bear the economic costs of rearing a child. This is especially clear in mammals where males lack a uterus and mammary glands. Even at the level of gametes, and over the whole animal kingdom, there is a basic economic imbalance between large, nutritious eggs and small, swimming sperm. A sperm is well equipped to find an egg. It is not economically equipped to grow on its own. Unlike an egg, it does not have the option of dispensing with the other gamete.

The economic imbalance between the sexes can be redressed

later in development, through the medium of paternal care. Many bird species are monogamous, with the male playing an approximately equal role in protecting and feeding the young. In such species the twofold cost of sex is at least substantially reduced. The hypothetical cloning female still exports her genes twice as efficiently to each child. But she has half as many children as her sexual rival, who benefits from the equal economic assistance of a male. The actual magnitude of the cost of sex will vary between twofold (where there is no paternal care) to zero (where the economic contribution of the father equals that of the mother, and the productivity in offspring of a couple is twice that of a single mother).

In most mammals paternal care is either nonexistent or too small to make much of a dent in the twofold cost of sex. Accordingly, from a Darwinian point of view, sex remains something of a paradox. It is, in a way, more "unnatural" than cloning. This piece of reasoning has been the starting point for an extensive theoretical literature with the more or less explicitly desperate aim of finding a benefit of sex sufficiently great to outweigh the twofold cost. A succession of books has tried, with no conspicuous success, to solve this riddle (Williams, 1975; Maynard Smith, 1978; Bell, 1982; Michod & Levin, 1988; Ridley, 1993). The consensus has not moved greatly in the twenty years since Williams's 1975 publication, which began:

> This book is written from a conviction that the prevalence of sexual reproduction in higher plants and animals is inconsistent with current evolutionary theory . . . there is a kind of crisis at hand in evolutionary biology. . . .

and ended:

> I am sure that many readers have already concluded that I really do not understand the role of sex in either organic or biotic

evolution. At least I can claim, on the basis of the conflicting views in the recent literature, the consolation of abundant company.

Nevertheless, outside the laboratory, asexual reproduction in mammals, as opposed to some lizards, fish, and various groups of invertebrates, has never been observed. It is quite possible that our ancestral lineage has not reproduced asexually for more than a billion years. There are good reasons for doubting that adult mammals will ever spontaneously clone themselves without artificial aid (Maynard Smith, 1988). So far removed from nature are the ingenious techniques of Dr. Wilmut and his colleagues; they can even make clones of *males* (by borrowing an ovum from a female and removing her own DNA from it). In the circumstances, notwithstanding Darwinian reasoning, ethicists might reasonably feel entitled to call human cloning unnatural.

I think we must beware of a reflex and unthinking antipathy, or "yuk reaction" to everything "unnatural." Certainly cloning is unprecedented among mammals, and certainly if it were widely adopted it would interfere with the natural course of the evolutionary process. But we've been interfering with human evolution ever since we set up social and economic machinery to support individuals who could not otherwise afford to reproduce, and most people don't regard that as self-evidently bad, although it is surely unnatural. It is unnatural to read books, or travel faster than we can run, or scuba dive. As the old joke says, "If God had intended us to fly, he'd never have given us the railway." It's unnatural to wear clothes, yet the people most likely to be scandalized at the unnaturalness of human cloning may be the very people most outraged by (natural) nudity. For good or ill, human cloning would have an impact on society, but it is not clear that it would be any more momentous than the introduction of antibiotics, vaccination, or efficient agriculture, or than the abolition of slavery.

If I am asked for a positive argument in favor of human cloning,

my immediate response is to question where the onus of proof lies. There are general arguments based on individual liberty against prohibiting anything that people want to do, unless there is good reason why they should not. Sometimes, when it is hard to peer into the future and see the consequences of doing something new, there is an argument from simple prudence in favor of doing nothing, at least until we know more. If such an argument had been deployed against X rays, whose dangers were appreciated later than their benefits, a number of deaths from radiation sickness might have been averted. But we'd also be deprived of one of medicine's most lifesaving diagnostic tools.

Very often there are excellent reasons for opposing the "individual freedom" argument that people should be allowed to do whatever they want. A libertarian argument in favor of allowing people to play amplified music without restriction is easily countered on grounds of the nuisance and displeasure caused to others. Assuming that some people want to be cloned, the onus is on objectors to produce arguments to the effect that cloning would harm somebody, or some sentient being, or society or the planet at large. We have already seen some such arguments, for instance, that the young clone might feel embarrassed or overburdened by expectations. Notice that such arguments on behalf of the young clone must, in order to work, attribute to the young clone the sentiment, "I wish I had never been born because . . ." Such statements can be made, but they are hard to maintain, and the kind of people most likely to object to cloning are the very people least likely to favor the "I wish I didn't exist" style of argument when it is used in the abortion or the euthanasia debates. As for the harm that cloning might do to third parties, or to society at large, no doubt arguments can be mounted. But they must be strong enough to counter the general "freedom of the individual" presumption in favor of cloning. My suspicion is that it will prove hard to make the case that cloning does more harm to third parties than pop festivals, advertising hoardings, or mobile telephones in trains—to name three pet hates

of my own. The fact that I hate something is not, in itself, sufficient justification for stopping others who wish to enjoy it. The onus is on the objectors to press a better objection. Personal prejudice, without supporting justification, is not enough.

A convention has grown up that prejudices based upon religion, as opposed to purely personal prejudices, are especially privileged, self-evidently exempt from the need for supporting argument. This is relevant to the present discussion, as I suspect that reflex antipathy to advances in reproductive technology is frequently, at bottom, religiously inspired. Of course people are entitled to their religious, or any other, convictions. But society should beware of assuming that when a conviction is religious this somehow entitles it to a special kind of respect, over and above the respect we should accord to personal prejudice of any other kind. This was brought home to me by media responses to Dolly.

A news story like Dolly's is always followed by a flurry of energetic press activity. Newspaper columnists sound off, solemnly or facetiously, occasionally intelligently. Radio and television producers seize the telephone and round up panels to discuss and debate the moral and legal issues. Some of these panelists are experts on the science, as you would expect and as is right and proper. Others are distinguished scholars of moral or legal philosophy, which is equally appropriate. Both these categories of person have been invited to the studio in their own right, because of their specialized knowledge or their proven ability to think intelligently and express themselves clearly. The arguments that they have with each other are usually illuminating and rewarding.

But there is another category of obligatory guest. There is the inevitable "representative" of the so-and-so "community," and of course we mustn't forget the "voice" from the such-and-such "tradition." Not to mince words, the religious lobby. Lobbies in the plural, I should say, because all the religions (or "cultures" as we are nowadays asked to call them) have their point of view, and they all have to be represented lest their respective "communities" feel

slighted. This has the incidental effect of multiplying the sheer number of people in the studio, with consequent consumption, if not waste, of time. It also, I believe, often has the effect of lowering the level of expertise and intelligence in the studio. This is only to be expected, given that these spokesmen are chosen not because of their own qualifications in the field, or because they can think, but simply because they represent a particular section of the community.

Out of good manners I shall not mention names, but during the admirable Dolly's week of fame I took part in broadcast or televised discussions of cloning with several prominent religious leaders, and it was not edifying. One of the most eminent of these spokesmen, recently elevated to the House of Lords, got off to a flying start by refusing to shake hands with the women in the television studio, apparently for fear they might be menstruating or otherwise "unclean." They took the insult more graciously than I would have, and with the "respect" always bestowed on religious prejudice—but no other kind of prejudice. When the panel discussion got going, the woman in the chair, treating this bearded patriarch with great deference, asked him to spell out the harm that cloning might do, and he answered that atomic bombs were harmful. Yes indeed, no possibility of disagreement there. But wasn't the discussion supposed to be about cloning?

Since it was his choice to shift the discussion to atomic bombs, perhaps he knew more about physics than about biology? But no, having delivered himself of the daring falsehood that Einstein split the atom, the sage switched with confidence to geological history. He made the telling point that, since God labored six days and then rested on the seventh, scientists too ought to know when to call a halt. Now, either he really believed that the world was made in six days, in which case his ignorance alone disqualifies him from being taken seriously, or, as the chairwoman charitably suggested, he intended the point purely as an allegory—in which case it was a lousy allegory. Sometimes in life it is a good idea to stop, sometimes

it is a good idea to go on. The trick is to decide *when* to stop. The allegory of God resting on the seventh day cannot, in itself, tell us whether we have reached the right point to stop in some particular case. As allegory, the six-day creation story is empty. As history, it is false. So why bring it up?

The representative of a rival religion on the same panel was frankly confused. He voiced the common fear that a human clone would lack individuality. It would not be a whole, separate human being but a mere soulless automaton. When I warned him that his words might be offensive to identical twins, he said that identical twins were a quite different case. Why? Because they occur naturally, rather than under artificial conditions. Once again, no disagreement about that. But weren't we talking about "individuality," and whether clones are "whole human beings" or soulless automata? How does the "naturalness" of their birth bear upon that question?

This religious spokesman seemed simply unable to grasp that there were two separate arguments going on: first, whether clones are autonomous individuals (in which case the analogy with identical twins is inescapable and his fear groundless); and second, whether there is something objectionable about artificial interference in the natural processes of reproduction (in which case other arguments should be deployed—and could have been—but weren't). I don't want to sound uncharitable, but I respectfully submit to the producers who put together these panels that merely being a spokesman for a particular "tradition," "culture" or "community" may not be enough. Isn't a certain minimal qualification in the IQ department desirable too?

On a different panel, this time for radio, yet another religious leader was similarly perplexed by identical twins. He too had "theological" grounds for fearing that a clone would not be a separate individual and would therefore lack "dignity." He was swiftly informed of the undisputed scientific fact that identical twins are clones of each other with the same genes, like Dolly except that Dolly's clone is older. Did he really mean to say that identical twins

(and we all know some) lack the dignity of separate individuality? His reason for denying the relevance of the twin analogy was even odder than the previous one. Indeed it was transparently self-contradictory. He had great faith, he informed us, in the power of nurture over nature. Nurture is why identical twins are really different individuals. When you get to know a pair of twins, he concluded triumphantly, they even *look* a bit different.

Er, quite so. And if a pair of clones were separated by fifty years, wouldn't their respective nurtures be even *more* different? Haven't you just shot yourself in your theological foot? He just didn't get it—but after all he hadn't been chosen for his ability to follow an argument.

Religious lobbies, spokesmen of "traditions" and "communities," enjoy privileged access not only to the media but also to influential committees of the great and the good, to governments and school boards. Their views are regularly sought, and heard with exaggerated "respect," by parliamentary committees. You can be sure that, if a royal commission were set up to advise on cloning policy, religious lobbies would be prominently represented. Religious spokesmen and spokeswomen enjoy an inside track to influence and power which others have to earn through their own ability or expertise. What is the justification for this? Maybe there is a good reason, and I'm ready to be persuaded by it. But I find it hard to imagine what it could be.

To put it brutally and more generally, why has our society so meekly acquiesced in the idea that religious views have to be respected automatically and without question? If I want you to respect my views on politics, science or art, I have to earn that respect by argument, reason, eloquence, relevant knowledge. I have to withstand counterarguments from you. But if I have a view that is part of my religion, critics must respectfully tiptoe away or brave the indignation of society at large. Why are religious opinions off limits in this way? Why do we have to respect them, simply because they are religious?

It is also not clear how it is decided which of many mutually contradictory religions should be granted this unquestioned respect, this unearned influence. If we decide to invite a Christian spokesman into the television studio or the royal commission, should it be a Catholic or a Protestant, or do we have to have both to make it fair? (In Northern Ireland the difference is, after all, important enough to constitute a recognized motive for murder.) If we have a Jew and a Muslim, must we have both Orthodox and Reformed, both Shiite and Sunni? And then why not Moonies, Scientologists and Druids?

Society accepts that parents have an automatic right to bring their children up with particular religious opinions and can withdraw them from, say, biology classes that teach evolution. Yet we'd all be scandalized if children were withdrawn from art history classes that teach about artists not to their parents' taste. We meekly agree, if a student says, "Because of my religion I can't take my final examination on the day appointed, so no matter what the inconvenience, you'll have to set a special examination for me." It is not obvious why we treat such a demand with any more respect than, say, "Because of my basketball match (or because of my mother's birthday party, etc.) I can't take the examination on a particular day." Such favored treatment for religious opinion reaches its apogee in wartime. A highly intelligent and sincere individual who justifies his personal pacifism by deeply thought-out moral philosophic arguments finds it hard to achieve conscientious objector status. If only he had been born into a religion whose scriptures forbid fighting, he'd have needed no other arguments at all. It is the same unquestioned respect for religious leaders that causes society to beat a path to their door whenever an issue like cloning is in the air. Perhaps, instead, we should listen to those whose words themselves justify our heeding them.

Science, to repeat, cannot tell us what is right or wrong. You cannot find rules for living the good life, or rules for the good governance of society, written in the book of nature. But it doesn't follow

from this that any other book, or any other discipline, can serve instead. There is a fallacious tendency to think that, because science cannot answer a particular kind of question, religion can. Where morals and values are concerned, there are no certain answers to be found in books. We have to grow up, decide what kind of society we want to live in and think through the difficult pragmatic problems of achieving it. If we have decided that a democratic, free society is what we want, it seems to follow that people's wishes should be obstructed only with good reason. In the case of human cloning, if some people want to do it, the onus is on those who would ban it to spell out what harm it would do, and to whom.

References

Bell, G. (1982). *The Masterpiece of Nature.* London: Croom Helm.

Dawkins, R. (1998). "The Values of Science and the Science of Values." In J. Ree and C. W. C. Williams (eds.), *The Values of Science: The Oxford Amnesty Lectures 1997.* New York: Westview.

Glover, J. (1984). *What Sort of People Should There Be?* London: Pelican.

Maynard Smith, J. (1978). *The Evolution of Sex.* Cambridge: Cambridge University Press.

Maynard Smith, J. (1988). "Why Sex?" In J. Maynard Smith (ed.), *Did Darwin Get It Right?* London: Penguin.

Michod, R. E., and Levin, B. R. (1988). *The Evolution of Sex.* Sunderland, Mass.: Sinauer.

Ridley, Mark (1996). *Evolution* (second edition). Oxford: Blackwell Scientific Publications.

Ridley, Matt (1993). *The Red Queen.* London: Viking.

Ridley, Matt (1996). *The Origins of Virtue.* London: Viking.

Williams, G. C. (1975). *Sex and Evolution.* Princeton, N.J.: Princeton University Press.

This article contains elements from shorter pieces that appeared in two London newspapers early in 1997, the *Evening Standard* and the *Independent.*

Soul Searching

George Johnson

Explorers returning from distant lands tell of aborigines so afraid of cameras that they recoil from the sight of a lens as if they were looking down the barrel of a gun. Taking their picture, they fear, is the same as stealing their soul.

You might as well just shoot them dead on the spot. Knowing that a photograph is only skin deep, people in the developed lands find such terror absurd. But the fear that one's very identity might be stolen, that one could cease to be an individual, runs deep even in places where cameras seem benign.

The queasiness many people feel over the news that a scientist in Scotland has made a carbon copy of a sheep comes down to this: If a cell can be taken from a human being and used to create a genetically identical double, then any of us could lose our uniqueness. One would no longer be a self.

There are plenty of other reasons to worry about this new divide the biologists have trampled across. Nightmare of the week goes to those who imagine docile flocks of enslaved clones raised for body parts. But the most fundamental fear is that the soul will be taken by this penetrating new photography called cloning. And here, at least, the notion is just as superstitious as the aborigines'. There is one part of life biotechnology will never touch. While it is possible to clone a body, it is impossible to clone a brain.

That each creature from microbe to man is unique in all the

world is amazing when you consider that every life-form is assembled from the same identical building blocks. Every electron in the universe is indistinguishable, by definition. You can't tell one from the other by examining it for nicks and scratches. All protons and all neutrons are also precisely the same.

And when you put these three kinds of particles together to make atoms, there is still no individuality. Every carbon atom and every hydrogen atom is identical. When atoms are strung together into complex molecules—the enzymes and other proteins—this uniformity begins to break down. Minor variations occur. But it is only at the next step up the ladder that something strange and wonderful happens. There are so many ways molecules can be combined into the complex little machines called cells that no two of them can be exactly alike.

Even cloned cells, with identical sets of genes, vary somewhat in shape or coloration. The variations are so subtle they can usually be ignored. But when cells are combined to form organisms, the differences become overwhelming. A threshold is crossed and individuality is born.

Two genetically identical twins inside a womb will unfold in slightly different ways. The shape of the kidneys or the curve of the skull won't be quite the same. The differences are small enough that an organ from one twin can probably be transplanted into the other. But with the organs called brains the differences become profound.

All a body's tissues—bone, skin, muscle, and so forth—are made by taking the same kind of cell and repeating it over and over again. But with brain tissue there is no such monotony. The precise layout of the cells, which neuron is connected to which, makes all the difference. Linked one with the other, through the junctions called synapses, neurons form the whorls of circuitry whose twists and turns make us who we are.

In the reigning metaphor, the genome, the coils of DNA that

carry the genetic information, can be thought of as a computer directing the assembly of the embryo. Back-of-the-envelope calculations show how much information a human genome contains and how much information is required to specify the trillions of connections in a single brain. The conclusion is inescapable: The problem of wiring up a brain is so complex that it is beyond the power of the genomic computer.

The best the genes can do is indicate the rough layout of the wiring, the general shape of the brain. Neurons, in this early stage, are thrown together more or less at random and then left to their own devices. After birth, experience makes and breaks connections, pruning the thicket into precise circuitry. From the very beginning, what's in the genes is different from what's in the brain. And the gulf continues to widen as the brain matures.

The genes still exert their influence—some of the brain's circuitry is hardwired from the start and immutable. People don't have to learn to want food or sex. But as the new connections form, the mind floating higher and higher above the genetic machinery like a helium balloon, people learn to circumvent the baser instincts in individual ways.

Even genetically identical twins, natural clones, are born with different neural tangles. Subtle variations in the way the connections were originally slapped together might make one twin particularly fascinated by twinkling lights, the other drawn to certain patterns of sounds. Even if the twins were kept in the same room for days, these natural predilections would drive them each in different directions. Experience, pouring in through the senses, would cause unique circuitry to form. Once the twins left the room, the differences between them would increase.

Send one twin around the block clockwise and the other counterclockwise and they would return with more divergent brains. For artificial clones the variations would accumulate even faster, for they would be born years apart, into different worlds.

Photography is only skin deep. Cloning is only gene deep. But what about the ultimate cloning—copying synapse by synapse a human brain?

If such a technological feat were ever possible, for one brief instant we might have two identical minds. But then suppose neuron No. 20478288 were to fire randomly in brain 1 and not in brain 2. The tiny spasm would set off a cascade that reshaped some circuitry, and there would be two individuals again.

We each carry in our heads complexity beyond imagining and beyond duplication. Even a hard-core materialist might agree that, in that sense, everyone has a soul.

This essay first appeared in The Week in Review of *The New York Times,* March 2, 1997.

PART II
Commentary

Sasha

Andrea Dworkin

I *would* like to have my cat Sasha back again. He died maybe ten years ago. His death was terrible—episodic and prolonged. When he was taken to New York City's Animal Medical Center for an intractable case of constipation, the doctors admitted him to the hospital. A few days later he was deemed cured and John Stoltenberg and I could bring him home. But he didn't come home. Before releasing him, some attendants gave him a cold bath. He went into shock, and for days he lay nearly dead, tiny as if his body was sinking into itself and he was disappearing, smaller and smaller, so that eventually he would be soft bone and empty skin. He was so fragile that it hurt to look at him. John went to see him every day—from Brooklyn to the Upper East Side of Manhattan—and sat by the incubator in which he lay, talked to him, trying both to comfort him and to reach his will to live.

I think Sasha was there two weeks. He turned the corner to life, back to us, and one day John was able to bring him home. Our other cats—George, older, brilliant and dominating, and Cady, younger, female, quiet in her feline hauteur—were mean to him, because he smelled alien and different; and so Sasha sat alone on my bed, slowly recovering some strength and his native temperament, which was a beautiful and elegant sweetness, a tenderness of spirit. Sasha was kind. In cats or humans it is an uncommon quality. He had a big soul.

He never fully recovered. He was somehow weaker, a shade paler, less vibrant; and after not too long a time he had heart failure. Though we desperately tried to save him, he eventually could not sustain the effort of moving or breathing. We put him to sleep.

When I heard about the Scottish cloned sheep, I wondered if it meant that I could have had Sasha again, another Sasha but the same, my darling kind cat.

I have no warm spot for reproductive technologies of any kind except for contraception, condoms, and spermaticides. One mean theme of history, as I see it, is the ambition of men to control the reproductive capacities of women. Control of the whole woman was the best way to segregate her from a world of choice and possibility; and so in society after society, from the ancient Greeks to contemporary Saudis, women were and are imprisoned in homes and owned as reproductive chattel. While it continues to astonish me that men were and are willing to destroy the creativity and freedom of women in order to have children with whom they have, for the most part, little to do, I have no doubt that reproductive technologies continue rather than change this story of domination.

In *Right-wing Women* (Coward-McCann, 1983) I wrote about men's control of women's reproduction and sexuality in terms of what I called the *brothel model* and the *farming model:*

> The brothel model relates to prostitution, narrowly defined; women collected together for the purposes of sex with men; women whose function is explicitly nonreproductive, almost antireproductive; sex animals in heat or pretending, showing themselves for sex, prancing around or posed for sex.
>
> The farming model relates to motherhood, women as a class planted with the male seed and harvested; women used for the fruit they bear, like trees; women who run the gamut from prized cows to mangy dogs, from highbred horses to sad beasts of burden. (p. 174)

The farming model is extravagantly wasteful: Most women had to have children repeatedly so that some women would have some children that some men would want. In the brothel model, women are used for sexual release and pleasure—and their children are refuse, social garbage. The contemporary family headed by a single mother is stigmatized and disenfranchised because she has the social status of a whore, not a tamed, domesticated (married and fertile) female. (Whores are also pretty tame—do sexual tricks by rote—but men like to believe that in using whores they are walking on the wild side. And whores rarely have homes, even on sufferance, whereas farmed women are supposed to have homes—it's part of the deal.)

With the growth and legitimacy of the pornography industry in the United States and other Western countries, there is an increasingly potent social imperative that all women appropriate the sexuality of whores, which is to say, that all women be available and accessible to all men all the time and that all women submit (with a smile, unless gagged) to all brutal and exploitative sex acts, in private and in public, in "representation" and in life.

Of course, all women do not. Nonetheless, it is shocking to see a new desperation in women to be married mothers—to be in the most protected social circle—so as not to be exiled into the desolate dystopia of the pornographically liberated woman. Married, infertile women turn themselves into lab rats to achieve a technologized pregnancy. The process is painful and humiliating by all accounts; there is failure after failure; the woman's desperation to conceive grows with the physical torment of being worked on; and her sense of needing a baby more than she needs her own life can push her past decency, into the wombs of other women, less valued, women who will do (the new) reproductive prostitution because they need the money, the food, the shelter, all of which will be provided for the duration of the pregnancy. A live birth means the end of care and attention, thus the fairly common extortionate

refusal to give up the baby. The stand-in, of course, may also feel love. Her body has fed the fetus; she has shared her blood, experienced morning sickness and an assault of hormonal change and disruption. She has carried the fetus inside herself, in her body, and then she is supposed to move on, childless from that pregnancy. This is cruel. This is wrong.

In a world in which cloning works, only compliant women will live. Cloning is the absolute power over reproduction that men have wanted and have destroyed generations upon generations of women to approximate. This, of course, is not the logical social consequence. The technology used to make the cloned sheep is perfectly adequate to induce parthenogenesis such that women could, if we choose, reproduce ourselves—and eventually this would be an all-female world, which would, probably, end at least rape, prostitution, incest, and forced pregnancy. Men would not have to be killed—an important point, since we seem so reluctant to kill them. They would just die out over time.

But they won't, will they? If they did not already have the real power over reproductive technologies, they would take it—using the violence that we will not use. But they do have it, don't they? They have it and they will use it. Women with attitudes will die or be killed or be exiled or marginalized to eventual death—well, just like now, but as transition, a gynocidal devastation. Within reach is a world with fewer but better women. They can be used exclusively for reproduction; they can be genetically copied; they will be captives as women mostly have been; and the defiant will be rooted out, the ambitious purged, the rebellious destroyed. Every man will be able to have the girl he wants when and how he wants her; and women finally will be less than human, as low and objectlike as men have wanted us to be, without will or freedom or dignity.

So, in the meantime, would I be able to have my Sasha back, another Sasha, to console me for the coming loss? In thinking about Sasha I understood that death is necessary. It forces change. It forces

movement. Death makes it impossible for any of us to stand still. We try to hold on, but those we love die. We try to keep our small lives the same, but someone we cherish dies and our small lives change. Death forces us, while we live, to keep seeking, to risk, to love, someone different, not the same. To have another Sasha would be the first step toward stasis, toward turning life into a museum, a set-piece, a site of archeology and misplaced time. No, I must not be able to have another Sasha. He made me happy; losing him made me sad. Life pushes on, relentless, unsentimental; and we need passion, courage, and will to endure. Love and tenderness give endurance meaning, but we do not get to keep them.

And so I think the men who will clone the compliant women will control them both reproductively and sexually; and, in the process, they will destroy all human meaning: The men will abandon change for absolute control, any chance of intimacy for absolute power. Through cloning especially, men will defeat death; and change, too, will die. Life will be power without love or freedom or grace.

Sheep, Joking, Cloning and the Uncanny

William Ian Miller

The sheep has its own genre of joke, the sheep joke. This charming little subset of the vast domain of jokes has been around for centuries; the earliest instance I know of dates from an Icelandic saga of the thirteenth century. Cows, horses, dogs and cats cannot make this claim. They do not have their own genre of joke. Humans, however, do. Of course, it is we who are the chief butt of the sheep joke, since its defining subtext is the human male's lack of particularity as to choice of sexual object. With not much tweaking, the misanthropy of the sheep joke can easily be given a misogynistic bent as when the choice of sheep is not thrust upon some lonesome shepherd in the uplands removed from his conspecifics in the valley below, but when a so-called normal male actually prefers the comfort of sheep to the embrace of available women. Needless to say, there exists a Web site devoted to such tasteless jokes and one of their equally tasteless subgenres: the Scottish joke in which sheep also figure prominently.

Sheep jokes are sex jokes and although it may be the case that humans are not the only species that can joke, we may well be the only species that feels compelled to joke about sex. Even Dolly's creators, after all, were making a not very good sex (and sheep) joke, and perhaps an inadvertent Scots joke, when they rather tastelessly named her after Dolly Parton. These sophisticated researchers will still be boys (and Scotsmen). Sex and sheep seemed to come to-

gether by some inevitable association of ideas. The boy in them could not ignore prurient possibility in the fact that Dolly was generated from a cell taken from mammary tissue, a ewe's breast, 'tis true, but no matter; the fetishization of mammary tissue is not, it seems, particularly heedful of which mammal it comes from. The same Lockean association of ideas inevitably suggested Dolly Parton whose breasts, one suspects, also involved some scientific intervention. So we come full circle: sheep, breasts, sex, Dolly and science. The joke has even more twists: For where Dolly P's plastic surgeon merely made a breast into a larger breast, these researchers made a breast into a woman, of a different species to be sure, but still, as one form of the sheep joke has it, an object of desire in the heart of Midlothian.

With Dolly, however, the sheep joke of ancient lineage met the clone joke of more recent vintage. Some scholars may claim ancient pedigree for clone jokes too, citing Plautine comedies in which identical twins play havoc with the usual human presumption that we are all supposed to look enough like ourselves not to be mistaken for another, but let that pass as too scholarly a quibble even to engage scholars. The Plautine comedies suggest, however, no differently than clone jokes do, that when we are doubled it is a matter for joking (or as we will soon discuss, a matter for horror and disgust).

The meeting of sheep joke and clone joke is my theme or, if not quite my theme, it will be my point of departure. Sheep jokes have also of late been the theme of editorials in standard science journals. There the tone is of impatient contemptuous annoyance with the "terrible sheep jokes" in *Nature*'s words, which, to the editors' minds, along with sensationalized sci-fi horror riffs on cloning, trivialize the seriousness of the scientific issues raised by cloning. But then it was not the hoi polloi that began the sheep jokes, was it? It was Ian Wilmut himself, not only by naming Dolly Dolly, but by choosing a sheep rather than some other mammal whose reputation among humans would not have allowed for the easy coupling

of our concerns about perverse sexuality and plainly reproductive sexuality, our anxiety about duplication with our anxieties about reproduction. In some unconscious stroke of inspiration, Wilmut, like the child of nature we suppose Shakespeare to have been, knew that literary and imaginative possibility were enhanced by the coming together of the sheep joke and the clone joke.

There were also other poetic impulses unconsciously and inexorably making the sheep the most appropriate choice of animal. Is it not a virtually universal belief that sheep, if not clones already, wish they were, or act so as to give us that impression? They long ago decided that there was no payoff in being a unique sheep. Doesn't the richly significant notion of the black sheep prove that? Even a mother sheep refuses or is simply unable to recognize her own offspring if it doesn't at least have a good chance of looking just like her. But do we think it a sign of sheep's stupidity that they recognize their own only when their children approach identity with themselves? Or do we rather think sheep much wiser, at the cost, it is true, of being much unkinder, than those poor little birds who stupidly raise the offspring of cowbirds only to have the thuggish impostors they raised push their real chicks out of the nest?

If we think of sheep as aggressively evincing a will to clonedom, as desperately aspiring to what comes as second nature to an amoeba and *E. coli,* we as humans are ambivalent, more than ambivalent. We are in many ways unnerved by the uncanniness of cloning, no less than we are by sex itself. And the most certain sign of our uneasiness, our being unnerved, is the compulsion to joke about it: In this case, we feel, perhaps, that this joking in the face of a new possibility for mass-produced life is in fact joking in the face of death, death of the spirit and death of the (male) body.

Joking (along with laughter, it seems) bears some inevitable, maybe even necessary, connection to certain vaguely uneasy and unnerving states: to the horrific, to the disgusting, to the uncanny on one hand and to the sacred, the pure and pious on the other. Joking seems to serve protective functions, by relief and release, as

well as other ways; but it often finds itself paying a kind of inadvertent homage to what it mocks. The intense presence of the urge to joke is as sure an indication as there is that we are approaching the dangerous, the sacred and the magical. Pious and grave talk about human dignity is so often untrustworthy (we suspect it as the style of the hypocrite), so unfelt, so by rote, so safe and predictable, that some feel it necessary to retreat to the joke to pay serious homage.*

The merging of the sheep joke with the clone joke, in an indirect way, reveals just how much cloning appalls us, unnerves us, disgusts, horrifies and revolts us, precisely because it engages our deepest concerns about personhood, identity, life and sex. And if horror and disgust are too strong (not for me), there is no doubt that the possibility of perfect doubling disconcerts us, and suggests we are in the presence of the uncanny, however loosely we may want to understand that term.

Admit that there is something about duplication that partakes of the uncanny that even decades of xeroxing, nearly a century of assembly lines, a century and a half of photography and five centuries of the printing press have not quite inured us to. When young, we learn to grow used to our own reflection, even become fascinated by it; but it inverts us after a fashion, exchanging right and left so that our good side is to the Other our bad, our dexter is sinister to the Other. But when older, quite older, we are more likely to loathe what we see in the mirror if we even bother to at-

*I am seriously tempted to believe that the adolescent sick joke, the shocking joking about deformity, famine, death and degradation, is as certain a sign of real fear and respect of the positive norms at stake as the usual forms of piety might be. (Admittedly, the mockery is completely parasitical on the continued vitality of the usual forms of piety.) In adolescence, when our disgust mechanisms are at their most sensitive, we may have already achieved our most sensitive engagement with moral sensation. The engagement, to be sure, is via the *via negativa,* but it is moral engagement, not lack of it, that drives the joking. Contrast the maturer style of adulthood in which we often utter the right views in the accepted way as either a kind of cowardice or a kind of slothfulness.

tend to it. It is not being inverted that gets to us then (we never were really aware of the inversion except by way of finding that photos deviated from reflections in some small unnerving way), but representation itself, a representation that reveals the subversion of health and bodily decorum, makes known to us hairs that obtrude, spots that appear. We start to avoid mirrors because we feel that what we see is not just a representation of decay, but also a reproduction, that is, an augmentation, a doubling, of it.

We can tolerate photos of ourselves that flatter our most self-indulgent posturings in front of the mirror or before our mind's eye, but more primitive people, new to the technology, often feel that the photo captured their spirit, or perhaps reduced theirs by half at least. To show how we moderns still believe a representation of us somehow captures us, try ripping up a picture of yourself or poking a pin through its eyes or doing the same to a picture of your children or parents. It may be we have been cured of our ancient voodooism with regard to two-dimensional representations, although the fact that Dorian Gray's picture still inspires some dread suggests otherwise. Imagine, however, burning yourself or a loved one in effigy, rounded into 3-D? I suspect that even when a picture is being destroyed out of homage to the representee, because it is not a flattering likeness, there still lingers a little twinge or some small wonder that no twinge occurred. Note too that we blame the nonflattering photo not because it lies, but because it tells one kind of truth we do not like. Just as well-mannered people avoid the truth, so must well-mannered photographs.

Identical twins, although largely denatured of their danger, still are more likely to discombobulate us than "normals" do. The duplication is uncanny, which uncanniness can be experienced as a small twinge of the heebie-jeebies, or a small mirth or as a small occasion for wonderment or ambivalence. Some cultures find identicals so monstrous that they kill one or both; some cultures find them so special as to place them at the core of their foundational myths. But in either case they grab our attention, for they are man-

ifestly disruptions in the proper ordering of things. And then they inspire in us all kinds of fantasy of what their experience must be: Imagine the limited horizons of certain kinds of self-deceptions that identicals must face. They must suffer seeing themselves exactly as others see them. I might be able to self-deceive regarding the attractiveness of the image strutting in the mirror, but what if I agree with everyone else that my identical brother whom no one can tell apart from me seems homely as a mudpuppy? I might deceive myself into thinking that the subtle differences between him and me make me the attractive sib, but how can I maintain that view when everyone calls me my brother's name? However, should my identical be obviously good looking, then I can assume a confidence about my self-presentation with an ease that comes seldom to normals.

Cloning from adult cells will prevent this particular kind of twin anxiety by interposing a generation or more between the twins. From the perspective of the older donor twin, seeing oneself as one once was will not be much more disconcerting than old home movies (which often have their own tale of woe and humiliation to tell). But what of the young clone looking up, knowing exactly what age and decay, what physical possibility holds in store. This is even worse I presume for strategies of self-deception than the ones identical twins must construct to make themselves believe they are better looking than their manifestly homely sib.

Sheep jokes tell us that we are painfully ambivalent about, I would even say scared out of our wits by, sex. It is not just the sex act or the rituals of courtship that frequently make either cowards or fools of us, it is also that we are more than a little ambivalent about the reproductive aspect of the sex act. Sex and reproductive fecundity immerse us fully in the realm of the disgusting. Not just the obvious bodily secretions and their minglings, not just the odors or unfortunate placement of the genitals, but reproductive fecundity itself leaves us immersed in too much flesh, too much ooze, too much life soup for many of our tastes. Now imagine the hor-

rors of cloning—reduplication, perfect reduplication. Sure, we get rid of the messiness of sex or just turn it into the recreational sideshow most of us have always wanted it to be except for the three or four moments we decided it was time for kids. Suddenly fecundity and the disgustful side effects of it overwhelm us. Amoebae, algae, pond scum, fetid rank swampy ur-life. We replace the yuckiness of sexual reproduction (yes, I know it also has its allure, but most of that is parasitical on the yuckiness), with the yuckiness of pure pond scum. The last thing we need is more fertility, more ways of making more of us.

Contrary to most people's image of cloning as a fleshless, futuristic, hypersterile technological mode of "reproduction," I see it as the urge for an even more fecund fetidness than fleshly indulgent sex ever offered us. Cloning is about making us pond scum, with all its disgustful associations with excess, surfeit and eternal reduplicative recurrence. (Do we start to hear now the faint strains of the scary music that I wish to score my account with?) And we have not even added to the horror of amoebic excess, of triumphant bacteria, the horror of doubling, which I touched on briefly with my discussion of identical twins, but which I would like to repair to again for some added brief suggestions.

Doubling is invariably a theme of horror. What is it about effigies, wax museum figures, just plain dolls that are not toylike enough, that makes them sources of fear, nervousness or fascination? Even God is nervous about it; he feared images of Himself and prohibited them. The story is usually told that He did this because the image would be a false representation and the veneration of it would be a regression to idol worship. Idol worship was not His concern; it could hardly have been if He were omnipotent. His real concern was that He too would be subject to soul capture, that in being represented, he would be duplicated, doubled, that in the end the faithful would find God indistinguishable from his representation, or, worse, but a pale reflection of it; the faithful, He knew, could clone him more easily than He could ever let on. So

he played the game in a minor key: He became the first to mimic vertical generational cloning, by making His son Him. The problem, we see, in representation is not that it represents, but that it in fact may duplicate.

But there are other fears that are prompted by doubling, among which we may include the horror that subtends Dorian Gray and on a more comic note, the incredibly bizarre and eerie self-refashioning of Michael Jackson as Diana Ross. Consider that the usual paranoid vision of duplication is a world of utterly fungible beings with no variation whatsoever. Anyone who has lived in a suburb or attended a rally of one's favorite cause knows we have pretty much achieved that already. The danger that is frequently alleged is that with perfect duplication, with perfectly identical looks at least, we will collapse into a gray undifferentiated mass. What will occur, I would bet, is exactly the opposite. The smallest difference will become charged with the greatest and most magical value. We will fight for differentiation with a vengeance and find it whether it is there or not. Academics, for instance, who are seen as perfect clones to the legislator downstate or upstate, manage to construct an honor culture in which some are esteemed and others ignored or mocked, with the subtlest differentiations in status noted, struggled for and worried about. Doubling then will give rise to a culture that will be ranked, be hierarchical and possess a foliated differentiation of exquisite subtlety.

Carry this a step farther as Dostoyevsky does in *The Double.* Suppose that one's perfect double should appear one day, even bear your name, work in your office, compete for the same rewards in the same circles. Suppose too, as Dostoyevsky does, that your double, your genetic twin, is loathsome, not to the sight, but morally reprehensible. He is insolent and mean to those beneath him, servile to those above, bowing and scraping in total disregard of his dignity. And then suppose, too, that precisely this flattering unctuousness causes him to advance at your expense. In the typical Dostoyevskian nightmarish and paranoid world the problem is not that

one's double duplicates, but that with duplication comes, unavoidably and necessarily, *duplicity.* The double is the cheat, the crook, the shifty conniver who manipulates identity, your identity, to his advantage. The double runs up debts that you must discharge. Personhood decays into impersonation, is, in fact, indistinguishable from it. Cloning runs the risk of making us all impostures.

Pascal made the observation long ago that, as an existential matter, we humans are relegated to the middle of things; that we risk annihilation from the infinitely large and infinitely small. The ancient Norse cultures thought so too, putting us in middle earth, half way between the heat and cold, the giants and the gods. All this is a windy way of getting at the proper balance between representation, reproduction and duplication. Here I will personalize my account somewhat by making a confession. I have four kids, all of whom look like my wife. Sure, two of them have the shape of my feet. Three have my build. But they do not look like me, not in the least. But strangely they do not look like each other either, so that somehow my wife has the magical power to be looked like yet preserve their individuation with a vengeance.

I am, it should by now be clear, disgusted, even revolted by the idea of cloning: not just the idea of cloning humans, but the idea of cloning sheep too. I am quite frankly disgusted by Dolly. But here's the rub. I must admit that I also resent that my kids don't look like me, even though it is clearly to their social advantage that they favor my wife. Is it my egoism, my narcissism? I think it is rather my keen sense of honor and shame. My genes are just a bunch of wimps. They can't win any fight with my wife's genes unless the stakes are low, as in the battle for the exact shape of our kids' second toe. But it is also manifestly the case that I do not want my kids to look like me so that my paternity is clear, or that I can take some unfathomably greater pride in my reproductivity, or that I can just get a kind of uncanny feeling by seeing some vague resemblance to myself. I do not want identity; I just want some vague resemblance of the kind kids usually have to their parents. All I want, in other

words, is to be right in the middle of things. We weren't meant to be duplicated except by a sibling born of the same mother and father within a few hours of each other and even then at a fairly low probability; but neither are we meant to be erased from the not too small statistical probability that we will be *vaguely* represented, not duplicated, via sexual reproduction. We must also discount the likelihood by the chances of infertility, of infant mortality, or, as in my case, of the likelihood of sexually reproducing with a partner whose genes outmuscle yours at every turn.

We were not meant to be duplicated across generations, only represented vaguely. I know, saying such a thing makes me out to be something of a know-nothing, who gives ready credence to an immutable human nature and who believes in some divinely or satanically ordered telos. But I mean no such thing. All I mean to say is that there are certain large constraints on being human and we have certain emotions that tell us when we are pressing against those constraints in a dangerous way. This is part of the job that disgust, horror and the sense of the uncanny do; they tell us when we are leaving the human for something else; either downward toward the material, mechanical and bestial, or upward toward the realm of spirit or the world of pure hokum. Nature gave us just about as much doubling as we can handle without getting too spooked.

Sameness Is All

Adam Phillips

It seems somehow appropriate—whatever the scientific equivalent of poetic justice may be—that the first animal to be successfully cloned was a sheep. Sheep, after all, are not famous for their idiosyncracy, for the uniqueness of their characters. We had assumed that sheep were virtually clones of each other; and now we have also been reminded that they are inevitably—all but two of them—genetically different. Now that what was once a figure of speech has become a reality—now that cloning has become a practicable possibility—it may be timely to wonder why describing someone as a clone has never been a compliment. That is to say, is cloning the death or the apotheosis of individualism?

One of the characteristics of contemporary culture has been a longing for community, for a sufficient sense of sameness with others; and at the same time a suspicion of people's wish to believe themselves to be too similar to each other. Or, indeed, identical to—overly convinced by—the images they have of themselves. From our experience of small-scale cults and large-scale fascism we have become fearful when too many people seem to agree with each other—seem to be of the same mind about something—or claim to know who they really are. Democracies, in other words, have to be ambivalent about consensus. Too little and there is fragmentation; too much and there is a (spurious) homogeneity. But with the advent of cloning—when the same has, as it were, been

literalized as the identical, when the identical, at long last, supposedly exists—a whole range of political and psychological vocabularies are stopped in their tracks. Cloning, among many other things, seems to be a final solution to the problem of otherness. And, of course, the end of any continuing need—at least in the mass production of animals—for two sexes in the task of reproduction. In one fell swoop, cloning is a cure for sexuality and difference.

From a psychoanalytic point of view, one of the individual's formative projects, from childhood onwards, is to find a cure for—or, less strictly speaking, some kind of solution to—exactly these two things: sexuality and difference, the sources of unbearable conflict. And it is this that makes children's fascination with, and interpretation of cloning—and the whole science of genetics—so interesting. Indeed children should be consulted about all the great scientific issues of the day because they usefully anthropomorphize these issues for us (for them it's all about bodies and the connections between them: about mummy and daddy and me and you). So from the child's point of view, what might the appeal of cloning be, and what might be the conscious and unconscious fears associated with it? Since there could be no general answer to these questions, even if cloning itself radically changes our sense of what generalization might entail, I want to use two brief clinical vignettes that are suggestive and perplexing rather than exemplary—suggestive of what these particular children are using their ideas about cloning to say and to solve; and perplexing if for no other reason than the fact that one new thing adults can do now that children can't, but can aspire to do, is clone. In other (old) words—that once again cloning ironizes, shall we say?—children have a new role model on their horizon.

An eight-year-old girl who was referred to me for school phobia—which began a year after her sister was born—told me in her second session that when she grew up she was "going to do clothing." I said, "Make clothes for people?" and she said, "No, no cloth-

ing . . . you know, when you make everyone wear the same uniform, like the headmistress does . . . we learned about it in biology." I said, "If everyone wears the same uniform, no one's special." She thought about this for a bit and then said, "Yes, no one's special but everyone's safe." I was thinking then, though I couldn't find a way of saying it, that if everyone was the same there would be no envy; but she interrupted my thoughts by saying, "The teacher told us that when you do clothing you don't need a mummy and daddy, you just need a scientist. A man . . . it's like twins. All the babies are the same." There was so much in all this that I couldn't choose which bit to pick up; I could only apparently carry on with the conversation. I said, "If your sister was exactly the same as you, maybe you could go to school," and she said, "Yes," with some relish, "I could be at home and school at the same time . . . everything!"

In this little girl's strong misreading—to use Harold Bloom's phrase—of cloning, there seemed to be several theories afoot. Firstly, that what she called "clothing" was a uniformity imposed by a powerful solo individual, either the female headmistress or the male scientist. And that if specialness or uniqueness was what was lost at the birth of a sibling, then "clothing" was the last punitive act in the drama—a drama that in actuality begins with the parents' sexuality. You lose your place in the family when your sister arrives, then you begin to experience your school uniform as the ultimate proof of your loss of individuality. She wanted to "do clothing" perhaps because then she would at least be the active agent, not the passive victim; the appeal here is of a certain kind of omnipotence that in and of itself differentiates the cloner from the cloned. The headmistress has one unique talent—to make the children the same—but not the same as her. In other words, the scientist who clones acquires a paradoxical (and enviable) uniqueness (as though the new law of the genetic jungle is clone or be cloned).

The theory I seemed to want to introduce is that because she and her sister are different, there is a competition (for the mother) that she loses. Cloning, in other words, is a cure for the terrors and de-

lights of competition. If the two children were identical, they would, by definition, be getting the same things. If the parents don't have to have sex—"you don't need a mummy and daddy"—then the child doesn't need to be preoccupied by the relationship between the parents; nor indeed need she then see the primary relationship—the "source" that babies apparently come from—as one between two people of similar status, and that involves difference. My patient keeps her (symbolized) parents apart, the female headmistress and the male scientist, both doing the similar thing, but separately. She imagines one person having a mysterious talent, rather than two people doing something to each other that they can't do by themselves. What is interestingly obscure or ambiguous in this child's account is whether, or in what sense, the cloner and the clones are looked after—"you don't need a mummy and a daddy," as though the unconscious fear might be that the cloner is a tyrannical parent, oblivious or hostile to difference and the individuality of need.

It is also possible, of course, that the child is wondering about whether I am going to clone her, remake her out of my words. What Freud called *transference*—the way we invent new people on the basis of our earliest relationships—was evidence for him that a kind of psychic cloning went on between people, that we unwittingly treat people as though they were the same as us (the same as ourselves or our parents). The analyst interprets to show the patient that the analyst is not the same as anyone in his past, that the patient's cloning of the analyst is his defense against the shock of the new. The analyst, in other words, contests the patient's strong wish to clone him (psychoanalysis, one could say, was a cure for cloning before cloning itself existed, the cure as precursor of the problem). Psychoanalysis calls the simulation of sameness narcissism, which it tends to treat as the saboteur of development; Narcissus wanted to be the same as himself, the same as the image of himself, a distinction he didn't have it in himself to make. From a psychoanalytic point of view, successful psychic cloning—making peo-

ple, including ourselves, in our own image of them—is a denial of difference and dependence, and therefore a refusal of need. The art of self-cloning is an attempt to stop time by killing desire. Replicating myself, I keep finding nothing else. I depend on something other than myself to actually nourish me.

Adolescents, of course, are preoccupied by the relationship between dependence and conformity, between independence and compliance. So it's not surprising perhaps that in the cultic jargon of adolescents, to be called a clone is an ultimate insult. And yet it may be worth wondering exactly what is being repudiated—what longings or pleasures may be encoded in the word—in this particular, increasingly topical, form of scapegoating. In other words, cloning gives us the opportunity to rewonder what's wrong with being apparently or exactly the same as someone else. And this is a question not only about why we may be frightened of being like other people—what it is we imagine we lose in this process—but about why we may be frightened of other people being just like us.

If cloning as analogy captures the adolescent imagination, then this tells us as much about cloning as it does about adolescence. And one thing it tells us, I think, is that there is, for some people, a deep fear of not being a clone, of not being identical to someone, or identical to someone else's wishes for oneself (the child enacting the parents' conscious and unconscious projects being the model for this). As though we can only work out what or who we are like from the foundational belief—the unconscious assumption—that there is someone else that we are exactly like. For the adolescent the question is: If I'm not the same as someone else, what will I be like? And this is where cloning comes in. The adolescent lives as if she has been cloned, and is trying and not trying to find out what else there is to her. But now, of course, she can also find a more accurate and exacting description—an unprecedented picture—of this predicament which recreates it anew. Once there were twins and mirrors and doubles; now cloning is available for adolescent

consumption. Ideas about development are themselves developed by fresh analogy.

A sixteen-year-old boy given to disparaging some of his male contemporaries as clones—kids who, in his view, were rather too keen to please their teachers, rather too timid to defy their parents—mentioned one day in a session that he wanted to find a girlfriend who would be his clone: "Just like me so we'd have lots of things in common . . . anyway, girls are so good at being clones." I asked him what that meant, that they were good at, and he replied, "Being like the people they like." I wondered aloud whether if this was true, it was because some girls picked up how frightened boys were of them. And he said, a bit too quickly, with that dazzling logic we all have recourse to when ruffled, "Well I'm not scared of them, that's why I want a clone girlfriend." I suggested that having things in common with people was overrated. This interested him, so after a pause I continued with this impromptu lecture that was stirring in me, elaborating what I meant—because he had asked—and ending, for some reason, with a slightly impatient question: "Anyway, what would two people who were exactly the same do together?" I was, at this moment, genuinely confounded by this and didn't expect him to answer (it's often surprisingly difficult to work out who one's questions are addressed to). We both sat there for a few minutes and then he said, as if he was stumbling over what I'd said, "They couldn't ask each other . . . because they'd get the same answer, so they'd have to ask someone else." And I said, clearly helped by him, "So they'd need a third person. They'd still need somebody different?" And he said, "Yes," perking up, "Me and my clone would need you to guide us!"

The fantasy of the clone girlfriend—not exactly a rarity—was for this boy an all-purpose magical solution, a way of preempting what you do about, or with, the parts of yourself that have nothing "in common" with an object of desire. What is of interest is that the (narcissistic) solution of creating absolute sameness, the clone,

unconsciously kills desire. The fantasy of cloning a girlfriend is a fantasy of not needing a girlfriend. The exact replication of the self merely replicates the problem. That men must not be clones, but must clone women—one contemporary description of a war between the sexes—suggests, among other things, that men already experience themselves as having been cloned by women. The fantasy of cloning—made puzzlingly real by the actuality of it—raises the question now of what the alternative analogies are for relationship? The cloning has already happened; the problem is where we can go from here?

Cloning is, for obvious and not quite so obvious reasons, a compelling way of talking about what goes on between people. But of course the fantasies about cloning—the cultural gossip about it—are informed by wishes. Genetic inheritance, for example, is always a potential: It doesn't predict growth, but it provides (often unknowable) constraints. The environment is an essential part of the equation. The cloned sheep will be identical genetically, but they will have different histories. As my two examples suggest—though for quite different reasons given the ages of the children—cloning is used to get around history, as though in the total fantasy of cloning, history as difference is abolished. People, in actuality, can never be identical to each other. Perhaps this relentless wish for absolute identity—that even real cloning cannot satisfy—conceals, tries to talk us out of, a profound doubt about our being the same as anything. Wishes always return us to the scene of a crime.

Queer Clones

William N. Eskridge, Jr.
Edward Stein

Reproduction has been part of the controversies surrounding homosexuality for as long as there have been such controversies. Homophobes of various stripes (as well as others) have been concerned that condoning homosexuality might lead to a decline in the ability of the human species to reproduce, while at the same time being worried about the ways in which homosexuals might try to reproduce themselves. Lesbians, gay men, and bisexuals (collectively, queers),[1] for their part, often want to have children, typically for the same, other-regarding reasons other people desire them. Lesbian and gay parents have thereby exercised their right to create "families we choose," less encumbered by traditionalist notions of family, marriage, and the like. Queer families have, in turn, been a source of concern to some homophobes who are affronted that lesbians and gay men would appropriate heterosexual institutions, including marriage and childrearing.[2]

The children in queer families of choice sometimes were begat in previous relationships with a partner of the opposite sex. Increasingly, children are begat within a same-sex union through artificial insemination, various forms of surrogacy, co-parenting schemes, and adoption.[3] The law has not been friendly to such families; courts and agencies in various states regularly deprive gay and lesbian parents of custody of their children at the behest of nongay co-parents or even relatives, deny adoption rights to lesbian and

gay individuals or couples, and create legal difficulties for gay surrogacy and lesbian artificial insemination efforts.[4]

Given the difficulties, many of them legal, with these various reproductive methods, the advent of a reliable technique for human cloning would, at first glance, offer queer families of choice a fascinating and useful alternative for reproduction. Under this technology, already explicitly accomplished with sheep,[5] genetic material would be taken from one person (call her the *clonee*) and grafted into an egg of another person (call her the *ovum surrogate*) in such a way as to create the equivalent of a fertilized egg (a zygote). This zygote would have the same genetic makeup as the clonee. The zygote would contain none of the genetic material of the ovum surrogate, which would only provide the "structural" material, the "shell," for the zygote. The resulting zygote would then be implanted into the womb of yet a third person (call her the *gestational surrogate*) and would develop into a fetus and then be delivered as a human baby. There seems no biological reason why the roles of clonee, ovum surrogate, and gestational surrogate cannot be combined, and one female could provide the genetic material, the "shell" for the zygote, and the womb in which the zygote gestates.

Under cloning technology as we imagine it, a single lesbian or bisexual woman, or a gay or bisexual man or a transsexual[6] with the assistance of a woman, could be the clonee parent of a child with her or his genetic material. Furthermore, once the technology exists for grafting genetic material into an egg to produce a zygote, there should follow technology for *gene-splicing,* whereby the genes of two people of the same sex could be spliced together to produce a zygote that shares genetic material with both. With the advent of gene-splicing, same-sex unions could not only produce children, but also produce children who are genetic hybrids of the parents, just like those produced in different-sex unions. Cloning and gene-splicing would also offer reproductive possibilities for transsexuals and people infected with the virus that causes AIDS. These persons

often cannot easily reproduce or reproduce at all under current technologies; cloning would offer a better and safer (for infected people) means for them to have children, and gene-splicing would offer a broad array of partnerings fresh possibilities for reproduction.

The implications of these scientific and social developments are as unpredictable as they are profound. This essay explores some implications whose contours are suggested by reflection on the practical, legal, historical, and biological features of lesbian and gay families of choice. (Although our analysis, especially our legal analysis, will focus on the United States, some of the general points should have broader, transnational application.) These implications flow from the following ideas. To begin with, queer cloning and gene-splicing will almost certainly be easier (both mechanically and legally) for lesbians than for gay men. Thus, one result of the development of these technologies will be to reinvigorate the feminist utopian idea of women reproducing without men. Moreover, some queer people may be attracted to cloning because they think it will be a way to have queer children. The thought is that a child who is the product of queer cloning—because he or she would be genetically linked only to a queer parent (in the case of cloning) or two queer parents (in the case of a couple opting for gene-splicing)—would inevitably or very likely be queer as well.

Finally, and most importantly, cloning has the potential to complete the radical transformation that queer people offer society: Gay people have always engaged in *mutual sex without reproduction,* a pattern now typical of straight people as well; with cloning, gay people (and others) would have the option of engaging in *mutual reproduction without sex.* This would expand the options that lesbians and gay men have for reproducing. This complete separation would also have far-reaching implications for the diversity of families in America. For people infected with the virus that causes AIDS and for transsexuals, cloning and gene-splicing will in some cases allow people to reproduce who would not otherwise have that option.

Gendered Asymmetries

The biology of cloning and the current legal regimes ensure that *queer cloning,* by which we mean the use of cloning or gene-splicing technologies by lesbians, gay men, bisexuals, and transsexuals, will be much easier for lesbians than for gay men and for transsexuals. Assuming the development of the necessary technology, a lesbian who wants to clone herself could carry her own clone to term, and the current law in every American jurisdiction would recognize her as the mother of the child. There would, of course, be no legal father (unless the lesbian were married to a man). In an increasing number of jurisdictions, however, the lesbian's female partner (if she had one) could petition for a "second-parent adoption," in which she would legally become the child's second parent.[7] Current law does not, however, provide for gene-splicing. Under current law, if two women together provide the genetic material for a child and one of them carries the baby to term, the woman who plays the gestational role would be a legal mother, but it is not clear what legal rights the other genetic mother would have. The law in these cases should follow the policy of the second-parent adoption cases and recognize *both* women as legal as well as the biological mothers. Like the second-parent adoption decisions, however, this approach would require a creative interpretation of the governing statutes, a move that some judges will not be willing to take.

Queer cloning would be a boon to lesbians and would probably contribute to an even more pronounced lesbian baby boom.[8] Under current (that is, precloning) practices, many lesbians are reluctant to have children by known sperm donors because of legitimate fears that the male donors will assert parental rights and interfere with their raising of the children, or that the male donors may carry a disease (prominently, the virus that causes AIDS) that could be passed on through insemination. Women having these

concerns can turn to sperm banks, but some sperm banks will not deal with unmarried women. Moreover, some women are uninterested in sperm banks, because they would prefer to know the person who is the genetic partner in creating their children. The advantage of cloning (or gene-splicing) is that sperm—and hence men—become unnecessary. With cloning, a lesbian with a functional womb could clone herself and carry the resulting zygote to term or, if she wants to mix her genes with those of her life partner or a close friend, gene-splicing could do the trick.

Queer cloning, therefore, makes possible the feminist utopian notion, propounded by some women in the early 1970s, of a community of women, unencumbered by men. To be sure, not all women shared this vision in the 1970s, and most probably do not today, but with the advent of queer cloning this possibility will become a live one. Technological change might broaden the appeal of women's communities, not just for lesbians and bisexual women, but also for many heterosexual and asexual women. Nonqueer women would also have the option of having children with other women, but without having sex with them. If this occurred, we wonder whether the concept of sexual orientation itself might not carry diminished power or even disappear over time.

The foregoing is at this point speculative, because queer cloning is neither technologically available for humans nor currently legal. Even if they were available in the foreseeable future, such reproductive technologies would be quite expensive, and health insurance companies would be unlikely to pay for use of such expensive technologies. In the short term, therefore, queer cloning would only be available to the wealthiest women. And, contrary to popular myth, lesbians (at least those who identify themselves as such) are at the bottom of the income scale, making much less income on average than straight or gay men and somewhat less than straight women.[9]

Whatever the limitations of cloning and gene-splicing for lesbians, they are magnified for gay men and for most transsexuals.

The main impediment is practical: Even under cloning technology as currently envisioned, gay men and male-to-female (and some female-to-male) transsexuals would still need the cooperation of a woman to bear a child. While cloning would be able to create a zygote from one male or, with gene-splicing, two males, the zygote would still need a human womb in which to gestate. In the foreseeable future, therefore, men would still need women to make use of cloning, even though women would not need men. This practical fact, alone, would discourage gay men and transsexuals from queer cloning in the foreseeable future, for they would have to find a woman willing to carry the embryo to term. In most cases, such an arrangement would involve a fee. Thus, all the expenses women would bear in such a cloning arrangement would be borne by those seeking surrogates, who would also bear the additional expenses of finding and compensating a woman to carry the child. Only well-to-do people would be able to afford this. There is also the possibility (although this is more speculative) that what might be called *incubation* technology will advance to the point whereby a human zygote could be gestated inside a machine, a female of another species, or even a human male. Even if this becomes possible and men are able to reproduce without women, the costs involved would be exceedingly high. While the myth of gay wealth holds in part for men—gay men's average income is higher than that of straight women or lesbians—gay men on average earn less than straight men.[10]

Setting aside the possibility of gestation without females (there are, of course, no legal structures for dealing with offspring who have no gestational mother and no female genetic parent), there is also a legal impediment to queer cloning for men and most transsexuals.[11] Surrogacy arrangements, where a person pays a woman to be impregnated and bear a child, are unenforceable in most jurisdictions, such as New York and New Jersey,[12] and criminally illegal in some, such as the District of Columbia and Michigan.[13] In other jurisdictions, such as Florida and Virginia, a surrogacy

arrangement is only enforceable if the recipients of the child are a married couple, a requirement that excludes most gay men (as well as lesbians who want to make use of surrogacy because they are unable or unwilling to be pregnant).[14] In other jurisdictions, the state of the law is unclear or in flux. In California, Governor Wilson in 1993 vetoed a bill that would have explicitly allowed surrogacy arrangements. Does that mean that such arrangements are void? In the same year, the California Supreme Court held that gestational surrogacy is permissible under state law.[15] Does that reasoning apply to queer cloning? The law is not completely clear in California, and it is substantially less clear in the many other jurisdictions where there are no statutes or judicial decisions addressing surrogacy issues.

What is clear is that the regulatory schemes in place for virtually all American jurisdictions were conceived with an infertile straight couple in mind; male couples fall outside, or not clearly inside, their ambits. "Surro-gay" arrangements, as Marla Hollandsworth calls them, are carried out every week in the United States, but usually "around" rather than "within" the law. Without the force of law, such arrangements are unenforceable, which means that the surrogate mother can decide to keep the baby to which she has contributed genetic material. Would this presumptive policy be extended to gestational surrogates? Logically not, as California's Supreme Court held, but logic is not the surest guide in this area of law. At the very least, until the law is clarified, queer cloning by gay men runs the risk of losing the child to the gestational mother in most American jurisdictions. This lack of clarity increases the legal risk, and probably the price as well, of queer cloning and could be expected to discourage gay men and transsexuals from taking advantage of it.

Even in states that ultimately allow surrogacy arrangements, parentage statutes may create problems for gay men and transsexuals seeking to clone. When the surrogate is a married woman and the arrangement is carried out under a physician's guidance, as

many as half the states provide by statute that the woman's husband, and not the sperm donor, is the legal father of the child.[16] This is an odd legal regime in the case of gay cloning (or any instance of gestational surrogacy), for neither "legal" parent would have any biological connection with the child, and the only person(s) with a biological connection, the gay man or the transsexual, would have no legal rights. This would not be an inevitable result even in those states, because it is likely in at least some of those states that (1) a gestational surrogate is not regulated, (2) the legal regime can be avoided by using unmarried women as surrogates, or (3) the legal regime can be avoided by not using a licensed physician, as the California courts have held.[17]

In addition to the practical and legal difficulties of queer cloning by gay men, there are moral difficulties. Some gay men, including the authors of this essay, are feminists and would be ethically concerned about critiques of surrogacy as exploiting women's bodies, commodifying an inalienable feature of female personhood, and reinforcing gender stereotypes of women as "breeders."[18] On the other hand, many feminists powerfully defend surrogacy as a freedom that women have to deploy their bodies; some of the same prochoice arguments that support the right to abortion also support the right to surrogacy.[19] The feminist debate itself presents intractable ethical issues (which we do not attempt to resolve here); other normative as well as descriptive theories further complicate matters.

The moral quandaries buttress our argument that queer cloning would be a less desirable option for gay men and most transsexuals than for lesbians. Further, queer cloning might undermine current options gay men have for forming families of choice. Under current practice, where sperm is needed for reproduction, gay men are able to form family clusters with lesbians; that is, one or two gay men contribute sperm to one or two lesbians, and the child is raised with gay and lesbian parents—often two mommies and two daddies. If it comes to pass that sperm is no longer needed

to reproduce, men would no longer be biologically necessary, and the impetus for such family clusters would diminish. (It would not disappear if women believed that, in our culture, having a father as well as a mother is psychologically important to the child or if queer cloning was prohibitively expensive for many people.)

The Perpetuation of Queer Culture?

People want to have children for all sorts of reasons. The reasons that lesbians, gay men, and bisexuals have for wanting children are pretty much the same as the reasons why straight people want to have children—the joy of nurturing another human being, the perpetuation of the species, carrying on an extended family, and providing one's own parents with grandchildren. One distinctive reason some lesbians and gay men desire children involves their desire to perpetuate queer culture by having queer children. Such people usually operate under the assumption that gay people will have gay children or that they are more likely to do so than straight people. If this is true because sexual orientation has a genetic component, then queer cloning offers a way for queer people to produce queer children, or at least to increase the odds of doing so. If I am gay, surely my clone will also be gay, right? Not necessarily. Like so many of the other myths about sexual orientation, this one is beset by complexities, inaccurate beliefs, and unanswered questions.

A person and his or her clone are genetically identical, but that does not mean they will share all of the same traits. A person's physical and psychological characteristics are not simply read off a person's genes, not even on the most genetically deterministic view of things; genes in themselves do not directly specify any behavior or psychological phenomenon. Instead, genes direct patterns of RNA synthesis, that in turn specify the production of proteins, that in turn may influence the development of a psychological char-

acteristic, that in turn causes behaviors. At every step of this process linking genes and psychological properties or behaviors, nongenetic factors (environmental factors, broadly construed) play a role. A person's development is significantly affected by a wide range of nongenetic factors, such as prenatal hormonal levels and diet during puberty, to pick two among many examples. The upshot with respect to sexual orientation is that, due to the panoply of developmental factors, it is quite possible for genetically identical individuals to have different sexual orientations.

Concrete evidence of this can be found by looking at twin studies of sexual orientation. The most recent and sophisticated twin study, done by Michael Bailey, the most prominent researcher using twins to study sexual orientation, reported that between 20 and 38 percent (depending on how broad a notion of being gay or bisexual is used) of the identical twins of gay and bisexual men (and who have identical twins) were also gay or bisexual and that between 24 and 30 percent of identical twins of gay and bisexual women were also gay or bisexual.[20] This is lower than the percentage reported in earlier studies by Bailey, which showed that about 50 percent of the identical twins of gay and bisexual people were also gay or bisexual.[21] (Bailey's own assessment of his earlier studies is that the population sample he used may have been biased.)[22] The most interesting and consistent finding of recent twin studies is that at least half of identical twins had different sexual orientations.[23] This is the case even though the identical twins in these studies shared all of their genes and most environmental factors. It is not clear how to use twin studies to disentangle the genetic and environmental influences that operate on identical twins.[24] Genetic factors no doubt play *some* role in shaping a person's sexual orientation (similarly, genetic factors play *some* role in shaping a person's dietary and religious preferences, for example), but how much of a role they play and how the role is mediated are far from clear. The consequence for queer cloning is that neither cloning nor gene-splicing of queer people will guarantee queer children. Given

the role that the environment is likely to play in the development of sexual orientation and the fact that sexual orientation is a cognitively mediated property, it is not clear that queer cloning will produce queer children. We think there is not even enough evidence to speculate about the odds.

Nonetheless, queer cloning could improve the conditions of lesbians and gay men, perhaps substantially so. The biggest improvement could be that cloning would provide a way for some gay men and lesbians, who would otherwise not be able to have children, to do so. While it would be foolish for them to have children in order to replicate their sexual orientation, few queer people want children for this reason only, and most queer people with children find the nurturing, sharing, and other generative experiences to be among the most rewarding of their lives—just as straight people do. Moreover, even though queer cloning would not necessarily produce more queer children, there is good reason to think it will contribute to a more "queer-friendly" culture in general. Social scientific studies and anecdotal evidence suggest that the (nonclone) offspring of gay men and lesbians are more likely than people in general to be queer-friendly, that is, nonhomophobic, more supportive of lesbian and gay rights, and so forth.[25] Queer parenting, including cloning, would then have benefits for the queer community and would help in the development and maintenance of a just society.

Ideological Land Mines

Queer cloning offers the possibility of completing the perfect segregation of sex and reproduction that is already increasingly characteristic of lesbian and gay couples. Same-sex sexual activity does not lead to reproduction, as everybody already knows; with the advent of queer cloning, queer reproduction could be completely divorced from sex and even the mechanical simulation of sex, namely,

artificial insemination. Queer cloning is also, potentially, the apotheosis of some versions of lesbian feminism. It would further fuel the lesbian baby boom, and maybe initiate a tiny transsexual baby boomlet. Finally, even skeptics such as the authors of this essay concede that there is *some* kind of genetic component to sexual orientation (but whether it is primarily or significantly genetic is unproved at this point, but not refuted either). Given this, queer cloning could be a way to increase the relative number of queers in our society.

Any potential benefits of queer cloning will inevitably be tempered by individual and societal homophobia. The depth of homophobia in American culture derives in part from the way in which it is cumulative of several related anxieties: In the minds or hearts of many Americans, same-sex intimacy violates natural law (whether defined religiously or philosophically) because it involves sex without reproduction, inverts proper gender roles by suggesting to women that they do not need men for their well-being, and is sexually threatening to straight people, whom "homosexuals" allegedly prey upon or recruit.[26] Americans, in general, tend to be nervous about the breakdown of traditional standards of sexual and gender morality *or* women's taking over men's traditional roles and leaving the home *or* the unleashing of the libido. This nervousness is likely to manifest itself as anxiety towards queer people—as outside traditional sexual morals, as inherently gender-bending (partly because many people connect homosexuality with sissy boys, butch girls, boys who want to be girls, and vice versa), and as more sexualized than other people. Nervousness with respect to all three phenomena has in the past produced hysterical manias and witch-hunts against queer people.

If queer cloning occurred on a significant enough scale that mainstream society attended to it, many would certainly be alarmed, because queer cloning would trigger all the anxieties that inspire homophobia in so many Americans. That same-sex couples not only have "unnatural sex" (that is, sex unlinked to reproduction)

is bad enough to a traditionalist, but that they might also have "unnatural reproduction" (that is, reproduction unlinked to sex) is even worse. That lesbians can abandon relations with, and dependence on, straight men is bad enough to a sexist, but that they do not even need men (sperm) for the most male of activities (impregnation) is not only worse but a catastrophe. That homosexuals not only allegedly threaten children with molestation and recruitment is bad enough to the homophobic parent, but that they can create their own recruits as well is, to such a person, a social nightmare. The worst, and most far-fetched, hetero-nightmare is that, after a few generations of self-procreating homosexuals, queers might outnumber straight people and subject straights to the same sorts of discrimination and abuse to which homosexuals have traditionally been subjected.

These comments are not abstract musings. This sort of thinking is currently propelling social and legal reaction. In 1993, Hawaii's Supreme Court held that the state prohibition of same-sex marriage is sex discrimination that must be justified by a neutral and strong state interest, a task even committed homophobes recognize as unlikely.[27] Even though American society allows divorce on demand, tolerates adultery and fornication, and does too little to address the violence of rape and molestation of women and girls, many people have become so enflamed at the mere possibility of same-sex marriage that one state legislature after another has enacted measures to ensure that same-sex marriages will not be recognized in their jurisdictions, and Congress in 1996 enacted the Defense of Marriage Act (DOMA) that not only reassured the states the power to avoid recognition, but also assured that 1049 federal statutes would never be construed to benefit the same-sex couples that Hawaii might join in matrimony.[28] In a nation where so many more tangible problems are pressing, the legislative response to the possibility of same-sex marriage has been astounding. It is comprehensible only in light of the fact that same-sex marriage triggers all the anxieties that contribute to homophobia: It would

be unnatural; marriage "must" be gendered; "real" marriages would be threatened (and were "defended" in 1996 with the passage of the DOMA).

As with the *possibility* of same-sex marriage, the *possibility* of queer cloning might be a stimulus for a preemptive antigay reaction. States could, for example, criminalize or void gestational surrogacy unless the intended parents were a married couple. Such measures would only affect gay male or transsexual cloning; it is doubtful that state family law could much affect lesbian cloning, for if a state tried to do so, lesbian cloning would just go underground. To deal with lesbian cloning, the federal government could prohibit gene-splicing or cloning altogether or limit such methods to different-sex couples, although the latter is less likely because of constitutional objections. Under some circumstances, it is also conceivable that queer cloning would contribute to a more general antigay backlash. Conversely, antigay sentiments probably contribute to anticloning sentiments. Because cloning would, in fact, be the apotheosis of "unnatural" reproduction and would, in fact, free up women to reproduce without the aid of men and would, in some people's fantasies, allow narcissists to reproduce themselves, some of the same impulses that form intense homophobic reactions would generate reactions to the possibility of cloning: Thus, cloning is unnatural, it divides the sexes, people who do it are self-absorbed.

Another way that the advent of cloning and related technologies might positively harm queer people involves potential attempts to use such technologies to prevent the birth of queer or potentially queer children. Some heterosexuals might use cloning or gene-splicing to try to ensure that their children would be heterosexual. Given the widespread prejudice and discrimination against lesbians, gay men, and bisexuals, it seems quite likely that many parents will try to ensure that their children are heterosexual. This is especially plausible, as parents worldwide sometimes choose to abort a fetus if it is not of the sex they desire.[29] Using cloning tech-

nologies (as well as other genetic interventions) to prevent the birth of queer children treats lesbians, gay men, bisexuals, and transsexuals as diseased, not worthy of living, and the like. The advent of cloning could lead to a proliferation of such attitudes. Such proliferation would increase the pressure to hide one's homosexuality and would decrease the collective power of lesbians and gay men. The availability of cloning and splicing procedures that some might use to try to ensure that their children would be heterosexual would engender and perpetuate (1) attitudes that lesbians and gay men are undesirable and not valuable, (2) policies that discriminate against lesbians and gay men, and (3) the very conditions that give rise to such attitudes and policies. Even if such procedures do not work, which they would not (for the same reasons that queer cloning would not guarantee queer children), their mere availability may well engender these results. Biological procedures do not have to be valid to be implemented.[30]

We doubt that any state regulatory response would be the end of queer cloning (or cloning to ensure heterosexuality), unless a worldwide effort simply halted the development of cloning and gene-splicing technologies. Once the technology becomes available anywhere in the Western world, it will become available to some Americans. Thus, lesbians with sufficient resources could travel to France or traffic in domestic black-market cloning or gene-splicing to create their families if they really desire; some gay men could try some of these approaches but with greater trouble and expense.

* * *

Queer cloning can be viewed as the next logical step in queer people's formation of families of choice. Queers have always begat and reared children, but traditionally in different-sex marriage settings or in the wake of their break-up. The last generation has seen the formation of lesbian and gay families in which children have been conceived or adopted within the context of same-sex unions. The

next generation will see the formation of lesbian, gay, and transsexual families whose children may sometimes be the consequence of cloning or gene-splicing technologies. In short, queer cloning has the potential to give queer people more ways to make families (thereby overcoming present restriction on their doing so) and allows for the further separation of reproduction and sex.

On the other hand, queer cloning or gene-splicing will in the short term be costly, especially for men, and risky for all queer people. Because family law has been conceived with heterosexual married couples in mind, it yields gaps and barriers to queer families generally, and families with clones in particular. In some jurisdictions, family law is already pervaded with antigay bias. Our fear is that even the possibility of queer cloning will trigger further antigay measures, and perhaps even anticloning measures as well. Nevertheless, we remain essentially optimistic that queer cloning will in the long run expand gay people's options for family formation, "normalize" queer people as more of them beome parents as well as partners, and perhaps even contribute in some modest way to the erosion of gender, sex, and sexual orientation as stigmatizing traits.

Endnotes

1. There has been considerable controversy about the use and meaning of the term *queer.* We use it as a general term for people who are not heterosexual in their sexual orientation.
2. See Kath Weston, *Families We Choose* (New York: Columbia Univ. Press, 1992), as well as Laura Benkov, *Reinventing the Family: The Emerging Story of Lesbian and Gay Parents* (New York: Crown, 1994); William N. Eskridge, Jr., *The Case for Same-Sex Marriage* (New York: Free Press, 1996); David Estlund and Martha Nussbaum, editors, *Sex, Preference, and Family* (New York: Oxford Univ. Press, 1997).
3. On alternative reproductive techniques, see, for example, John Robertson, *Children of Choice: Freedom and the New Reproductive Technologies* (Princeton: Princeton Univ. Press, 1994).

4. See Benkov, *Reinventing the Family;* William Eskridge, Jr., and Nan D. Hunter, *Sexuality, Gender, and the Law,* 827–867 (Westbury, NY: Foundation Press, 1997), surveying legal debates and obstacles to lesbian and gay parenting.
5. I. Wilmut *et al.,* "Viable Offspring Derived from Fetal and Adult Mammalian Cells," *Nature* 385 (Feb. 27, 1997), 810–813. See also Gina Kolata, "Rush Is on for Cloning of Animals," *New York Times,* June 3, 1997.
6. A transsexual is a person whose gender identity does not match his or her sex at birth *and* who has undergone or plans to undergo surgery to change his or her sex. To be contrasted are hermaphrodites, or intersexed persons, whose sex at birth is in some way or another ambiguous. Many transsexuals after surgery are infertile; some intersexed persons are infertile as well. In the discussion in text, we use the term *transsexual* to denote infertile transsexuals. See generally Bernice Hausman, *Changing Sex: Transsexualism, Technology and the Idea of Gender* (Philadelphia: Temple Univ. Press, 1995).
7. See *In re* Jacob, 660 N.E.2d 397 (N.Y. 1995); *In re* Adoption of B.L.V.B., 628 A.2d 1271 (Vt. 1993); Adoption of Tammy, 619 N.E.2d 320 (Mass. 1994); *In re* Adoption of Two Children by H.N.R., 666 A.2d 535 (N.J. Super. 1995). Contra, *In re* Angel Lace M., 516 N.W.2d 678, 683 and nn. 8–9, 11 (Wis. 1994) (unmarried mother's life partner could not adopt child without terminating mother's parental rights because statute literally required such termination unless birth parent is spouse of adoptive parent).
8. The "lesbian baby boom" has been going on since the 1980s, when many lesbians and lesbian couples decided to have babies and rear children in lesbian households. See Nancy Polikoff, "This Child Does Have Two Mothers: Redefining Parenthood To Meet the Needs of Children in Lesbian-Mother and Other Nontraditional Families," 78 *Geo. L. J.* 459 (1990).
9. According to M. V. Lee Badgett, "The Wage Effects of Sexual Orientation Discrimination," 48 *Indust. & Labor Rels. Rev.* 726 (1995), the annual average earnings of employees by sex and sexual orientation were as follows:

Heterosexual Men	$28,312
Homosexual/Bisexual Men	$26,321
Heterosexual Women	$18,341
Homosexual/Bisexual Women	$15,056

Badgett's data reflect the previously documented wage gap between women and men and suggest that a similar wage gap exists between gay/bisexual and straight employees for each sex. Admittedly, Badgett's findings are preliminary. Because the sexual orientations of the employees were based on self-reporting to the surveyors, it is hard to be sure the numbers capture the nuances of the workplace. For example, would the incomes of completely closeted but apparently queer employees reflect this disparity?

10. See note 9 above.

11. See Marla Hollandsworth, "Gay Men Creating Families Through Surro-Gay Arrangements: A Paradigm for Reproductive Freedom," 3 *Am. U. J. Gender & L.* 183 (1995), as well as Eskridge and Hunter, *Sexuality, Gender, and the Law,* 774–778, 849–853.

12. See, e.g., N.Y. Dom. Rel. Law § 122; *In re* Baby M, 537 A.2d 1227 (N.J. 1988).

13. D.C. Code § 16-401 (1993); Mich. Stat. Ann. § 25-248 (1994).

14. Fla. Stat. Ann. ch. 742.15, 742.16 (1994); Va. Code Ann. §§ 20-159 to -165 (1994). Arkansas is the only state that explicitly provides that an unmarried man can enter into an enforceable surrogacy contract with a woman. Ark. Code Ann. § 9-10-201 (1993).

15. *Johnson v. Calvert,* 851 P. 2d 776 (Cal. 1993).

16. This is the rule of the Uniform Parentage Act, § 5(a)-(b), which has been adopted verbatim in at least thirteen states. See Hollandsworth, "Surro-Gay Arrangements," 208 & n.110. Other states have a similar rule even though they do not otherwise follow the uniform law. See *id.* at 209 n.112.

17. *Jhordan C. v. Mary K.,* 224 Cal. Rptr. 530 (Cal. App. 1986).

18. See, e.g., Martha Field, *Surrogate Motherhood* (Cambridge, MA: Harvard Univ. Press, 1990); Elizabeth Anderson, "Is Women's Labor a Commodity?," *Phil. & Pub. Affs.,* Winter 1990, at 71; Margaret Radin, "Market Inalienability," 100 *Harv. L. Rev.* 1849 (1987); Debra Satz, "Markets in Women's Reproductive Labor," *Phil. & Pub. Affs.,* Spring 1992, at 107, all discussed in Eskridge and Hunter, *Sexuality, Gender, and the Law,* 779–780.

19. See, e.g., Lori Andrews, *Between Strangers: Surrogate Mothers, Expectant Fathers, and Brave New Babies* (New York: Harper & Row, 1989); Carmel Shalev, *Birthpower* (New Haven, CT: Yale Univ. Press, 1989), discussed and analyzed in Eskridge and Hunter, *Sexuality, Gender, and the Law,* 779–780.

20. J. Michael Bailey, Michael Dunne, and Nicholas Martin, "Sex Differences in the Distribution and Determinants of Sexual Orientation in a National Twin Sample," unpublished manuscript.

21. J. Michael Bailey and Richard Pillard, "A Genetic Study of Male Sexual Orientation," *Arch. Gen. Psychiatry* 48 (1991), 1089–1096; and J. Michael Bailey, Richard Pillard, Michael Neale, and Yvonne Agyei, "Heritable Factors Influence Sexual Orientation in Women," *Arch. Gen. Psychiatry* 50 (1993), 217–223.

22. Bailey, Dunne, and Martin, "Sex Differences in the Distribution and Determinants of Sexual Orientation in a National Twin Sample."

23. William Byne and Bruce Parsons, "Sexual Orientation: The Biological Theories Reappraised," *Arch. Gen. Psychiatry* 50 (1993), 228–239.

24. Byne and Parson, "Sexual Orientation: The Biological Theories Reappraised"; Edward Stein, *Sexual Desires: Science, Theory and Ethics* (New York: Oxford Univ. Press, in press).

25. On queers who parent, see Charlotte Patterson, "Lesbian Mothers, Gay Fathers and Their Children," in Anthony D'Augelli and Charlotte Patterson, editors, *Lesbian, Gay and Bisexual Identities over the Lifespan* (New York: Oxford, 1995), 262–290; also several essays in *Dev. Psychol.* 31 (January 1995) [special issue on sexual orientation and human development].
26. An historical explication of these mutually reinforcing anxieties is in William N. Eskridge, Jr., *Gaylaw: Challenging the Apartheid of the Closet,* chs. 1–3 (Cambridge, MA: Harvard Univ. Press, in press).
27. *Baehr v. Lewin,* 852 P.2d 44 (Haw. 1993). In December 1996, the trial judge, on remand from the Hawaii Supreme Court, ruled that the state had not carried its burden of justification and therefore could not constitutionally bar same-sex couples from civil marriage. As we go to press, the state has appealed that ruling, and an initiative that could ultimately override the state courts on this issue will be voted on later in 1998.
28. Defense of Marriage Act of 1996.
29. Mary Anne Warren, *Gendercide: The Implications of Sex Research* (Totowa, NJ: Rowman and Allenheld, 1985).
30. Edward Stein, "Choosing the Sexual Orientation of Children," *Bioethics* 12 (1998); William Byne and Edward Stein, "Ethical Implications of Medical and Biological Research on the Causes of Sexual Orientation," *Health Care Analysis* 5 (1997), 136–148; and Edward Stein, Udo Schüklenk, and Jacinta Kerin, "Scientific Research on Sexual Orientation," in Ruth Chadwick, editor, *Encyclopedia of Applied Ethics* (San Diego: Academic Press, 1997).

Sex and the Mythological Clone

Wendy Doniger

A *recent* item from the Associated Press was briefly but pithily recounted by the *New York Times* (Wednesday, June 25, 1997) under the headline, "Vatican Warns Against Cloning": "Human cloning would not lead to identical souls because only God can create a soul, a panel set up by Pope John Paul II has concluded. The Pontifical Academy of Life said the spiritual soul, 'the constitutive kernel' of every human created by God, cannot be produced through cloning." This consideration may not rank very high on the list of objections to cloning that are now raging in medical, legal, and political circles, but it is very deep-seated indeed, and may be subconsciously fueling the other, more "rational" objections. Though science has only recently learned how actually to produce clones, mythology has imagined for millennia that doubles could be produced by the ancient counterpart of science—magic—and has generally regarded it as a lousy idea. When medicine, confronting the achievement of cloning, exclaims, all dewy-eyed, "O brave new world," mythology mutters, " 'Tis new to thee." [Shakespeare, *The Tempest* 5.1]

Just about a century ago, European mythology reacted to dramatic new medical advances by imagining various sorts of cloning, all depicted as evil for many of the reasons that still animate the Pontifical Academy of Life. Inspired by the earlier, classic Romantic text about the use of cadavers and galvanization to create a

human clone (Mary Shelley's *Frankenstein,* 1818), three other great Gothic novels on this theme were published in the last decades of the nineteenth century and remain, with *Frankenstein,* a part of our own contemporary mythology of cloning. These novels speak of our horror not of the ghosts of the past but of the ghosts of the future, of the medical science that is yet to come; they speak of the production of morally (and hence physically) flawed doubles cloned through the use of psychotropic drugs (Robert Louis Stevenson's *The Strange Case of Dr. Jekyll and Mr. Hyde,* 1887), vivisection (H. G. Wells's *The Island of Dr. Moreau,* 1896), and blood transfusion and hypnosis (Bram Stoker's *Dracula,* 1897).

These novels were reacting to specific scientific advances that galvanized (if I may use the term) British society in ways similar to those in which the recent advances in cloning have affected our own society. To us, now, these texts are classics with many spin-offs, notably their many, many clones in film versions from Hammer and Hollywood, some of which I consider here. But in their own day they themselves were just reruns of much older ideas about splashing around in and mucking about with what we would now call the gene pool. Enhancing the power of the new terrors by analogizing them to the ancient terrors expressed in myths, these novels kept the old myths alive by giving them the transfusion, as it were, of new scientific terrors. Myths, like vampires, are un-dead. In this essay, I will attempt to track the myth of cloning back to its lair in the mythological roots of European civilization, to excavate the soil to which, like Dracula with his Transylvanian coffin, the myth returns again and again to be revived.

The premodern mythology of cloning deals with two basic issues, often in separate narratives: One is eugenics, the active attempt to influence the human embryo, and the other is the problem of the erasure of individuality, the challenge set by the confrontation of multiple copies of a human being. Many myths have imagined this second problem as happening to adult twins (who are, in mythology, overwhelmingly male or male/female, seldom female)

and nontwins (both men and women). The narratives about men are entirely different from those about women, and there are, moreover, two different sorts of narratives told about all of them (twins and nontwins, male and female): stories about the people who actively produce clones, and stories about people who passively encounter clones that someone else has produced. Let us consider the various situations one by one.

Embryos: Paternal Insecurity and Resemblance

A surprisingly large number of male authors, in different cultures over many centuries, have believed that a woman who imagines or sees someone other than her sexual partner at the moment of conception may imprint that image upon her child, thus predetermining either its appearance or aspects of its character, or both. This belief in mind over matter—what you think about is what you get—is called by various names: maternal imagination (a woman's fantasy about something or someone who may not be physically present), impression (the mental reception, and transmission to the embryo, of a visual image that is physically present), or imprinting. Since the father, though less often, is said to participate in these processes too, it is probably best called parental imprinting.[1]

This concept is attested first in stories about animal husbandry, such as the Hebrew Bible story of Jacob, who put speckled rods in front of the ewes being covered by rams, so that they would bring forth speckled lambs (Genesis 30:25–43 and 31:1–12), and in Greek texts such as the *Knyegetika,* attributed to Oppian, a Syrian of the late second or early third century C.E., who veers from his main line, horses and hounds, just long enough to apply the principles of their breeding to humans, too.[2] The *Gynecology* of Soran, an authority on obstetrics who lived at the turn of the second century C.E. in Rome and Alexandria, also assumes a correlation be-

tween human procreation and animal husbandry; Soran tells of a misshapen tyrant of the Cyprians who compelled his wife to look at beautiful statues during intercourse and became the father of well-shaped children; without drawing breath, he mentions horse-breeders who place handsome stallions (real ones, not pictures) in front of mares being covered by (presumably other) stallions.[3] In effect, the tyrant is cloning the statue. But how did the mere sight of the real stallions or statues influence the quality of the offspring?

A lost and probably apocryphal text attributed to Empedocles, a pre-Socratic poet (circa fifth century B.C.E.), is quoted by Aetius, who asks: "How do offspring come to resemble others rather than their parents? [Empedocles says that] foetuses are shaped by the imagination [*phantasia*] of the woman around the time of conception. For often women have fallen in love with statues of men and with images and have produced offspring which resemble them."[4] Soran seems to have taken the folk wisdom recorded by Empedocles, that women *do* fall in love with statues, and connected it with the folk wisdom of animal husbandry recorded by the Hebrew Bible (and elsewhere), that females can be *made* to desire obstetrically, as it were, the images that the husband desires eugenically; in the process, he has moved from the herd animals favored in the Bible (sheep and goats) to the favorite animals of the Greeks, horses. The result is an active attempt by the husband to treat his wife like a mare (or a ewe): He shows her pictures of what he wants her to give birth to.

This sort of mythological embryology involves a kind of prescientific cloning: It investigates ways of producing copies of desired stock. But, we must ask, desired by whom? One factor that seems to pervade all the ancient texts on this subject is the male desire to control female desire. For when the positive approach to eugenics on the animal husbandry model, in early Greek texts, was reintroduced into later Jewish and Christian texts, it was soon overwhelmed by male paranoia. In comparison with the earlier texts on animal husbandry, these later texts about human embryology deal

largely with the fear of *negative* cloning: the influence of some man other than the father, to make the child *fail* to resemble the father. As long as the father controlled the process, he regarded it as a good idea; but when the mother had ideas of her own, the male authors of our texts generally regarded it as unacceptable.[5] The fear that his son will not look like him drives him to make sure what his woman is looking at, in the hope that she will not imagine some other man. It comes down to the matter of who initiates the fantasy: Her fantasy is only acceptable if it is, in fact, *his* fantasy, his idea of what she should be seeing while he makes love to her; and it is certainly easier to regulate external vision than internal vision.

Premodern theories of parental imprinting, motivated primarily by concerns about paternity and inheritance, usually assume that the male child (the only sort of child the authors of these texts cared about) will normally resemble its father (and, sometimes, to some extent, its mother). If he happens to resemble his father's best friend, some texts drew what seems to us the most obvious conclusion, namely, that the mother was sleeping with the father's best friend. Other texts, however, imagined that she might merely have *thought* about him, or looked at a *picture* of him, and that this was sufficient to imprint that false image on the baby's face. But the repressed knowledge of adultery is always there, and bursts out in various paranoid forms. Thus, Jewish midrashic texts, dating from the third or fourth century C.E., regarded maternal imprinting, whether by pictures or just by the woman's fantasy, as a form of mental adultery, better than physical adultery,[6] but still bad enough to brand the child a kind of bastard.[7] To men who fantasized that mental acts influenced the quality of their offspring, the very survival of the species depended upon the sexual fantasies of their women. Thomas Laqueur states the case very well: "Since normal conception is, in a sense, the male having an idea in the woman's body, then abnormal conception, the mola, is a conceit for her having an ill-gotten and inadequate idea of her own."[8] The eye was therefore an instrument of eugenics, passively and externally re-

ceiving the images produced by the father, while the mind (hidden inside the woman) was an instrument of adultery.

As if this were not bad enough, the theory was turned on its head to show that resemblance, too, could dissemble. In the seventeenth century in Europe, it was argued "that a woman who thinks strongly about her husband in the midst of illicit pleasures can produce, through the force of her imagination, a child that *perfectly resembles him who is not the father . . . Resemblance is not proof of filiation . . .*"[9] Now, it is easy enough to imagine that a woman might dream of her lover while in the embrace of her husband, but why, one might ask, would she think of her husband while in the embrace of her lover? One answer is that if she, too, subscribes to the theory of maternal imprinting, she will think about her husband when she is with her lover on purpose, in order to conceal her adultery. Thus, the mother controls her own imagination and produces "not a monster but its exact opposite: a child who actually resembles the legitimate spouse who did not father it."[10] This aspect of resemblance furnished yet another black mark in the copybook of cloning: a son who resembled his father *too closely* posed a threat, sometimes projected from the supposed cuckolder onto the son himself in stories in which a woman mistook her too-resembling son for her husband and slept with him, the old Freudian nightmare.[11]

The backlash from this switchback was very serious. For where the theory of maternal imprinting doubtless saved the necks of a number of adulteresses whose children did not resemble their fathers, the corollary (that an adulteress could imprint her lover's child with her husband's features) cast suspicion upon *all* women, indeed particularly upon faithful women, whose children *did* resemble their legitimate fathers.[12] Women as a whole were cast as body snatchers, who could at will replace a seemingly normal child with a monster conceived in the pods of adulterous beds. This was truly a no-win situation; women were damned if they did, and damned if they didn't, produce children who resembled their husbands. And the cognitive dissonance that resulted from this uncer-

tainty drove men both to accelerate their attempts to control women's sexuality and to project their images, obsessively, upon their sons. Thus M. Boursicot, the French diplomat in the real-life affair that inspired David Henry Hwang's *M. Butterfly,*[13] explained why he thought his (male) Chinese lover was a woman and that she had borne him a son; speaking of that son, he said, "He looked like me."[14] Since cloning is about reproducing humans, which is to say it is about sex (or possible substitutes for sex), it is no wonder that sexual fears play such a large part in the mythology of cloning.

Male Twins: Identity and Resemblance

The scenario of parental imprinting assumes that the other man whom your son might resemble is either your rival (in negative cloning) or someone who will improve what we would call your genetic stock (in positive cloning). But this situation, nervous enough, is exacerbated by a fear not of nonresemblance but of resemblance, the fear that your rival—in flesh or in a picture—will *look like you,* and that your wife will mistake him for you and therefore betray you with him. Thus, fears of both nonresemblance and resemblance are keyed to the father's desire to imprint his child himself, usually with his own image; the interference either of the mother's imagination of another man (the problem of nonresemblance) or of the physical or mental presence of another man who resembles the husband is a threat to paternity and inheritance.

The most obvious natural clones are identical twins, who play a major role in many of the creation myths of the world, often negative; many premodern cultures believe that one, or both, of twins should be killed at birth. Of the many aspects of this mythology, the one that concerns my argument here is the problem of sexual identity. In Plautus' *Menaechmi,* composed in the early second century B.C.E., Menaechmus unwittingly masquerades as his brother and enjoys both his brother's dinner and his courtesan. In another play

by Plautus, *Amphitryon,* the natural cloning of twins is replaced by the magic cloning of two gods (Jupiter and Mercury), who magically assume the forms of Amphitryon and his servant, Sosia, so that Jupiter can seduce Amphitryon's faithful wife. The story of Amphitryon was retold a number of times, notably by Molière (1668), Heinrich von Kleist (1807), Jean Giraudoux (1929), and S. N. Behrman (1938). Shakespeare combined and adapted both plays to produce his great slapstick tale of twin brothers *and* their twin servants, no longer doublets but quartets: *The Comedy of Errors.* The innocence and comedy inheres in the fact that, like the brothers in *Menaechmi* rather than the gods in *Amphitryon,* the double, the clone, *does not intend* to seduce his twin brother's wife; on the contrary, the joke is that he does *not* desire her as she expects he will. Here is a brief summary of the plot:

> Twin brothers, both named Antipholus, were separated in youth as the result of a shipwreck; one lived in Ephesus (E. Antipholus, henceforth E.), the other in Syracuse (S. Antipholus, henceforth S.), and each had a servant named Dromio (E. Dromio and S. Dromio). E. was married to Adriana but S. was not attached. One day, S. came by chance to Ephesus, with S. Dromio, and was mistaken for E.

The sexual "errors" turn upon the question of sexual jealousy and rejection: Adriana wonders why S. (her husband, she thinks) does not love her, and, indeed, her worries are not unfounded: For E. is suspiciously friendly with a courtesan, as he himself admits, and Adriana worries that she is growing old and losing her husband's love. Thus, where the wife (rightly or wrongly) suspects what we have come to call "the other woman," she begins to believe that her husband actually is "the other man"—which he, or rather his twin brother, really is. Similarly, the unattached S. Dromio is puzzled to discover that E. Dromio's girlfriend, who of course seems to him to be a total stranger, regards him as her lover.

The Comedy of Errors is about dissymetry in sexual love: One partner expects intimacy, while the other regards him or her as a stranger. When Adriana mistakes S. for her (straying) husband, she says, "I am not Adriana, nor thy wife," and explains that since she is part of him, and he is false, she is false. "I know you not," he replies, and means it literally (in both senses of "know," intellectual and carnal knowledge), while she thinks he is merely speaking metaphorically, as she was. Adriana says that for weeks E. has been "much, much different from the man he was." (5.1) And now he is really really different. The unusual accident of double twins triggers the not so unusual accident of marital infidelity and estrangement: The feeling that one simply *does not recognize* one's official partner is expressed in the dream (or nightmare) that that partner actually is a total stranger.

The Comedy of Errors was adapted, centuries later, a number of times, into various Gilbert and Sullivan operettas and the musical comedies *The Boys from Syracuse, A Funny Thing Happened to Me on the Way to the Forum,* and *Don't Start the Revolution Without Me*). The theme is a perennial favorite. It even inspired a female variant, in *Big Business* (1988, directed by Jim Abrahams), in which both Bette Midler and Lily Tomlin play identical twins:

> The Midler twins are born of a couple from New York, and the Tomlin twins of a couple from a small Tennessee town, simultaneously in the same hospital. A nurse switches one of each, in the Gilbert and Sullivan manner, so that one Midler and one Tomlin is left with each set of parents. The Midler twin in the country and the Tomlin twin in the city have a sense that they are misfits who belong somewhere else; the Midler twin in the city and the Tomlin twin in the country, on the other hand, are successful in their work and with men, though they break away from them (the city Midler divorces her husband and the country Tomlin abandons her boyfriend). Eventually the twins meet in New York, and the men who have been rejected by the suc-

> cessful twins are encouraged by the misfit twins, but since no one knows that there are doubles, the stop-go, hot-and-cold effect drives the men crazy. Finally they switch back to where they should have been, and the misfit twins end up happily with the men who had been rejected by their successful twins, while the successful city Midler finds a new man and the successful country Tomlin accepts the man rejected by the misfit city Tomlin.

Now country mouse and city mouse have been added to the mix; when the women meet their twins, the city Midler says scornfully, "It's me with a bad haircut," and the city Tomlin moans, "I hope I'm me." The country Midler shrieks, "They're pod people! I saw the movie!" to which the country Tomlin replies, "You watch too many movies." The Shakespearean problems remain: The men don't know why they have been accepted or rejected, and they offer a modern version of the old answer to the question of inconsistent (female) behavior: "Do you suppose it's hormonal?"

The many variants of the tale of twin brothers, from ancient folklore to the contemporary cinema, can be divided into two main groups: those in which (as in *Menaechmi* and *The Comedy of Errors*) one twin is unaware of the other's existence, unwittingly masquerades as the other, or rejects the other's beloved; and those in which (as in *Amphitryon*) one twin purposely masquerades as the other in order to bed the other's beloved. In the first group we might include the many variants of the folk tale of "The Two Brothers," best known to us in the variant recorded by the brothers Grimm,[15] in which the double lays a sword in the bed between himself and his twin brother's wife. (The sword motif recurs in stories not about twins but about magical doubles—like Jupiter/Amphitryon—in the Welsh story of Pwyll in the *Mabinogion*[16] and in the story of Siegfried, recorded in Norse mythology,[17] and in Richard Wagner's opera, *Götterdämmerung;* a variant also occurs in African mythology).[18] The theme of the unwitting masquerade remained popular in Hollywood, where Danny Kaye

practically cornered the market on male twins who find themselves innocently mistaken for their doubles: *Wonder Man* (1945), *On the Riviera* (1951), *On the Double* (1961). And in the same year—1944—that Betty Hutton sang duets with herself in *Here Come the Waves,* Gene Kelly danced with his alter ego in *Cover Girl.*

In the second group, where the seduction is intended, we might include the folk variants listed by Stith Thompson under the motif of a twin who deceives the wife of his brother (motifs K 1915–1917, K 1311);[19] E. T. A. Hoffmann's "The Doubles" (*Die Doppelgänger,* 1821); *Lives of the Twins* by Rosamond Smith (Joyce Carol Oates, 1987); and many films, from *The Corsican Brothers* (1941), in which Siamese twins, separated shortly after birth, later become bitter rivals when one falls in love with the woman who loves the other, to the Canadian film *Dead Ringers* (1988), based upon the 1975 suicide of two real twin gynecologists, Cyril and Stewart Marcus, who often impersonated one another with women.

Male Clones: The Double Bind

Men, or male gods, who are not natural twins may use magic to make themselves into clones of other men. This happens in two sorts of narratives, really the same story told from two different points of view. Sometimes a man or a god (like Jupiter) will produce a double of himself in order to get to the woman he wants (the woman who then may react by splitting off *her* clone). But sometimes a man suddenly encounters a double he didn't know he had (as Amphitryon encounters Jupiter in the form of Amphitryon). In the European retellings, the emphasis shifts from the motives of the cloner to the reaction of the clonee, the man who suddenly confronts a double he did not know he had. The Amphitryon reaction lies at the heart of our own adverse reaction to cloning: the gut feeling that there should not be two identical forms of anything, especially of me.

Let us take another look at Amphitryon. The name of his servant, cloned by Mercury, is Sosia, which comes to mean "a double" in both French and Italian; in French, *sosie* means "a person who bears a perfect resemblance to someone else."[20] Robert's French dictionary, citing occurrences in J. de Rotrou's *Les Sosies* (1638) and Molière's *Amphitryon* (1668),[21] summarizes this character in Plautus: "Sosia finds himself face to face with another Sosia. . . . He comes to doubt his own identity." Sosia becomes hopelessly confused and finally asks the god Mercury (in the form of Sosia), "Then who am I, if I'm not Sosia, will you kindly tell me that?" To which Mercury replies, "Well, when *I* don't want to be Sosia, *you* can be Sosia yourself."[22]

Different retellings of the Amphitryon story raised different questions about the sense of self threatened by the confrontation with the clone, not only in the humans—Sosia, Amphitryon, and his wife Alcmena—but even in the god, Jupiter. For Jupiter experiences the usual paradox of the double bind that plagues all intentional doubles who engage in sexual masquerades: You disguise yourself in order to extend your powers, to get into bed with someone else's woman, but then it isn't you she loves, but the other, of whom you are insanely jealous. Jupiter keeps asking Alcmena, "Wasn't the sex better last night than on other nights?" but she resolutely insists that she couldn't tell the difference—which was, but also was not, what Jupiter intended.

The myth of the sexual double is often set in the context of some other (often related) concern that a particular culture regards as even more basic than sex, such as fraternal succession or political rivalry. Many clones are about death; Otto Rank summarizes well the theme of the double in literature of the nineteenth-century Romantics, such as Hoffmann:

> We always find a likeness which resembles the main character down to the smallest particulars, such as name, voice, and clothing—a likeness which, as though "stolen from the mirror" (Hoff-

> mann), primarily appears to the main character as a reflection. Always, too, this double works at cross-purposes with its prototype; and, as a rule, the catastrophe occurs in the relationship with a woman, predominantly ending in suicide by way of the death intended for the irksome persecutor. In a number of instances this situation is combined with a thoroughgoing persecutory delusion or is even replaced by it, thus assuming the picture of a total paranoiac system of delusions.[23]

In stories like Edgar Allan Poe's "William Wilson" (1840), Théophile Gautier's *Avatar* (1856), and Maurice Renard's *Le docteur Lerne, sous-dieu* (1919), the protagonist, intent on seducing another man's wife, encounters his double and, in killing him, kills himself.

Other nineteenth-century clones were bureaucratic (the mindless, faceless doubles that run the world), like Golyadkin, the pitiful protagonist of Dostoyevski's *The Double* (1846); but Golyadkin loses to his bolder and more successful double not only his job but also the woman whom he loves from afar.[24] So, too, a number of nonmagical clones were produced, with the mere application of a bit of makeup, for the purposes of spying, or of protecting a powerful political figure. Alexander Dumas's novel *The Man in the Iron Mask* (1847), in which King Louis XIV has a twin who replaces him, was cloned several times, in films by Douglas Fairbanks (1929) and Warren William (1939). The novel was cloned in a book by Sir Anthony Hope, *The Prisoner of Zenda* (1894), in which an Englishman takes the place of a "Ruritanian" monarch whom he resembles exactly (though they are only distantly related). This, then, was cloned in several films, a serious swashbuckler with Ronald Colman (1937), a satire by Peter Sellers (1979), and several more distant relatives: *Moon Over Paradour* (with Richard Dreyfuss, 1988) and *Dave* (with Kevin Kline as the clone of the American president, 1993). In each of these, despite the political premise, the identity crisis occurs in the bedroom, when the princess or First Lady tempts the clone to give up his true identity forever.

Then there are the science fiction clones in films, beginning with a great political film of the silent era, Fritz Lang's futuristic *Metropolis* (1926), in which a robot clone of the heroine fools everyone except the hero who loves her. In *Invasion of the Body Snatchers* (1956), seed pods from outer space land in a small town and begin to replace its inhabitants one by one with mindless clones. Their goal is political, as is the agenda of the filmmaker: The assumption that the clones have no emotions, no feelings at all, is a clue to the movie's function as a thinly veiled anticommunist tract, in which the possessed hand over their minds to Mars, aka Moscow; the anticommunist party line traditionally depicted communists as emotionless (recall *Ninotchka* [1939]). But the test of identity is still sexual: When the hero's girlfriend has been replaced by a clone, he does not realize this until he kisses her, an act that he later recalls with the immortal line, "I've been afraid a lot of times in my life, but I didn't know the real meaning of fear until I'd kissed Becky." And the cloning becomes explicitly sexual in *The Stepford Wives* (1974, written by William Goldman from the novel by Ira Levin), in which suburban husbands replace their wives with computerized robots who love to clean house and praise their husbands' sexual performances, and who lose their desire to do anything that makes them individuals. That is, the clones are created precisely for their mindless sexuality.

The Manchurian Candidate (1962, from the novel by Richard Condon) used vaguely "Commie" brainwashing techniques to implant false memories in Lawrence Harvey; *Blade Runner,* directed by Ridley Scott in 1982, from Philip K. Dick's short story "Do Androids Dream of Electric Sheep?" used more complex and explicitly clone-like techniques (quickly satirized, in 1983, in *The Man with Two Brains,* in which Steve Martin plants the disembodied brain he loves in the gorgeous body of his despised wife, Kathleen Turner). False identity, more precisely false memory, remained the basic issue in later films about scientific clones, like *Total Recall* (1990) and *Duplicates* (1992), in which evil surgeons implant false memories in

the brains of innocent people. In another branch of this genre, it is the face, rather than the brain, that is cloned, producing a more superficial identity crisis. In *Shattered* (1991), the amnesiac victim is given both memory and (through plastic surgery) the face of another man; since he is still loved by the woman who had loved *him,* presumably his memory and his face, the film asks, if you don't have your face or your memories, who are you? *Face/Off* (1997) simplifies the problem: The memory remains, and only the faces are transferred from one man to another. Despite the political basis of most of these films (*Total Recall* is about a political tyranny and resistance on Mars; *Duplicates* about a government plan to replace the memories of socially undesirable people; *Face/Off* about an FBI man and the terrorist he is hunting), the crunch still usually comes in the bedroom, where the victim regains a kind of physiological memory that has escaped the quasi-cloning process.[25] In *Face/Off,* the terrorist, with the face of the FBI man, successfully fools the FBI man's wife in bed; when he tells the people at the FBI how to find the terrorist, and they get suspicious and ask, "How do you know so much about this guy?" he replies, "I'm sleeping with his wife" (which is true only of the invisible self beneath the face—the terrorist, not of the apparent self in the face—the FBI man).

Many of these themes combine in a hilarious satire on the theme of cloning, the 1996 film *Multiplicity,* in which the twin who tries not to sleep with his brother's wife fails hilariously, several times:

> Doug (Michael Keaton) wants more time to do the increasing number of tasks demanded of him in his work as an engineer and more "quality time" with his kids and his wife Laura (Andie MacDowell), who wants to go back to her job in real estate. He lets a geneticist create two clones of himself (Doug 2 and Doug 3), and Doug 2 on his own produces a clone of himself, Doug 4, who is, like the blurry photocopy of a photocopy, an idiot. Doug warns the clones away from his wife (Rule Number One), but one night when Doug is away, though Doug 3 loyally puts a pil-

> low between them in the bed, Laura aggressively and irresistably seduces first him and then the other two clones.

Laura notices the discrepancies, memory lapses, and so forth; "I feel like I don't know you anymore," she says, like the wife of the twin in *The Comedy of Errors.* But she still thinks there is just one of him. And when she threatens to leave Doug in fury at something one of the clones did, he protests, "It wasn't me," invoking the split-level alibi that we will encounter below in classical myths about raped women.

At one point, one of the clones suggests that they "clone Laura," but in fact it is because Laura is already about to do the opposite of cloning, because she is about to split (into mother and real-estate agent), that her husband in desperation doubles himself (and then, to outdo her, trebles and quadruples himself into the mythological lineup). At the end, he defends himself by accusing her: "It's happened to you, too. You want to be a mom but you also want to work." Moreover, in justifying the infringement of Rule Number One, the clones say that she was "unstoppable," "a very powerful woman"; they suggest that she is insatiable (an idea confirmed by our own witnessing of the three seduction scenes). Believing that they must resist her, the magical doubles invoke the mythological technique of the sword (here a pillow) laid between them in the bed, but to no avail.

Doug has to get rid of them because he finds himself in the usual double bind of the man who both does and does not want his double to sleep with his wife: He is jealous of the clones, and feels that he has not doubled himself, as he hoped, but rather halved himself. When he finds out that Rule Number One has been broken, and reacts with shocked fury, the clones reassure him: "She thought I was you"; "She thought *I* was you too." And then: "We're not perfect." This last statement ostensibly means just, "We were susceptible to her," but in this context it also means, "We are not perfect copies; you alone are you." Now Doug asks them, as Jupiter asked Am-

phitryon's wife Alcmena, "Do you think she liked you more than she likes me?" "Of course not," Doug 2 says, "I *am* you; you're me."

But since this clearly does not address the problem, Doug 3 (the sensitive one) assures him, "I know she loves you, Doug. I wasn't really *there* for her. Even when I was there, I wasn't *there*." The psychobabble cliché is here cunningly applied to a liminal situation in which "there" means simultaneously "existentially real," "sexually intimate," and "orgasmically on the G-spot." But the best line of all, the one that sums up the double bind in a phrase worth hundreds of pages of Freud and Otto Rank, is what Doug calls Rule Number One: "No clone nookie; original nookie only."

Female Twins: Good and Evil

Female twins, too, can play these tricks, often, like male twins, in order to commit adultery—betraying their twin sisters, rather than their husbands (their victims in the scenario of imprinting); but they are worse than male twins, because they lack the balancing scenario of the loyal twin (with the sword in the bed) that marks the mythology of male twins. Prepubescent twin girls can be quite charming and even useful (like the two Hayley Mills characters in *The Parent Trap* [1961], and even the Doublemint Girls who double your [unspecified] fun), but when they grow up and become sexually active (and threatening), they usually become murderous. (The Hayley Mills twins remained essentially prepubescent; twenty-five years later, in *The Parent Trap: II* [1986], the grown-up Mills replaced her sister on an innocent date with a man she wanted to win for her shy sister.) The folk theme of the "Substitute Bride" or "The Black and White Bride" (Stith Thompson's Tale Type 403), which often involves twin sisters, fuels an entire genre of Hollywood films of "the good and evil twin," that Jeanine Basinger calls the "My God! There's two of her!" theme (from the poster for *Dark Mirror*).[26] ("There's two of them!" says the villain who first sees the

two Jean-Claude Van Dammes together in *Double Impact* [1991]). Special effects allowed the grande dame to play two parts simultaneously on the screen, resulting in all of those melodramatic tours de force such as *The Divorce of Lady X* (1938, Merle Oberon) and *Two-Faced Woman* (Greta Garbo's last film, made in 1941). So widespread is the film scenario that when a real woman impersonated her real (and murdered) sister in 1997, the police chief remarked, "I don't know if bizarre quite describes it; this is the stuff of a Hollywood movie."[27]

Filmes noires often depicted the evil twin as a successful murderer, such as *The File on Thelma Jordon* (1949, Barbara Stanwyck), which ends with the dying woman saying, "In a way, I'm glad it's over, the struggle, the good and evil. Willis [her lawyer] said I was two people; he was right. You don't suppose they could let just half of me die?" Bette Davis and Olivia de Havilland competed for the crown of queen of the good-and-evil twins, beginning in a film, *In This Our Life* (1942), in which Davis and de Havilland played together, not as twins but as sisters: Davis, the bad sister, stole the man who belonged to de Havilland, the good sister.

In subsequent films, Davis and de Havilland played separately, and each became both the good twin with the guy and the evil twin who took him away. In 1946, Olivia de Havilland made *The Dark Mirror,* which ends with the psychiatrist saying, only half jokingly, to the remaining, good, identical twin, "Why are you so much more beautiful than your sister?" In that same year, Bette Davis made *A Stolen Life* (the remake of a 1939 film with Elisabeth Bergner), in which, as usual, the evil Davis steals the good Davis's fiancé; the twist comes when the masquerader learns that the envied original was not in fact loved (a cinematic surprise already known from the film of Daphne Du Maurier's *Rebecca,* in 1940), so that she has gained nothing by the masquerade. As one critic remarked of this film, "What I'm waiting for is a film about beautiful identical quintuplets who all love the same man."[28]

Davis stamped the genre as her own by starring in the clone of

this film almost twenty years later: *Dead Ringer* (1964), this time involving murder as well as sexual betrayal: The evil twin is killed by the good twin, who gets away with it but then is hanged for the murder that her sister had committed (the murder of the man that the good twin loved). This is another variant of the theme of discovering that the one whom you clone in fact has a worse life, not a better life, than you do. *Killer in the Mirror,* made in 1986 (with Ann Jillian), appears, at first, to be yet another clone of the old Bette Davis film, but it adds a new twist: The evil sister is not in fact dead, but pretends to be dead—indeed, engineers the whole switch of identities—in order to take over the life of the good sister in order to avoid hanging for the murder that (as in *Dead Ringer*) she herself committed.

In Hollywood films about twin sisters made in the 1990s, too, murder often played the leading role. Sometimes the women are not twins but unrelated women, one of whom turns herself into a clone of the other and commits a murder for which the other is suspected. This is the case with a number of films ranging from Alfred Hitchcock's classic *Vertigo* (1958), in which Kim Novak masquerades as a woman she has in fact helped to kill, to *Basic Instinct* (1991), in which Jeanne Tripplehorn masquerades as Sharon Stone when she commits a murder. The same thing happens in *Single White Female* (1992), made from a novel by John Lutz whose excellent title, *Single White Female Seeks Same,* expresses the longing for sameness that characterizes both urban paranoia and sexual paranoia.

Some contemporary films about twin sisters are about politics, rather than murder. In a Hungarian film, *My Twentieth Century* (directed by Enyeko Ildiko, in 1990), there are twin sisters—one, in the West, sexy and given to luxurious tastes like diamond necklaces and champagne; the other, in the East, poor and dowdy and revolutionary, given to throwing bombs. A clone of *My Twentieth Century* is the Polish/French film *The Double Life of Véronique,* issued just one year later (1991), about two women, Véronique and Weronika

(Irene Jacob), born at precisely the same time, one in France and one in Poland. In these films, the twins are separated not by a magic mirror but by an Iron Curtain, yet here, too, they invade one another's sex lives. Finally, and predictably, the story of the good-and-evil twins generated at least one pornographic double, *Mirror Images* (1991), in which Delia Sheppard plays a promiscuous and sexually repressed set of twin sisters (a distinction that also characterized some of the good-and-evil sisters), who replace one another in various beds belonging to men who do not really seem to care who they are in bed with; the surviving sister sums it up with a classic sexist remark in the last line of the movie: "Does it really make any difference?" This is the bottom line in female cloning: All women are alike, anyway.[29] Indeed, the assumed genetic transparency of women, the assumption that a woman is just a man's way of making another man, just as a chicken is just an egg's way of making another chicken, is what made maternal imprinting a problem for men in the first place.

Female Clones: Sexual Abuse and Flight

Women in the mythologies of female twins thus share the evil propensities of male twins, and then some. But, just as male clones took two basic forms, the *Menaechmi* (inadvertent masquerade by natural twins) and the *Amphitryon* (intentional masquerade by artificial clones), females too have another sort of clone in addition to natural twins. But the female clone of this type is the very opposite of the *Amphitryon* model: Whereas males clone to win something, inevitably to the loss (or, occasionally, destruction) of their rivals and often of themselves as well, the female clone in this scenario is produced in order to avoid, rather than to steal, a lover—or even a husband. And despite the male bias of the texts in which these narratives appear, the stories themselves often express sympathy for the women forced to act in this way.

In the *Rig Veda* (circa 1000 B.C., in northern India) a woman who cannot stand her husband, or a stranger who is attempting to rape her, goes away and leaves an identical clone in her place, her shadow or reflection; in ancient Greek mythology, too, a phantom stands in for Helen when Paris comes to carry her off to Troy.[30] (In later, more realistic texts, the woman may just send her sister, or a servant—as Isolde sends Brangane, in *Tristan and Isolde).*[31] Stories such as these may express a kind of dissociation in reaction to a rape: "This happened to some other woman, not to me." The clone implies that the "real self" did not experience the event.[32] These are stories of denial, and of the asymmetry even in many less violent sexual acts, where one partner is "there" and the other is not. Thus, the meaning of the splitting as perceived by the person who clones is not merely "I am one, but I am also two," but "This is happening to me and this is not happening to me," and "I am here and I am not here." The mind/body separation experienced by victims of rape is often invoked in contemporary discussions of sexual violence.[33] In myths of rape, the clone serves to exonerate the woman herself from any possible defilement at the hands of the demonic rapist or unwanted husband.

Sexual aversion may lead to maternal imprinting, too: The animal husbandry model of Jacob's rods model that we considered previously works simply enough in the European folk belief that a woman frightened by the sight of a deformed man or a knife will bring forth a deformed child or a child with a birthmark in the shape of a knife.[34] But what if that "thing" or "object" is her husband? Jewish and Christian texts do not seem to have devoted much attention to this possibility, but an important ancient Indian myth tells of a woman, forced to accept a man she finds sexually loathesome, who closes her eyes and therefore brings forth a blind child. Her sister, subjected to the same man, takes the realistic-clone measure and sends her serving girl in her place, thereby virtually equating the uses of maternal imprinting and female cloning.[35] Just as the sisters in this story, forced to be impregnated by a man who disgusts

them, take measures to avoid him, measures that imprint the resulting children, so too European patriarchy and the *droit du seigneur* force women to be impregnated by men they don't want—and therefore, according to the theory, to imagine men they do want and to imprint the resulting children.

The women in these texts have limited options, but within them they have agency, an instinct for self-preservation, and a desire for sexual choice that the narratives seem to validate. To a female, let alone a feminist, reader, these stories depict women in a more positive light than the stories of female twins, or the tales of maternal imprinting and male cloning (which usually pay no attention at all to the women who are the objects of the male clone's desire). But from the standpoint of a male reader (or, more to the point, author), these are evil women: They abandon their husbands (and, as the texts make clear, their children). Thus, through either seduction or rejection, the female clone poses a sexual problem for men.

Conclusion

Each of these prescientific clones (embryos, twins, men, women) turns out to be at the very least nasty, at the very most totally destructive; mythology comes down strongly against cloning. The case against cloning is made over and over; even the comedies have a tragic aspect, and the tragedies are grim indeed. Many of these stories of clones are about things other than sex—they are about trying in vain to cheat death, and discovering one's identity, and politics, and (as the Pope says) about the uniqueness of souls. But time and again one clone somehow or other stumbles in the other's bed, and this feel of advertent or inadvertent sexual betrayal is, I think, an inescapable part of the terror of cloning.

The Pope's argument is deeply embedded in these myths; though more secular critics might use another word than *soul* to designate "the constitutive kernel" of a person, a word like *personality,* or *self,*

or *ego,* or *memory,* the myths resist the idea of two identical souls (or their equivalents) in two identical bodies. (Some contemporary Buddhists apparently wonder whose karma the clone would have.)[36] Christian missionaries in Africa argued that identical twins had two different souls, one each, and the missionaries' intervention did much to curtail the African practice of murdering one or both twins at birth.[37] Yet the very myths that assume that identical *twins* may have very different personalities (or souls) resist the idea that a *clone*—that is, a magically created double—could have a separate soul, that in creating a body de novo, the magician could create a soul de novo too. We, too, instinctively feel that the soul is inextricably linked to the body, and so if we see someone else with our body, we presume that he or she must have taken something of our soul. The question that we ask the mythological clone is, "If you are me, who am I?"

Endnotes

1. See Wendy Doniger and Gregory Spinner, "Misconceptions: Female Imaginations and Male Fantasies in Parental Imprinting," in *Daedalus,* in press.
2. Oppian, *Kynegetica,* 1.327–8. Text and translation in *Oppian Colluthus Tryphiodorus* (translated by A. W. Mair; Loeb Classical Library, vol. 80; New York: G. P. Putnam's Sons, 1928), pp. 34–5.
3. Soran, *Gynecology* 1, par. 39; text in *Soranos d'Éphèse: Maladies des Femmes* (text and translation by Paul Burguière and Danielle Gouryevitch; Paris: Les Belles Lettres, 1988), p. 36; see also translation by Oswei Temkin, *Soranus' Gynecology* (Baltimore: Johns Hopkins, 1956), pp. 37–8.
4. Empedocles, cited by Aetius 5.12.2, *Doxographi Graeci* (edited by Herman Diels; Berlin: Walter de Gruyter, 1965), p. 432. See also *The Poem of Empedocles* (text and translation by Brad Inwood; Toronto: University of Toronto Press, 1992), p. 185.
5. An important exception is offered by Paracelsus, writing in the sixteenth century in Germany, who granted that a woman's imaginations, too, could affect the embryo in positive—intellectually as well as physically positive—ways: If, at the moment of conception, she imagined a learned wise man, such as Plato or Aristotle,

or a warrior, Julius or Barbarossa, or a great artist, like the painter Dürer, she would bear a child like him. Paracelsus, *De Morbis Invisibilis,* in Hans Ranser, editor, *Schriften, Theophrasts von Hohenheim gennant Paracelsus* (Leipzig: Insel Verlag, 1921), Section 202, "Wirkung der Imagination," pp. 314–15.

6. Bemidbar Rabba 9:34; edited by M. A. Mirkin, *Midrash Rabba* (Tel Aviv: Yavneh, 1977), pp. 213 ff.
7. Kallah 50b, Kallah Rabbati 52a; Isaiah Tishby, *The Wisdom of the Zohar: An Anthology of Texts* (3 vols; translated by David Goldstein; Oxford University Press, The Littman Library, 1991 [1949]), vol. 2, pp. 646–9.
8. Thomas Laqueur, *Making Sex: Body and Gender from the Greeks to Freud* (Cambridge, MA: Harvard University Press, 1990), p. 59.
9. Marie-Hélène Huet, *Monstrous Imagination* (Cambridge, MA: Harvard University Press, 1993), pp. 79–80.
10. *Ibid.,* p. 80.
11. See the ancient story of Indra and Kutsa, *Jaiminiya Brahmana* (edited by Raghu Vira and Lokesha Chandra; Series 31; Nagpur: Sarasvati-vihara, 1954) 3.199–200; Wendy Doniger O'Flaherty, *Tales of Sex and Violence: Folklore, Sacrifice, and Danger in the Jaiminiya Brahmana* (Chicago: University of Chicago Press, 1985), pp. 75–6.
12. *Ibid.,* p. 81.
13. David Henry Hwang, *M. Butterfly* (New York: Plume [Penguin], 1989).
14. Eric Gerber, "Not-so-hot a Lover," *Houston Post,* Wednesday, May 21, 1986.
15. "The Two Brothers," in The Brothers Grimm, *The Complete Grimms' Fairy Tales* (translated by Margaret Hunt and James Stern; New York: Pantheon Books, 1944), pp. 308–11.
16. *The Mabinogion and Other Medieval Welsh Tales* (translated by Patrick K. Ford; Berkeley: University of California Press, 1977), pp. 37–56.
17. *Volsungasaga (The Saga of the Volsungs)* (translated by Jesse Byock; Berkeley: University of California Press, 1990), #29, "Sigurd Rides through the Wavering Flames of Brynhild," p. 80.
18. Susan Feldmann, "The Twin Brotheres," in *African Myths and Tales* (New York: Dell, 1963), pp. 272–6.
19. Stith Thompson, *Motif-Index of Folk Literature* (6 vols.; Bloomington, IN: Indiana University Press, 1955–58).
20. *Le Petit Robert 2,* p. 1690: Sosie, nom de l'esclave d'Amphitryon dont Mercure prend l'aspect. Personne qui a une parfaite ressemblance avec une autre. Paul Robert, *Le nouveau petit Robert, Dictionnaire alphabetique et analogique de la langue francaise.* Nouvelle edition. Paris: Dictionnaires Le Robert, 1996.
21. *Le Petit Robert 1,* p. 1838.
22. Plautus, *Amphitryon,* 1. 422, translated by James. H. Mantinband, in Charles E. Passage and James H. Mantinband, editors and translators, *Amphitryon: Three Plays*

in New Verse Translation (Plautus, Moliere, Kleist), Together with a Comprehensive Account of the Evolution of the Legend and Its Subsequent History on the Stage (Chapel Hill: University of North Carolina Press, 1974), p. 58.

23. Otto Rank, *The Double: A Psychoanalytic Study* (translated by Harry Tucker, Jr.; New York: New American Library, 1971 [1925]), p. 33.

24. Fyodor Dostoyevski, *The Double: Two Versions* (translated by Evelyn Harden; Ann Arbor, MI: Ardis, 1985 [*Dvoynik,* 1846]).

25. Wendy Doniger, "When a Kiss Is Still a Kiss: Memories of the Mind and the Body in Ancient India and Hollywood," in *Kenyon Review* (XIX:1, Winter, 1997), pp. 118–33.

26. Jeanine Basinger, *How Hollywood Spoke to Women, 1930–1960* (New York: Alfred Knopf, 1993), p. 100.

27. "Sister Charged with Murder, and Identity Switch," *New York Times,* Thursday, July 17, 1997, p. A16.

28. Richard Winnington, cited by Leslie Halliwell (*Halliwell's Film Guide,* edited by John Walker; New York: Harper, 1995).

29. Wendy Doniger, "Myths and Methods in the Dark," in *Journal of Religion* (76:4, October, 1996), pp. 531–47.

30. Wendy Doniger, *Splitting Women in Indian and Greek Myths* (The 1996–7 Jordan Lectures at the University of London).

31. *Tristan,* of Gottfried von Strassburg. Translated by A. T. Hatto and supplemented with the surviving fragments of the *Tristan* of Thomas (Harmondsworth: Penguin Books, 1960).

32. Wendy Doniger O'Flaherty, *Dreams, Illusion, and Other Realities* (Chicago: University of Chicago Press, 1984), pp. 95–6.

33. Cathy Winkler, "Rape Trauma: Contexts of Meaning," in *Embodiment and Experience: The Existential Ground of Culture and Self* (edited by Thomas Csordas; Cambridge: Cambridge University Press, 1994), pp. 256–7.

34. Havelock Ellis, "The Psychic State in Pregnancy," in *Studies in the Psychology of Sex* (Philadelphia: F. A. Davis, 1906), vol. 5, pp. 201–29.

35. *Mahabharata* (Poona: Bhandarkar Oriental Research Institute, 1933–69) 1.99–100; Wendy Doniger O'Flaherty, *Textual Sources for the Study of Hinduism* (Chicago: University of Chicago Press, 1990), pp. 46–51.

36. Peter Steinfels, "Beliefs," *New York Times,* Saturday, July 12, 1997, p. 9.

37. See Chinua Achebe, *Things Fall Apart* (New York: Knopf/Random House, 1992).

PART III
Ethics and Religion

Cloning Human Beings: An Assessment of the Ethical Issues Pro and Con

Dan W. Brock

The world of science and the public at large were both shocked and fascinated by the announcement in the journal *Nature* by Ian Wilmut and his colleagues that they had successfully cloned a sheep from a single cell of an adult sheep (Wilmut, 1997). But many were troubled or apparently even horrified at the prospect that cloning of adult humans by the same process might be possible as well. The response of most scientific and political leaders to the prospect of human cloning, indeed of Dr. Wilmut as well, was of immediate and strong condemnation.

A few more cautious voices were heard both suggesting some possible benefits from the use of human cloning in limited circumstances and questioning its too quick prohibition, but they were a clear minority. A striking feature of these early responses was that their strength and intensity seemed far to outrun the arguments and reasons offered in support of them—they seemed often to be "gut level" emotional reactions rather than considered reflections on the issues. Such reactions should not be simply dismissed, both because they may point us to important considerations otherwise missed and not easily articulated, and because they often have a major impact on public policy. But the formation of public policy should not ignore the moral reasons and arguments that bear on the practice of human cloning—these must be articulated in order to understand and inform people's more immediate emo-

tional responses. This essay is an effort to articulate, and to evaluate critically, the main moral considerations and arguments for and against human cloning. Though many people's religious beliefs inform their views on human cloning, and it is often difficult to separate religious from secular positions, I shall restrict myself to arguments and reasons that can be given a clear secular formulation.

On each side of the issue there are two distinct kinds of moral arguments brought forward. On the one hand, some opponents claim that human cloning would violate fundamental moral or human rights, while some proponents argue that its prohibition would violate such rights. While moral and even human rights need not be understood as absolute, they do place moral restrictions on permissible actions that an appeal to a mere balance of benefits over harms cannot justify overriding; for example, the rights of human subjects in research must be respected even if the result is that some potentially beneficial research is more difficult or cannot be done. On the other hand, both opponents and proponents also cite the likely harms and benefits, both to individuals and to society, of the practice. I shall begin with the arguments in support of permitting human cloning, although with no implication that it is the stronger or weaker position.

Moral Arguments in Support of Human Cloning

IS THERE A MORAL RIGHT TO USE HUMAN CLONING?

What moral right might protect at least some access to the use of human cloning? A commitment to individual liberty, such as defended by J. S. Mill, requires that individuals be left free to use human cloning if they so choose and if their doing so does not cause significant harms to others, but liberty is too broad in scope

to be an uncontroversial moral right (Mill, 1859; Rhodes, 1995). Human cloning is a means of reproduction (in the most literal sense) and so the most plausible moral right at stake in its use is a right to reproductive freedom or procreative liberty (Robertson, 1994a; Brock, 1994), understood to include both the choice not to reproduce, for example, by means of contraception or abortion, and also the right to reproduce.

The right to reproductive freedom is properly understood to include the right to use various assisted reproductive technologies (ARTs), such as in vitro fertilization (IVF), oocyte donation, and so forth. The reproductive right relevant to human cloning is a negative right, that is, a right to use ARTs without interference by the government or others when made available by a willing provider. The choice of an assisted means of reproduction should be protected by reproductive freedom even when it is not the only means for individuals to reproduce, just as the choice among different means of preventing conception is protected by reproductive freedom. However, the case for permitting the use of a particular means of reproduction is strongest when it is necessary for particular individuals to be able to procreate at all, or to do so without great burdens or harms to themselves or others. In some cases human cloning could be the only means for individuals to procreate while retaining a biological tie to their child, but in other cases different means of procreating might also be possible.

It could be argued that human cloning is not covered by the right to reproductive freedom because whereas current ARTs and practices covered by that right are remedies for inabilities to reproduce sexually, human cloning is an entirely new means of reproduction; indeed, its critics see it as more a means of manufacturing humans than of reproduction. Human cloning is a different means of reproduction than sexual reproduction, but it is a means that can serve individuals' interest in reproducing. If it is not protected by the moral right to reproductive freedom, I believe that

must be not because it is a new means of reproducing, but instead because it has other objectionable or harmful features; I shall evaluate these other ethical objections to it later.

When individuals have alternative means of procreating, human cloning typically would be chosen because it replicates a particular individual's genome. The reproductive interest in question then is not simply reproduction itself, but a more specific interest in choosing what kind of children to have. The right to reproductive freedom is usually understood to cover at least some choice about the kind of children one will have. Some individuals choose reproductive partners in the hope of producing offspring with desirable traits. Genetic testing of fetuses or preimplantation embryos for genetic disease or abnormality is done to avoid having a child with those diseases or abnormalities. Respect for individual self-determination, which is one of the grounds of a moral right to reproductive freedom, includes respecting individuals' choices about whether to have a child with a condition that will place severe burdens on them, and cause severe burdens to the child itself.

The less a reproductive choice is primarily the determination of one's own life, but primarily the determination of the nature of another, as in the case of human cloning, the more moral weight the interests of that other person, that is the cloned child, should have in decisions that determine its nature (Annas, 1994). But even then parents are typically accorded substantial, but not unlimited, discretion in shaping the persons their children will become, for example, through education and other childrearing decisions. Even if not part of reproductive freedom, the right to raise one's children as one sees fit, within limits mostly determined by the interests of the children, is also a right to determine within limits what kinds of persons one's children will become. This right includes not just preventing certain diseases or harms to children, but selecting and shaping desirable features and traits in one's children. The use of human cloning is one way to exercise that right.

Public policy and the law now permit prospective parents to conceive, or to carry a conception to term, when there is a significant risk or even certainty that the child will suffer from a serious genetic disease. Even when others think the risk or certainty of genetic disease makes it morally wrong to conceive, or to carry a fetus to term, the parents' right to reproductive freedom permits them to do so. Most possible harms to a cloned child are less serious than the genetic harms with which parents can now permit their offspring to be conceived or born.

I conclude that there is good reason to accept that a right to reproductive freedom presumptively includes both a right to select the means of reproduction, as well as a right to determine what kind of children to have, by use of human cloning. However, the specific reproductive interest of determining what kind of children to have is less weighty than are other reproductive interests and choices whose impact falls more directly and exclusively on the parents rather than the child. Even if a moral right to reproductive freedom protects the use of human cloning, that does not settle the moral issue about human cloning, since there may be other moral rights in conflict with this right, or serious enough harms from human cloning to override the right to use it; this right can be thought of as establishing a serious moral presumption supporting access to human cloning.

WHAT INDIVIDUAL OR SOCIAL BENEFITS MIGHT HUMAN CLONING PRODUCE?

Largely Individual Benefits

The literature on human cloning by nuclear transfer or by embryo splitting contains a few examples of circumstances in which individuals might have good reasons to want to use human cloning. However, human cloning seems not to be the unique answer to any great or pressing human need and its benefits appear to be limited at most. What are the principal possible benefits of human

cloning that might give individuals good reasons to want to use it?

1. Human cloning would be a new means to relieve the infertility some persons now experience. Human cloning would allow women who have no ova or men who have no sperm to produce an offspring that is biologically related to them (Eisenberg, 1976; Robertson, 1994b, 1997; LaBar, 1984). Embryos might also be cloned, by either nuclear transfer or embryo splitting, in order to increase the number of embryos for implantation and improve the chances of successful conception (NABER, 1994). The benefits from human cloning to relieve infertility are greater the more persons there are who cannot overcome their infertility by any other means acceptable to them. I do not know of data on this point, but the numbers who would use cloning for this reason are probably not large.

The large number of children throughout the world possibly available for adoption represents an alternative solution to infertility only if we are prepared to discount as illegitimate the strong desire of many persons, fertile and infertile, for the experience of pregnancy and for having and raising a child biologically related to them. While not important to all infertile (or fertile) individuals, it is important to many and is respected and met through other forms of assisted reproduction that maintain a biological connection when that is possible; that desire does not become illegitimate simply because human cloning would be the best or only means of overcoming an individual's infertility.

2. Human cloning would enable couples in which one party risks transmitting a serious hereditary disease to an offspring to reproduce without doing so (Robertson, 1994b). By using donor sperm or egg donation, such hereditary risks can generally be avoided now without the use of human cloning. These procedures may be unacceptable to some couples, however, or at least considered less desirable than human cloning because they introduce a third party's genes into their reproduction instead of giving their offspring only the genes of one of them. Thus, in some cases human cloning could be a rea-

sonable means of preventing genetically transmitted harms to offspring. Here too, we do not know how many persons would want to use human cloning instead of other means of avoiding the risk of genetic transmission of a disease or of accepting the risk of transmitting the disease, but the numbers again are probably not large.

3. *Human cloning to make a later twin would enable a person to obtain needed organs or tissues for transplantation* (Robertson, 1994b, 1997; Kahn, 1989; Harris, 1992). Human cloning would solve the problem of finding a transplant donor whose organ or tissue is an acceptable match and would eliminate, or drastically reduce, the risk of transplant rejection by the host. The availability of human cloning for this purpose would amount to a form of insurance to enable treatment of certain kinds of medical conditions. Of course, sometimes the medical need would be too urgent to permit waiting for the cloning, gestation, and development that is necessary before tissues or organs can be obtained for transplantation. In other cases, taking an organ also needed by the later twin, such as a heart or a liver, would be impermissible because it would violate the later twin's rights.

Such a practice can be criticized on the ground that it treats the later twin not as a person valued and loved for his or her own sake, as an end in itself in Kantian terms, but simply as a means for benefiting another. This criticism assumes, however, that only this one motive defines the reproduction and the relation of the person to his or her later twin. The well-known case some years ago in California of the Ayalas, who conceived in the hopes of obtaining a source for a bone marrow transplant for their teenage daughter suffering from leukemia, illustrates the mistake in this assumption. They argued that whether or not the child they conceived turned out to be a possible donor for their daughter, they would value and love the child for itself, and treat it as they would treat any other member of their family. That one reason they wanted it, as a possible means to saving their daughter's life, did not preclude their

also loving and valuing it for its own sake; in Kantian terms, it was treated as a possible means to saving their daughter, but not *solely as a means,* which is what the Kantian view proscribes.

Indeed, when people have children, whether by sexual means or with the aid of ARTs, their motives and reasons for doing so are typically many and complex, and include reasons less laudable than obtaining lifesaving medical treatment, such as having someone who needs them, enabling them to live on their own, qualifying for government benefit programs, and so forth. While these are not admirable motives for having children and may not bode well for the child's upbringing and future, public policy does not assess prospective parents' motives and reasons for procreating as a condition of their doing so.

4. Human cloning would enable individuals to clone someone who had special meaning to them, such as a child who had died (Robertson, 1994b). There is no denying that if human cloning were available, some individuals would want to use it for this purpose, but their desire usually would be based on a deep confusion. Cloning such a child would not replace the child the parents had loved and lost, but would only create a different child with the same genes. The child they loved and lost was a unique individual who had been shaped by his or her environment and choices, not just his or her genes, and more importantly who had experienced a particular relationship with them. Even if the later cloned child could not only have the same genes but also be subjected to the same environment, which of course is impossible, it would remain a different child than the one they had loved and lost because it would share a different history with them (Thomas, 1974). Cloning the lost child might help the parents accept and move on from their loss, but another already existing sibling or a new child that was not a clone might do this equally well; indeed, it might do so better since the appearance of the cloned later twin would be a constant reminder of the child they had lost. Nevertheless, if human cloning enabled some individuals to clone a person who had special meaning to

them and doing so gave them deep satisfaction, that would be a benefit to them even if their reasons for wanting to do so, and the satisfaction they in turn received, were based on a confusion.

Largely Social Benefits

5. *Human cloning would enable the duplication of individuals of great talent, genius, character, or other exemplary qualities.* Unlike the first four reasons for human cloning which appeal to benefits to specific individuals, this reason looks to benefits to the broader society from being able to replicate extraordinary individuals—a Mozart, Einstein, Gandhi, or Schweitzer (Lederberg, 1966; McKinnell, 1979). Much of the appeal of this reason, like much support and opposition to human cloning, rests largely on a confused and false assumption of genetic determinism, that is, that one's genes fully determine what one will become, do, and accomplish. What made Mozart, Einstein, Gandhi, and Schweitzer the extraordinary individuals they were was the confluence of their particular genetic endowments with the environments in which they were raised and lived and the particular historical moments they in different ways seized. Cloning them would produce individuals with the same genetic inheritances (nuclear transfer does not even produce 100 percent genetic identity, although for the sake of exploring the moral issues I have followed the common assumption that it does), but it is not possible to replicate their environments or the historical contexts in which they lived and their greatness flourished. We do not know the degree or specific respects in which any individual's greatness depended on "nature" or "nurture," but we do know that it always depends on an interaction of them both. Cloning could not even replicate individuals' extraordinary capabilities, much less their accomplishments, because these too are the product of their inherited genes and their environments, not of their genes alone.

None of this is to deny that Mozart's and Einstein's extraordinary musical and intellectual capabilities, nor even Gandhi's and

Schweitzer's extraordinary moral greatness, were produced in part by their unique genetic inheritances. Cloning them might well produce individuals with exceptional capacities, but we simply do not know how close their clones would be in capacities or accomplishments to the great individuals from whom they were cloned. Even so, the hope for exceptional, even if less and different, accomplishment from cloning such extraordinary individuals might be a reasonable ground for doing so.

Worries here about abuse, however, surface quickly. Whose standards of greatness would be used to select individuals to be cloned? Who would control use of human cloning technology for the benefit of society or mankind at large? Particular groups, segments of society, or governments might use the technology for their own benefit, under the cover of benefiting society or even mankind at large.

6. *Human cloning and research on human cloning might make possible important advances in scientific knowledge, for example, about human development* (Walters, 1982; Smith, 1983). While important potential advances in scientific or medical knowledge from human cloning or human cloning research have frequently been cited, there are at least three reasons for caution about such claims. First, there is always considerable uncertainty about the nature and importance of the new scientific or medical knowledge to which a dramatic new technology like human cloning will lead; the road to new knowledge is never mapped in advance and takes many unexpected turns. Second, we do not know what new knowledge from human cloning or human cloning research could also be gained by other means that do not have the problematic moral features to which its opponents object. Third, what human cloning research would be compatible with ethical and legal requirements for the use of human subjects in research is complex, controversial, and largely unexplored. Creating human clones solely for the purpose of research would be to use them solely for the benefit of others without their consent, and so unethical. But if and when human cloning was established to be

safe and effective, then new scientific knowledge might be obtained from its use for legitimate, nonresearch reasons.

Although there is considerable uncertainty concerning most of human cloning's possible individual and social benefits that I have discussed, and although no doubt it could have other benefits or uses that we cannot yet envisage, I believe it is reasonable to conclude at this time that human cloning does not seem to promise great benefits or uniquely to meet great human needs. Nevertheless, despite these limited benefits, a moral case can be made that freedom to use human cloning is protected by the important moral right to reproductive freedom. I shall turn now to what moral rights might be violated, or harms produced, by research on or use of human cloning.

Moral Arguments Against Human Cloning

WOULD THE USE OF HUMAN CLONING VIOLATE IMPORTANT MORAL RIGHTS?

Many of the immediate condemnations of any possible human cloning following Wilmut's cloning of Dolly claimed that it would violate moral or human rights, but it was usually not specified precisely, or often even at all, what rights would be violated (WHO, 1997). I shall consider two possible candidates for such a right: a right to have a unique identity and a right to ignorance about one's future or to an open future. Claims that cloning denies individuals a unique identity are common, but I shall argue that even if there is a right to a unique identity, it could not be violated by human cloning. The right to ignorance or to an open future has only been explicitly defended, to my knowledge, by two commentators, and in the context of human cloning, only by Hans Jonas; it supports a more promising, but in my view ultimately unsuccessful, argument that human cloning would violate an important moral or human right.

Is there a moral or human right to a unique identity, and if so would it be violated by human cloning? For human cloning to violate a right to a unique identity, the relevant sense of identity would have to be genetic identity, that is, a right to a unique unrepeated genome. This would be violated by human cloning, but is there any such right? It might be thought that cases of identical twins show there is no such right because no one claims that the moral or human rights of the twins have been violated. However, this consideration is not conclusive (Kass, 1985; NABER, 1994). Only human actions can violate others' rights; outcomes that would constitute a rights violation if deliberately caused by human action are not a rights violation if a result of natural causes. If Arthur deliberately strikes Barry on the head so hard as to cause his death, he violates Barry's right not to be killed; if lightning strikes Cheryl, causing her death, her right not to be killed has not been violated. Thus, the case of twins does not show that there could not be a right to a unique genetic identity.

What is the sense of identity that might plausibly be what each person has a right to have uniquely, that constitutes the special uniqueness of each individual (Macklin 1994; Chadwick 1982)? Even with the same genes, homozygous twins are numerically distinct and not identical, so what is intended must be the various properties and characteristics that make each individual qualitatively unique and different from others. Does having the same genome as another person undermine that unique qualitative identity? Only on the crudest genetic determinism, according to which an individual's genes completely and decisively determine everything else about the individual, all his or her other nongenetic features and properties, together with the entire history or biography that constitutes his or her life. But there is no reason whatever to believe that kind of genetic determinism. Even with the same genes, differences in genetically identical twins' psychological and personal characteristics develop over time together with differences in their life histories, personal relationships, and life choices;

sharing an identical genome does not prevent twins from developing distinct and unique personal identities of their own.

We need not pursue whether there is a moral or human right to a unique identity—no such right is found among typical accounts and enumerations of moral or human rights—because even if there is such a right, sharing a genome with another individual as a result of human cloning would not violate it. The idea of the uniqueness, or unique identity, of each person historically predates the development of modern genetics. A unique genome thus could not be the ground of this long-standing belief in the unique human identity of each person.

I turn now to whether human cloning would violate what Hans Jonas called a right to ignorance, or what Joel Feinberg called a right to an open future (Jonas, 1974; Feinberg, 1980). Jonas argued that human cloning in which there is a substantial time gap between the beginning of the lives of the earlier and later twin is fundamentally different from the simultaneous beginning of the lives of homozygous twins that occur in nature. Although contemporaneous twins begin their lives with the same genetic inheritance, they do so at the same time, and so in ignorance of what the other who shares the same genome will by his or her choices make of his or her life.

A later twin created by human cloning, Jonas argues, knows, or at least believes she knows, too much about herself. For there is already in the world another person, her earlier twin, who from the same genetic starting point has made the life choices that are still in the later twin's future. It will seem that her life has already been lived and played out by another, that her fate is already determined; she will lose the sense of human possibility in freely and spontaneously creating her own future and authentic self. It is tyrannical, Jonas claims, for the earlier twin to try to determine another's fate in this way.

Jonas's objection can be interpreted so as not to assume either a false genetic determinism, or a belief in it. A later twin might

grant that he is not determined to follow in his earlier twin's footsteps, but nevertheless the earlier twin's life might always haunt him, standing as an undue influence on his life, and shaping it in ways to which others' lives are not vulnerable. But the force of the objection still seems to rest on the false assumption that having the same genome as his earlier twin unduly restricts his freedom to create a different life and self than the earlier twin's. Moreover, a family environment also importantly shapes children's development, but there is no force to the claim of a younger sibling that the existence of an older sibling raised in that same family is an undue influence on the younger sibling's freedom to make his own life for himself in that environment. Indeed, the younger twin or sibling might gain the benefit of being able to learn from the older twin's or sibling's mistakes.

A closely related argument can be derived from what Joel Feinberg has called a child's right to an open future. This requires that others raising a child not so close off the future possibilities that the child would otherwise have as to eliminate a reasonable range of opportunities for the child autonomously to construct his or her own life. One way this right might be violated is to create a later twin who will believe her future has already been set for her by the choices made and the life lived by her earlier twin.

The central difficulty in these appeals to a right either to ignorance or to an open future is that the right is not violated merely because the later twin is likely to *believe* that his future is already determined, when that belief is clearly false and supported only by the crudest genetic determinism. If we know the later twin will falsely believe that his open future has been taken from him as a result of being cloned, even though in reality it has not, then we know that cloning will cause the twin psychological distress, but not that it will violate his right. Jonas's right to ignorance, and Feinberg's right of a child to an open future, are not not violated by human cloning, though they do point to psychological harms that a later twin may be likely to experience and that I will take up later.

Neither a moral or human right to a unique identity, nor one to ignorance and an open future, would be violated by human cloning. There may be other moral or human rights that human cloning would violate, but I do not know what they might be. I turn now to consideration of the harms that human cloning might produce.

WHAT INDIVIDUAL OR SOCIAL HARMS MIGHT HUMAN CLONING PRODUCE?

There are many possible individual or social harms that have been posited by one or another commentator and I shall only try to cover the more plausible and significant of them.

Largely Individual Harms

1. Human cloning would produce psychological distress and harm in the later twin. No doubt knowing the path in life taken by one's earlier twin might often have several bad psychological effects (Callahan, 1993; LaBar, 1984; Macklin, 1994; McCormick, 1993; Studdard, 1978; Rainer, 1978; Verhey, 1994). The later twin might feel, even if mistakenly, that her fate has already been substantially laid out, and so have difficulty freely and spontaneously taking responsibility for and making her own fate and life. The later twin's experience or sense of autonomy and freedom might be substantially diminished, even if in actual fact they are diminished much less than it seems to her. She might have a diminished sense of her own uniqueness and individuality, even if once again these are in fact diminished little or not at all by having an earlier twin with the same genome. If the later twin is the clone of a particularly exemplary individual, perhaps with some special capabilities and accomplishments, she might experience excessive pressure to reach the very high standards of ability and accomplishment of the earlier twin (Rainer, 1978). These various psychological effects might take a heavy toll on the later twin and be serious burdens to her.

While psychological harms of these kinds from human cloning are certainly possible, and perhaps even likely in some cases, they

remain at this point only speculative since we have no experience with human cloning and the creation of earlier and later twins. Nevertheless, if experience with human cloning confirmed that serious and unavoidable psychological harms typically occurred to the later twin, that would be a serious moral reason to avoid the practice. Intuitively at least, psychological burdens and harms seem more likely and more serious for a person who is only one of many identical later twins cloned from one original source, so that the clone might run into another identical twin around every street corner. This prospect could be a good reason to place sharp limits on the number of twins that could be cloned from any one source.

One argument has been used by several commentators to undermine the apparent significance of potential psychological harms to a later twin (Chadwick, 1982; Robertson, 1994b, 1997; Macklin, 1994). The point derives from a general problem, called the nonidentity problem, posed by the philosopher Derek Parfit, although not originally directed to human cloning (Parfit, 1984). Here is the argument. Even if all these psychological burdens from human cloning could not be avoided for any later twin, they are not harms to the twin, and so not reasons not to clone the twin. That is because the only way for the twin to avoid the harms is never to be cloned, and so never to exist at all. But these psychological burdens, hard though they might be, are not so bad as to make the twin's life, all things considered, not worth living. So the later twin is not harmed by being given a life even with these psychological burdens, since the alternative of never existing at all is arguably worse—he or she never has a worthwhile life—but certainly not better for the twin. And if the later twin is not harmed by having been created with these unavoidable burdens, then how could he or she be wronged by having been created with them? And if the later twin is not wronged, then why is any wrong being done by human cloning? This argument has considerable potential import, for if it is sound it will undermine the apparent moral importance of any bad consequence of human cloning to the later twin that is not so

serious as to make the twin's life, all things considered, not worth living.

I defended elsewhere the position regarding the general case of genetically transmitted handicaps, that if one could have a *different* child without comparable burdens (for the case of cloning, by using a different method of reproduction which did not result in a later twin), there is as strong a moral reason to do so as there would be not to cause similar burdens to an already existing child (Brock, 1995). Choosing to create the later twin with serious psychological burdens instead of a different person who would be free of them, without weighty overriding reasons for choosing the former, would be morally irresponsible or wrong, even if doing so does not harm or wrong the later twin who could only exist with the burdens. These issues are too detailed and complex to pursue here and the nonidentity problem remains controversial and not fully resolved, but at the least, the argument for disregarding the psychological burdens to the later twin because he or she could not exist without them is controversial, and in my view mistaken. Such psychological harms, as I shall continue to call them, are speculative, but they should not be disregarded because of the nonidentity problem.

2. Human cloning procedures would carry unacceptable risks to the clone. There is no doubt that attempts to clone a human being at the present time would carry unacceptable risks to the clone. Further research on the procedure with animals, as well as research to establish its safety and effectiveness for humans, is clearly necessary before it would be ethical to use the procedure on humans. One risk to the clone is the failure to implant, grow, and develop successfully, but this would involve the embryo's death or destruction long before most people or the law consider it to be a person with moral or legal protections of its life.

Other risks to the clone are that the procedure in some way goes wrong, or unanticipated harms come to the clone; for example, Harold Varmus, director of the National Institutes of Health,

raised the concern that a cell many years old from which a person is cloned could have accumulated genetic mutations during its years in another adult that could give the resulting clone a predisposition to cancer or other diseases of aging (Weiss, 1997). Risks to an ovum donor (if any), a nucleus donor, and a woman who receives the embryo for implantation would likely be ethically acceptable with the informed consent of the involved parties.

I believe it is too soon to say whether unavoidable risks to the clone would make human cloning forever unethical. At a minimum, further research is needed to better define the potential risks to humans. But we should not insist on a standard that requires risks to be lower than those we accept in sexual reproduction, or in other forms of ART.

Largely Social Harms

3. Human cloning would lessen the worth of individuals and diminish respect for human life. Unelaborated claims to this effect were common in the media after the announcement of the cloning of Dolly. Ruth Macklin explored and criticized the claim that human cloning would diminish the value we place on, and our respect for, human life because it would lead to persons being viewed as replaceable (Macklin, 1994). As I have argued concerning a right to a unique identity, only on a confused and indefensible notion of human identity is a person's identity determined solely by his or her genes, and so no individual could be fully replaced by a later clone possessing the same genes. Ordinary people recognize this clearly. For example, parents of a child dying of a fatal disease would find it insensitive and ludicrous to be told they should not grieve for their coming loss because it is possible to replace him by cloning him; it is *their child who is dying* whom they love and value, and that child and his importance to them is not replaceable by a cloned later twin. Even if they would also come to love and value a later twin as much as they now love and value their child who is dying, that would be to love and value that *different child* for its own sake, not as a replace-

ment for the child they lost. Our relations of love and friendship are with distinct, historically situated individuals with whom over time we have shared experiences and our lives, and whose loss to us can never be replaced.

A different version of this worry is that human cloning would result in persons' worth or value seeming diminished because we would come to see persons as able to be manufactured or "handmade." This demystification of the creation of human life would reduce our appreciation and awe of human life and of its natural creation. It would be a mistake, however, to conclude that a person created by human cloning is of less value or is less worthy of respect than one created by sexual reproduction. At least outside of some religious contexts, it is the nature of a being, not how it is created, that is the source of its value and makes it worthy of respect. For many people, gaining a scientific understanding of the truly extraordinary complexity of human reproduction and development increases, instead of decreases, their awe of the process and its product.

A more subtle route by which the value we place on each individual human life might be diminished could come from the use of human cloning with the aim of creating a child with a particular genome, either the genome of another individual especially meaningful to those doing the cloning or an individual with exceptional talents, abilities, and accomplishments. The child then comes to be objectified, valued only as an object and for its genome, or at least for its genome's expected phenotypic expression, and no longer recognized as having the intrinsic equal moral value of all persons, simply as persons. For the moral value and respect due all persons to come to be seen as resting only on the instrumental value of individuals and of their particular qualities to others would be to fundamentally change the moral status properly accorded to persons. Individuals would lose their moral standing as full and equal members of the moral community, replaced by the different instrumental value each has to others.

Such a change in the equal moral value and worth accorded to persons should be avoided at all costs, but it is far from clear that such a change would result from permitting human cloning. Parents, for example, are quite capable of distinguishing their children's intrinsic value, just as individual persons, from their instrumental value based on their particular qualities or properties. The equal moral value and respect due all persons simply as persons is not incompatible with the different instrumental value of different individuals; Einstein and an untalented physics graduate student have vastly different value as scientists, but share and are entitled to equal moral value and respect as persons. It is a confused mistake to conflate these two kinds of value and respect. If making a large number of clones from one original person would be more likely to foster it, that would be a further reason to limit the number of clones that could be made from one individual.

4. Human cloning might be used by commercial interests for financial gain. Both opponents and proponents of human cloning agree that cloned embryos should not be able to be bought and sold. In a science fiction frame of mind, one can imagine commercial interests offering genetically certified and guaranteed embryos for sale, perhaps offering a catalogue of different embryos cloned from individuals with a variety of talents, capacities, and other desirable properties. This would be a fundamental violation of the equal moral respect and dignity owed to all persons, treating them instead as objects to be differentially valued, bought, and sold in the marketplace. Even if embryos are not yet persons at the time they would be purchased or sold, they would be being valued, bought, and sold for the persons they will become. The moral consensus against any commercial market in embryos, cloned or otherwise, should be enforced by law whatever the public policy ultimately is on human cloning.

5. Human cloning might be used by governments or other groups for immoral and exploitative purposes. In *Brave New World,* Aldous Huxley imagined cloning individuals who have been engineered with lim-

ited abilities and conditioned to do, and to be happy doing, the menial work that society needed done (Huxley, 1932). Selection and control in the creation of people was exercised not in the interests of the persons created, but in the interests of the society and at the expense of the persons created; nor did it serve individuals' interests in reproduction and parenting. Any use of human cloning for such purposes would exploit the clones solely as means for the benefit of others, and would violate the equal moral respect and dignity they are owed as full moral persons. If human cloning is permitted to go forward, it should be with regulations that would clearly prohibit such immoral exploitation.

Fiction contains even more disturbing or bizarre uses of human cloning, such as Mengele's creation of many clones of Hitler in Ira Levin's *The Boys from Brazil* (Levin, 1976), Woody Allen's science fiction cinematic spoof *Sleeper* in which a dictator's only remaining part, his nose, must be destroyed to keep it from being cloned, and the contemporary science fiction film *Blade Runner*. These nightmare scenarios may be quite improbable, but their impact should not be underestimated on public concern with technologies like human cloning. Regulation of human cloning must assure the public that even such far-fetched abuses will not take place.

Conclusion

Human cloning has until now received little serious and careful ethical attention because it was typically dismissed as science fiction, and it stirs deep, but difficult to articulate, uneasiness and even revulsion in many people. Any ethical assessment of human cloning at this point must be tentative and provisional. Fortunately, the science and technology of human cloning are not yet in hand, and so a public and professional debate is possible without the need for a hasty, precipitate policy response.

The ethical pros and cons of human cloning, as I see them at this

time, are sufficiently balanced and uncertain that there is not an ethically decisive case either for or against permitting it or doing it. Access to human cloning can plausibly be brought within a moral right to reproductive freedom, but its potential legitimate uses appear few and do not promise substantial benefits. It is not a central component of the moral right to reproductive freedom and it does not uniquely serve any major or pressing individual or social needs. On the other hand, contrary to the pronouncements of many of its opponents, human cloning seems not to be a violation of moral or human rights. But it does risk some significant individual or social harms, although most are based on common public confusions about genetic determinism, human identity, and the effects of human cloning. Because most potential harms feared from human cloning remain speculative, they seem insufficient to warrant at this time a complete legal prohibition of either research on or later use of human cloning, if and when its safety and efficacy are established. Legitimate moral concerns about the use and effects of human cloning, however, underline the need for careful public oversight of research on its development, together with a wider public and professional debate and review before cloning is used on human beings.

References

Annas, G. J. (1994). "Regulatory Models for Human Embryo Cloning: The Free Market, Professional Guidelines, and Government Restrictions." *Kennedy Institute of Ethics Journal* 4,3:235–249.

Brock, D. W. (1994). "Reproductive Freedom: Its Nature, Bases and Limits," in *Health Care Ethics: Critical Issues for Health Professionals,* eds. D. Thomasma and J. Monagle. Gaithersbrug, MD: Aspen Publishers.

Brock, D. W. (1995). "The Non-Identity Problem and Genetic Harm." *Bioethics* 9:269–275.

Callahan, D. (1993). "Perspective on Cloning: A Threat to Individual Uniqueness." *Los Angeles Times,* November 12, 1993:B7.

Chadwick, R. F. (1982). "Cloning." *Philosophy* 57:201–209.

Eisenberg, L. (1976). "The Outcome as Cause: Predestination and Human Cloning." *The Journal of Medicine and Philosophy* 1:318–331.

Feinberg, J. (1980). "The Child's Right to an Open Future," in *Whose Child? Children's Rights, Parental Authority, and State Power,* eds. W. Aiken and H. LaFollette. Totowa, NJ: Rowman and Littlefield.

Harris, J. (1992). *Wonderwoman and Superman: The Ethics of Biotechnology.* Oxford: Oxford University Press.

Huxley, A. (1932). *Brave New World.* London: Chalto and Winders.

Jonas, H. (1974). *Philosophical Essays: From Ancient Creed to Technological Man.* Englewood Cliffs, NJ: Prentice-Hall.

Kahn, C. (1989). "Can We Achieve Immortality?" *Free Inquiry* 9:14–18.

Kass, L. (1985). *Toward a More Natural Science.* New York: The Free Press.

LaBar, M. (1984). "The Pros and Cons of Human Cloning." *Thought* 57:318–333.

Lederberg, J. (1966). "Experimental Genetics and Human Evolution." *The American Naturalist* 100:519–531.

Levin, I. (1976). *The Boys from Brazil.* New York: Random House.

Macklin, R. (1994). "Splitting Embryos on the Slippery Slope: Ethics and Public Policy." *Kennedy Institute of Ethics Journal* 4:209–226.

McCormick, R. (1993). "Should We Clone Humans?" *Christian Century* 110:1148–1149.

McKinnell, R. (1979). *Cloning: A Biologist Reports.* Minneapolis, MN: University of Minnesota Press.

Mill, J. S. (1859). *On Liberty.* Indianapolis, IN: Bobbs-Merrill Publishing.

NABER (National Advisory Board on Ethics in Reproduction) (1994). "Report on Human Cloning Through Embryo Splitting: An Amber Light." *Kennedy Institute of Ethics Journal* 4:251–282.

Parfit, D. (1984). *Reasons and Persons.* Oxford: Oxford University Press.

Rainer, J. D. (1978). "Commentary." *Man and Medicine: The Journal of Values and Ethics in Health Care* 3:115–117.

Rhodes, R. (1995). "Clones, Harms, and Rights." *Cambridge Quarterly of Healthcare Ethics* 4:285–290.

Robertson, J. A. (1994a). *Children of Choice: Freedom and the New Reproductive Technologies.* Princeton, NJ: Princeton University Press.

Robertson, J. A. (1994b). "The Question of Human Cloning." *Hastings Center Report* 24:6–14.

Robertson, J. A. (1997). "A Ban on Cloning and Cloning Research is Unjustified." Testimony Presented to the National Bioethics Advisory Commission, March 1997.

Smith, G. P. (1983). "Intimations of Immortality: Clones, Cyrons and the Law." *University of New South Wales Law Journal* 6:119–132.

Studdard, A. (1978). "The Lone Clone." *Man and Medicine: The Journal of Values and Ethics in Health Care* 3:109–114.

Thomas, L. (1974). "Notes of a Biology Watcher: On Cloning a Human Being." *New England Journal of Medicine* 291:1296–1297.

Verhey, A. D. (1994). "Cloning: Revisiting an Old Debate." *Kennedy Institute of Ethics Journal* 4:227–234.

Walters, W. A. W. (1982). "Cloning, Ectogenesis, and Hybrids: Things to Come?" in *Test-Tube Babies*, eds. W. A. W. Walters and P. Singer. Melbourne: Oxford University Press.

Weiss, R. (1997). "Cloning Suddenly Has Government's Attention." *International Herald Tribune*, March 7, 1997.

WHO (World Health Organization Press Office). (March 11, 1997). "WHO Director General Condemns Human Cloning." World Health Organization, Geneva, Switzerland.

Wilmut, I., et al. (1997). "Viable Offspring Derived from Fetal and Adult Mammalian Cells." *Nature* 385:810–813.

This essay is a shorter version of a paper prepared for the National Bioethics Advisory Commission.

I want to acknowledge with gratitude the invaluable help of my research assistant, Insoo Hyun, on this paper. He not only made it possible to complete the paper on the National Bioethics Advisory Commission's tight schedule, but also improved it with a number of insightful substantive suggestions.

Religious Perspectives

National Bioethics Advisory Commission

Religion and Human Cloning: An Historical Overview

It is possible to identify four recent overlapping periods in which theologians and other religious thinkers have considered the scientific prospects and ethics of the cloning of humans. The first phase, which began in the mid-1960s and continued into the early 1970s, was shaped by a context of expanded choices and control of reproduction (e.g., the availability of the birth control pill), the prospects of alternative, technologically-assisted reproduction (e.g., *in vitro* fertilization [IVF]), and the advocacy by some biologists and geneticists of cloning "preferred" genotypes, which, in their view, would avoid overloading the human gene pool with genes that are linked to deleterious outcomes and that could place the survival of the human species at risk.

Several prominent theologians engaged in these initial discussions of human genetic manipulation and cloning, including Charles Curran, Bernard Häring, Richard McCormick, and Karl Rahner within Roman Catholicism, and Joseph Fletcher and Paul Ramsey within Protestantism. The diametrically opposed positions staked out by the last two theologians gave an early signal of the wide range of views that are still expressed by religious thinkers.

Joseph Fletcher advocated expansion of human freedom and control over human reproduction. He portrayed the cloning of hu-

mans as one of many present and prospective reproductive options that could be ethically justified by societal benefit. Indeed, for Fletcher, as a method of reproduction, cloning was preferable to the "genetic roulette" of sexual reproduction. He viewed laboratory reproduction as "radically human" because it is deliberate, designed, chosen, and willed (Fletcher, 1971, 1972, 1974, 1979).

By contrast, Paul Ramsey portrayed the cloning of humans as a "borderline" or moral boundary that could be crossed only at risk of compromise to humanity and to basic concepts of human procreation. Cloning threatened three "horizontal" (person-person) and two "vertical" (person-God) border crossings. First, clonal reproduction would require directed or managed breeding to serve the scientific ends of a controlled gene pool. Second, it would involve nontherapeutic experimentation on the unborn. Third, it would assault the meaning of parenthood by transforming "procreation" into "reproduction" and by severing the unitive end (expressing and sustaining mutual love) and the procreative end of human sexual expression. Fourth, the cloning of humans would express the sin of pride or hubris. Fifth, it could also be considered a sin of self-creation as humans aspire to become a "man-God" (Ramsey, 1966, 1970).

A second era of theological reflection on cloning humans began in 1978, a year that was notable for two events, the birth in Britain of the first IVF baby, Louise Brown, and the publication of David Rorvik's *In His Image,* an account alleging (falsely) the creation of the first cloned human being (Rorvik, 1978).

This period also witnessed the beginning of formal ecclesiastical involvement with questions of genetic manipulation. In 1977 the United Church of Christ produced a study booklet on *Genetic Manipulation,* which appears to be the earliest reference to human cloning among Protestant denominational literature (Lynn, 1977). It provided a general overview of the science and ethics of cloning humans but stopped short of a specific theological verdict.

The discussions of the 1970s continued into the 1980s with par-

ticular attention to IVF, artificial insemination by donor, and surrogacy. These techniques challenged traditional notions of the family by separating genetic and rearing fatherhood and genetic, gestational, and rearing motherhood, as well as raising questions about whether the contractual and commercial ties in many of these arrangements were inimical to traditional religious views of the family.

A third era of religious discussion began in 1993 with the report from George Washington University of the separation of cells in human blastomeres to create multiple, genetically identical embryos. The Roman Catholic Church expressed vigorous opposition to the procedure, and a Vatican editorial denounced the research as "intrinsically perverse." Catholic moral theologians invoked norms of individuality, dignity, and wholeness in condemning this research (McCormick, 1993, 1994). While many Conservative Protestant scholars held that this research contravened basic notions of personhood such as freedom, the sanctity of life, and the image of God, some other Protestant scholars noted its potential medical benefits and advocated careful regulation rather than prohibition.

The fourth and most recent stage of religious discussion has come in the wake of the successful cloning of Dolly the sheep through the somatic cell nuclear transfer technique, as the cloning of a human once again appeared to be a near-term possibility. Several Roman Catholic and Protestant thinkers have reiterated and reinforced past opposition and warnings.

However, some Protestant thinkers, in reflecting on the meaning of human partnership with ongoing divine creative activity, have expressed qualified support for cloning research and for creating children using somatic cell nuclear transfer techniques. Likewise, some Jewish and Islamic thinkers encourage continuing laboratory research on animal models and even laboratory work on the possibility of cloning human beings (only in pursuit of a worthy objective), while expressing deep moral reservations, at least

at this time, about the transfer of a human embryo obtained by nuclear transfer techniques to a womb for purposes of gestation and birth.

Several conclusions emerge from this brief historical overview:

- Over the past twenty-five years, theologians have engaged in repeated discussions of the prospect of cloning humans that anticipate and illuminate much current religious discussion of this topic.
- Theological and ecclesiastical positions on cloning humans are pluralistic in their premises, their modes of argument, and even their conclusions. In short, they exhibit the pluralism characteristic of American religiosity.
- The religious discussion of cloning humans has connected it closely with ongoing debates about technologically assisted reproduction and genetic interventions.
- Despite changes in scientific research and technical capability, the *values* that underlie religious concerns about cloning humans have endured and continue to inform public debate.

Responsible Human Dominion Over Nature

Warnings Not To Play God. As often happens when a powerful new scientific tool is developed, the announcement that mammalian somatic cell nuclear transfer cloning was possible generated strong warnings against "playing God." This slogan is usually invoked as a moral stop sign to some scientific research or medical practice on the basis of one or more of the following distinctions between human beings and God:

- Human beings should not probe the fundamental secrets or mysteries of life, which belong to God.
- Human beings lack the authority to make certain decisions about

the beginning or ending of life. Such decisions are reserved to divine sovereignty.

- Human beings are fallible and also tend to evaluate actions according to their narrow, partial, and frequently self-interested perspectives.
- Human beings do not have the knowledge, especially knowledge of outcomes of actions, attributed to divine omniscience.
- Human beings do not have the power to control the outcomes of actions or processes that is a mark of divine omnipotence.

Even within religious communities, however, the warning against "playing God" may not be considered a sufficient argument against human cloning. Allen Verhey contends that this warning is simply too indiscriminate to provide ethical guidance. Furthermore, it overlooks moral invitations to play God, particularly in the realm of genetics (Verhey, 1995). While agreeing with Ramsey that human beings are not called to "play God," Protestant Ted Peters argues that this does not by itself define what is necessary for us to be human. Hence, we are responsible for using our creativity and freedom (features of the image of God) to forge a destiny more consonant with human dignity. In "playing human," Peters contends, there is no theological reason to leave human nature unchanged, and no theological principles that the cloning of humans necessarily violates (Peters, 1997).

Human Dignity

Appeals to human dignity are prominent in Roman Catholic analyses and assessments of the prospects of human cloning, which base "human dignity" on the creation story and on the Christian account of God's redemption of human beings. The Catholic moral tradition views the cloning of a human being as "a violation of human dignity" (Haas, letter from the Pope John Center, 1997).

Religious thinkers generally do not question whether a person created through cloning is a human being created in God's image. They extend to persons created through cloning the same moral protections that already apply to other persons created in the image of God. For instance, Rabbi Elliot Dorff argues that "[n]o clone may . . . legitimately be denied any of the rights and protections extended to any other child" (Dorff, 1997, p. 5). However, many fear that the human dignity of persons created through cloning will be violated by the denial of such rights and protections, for instance, through enslavement to others and other forms of "man's mastery over man" (Tendler, 1997).

Human cloning would violate human dignity, according to some religious opponents, because it would "jeopardize the personal and unique identity of the clone (or clones) as well as the person whose genome was thus duplicated" (Haas, 1997). This problem does not arise in the case of identical twins, because neither is the "source or maker of the other" (Haas, 1997). Religious concerns about identity and individuality focus mainly on how persons created through cloning will inevitably or possibly be treated, rather than whether such persons are actually unique creatures in God's image. Rejecting genetic determinism, religious thinkers hold that cloning humans would "produce independent human beings with histories and influences all their own and with their own free will" (Dorff, 1997, p. 6). The person created through cloning will be "a new person, an integrated body and mind, with unique experiences." However, it will doubtless be harder for such persons "to establish their own identity and for their creators to acknowledge and respect it" (Dorff, 1997, p. 6). Even for absolute opponents, the process of cloning humans only *violates* human dignity; it does not *diminish* human dignity: "In the cloning of humans there is an affront to human dignity. . . . Yet, in no way is the human dignity of that person [the one who results from cloning] diminished" (Haas, 1997, p. 3).

Sanctity of life is one norm associated with human dignity. For

instance, the prohibition of the shedding of human blood is connected with God's creation of humans in his own image (Genesis 9:6). Opponents often view the cloning of a human as a breach, or at least as a potential breach, of the sanctity of life. In rejecting human cloning, Joseph Cardinal Ratizinger of the Vatican insisted that "the sanctity of [human] life is untouchable" (quoted in Haas, 1997, p. 2). Even those who offer limited support for human cloning, in part on the grounds that it could be used in support of life, argue that it is necessary to set conditions and limits in order to prevent harm to persons who are created through cloning. Not only do they rule out such egregious violations of the sanctity of life as sacrificing persons created through cloning in order to obtain their organs for transplantation, they also worry about what will be done with the "bad results," that is, the "mistakes" that will be inevitable at least in the short term (Dorff, 1997, pp. 3–4). In addition, most recognize that the risks to persons created through cloning are now so unknown that we should virtually rule out human cloning for the present, because those who create children in this manner could not be sure that they are "doing no evil" (Tendler, 1997).

Objectification also represents a fundamental breach of human dignity. To treat persons who are the sources of genetic material for cloning or persons who are created through cloning as mere objects, means, or instruments violates the religious principle of human dignity as well as the secular principle of respect for persons. Cloning humans would necessarily involve objectification, some religious thinkers argue, because it would treat the child as "an object of manipulation" by potentially eliminating the marital act and by attempting "to design and control the very identity of the child" (Haas, 1997). Cloning humans is wrong, in short, because "it subjects human individuals at their most vulnerable, at their very coming-into-being, to the arbitrary whim, power and manipulation of others" (Haas, 1997). For other religious thinkers who accept human cloning under some circumstances, it is necessary to reduce

the effects of objectification, for example, by a commitment to accept and care for the "mistakes" made in cloning (Dorff, 1997).

Objectification can become commodification when commercial and economic forces determine whether and how a person is treated as an object. Religious opponents of human cloning stress that objectification through commodification is a major risk and worry that "economic incentives will control when humans will be cloned" (Cahill, 1997, p. 3). Commodification would deny "the sacred character of human life depicted in the Jewish tradition, transforming it instead to fungible commodities on the human marketplace to be judged by a given person's worth to others" (Dorff, 1997, p. 2).

Procreation and Families

Procreation and Reproduction. In the initial phase of theological debate about cloning humans, Paul Ramsey argued that the covenant of marriage includes the goods of sexual love and procreation, which are divinely ordained and intrinsically related: Human beings have no authority to sever what God had joined together. On this basis, Ramsey, a Protestant, joined with several Roman Catholic moral theologians, such as Bernard Häring and Richard McCormick, in objecting to the cloning of humans as part of the panoply of reproductive technologies. They claimed that such technologies separate the unitive and procreative ends of human sexuality and transform "procreation," which at most puts humans in a role of co-creator, into "reproduction." The Vatican's 1987 *Instruction on Respect for Human Life (Donum Vitae)* rejected human cloning either as a scientific outcome or technical proposal: "Attempts or hypotheses for obtaining a human being without any connection with sexuality through 'twin fission,' cloning, or parthenogenesis are to be considered contrary to the moral law, since they are in opposition to the dignity both of human procreation and of the con-

jugal union" (Congregation for the Doctrine of the Faith, 1987).

A similar critique distinguishes "begetting" (procreating) from "making" (reproducing). According to the Nicene Creed of early Christianity, Jesus, as the authentic image of God and the normative exemplar of personhood, is "begotten, not made" of God. The theological interpretation of "begetting" emphasizes likeness, identity, equality; begetting expresses the parent's very being. By contrast, "making" refers to unlikeness, alienation, and subordination; it expresses the parent's will as a project.

However, many religious thinkers do not accept the sharp separation between begetting and making, because it could rule out various reproductive technologies that they find acceptable, just as many do not accept the absolute connection between unitive and procreative meanings of sexual acts, in part because it would rule out artificial contraception, which they find acceptable. They may, nevertheless, still reject the cloning of humans to create children because they perceive it to be radically different from all other methods of technologically-assisted reproduction. Thus, they may stress the radically new features of human cloning, perhaps even viewing it as a "genuine revolution" in reproduction.

Concerns About the Family. Religious traditions usually approach the cloning of humans to create children from the standpoint of familial relationships and responsibilities rather than from the standpoint of personal rights and individual autonomy. Hence, a primary moral criterion is the impact of cloning humans on the integrity of the family, a concern that includes but also goes beyond the inseparable goods of marriage and the primacy of begetting over making.

Lisa Cahill, a Roman Catholic moral theologian, argues that "the child who is truly the child of a single parent is a genuine revolution in human history, and his or her advent should be viewed with immense caution." She further contends that cloning violates "the essential reality of human family and . . . the nature of the socially related individual within it. We all take part of our identity, both

material or biological and social, from combined ancestral kinship networks. The existing practice of 'donating' gametes when the donors have no intention to parent the resulting child is already an affront to this order of things. But, in such cases, as in cases of adoption where the rearing of a child within its original combined-family network is impossible or undesirable, the child can still in fact claim the dual-lineage origin that characterizes every other human being. Whether socially recognized or not, this kind of ancestry is an important part of the human sense of self (as witnessed by searches for 'biological' parents and families), as well as a foundation of important human relationships." Cloning humans to create children, Cahill concludes, would constitute an "unprecedented rupture in those biological dimensions of embodied humanity which have been most important for social cooperation" (Cahill, testimony, 1997). At the extreme, cloning humans would not only free human reproduction from marital and male-female relationships, but would "allow for the emancipation of human reproduction from *any* relationship" (Mohler, 1997).

Concerns about lineage and intergenerational relations in other religious traditions also set limits on or challenge the cloning of humans to create children. For example, Islamic scholar Abdulaziz Sachedina suggests that Islam could accept some therapeutic uses of human cloning "as long as the lineage of the child remains religiously unblemished" (Sachedina, 1997, pp. 6–7). And some Jewish thinkers worry that cloning humans may diminish the ethic of responsibility because of changed roles (father, mother, child) and relationships (spousal, parental, filial).

Assessments of Acts and Public Policies

Religious perspectives on public policies regarding human cloning vary for several reasons. One critical factor is whether the tradition views every possible act of cloning humans as intrinsically evil (as,

for example, Roman Catholicism does) or whether it recognizes that cloning humans could conceivably be justified in some circumstances, however few they may be (as, for example, many in the Jewish tradition do). The Roman Catholic tradition argues that the very *use* of cloning techniques to create human beings is contrary to human dignity: "One may not use, even for a single instance, a means for achieving a good purpose which intrinsically is morally flawed" (Haas, 1997, p. 4). And, for that tradition, creating a child through human cloning is intrinsically morally flawed. Some thinkers in other traditions also hold that such an action is always morally wrong, whatever good might come from it (see Meilaender, 1997).

By contrast, some other religious thinkers believe that cloning a human to create a child could be religiously and morally acceptable under certain conditions. They may view the technology as "morally neutral" (Dorff, 1997) and then consider which uses are morally justified; or they may oppose human cloning from matured (differentiated) cells except in the most exceptional circumstances and then identify those exceptional circumstances.

Two hypothetical scenarios are quite common. The first one involves cloning a sterile person to create a child. Rabbi Tendler poses the case of "a young man who is sterile, whose family was wiped out in the Holocaust, and [who] is the last of a genetic line." Rabbi Tendler says "I would certainly clone him" (Tendler, 1997, transcript, p. 35). The debate about this type of case hinges in part on different views of infertility. The Jewish tradition often views infertility as an "illness" and thus brings it under the responsibility to heal. According to others, for example, some in the Protestant tradition, the problem of infertility is not serious enough to warrant research into or actual human cloning (see Duff, 1997, p. 5).

A second case involves cloning a person who has a serious and perhaps fatal disease and needs a compatible source of biological material, such as bone marrow. Rabbi Dorff, for instance, holds that it would be "legitimate from a moral and a Jewish point of view"

to clone a person with leukemia with the intent of transplanting bone marrow from the created child as long as the "parents" intend to raise the child as they would raise any other child (Dorff, 1997, pp. 4–5; see also Tendler, 1997). Some Protestants concur on this case, even when they reject the first type of case (see Duff, 1997, p. 4). Those who consider the second type of case justifiable rule out destruction or abandonment of the created child, as well as the imposition of serious risks of harm. Indeed, acceptance of either type of hypothetical case—as well as a third type of case involving the cloning of a dying child—presupposes that the procedure is safe for the child created by cloning. Other conditions include the protection of the created child's rights and the lack of acceptable alternatives to cloning persons in such cases.

Those who view cloning humans as intrinsically wrong may also respond sympathetically and compassionately to people's suffering when they are infertile or have a disease that brings death or disability. However, they usually hold that the good of overcoming this suffering does not justify cloning humans: Cloning "is entirely unsuitable for human procreation even for exceptional circumstances" (Haas, 1997, p. 4). Indeed, religious critics may view the exceptional circumstances featured in the cases as "temptations" to be resisted (see Meilaender, 1997, p. 5).

Some rough correlations hold between evaluations of particular cases and proposals for public policy. Religious thinkers who view the cloning of a human being as intrinsically wrong, i.e., wrong in and of itself, under any and all circumstances, tend to support a permanent ban on cloning humans through legislative and other means. Any use of cloning technology to create a human child abuses that technology, which is, however, acceptable in animal reproduction. By contrast, religious thinkers who hold that, in some conceivable circumstances, it could be morally justifiable to clone a person to create a child tend to support public policies that regulate the procedure, with varying restrictions, or that ban the procedure for the time being or until certain conditions are met. In

assessing public policies, this second group is particularly concerned to prevent potential abuses of the technology in cloning humans rather than condemning all uses.

Most religious thinkers who recommend public policies on cloning humans propose either a ban or restrictive regulation. A few examples will suffice. On March 6, 1997, the Christian Life Commission of the Southern Baptist Convention issued a resolution entitled "Against Human Cloning," which supported President Clinton's decision to prohibit federal funding for human-cloning research and requested "that the Congress of the United States make human cloning unlawful." The resolution also called on "all nations of the world to make efforts to prevent the cloning of any human being."

The Vatican's 1987 *Instruction on Respect for Human Life (Donum Vitae)* argued for a legal prohibition of human cloning, as well as many other reproductive technologies. Official Roman Catholic statements since that time have condemned nontherapeutic research on human embryos and human cloning and have called on governments around the world to enact prohibitive legislation. Most recently, in the wake of the cloning of Dolly, a Vatican statement reiterated the basic teaching of *Donum Vitae:* "A person has the right to be born in a human way. It is to be strongly hoped that states . . . will immediately pass a law that bans the application of cloning of humans and that in the face of pressures, they have the force to make no concessions."

By contrast, Rabbi Elliot Dorff argues that "human cloning should be regulated, not banned." He holds that "the Jewish demand that we do our best to provide healing makes it important that we take advantage of the promise of cloning to aid us in finding cures for a variety of diseases and in overcoming infertility." However, "the dangers of cloning . . . require that it be supervised and restricted." More specifically, "cloning should be allowed only for medical research or therapy; the full and equal status of clones with other fetuses or human beings must be recognized, with the

equivalent protections guarded; and careful policies must be devised to determine how cloning mistakes will be identified and handled" (Dorff, 1997). Although Dorff stresses legislation, particularly to regulate privately funded research, he recognizes that legislation will be only partially effective, and for that reason calls for increased attention to hospital ethics committees and institutional review boards, in part because of the self-regulation involved. Hence, although legislation is important "to ban the most egregious practices," most supervision "should come from self-regulation akin to what we already have in palce for experiments on human subjects" (Dorff, 1997, p. 15).

Conclusions

The wide variety of religious traditions and beliefs epitomizes the pluralism of American culture. Moreover, religious perspectives on cloning humans differ in fundamental premises, modes of reasoning, and conclusions. As a result, there is no single "religious" view on cloning humans, any more than for most moral issues in biomedicine. Nevertheless, discourse on many contested issues in biomedicine still proceeds across religious traditions, as well as secular traditions. Specifically with regard to cloning humans to create children, some religious thinkers believe that this technology could have some legitimate uses and thus could be justified under some circumstances if perfected; however, they may argue for regulation because of the danger of abuses or even for a ban, perhaps temporary, in light of concerns about safety. Other religious thinkers deny that this technology has any legitimate uses, contending that it always violates fundamental moral norms, such as human dignity. Such thinkers often argue for a legislative ban on all cloning of humans to create children. Finally, religious communities and thinkers draw on ancient and diverse traditions of moral reflection to ad-

dress the cloning of humans, a subject they have debated off and on over the last thirty years. For some, fundamental religious beliefs and norms provide a clear negative answer: It is now and will continue to be wrong to clone a human. Others, however, hold that more reflection is needed, given new scientific and technological developments, to determine exactly how to interpret and evaluate the prospect of human cloning in light of fundamental religious convictions and norms.

References

Cahill, L. S., "Cloning: Religion-Based Perspectives," Testimony before the National Bioethics Advisory Commission, March 13, 1997.

Congregation for the Doctrine of the Faith, *Instruction on Respect for Human Life in Its Origin and on the Dignity of Procreation* (Rome, 1987).

Dorff, R. E. N., "Human Cloning: A Jewish Perspective," Testimony before the National Bioethics Commission, March 14, 1997.

Duff, N. J., "Theological Reflections on Human Cloning," Testimony presented to the National Bioethics Advisory Commission, March 13, 1997.

Fletcher, J., *Humanhood: Essays in Biomedical Ethics* (Buffalo, NY: Prometheus Books, 1979).

Fletcher, J., *The Ethics of Genetic Control* (Garden City, NY: Anchor Press, 1974).

Fletcher, J., "New beginnings in human life: A theologian's response," *The New Genetics and the Future of Man,* M. Hamilton (ed.) (Grand Rapids, MI: Wm. B. Eerdmans Publishing Company, 1972, 78–79).

Fletcher, J., "Ethical aspects of genetics controls," *New England Journal of Medicine* 285(14):776–783, 1971.

Haas, J. M., letter from the Pope John Center, submitted to the National Bioethics Advisory Commission, March 31, 1997.

Lynn, B., *Genetic Manipulation* (New York: Office for Church in Society, United Church of Christ, 1977).

McCormick, R. A., "Blastomere separation: Some concerns," *Hastings Center Report* 24(2):14–16, 1994.

McCormick, R. A., "Should we clone humans?," *The Christian Century* 17–24:1148–1149, November 1993.

Meilaender, G. C., Testimony before the National Bioethics Advisory Commission, March 13, 1997.

Mohler, R. A., "The Brave New World of Cloning: A Christian Worldview Perspective," (unpublished manuscript, March 1997).

Peters, T., *Playing God? Genetic Discrimination and Human Freedom* (New York: Routledge, 1997).

Ramsey, P., "Moral and Religious Implications of Genetic Control," *Genetics and the Future of Man,* John D. Roslansky (ed.) (New York: Appleton-Century-Croffs, 1966).

Ramsey, P., *Fabricated Man: The Ethics of Genetic Control* (New Haven: Yale University Press, 1970).

Rorvik, D., *In His Image: The Cloning of a Man* (Philadelphia: J.B. Lippincott Company, 1978).

Sachedina, A., "Islamic Perspectives on Cloning," Testimony before the National Bioethics Advisory Commission, March 14, 1997.

Tendler, R. M., Testimony before the National Bioethics Advisory Commission, March 14, 1997.

Verhey, A., "Playing God and invoking a perspective," *Journal of Medicine and Philosophy* 20:347–364, 1995.

This is an abridged version of chapter 3 of NBAC report on human cloning (June 1997). Much of the material in the original version is derived from a commissioned paper prepared for the National Bioethics Advisory Commission by Courtney S. Campbell, Department of Philosophy, Oregon State University, titled "Religious Perspectives on Human Cloning."

To Clone or Not to Clone

Jean Bethke Elshtain

Cloning is upon us. The techno-enthusiasts in our midst celebrate the collapse of yet another barrier to human mastery and control. But for most of us, this is an extraordinarily unsettling development. Talk to the man and woman in the street and you hear murmurs and rumblings and much dark musing about portents of the end-times and "now we've gone too far." The airwaves and the street win this one hands down, a welcome contrast to the celebratory glitz of *USA Today* trumpeting "Hello Dolly!"—Dolly being the name of the fetching ewe that faced the reader straight-on in a front page color photo announcing her cloned arrival. The subhead read, "Sheep cloning prompts ethical debate." The sheep looked perfectly normal, of course, and not terribly exercised about her historic significance. That she was really the child of no one—no one's little lamb—will probably not haunt her nights and bedevil her days. But we—we humans—should be haunted, by Dolly and all the Dollies to come and by the prospect that others are to appear on this earth as the progeny of our omnipotent striving, our yearning to create without pausing to reflect on what we are destroying.

When I pondered cloning initially, a Chicago Bulls game was on television. The Bulls were clobbering the Spurs. Michael Jordan had just performed a typically superhuman feat, an assist that suggested he has eyes in the back of his head and two sets of arms. To one

buoyant citizen—a rare optimist among the worriers—who called a local program to register his two cents worth on cloning, the prospect of "more Michael Jordans" made the whole "cloning thing" worthwhile. "Can you imagine a whole basketball team of Michael Jordans?" he queried giddily. Unfortunately, I could. It seemed to me then and seems to me now a nightmare. If there were basketball teams fielding Jordans against Jordans, we wouldn't be able to recognize the one, the only, Michael Jordan. It's rather like suggesting that forty Mozarts are better than one. But there would be no Mozart were there forty Mozarts. We know the singularity of the one; the extraordinary genius—a Jordan, a Mozart—because they stand apart from and above the rest. Absent that irreducible singularity, their gifts and glorious, soaring accomplishments would come to mean nothing as they would have become the norm, just commonplace. Another dunk; another concerto. In fact, lots of callers made this point, or one similar to it, reacting to the Michael Jordon Clontopia scenario.

A research librarian at a small college in Indiana, who had driven me to her campus for the purpose of delivering a lecture, offered a spontaneous, sustained, and troubled critique of cloning that rivals the best dystopian fictions. Her cloning nightmare was a veritable army of Hitlers, ruthless and remorseless bigots and killers who kept reproducing themselves and were one day able to finish what the historic Hitler failed to accomplish. It occurred to me that an equal number of Mother Theresas would probably not be a viable deterrent, not if the Hitler clones were behaving like, well, Hitlers.

But I had my own nightmare scenario to offer. Imagine, I suggested to my librarian driver, a society that clones human beings to serve as spare parts. Because the cloned entities are not fully human, our moral queasiness could be disarmed and we could "harvest" organs to our heart's content—and organs from human beings of every age, race, phenotype at that. Harvesting organs from anencephalic newborns would, in that new world, be the

equivalent of the Model T—an early and, it turns out, very rudimentary prototype of glorious, gleaming things to come.

Far-fetched? No longer. Besides, often the far-fetched gets us nearer the truth of the matter than all the cautious, persnickety pieces that fail to come anywhere close to the pity and terror this topic evokes. Consider Stanislaw Lem's *The Star Diaries,* in which his protagonist, Ijon Tichy, described as a "hapless Candide of the Cosmos," ventures into space encountering one weird situation after another. Lem's "Thirteenth Voyage" takes him to a planet, Panta, where he runs afoul of local custom and is accused of the worst of crimes, "the crime of personal differentiation." The evidence against him is incriminating. Nonetheless, Tichy is given an opportunity to conform. A planet spokesman offers a peroration to Tichy concerning the benefits of his planet, on which there are no separate entities—"only the collective."

For the denizens of Panta have come to understand that the source of all "the cares, sufferings and misfortunes to which beings, gathered together in societies, are prone" lies in the individual, "in his private identity." The individual, by contrast to the collective, is "characterized by uncertainty, indecision, inconsistency of action, and above all—by impermanence." Having "completely eliminated individuality," on planet Panta they have achieved "the highest degree of social interchangeability." It works rather the way the Marxist utopia was to function. Everyone at any moment can be anything else. Functions or roles are interchangeable. On Panta you occupy a role for twenty-four hours only: one day a gardener, the next an engineer, then a mason, now a judge.

The same principle holds with families. "Each is composed of relatives—there's a father, mother, children. Only the functions remain constant; the ones who perform them are changed every day." All feelings and emotions are entirely abstract. One never needs to grieve or to mourn as everyone is infinitely replaceable. "Affection, respect, love where at one time gnawed by constant anxiety, by the fear of losing the person held dear. This dread we

have conquered. For in point of fact whatever upheavals, diseases or calamities may be visited upon us, we shall always have a father, a mother, a spouse, and children." As well, there is no "I." And there can be no death "where there are no individuals. We do not die." Tichy can't quite get with the program. Brought before a court, he is "found guilty and condemned to life identification." He blasts off and sets his course for Earth.

Were Lem writing an addendum for his brilliant tale, he might show Tichy landing, believing he is at last on terra firma in both the literal and metaphorical sense, only to discover that the greeting party at the rocket-port is a bit strange: There are forty very tall basketball players all in identical uniforms wearing No. 23 jerseys, on one side and, on the other, forty men in powdered wigs, suited up in breeches and satin frock coats and playing identical pieces on identical harpsichords. Wrong planet? No more.

Sure, it's amusing, up to a point. But it was anything but amusing to overhear the speculation that cloning might be made available to parents about to lose a child to leukemia or, having lost a child to an accident, in order that they might reproduce and replace that lost child. This image borders on an obscenity. Perhaps we need a new word to describe what it represents, to capture fully what order of things the cloning of children in order to forestall human loss and grief violates. We say to little Tommy, in effect: "Sorry to lose you. But Tommy 2 is waiting in the wings." And what of Tommy 2? What happens when he learns he is the pinch hitter? "There was an earlier Tommy, much loved, so Mommy and Daddy had a copy made." But it isn't really Mommy and Daddy—it's the two people who placed the order for him and paid a huge sum. He's their little product; little fabricated Tommy 2, a techno-orphan. And Tommy 1 lies in the grave unmourned; undifferentiated in death; unremembered because he had been copied and his individuality wrenchingly obliterated.

The usual nostrums are of no use here. I have in mind the standard cliché that, once again, our "ethical thinking" hasn't caught up

with technological "advance." This is a flawed way to reflect on cloning and so much else. The problem is not that we must somehow catch our ethics up to our technology. The problem is that technology is rapidly gutting our ethics. And it is *our* ethics. Ethical reflection belongs to all of us—all those agitated radio callers—and it is the fears and apprehension of ordinary citizens that should be paid close and respectful attention. The ethicists are cut from the same cloth as everybody else. They breathe the same cultural air. They, too, are children of the West, of Judaism, Catholicism, the Renaissance, the Reformation, the Enlightenment. In the matter of cloning, we cannot wait for the experts. The queasiness the vast majority of Americans feel at this "remarkable achievement" is appropriate and should be aired and explored fully.

Perhaps something remarkable will finally happen. We will put the genie back into the bottle for a change. We will say, "No, stop, we will not go down this road." This doesn't make us antiscience or antiprogress or stodgy sticks-in-the-mud. It makes us skeptical, alert, and, yes, frightened citizens asking the question: Whatever will become of the ancient prayer, "That I may see my children's children and peace upon Israel," in a world of cloned entities, peopled by the children of No Body, copies of our selves? These poor children of our fantasies and our drive to perfect and our arrogant search for dominion: What are we to say to them? Forgive us, for we knew not what we were doing? That tastes bitter on the tongue. We knew what we were doing and we did it anyway. Of whom will we ask forgiveness? Who will be there to listen? Who to absolve?

Are these the musings of an alarmist, a technophobe, a Luddite? Consider that there are now cloned calves in Wisconsin and cloned rodents in various laboratories worldwide. Cloned company is bursting out all over: thus far none of it human. The clone enthusiasts will surely find a way, however. Dolly's creator or producer or manufacturer—hard to know what to call him—thinks human cloning is a bad idea. But others are not nearly so reticent. Consider, then, some further developments on the cloning and related

fronts that promise, or threaten, to alter our relation to our bodies, our selves.

A big story of the moment—and a huge step toward human cloning—lies in the fertile field of infertility science: the world of human reproductive technology. Many procedures once considered radical are by now routine. These include in vitro fertilization, embryo flushing, surrogate embryo transfer, and sex preselection, among others. Now comes Dr. Mark Sauer, described by the *New York Times* as "an infertility expert at Columbia Presbyterian Medical Center in New York" who "dreams of offering his patients a type of cloning some day." It would work like this. You take a two- or three-day-old human embryo and use its cells—there are only about eight at this stage—to grow identical embryos where once there was only one. The next step is to implant "some" of these embryos in a woman's uterus immediately and freeze the extras. And what are the plans for the clonettes in cold storage? Well, initial attempts at impregnation may fail. So you have some spare embryos for a second, third, or fourth try. Suppose the woman successfully carries the initial implants to term. She may want more babies—identical babies—and the embryos are there for future use. The upshot, of course, is that a woman could wind up with "identical twins, triplets, or even quadruplets, possibly born years apart."

And why would anyone want this, considering the potentially shattering questions it presents to the identity and integrity of the children involved? Dr. Sauer has an answer. Otherwise there "might be no babies at all." To be sure, the premise of this procedure isn't as obviously morally repugnant as the scenario noted above, the speculation that cloning might be made available to parents about to lose a child to leukemia or, having lost a child to an accident, in order that they might reproduce and replace that child, as I noted already.

Rather, the debate about this latest embryo cloning scenario, by contrast, rages around whether or not this is, in fact, cloning at all or whether it is a version of cloning that is more or less question-

able than the standard or classic form: the Dolly scenario. Dr. Sauer and other enthusiasts say that because cloning is a "politically dirty word"—there is, apparently, no real ethical issue here—they hope that their proposed method of crypto-cloning may slip under the radar screen. Besides, he avers, it's much better for the women involved: You don't have to give them lots of drugs to "force their ovaries to pump out multiple eggs so that they could fertilize them and create as many embryos as possible."

Again, why are so many women putting themselves through this? And why has this been surrounded by the halo of "rights"? You can be sure, once word gets around, that the more "attractive" idea (in the words of another infertility specialist) of replicating embryos will generate political demands. A group will spring up proclaiming "embryo duplication rights" just as an outfit emerged instantly after Dolly was announced arguing that to clone oneself was a fundamental right. Several of the infertility specialists cited in the *Times* piece, all male doctors, interestingly enough, spoke of the pleading of women, of "the misery my patients are living through." But surely a good bit of that misery comes from having expectations lifted out of all proportion in relation to chances of success (with procedures like in vitro), only to find, time and time again, that the miracle of modern medicine has turned into an invasive, expensive, mind-bending, heart-rending dud. A doleful denouement to high-tech generated expectations and the playing out of "reproductive freedom."

Whatever happened to accepting embodied limits with better grace? There are many ways to enact what the late Erik Erikson called "generative" projects and lives. Biological parenthood is one but not the only one. Many of the women we call great from our own history—I think here of one of my own heroes—Jane Addams of Hull-House—were not mothers although they did an extraordinary amount of mothering. Either through necessity or choice, she and many others offered their lives in service to civic or religious projects that located them in a world of relationships over the

years with children not their own that involved loving concern, care, friendship, nurture, protection, discipline, pride, disappointment: all the complex virtues, habits, and emotions called forth by biological parenting.

And there is adoption, notwithstanding the frustrations many encounter and the fear instilled by such outrageous violations of decency as the holding in the "Baby Richard" and other recent cases in which children were wrenched from the only family they had ever known in order to be returned to a bio-parent claimant who had discovered belatedly the overwhelming need to be a father or mother. How odd that biology now trumps nearly all other claims and desires. In several texts I've encountered recently, adoption is surrounded with a faintly sinister odor and treated as an activity not all that different from baby selling. Somehow all these developments—the insistent urge to reproduce through any means necessary and the emergence of a multimillion-dollars-a-year specialty devoted to precisely that task; the diminution of the integrity of adoption in favor of often dubious claims from bio-parents; the possibility, now, of cloning embryos in order to guarantee more or less identical offspring to a desperate couple—are linked.

What common threads tie these disparate activities together? How does one account for the fact that the resurgence of feminism over the past thirty years and enhanced pressures on women, many of them placed on women by themselves, to reproduce biologically have emerged in tandem? Why are these developments surrounded by such a desperate aura and a sense of misery and failure—including the failure of many marriages that cannot survive the tumult of infertility high-tech medicine's intrusion into a couple's intimate lives? Let's try out one possible explanation. Here at the end of the twentieth century we all care mightily about identity: who we are. Sometimes this takes the form of identity politics in which one's own identity gets submerged into that of a group, likely a group defined in biological or quasi-biological terms on grounds of sex, race, or ethnicity. That's problematic enough as a

basis for politics, to say the least. But we've further compounded the biological urgencies, upping the ante to bear one's "own" child as a measure of the success or failure of the self.

Mind you, I do not want to downplay how heartbreaking it is for many couples who want to have a baby and cannot. But, again, there are many ways to parent and many babies desperate for loving families. Rather than to expand our sense of gracious acceptance of those who may not be our direct biological offspring, which means accepting our own limits but coming to see that these open up other possibilities, we rail against cruel fate and reckon ourselves nigh-worthless persons if we fail biologically. Perhaps with so much up for grabs, in light of the incessant drumbeat to be all we can be, to achieve, to produce, to succeed, to define our own projects, to be the sole creators of our own destinies, we have fallen back on the bedrock of biology. When all that is solid is melting into air, maybe biology seems the last redoubt of solidity, of identity. But, of course, this is chimerical. In demanding of our bodies what they sometimes cannot give, our world grows smaller, our focus more singular if not obsessive, and identity itself is called into question: our own and that of our future, identical offspring.

This article appeared, in slightly different form, as "The Hard Questions: Our Bodies, Our Clones," in the *New Republic,* August 4, 1997, pages 25 and following.

Human Cloning and the Public Realm: A Defense of Intuitions of the Good

David Tracy

The Dilemma

In 1947 a surprising discovery was made: The United Nations, in its desire to enlist cross-cultural agreements on basic human rights, appointed a committee of ethical, political, and religious thinkers to determine what rights did cross-cultures have and for what ethical, political, metaphysical, or religious reasons. A consensus on certain basic human, civic, and political rights emerged. But there proved to be no way for any philosopher to win agreement on anything like a common ethical, political, metaphysical, or religious answer to the question of *why* the most basic human rights were just that: basic human rights. Fortunately, the U.N. Declaration on Human Rights (1948) was passed anyway. Liberals agreed—but for their own ethical-political reasons; the same with Marxists, conservatives, and radicals. Jews and Christians, Muslims, Buddhists, Hindus, Taoists, Confucianists, and peoples of several indigenous religions found it possible to agree with the practical list of basic human rights—but each for their own ethical, metaphysical, or religious reasons. Desperate as the situations on human rights remain in many places of our globe (e.g., China, Sudan, North Korea, etc.) we are all far better off for that earlier U.N. Declaration on Human Rights even if a more far-ranging consensus on

the fundamental ethical reasons for those rights is still lacking—and is likely to remain lacking for the foreseeable future. At least the torturers may sleep a little less easily; at least some of the torture, false imprisonments, assaults on ethnic, racial, gender, civic, religious, and individual rights have been slowed down, although clearly not halted. At least there is a consensus document that all relevant parties agreed upon and can be held accountable to.

Many philosophers and ethicists at the time (including several who participated in the writing of the document, such as Jacques Maritain) lamented their failure to reach any common agreement on the reasons why certain human rights were indeed basic. Almost fifty years later, there is still no agreement on *why* certain rights are the most basic human rights. Does anyone seriously think that any agreement could possibly be achieved today on the much more complex ethical issues at stake in the present debate on human cloning? After all, that debate demands reflection not just on human rights but on every meaning of what constitutes an authentic human being. Is it possible in our situation, so much more pluralistic, complex, and global than that of 1948, to hope for any consensus at all this time, even on the practical step needed: a ban? a moratorium? research full speed ahead? The only serious hope is to increase the range of conversation-partners to the discussion: first, to educate ourselves as best we nonscientists can in the complex scientific procedures, techniques, and facts involved (here the media—at least the major print media—have performed admirably to inform us in lay terms); second, to endorse President Clinton's charge to his commission that all informed parties should join in the discussion.

Any philosophical, ethical, or religious individual or tradition that can help focus the discussion on human cloning by rendering available the ethical resources of their traditions should be welcome to this crucial and unavoidable discussion. None of us, to be sure, will be much aided by those familiar factions, secular and re-

ligious alike, who continue to function like "certainty-factories" with their quick, ready-made pronouncements based on clear and distinct ideas and very few of them.

If ever there was an issue that demanded both a sense for intellectual complexity and ethical ambiguity, human cloning is that issue. For somehow we must find a way together to go back to where the debates on human rights left off, in the hope of uncovering our most basic intuitions of what we ultimately believe to be human. We must be willing to force ourselves to try to articulate our basic moral feelings, emotions, intuitions on the human. What Albert Einstein famously said about the atomic age—"Everything has changed except our thinking"—is even more true on the issues raised by human cloning. How can we think well and responsibly without hearing all the voices and traditions that deserve to be heard?

Any reading of the growing literature on the possibility of human cloning (President Clinton's clear and surprisingly strong statement, his commission's first report, the many institutional or individual essays of the last year) shows that there is clearly no real consensus. Possibly there never will be. But there is enough consensus, I believe, on certain shared deeply troubling questions and moral intuitions raised.

1. Do we really want the emerging biotechnology, so overwhelming in both its promise and threat for the future, to proceed without serious ethical reflection? Clearly no. The danger is not technology nor biotechnology; the danger is an emerging market-driven biotechnocracy that is as dangerous (because it is as unthinking) as any other totality system of the past.

2. Do we acknowledge that in the emerging global monoculture every significant human cultural difference and otherness may be destroyed as the quiet regimes of economic and political power (indeed more the economic than the political) find ever more effective market strategies to enforce the rule of what Michael Foucault nicely called the reign of "more of the same"? Human cloning

certainly sounds like the ultimate contribution to an undesirable monoculture.

3. Are we not justly alarmed at the disturbing lack of agreement on some basic ethical understanding of what constitutes a human person as human? If the global market alone dictates the future on human cloning, the answers to this question will eventually drown out every other voice. As many of our most serious social critics have argued, we are already too inflicted by "possessive individualism." Would human beings desire to become what we have already made of the nonhuman world: manufactured and marketable commodities?

4. Does not the present debate have the danger of excluding sufficient reflection on the increasing gap between the rich and powerful countries and the poor and relatively powerless ones? If we already have a situation where the poor of the world sometimes have few options except to sell body organs for the health of the rich, where would the realities of human cloning take us? Would it become (as it easily could if only the market decides) a new luxury item for the rich, the beautiful, the talented, the famous?

5. On the other hand, opponents of human cloning (as I am) cannot afford to ignore the benefits that such cloning *might* provide for all humankind, for example, in helping to control or eliminate some genetic diseases, or as a possibility needed in some extreme situations such as the only viable alternative to survival if some literally uncontrollable virus were let loose on the globe? Or yet more speculatively, the late Carl Sagan is persuasive that it is more probable than not that there is intelligent life elsewhere in the universe. What if, in the future, the only way to contact those "others," given the limitations of our present bodies, was to devise new human bodies for the presently inconceivable journey to other galaxies? However, as several scientific commentators have observed, science may be able, with research already in progress, to solve some, if not all, of these dilemmas without crossing the moral

chasm of human cloning. Is that the case? What should we do if it were not the case?

President Clinton's commission is clearly wise to call for at least a moratorium on human cloning until the scientific facts are clear and the ethical consequences are widely discussed. Now the pressing issue is how to discuss these matters in a public way.

The Public Realm: Arguments and Intuitions of Human Goods

Consider the contemporary discussion of the nature of publicness itself. In a pluralist culture, it is important to know what will and will not count as public—that is, available to all intelligent, reasonable, and responsible members of that culture despite their otherwise crucial differences in belief and practice. A public realm assumes that there is the possibility of discussion (argument, conversation) among all participants. The only hope for such discussion in a radically pluralist culture is one based on reason. But today to state that reason is the solution is to restate the problem of publicness, not to resolve it.

At least this much seems clear on what seems to constitute a public realm. To produce public discourse is to provide reasons for one's assertions. To provide reasons is to render one's claims shareable and public. To provide reasons is to be willing to engage in argument. Argument is the most obvious form of public discourse. To engage in argument is minimally to make claims and to give the warrants and backings for those claims.

The move to explicit argument is the most obvious way to ensure publicness. If there is a public realm at all, this means at least that there is a space where argument is not merely allowed but demanded of all participants. This means, as well, that truth in the public realm will be fundamentally a matter of consensus—a consensus of the community of inquiry cognizant of and guided by the criteria and evidence of whatever the particular subject matter

under discussion demands. A community of inquiry must be democratic, even radically egalitarian, in the most fundamental sense: the sense that no one can be accorded privileged status in an argument; all are in principle equal; all are bound to produce and yield to evidence, warrants, backing. Any emerging consensus must be a consensus responsible to the best argument on both the scientific and ethical questions at stake.

The first responsibility of the public realm, therefore, is the responsibility to give reasons, to provide arguments—to be public. Argument has traditionally been, and must remain the primary candidate for publicness. And yet there is a second candidate as well: one related to, yet distinct from argument itself. That candidate is an inquiry into various intuitions of the good, including those expressed in art and religion.

Religions, for example, characteristically provide responses to questions at the limits of human argument and even human experience. These religious questions—these limit-questions, if you will—remain relatively stable across the wide and often conflicting responses of the religions. Since we do not really receive answers to questions we have never asked, it is important to find disciplined ways to formulate the peculiar kinds of questions, experiences, and intuitions to which religions typically appeal. Indeed, such questions abound for any thoughtful person: What, if anything, is the meaning of the whole? What, if any, is the significance of such positive experiences as a fundamental trust empowering the fact that we continue to go on at all, or such negative experiences as a fundamental anxiety in the face of no specific object (No-thing) as distinct from fear in the face of some specific object? What is our primordial intuitive response to finitude, to contingency, to mortality, to radical oppression or alienation, to joy, love, wonder, and those strange experiences mystics describe as a consolation without a cause? What do we ultimately feel, sense, intuit, think that a human being is as human?

What is the meaning of the fact that our best reflective enter-

prises seem to disclose limits at the edge of their argumentative inquiry which can seem to suggest some other dimension, perhaps even some glimpse of the character of the whole: the realization, for example, that some intelligible order must exist in order for scientific inquiry to function at all; the disturbing question of why be moral at all at the very limit of all our moral convictions? We may reasonably call all such genuinely religious questions "limit-questions."

To choose the category "limit" to describe the kind of questions that religions address is to recall, of course, Kant's definition of limit as "that which can be thought but not known." Insofar as we try to describe what can be thought but not known, we do not need to insist that the discussion employ the Western religious term of "God" or the Western philosophical category of the "Absolute." We can choose, as I did above, the more flexible and admittedly more vague category of "the whole" and thus find at least some initial way to use the Western category of "limit" without precluding its use for the intuitions on the whole of non-Western religions as well. To be able to sense some intuition of the whole, even when we cannot know the whole, suggests anew, as Emerson saw so clearly, the call within any reasonable person to allow for distinct modes of inquiry upon all human limit-experiences and limit-questions.

If we are willing to risk an interpretation of the religions for a discussion of basic intuitions on the good, moreover, we must also acknowledge that the risk is inevitably great. For the religious phenomenon is a deeply ambiguous phenomenon in human thought and history. It is likely to remain so. Religion is cognitively ambiguous as necessarily approached and expressed indirectly (e.g., through limit-language). That cognitive ambiguity often yields positive, if often indirect and symbolic, intuitive fruit for thought and life—as does religion's most natural analogue, art. Yet that cognitive ambiguity can also yield such negative intellectual fruits as ir-

rationality, obscurantism, and mystification with their attendant intellectual and ethical damage.

Religions release not only great creative possibilities for the good in individuals, societies, and whole cultures; religions also release frightening, even demonic realities—as the history of religion in any culture shows. And yet this cognitive and ethical ambiguity of religion, with its disclosure of the true and the false, the good and the evil, even the "beyond good and evil" possibilities of the holy, should be sufficient evidence to warrant the belief that religions are crucial phenomena for all in the public realm to risk interpreting. In the discussion on human cloning we should interpret religions as fundamentally intuitions and visions of the good. Thus interpreted, the religions could teach much about some of our most basic intuitions on a possibly shared humanity, especially on the central question of what constitutes a human being as human. That question eventually becomes a question not solely of rights (as it must be) but of some visions of the human good.

The kind of cultural pluralism that already exists in the contemporary public realm is matched by a similar pluralism in contemporary religion and art, in their sometimes complementary, sometimes conflicting intuitions and visions of the human good. In principle, pluralism is an enriching, not an impoverishing reality. In fact, pluralism is often an unnerving reality. For unless we learn to converse better and argue more clearly with one another on how to provide better descriptions of and reflection upon our distinct visions of the human good, we are all in danger of allowing the promise of cultural and religious pluralism to slide into a kind of Will Rogers pluralism—one where you never met an opinion you didn't like. Any responsible pluralist has met unacceptable opinions and intuitions and, when pressed, should be able to state clearly just why this opinion is wrong. As Isaiah Berlin, one of the great defenders of pluralism in politics and culture, once observed, a responsible pluralist will always be able to tell the better from the

good and the good from the bad and the downright awful. That is the kind of pluralism needed for a public discussion on intuitions and visions of the human good when facing the communal questions and unavoidable practical communal decisions demanded by the debate on the possibility of human cloning.

Religions as Intuitive Visions of the Good

Any contemporary discussion of intuitions, feelings, and visions of the good that will bear public use must be articulated with as much philosophical care as the subject matter allows. This is even more the case, as Hans Jonas argued, in a situation where technology has so great a role in forming and transforming our personal and societal intuitions, feelings, and visions of the good for human beings. Two great resources for discussing some of our most basic intuitions of the good are clearly art and religion, both read here as expressions, personal and communal, of intuitions and visions of the human good.

The difficulties for a fruitful discussion are, however, also quite clear: (1) Given the increasing power of the techno-economic realm (i.e., technological innovations driving and driven by the global market economy), even "reason" can become merely technical reason, that is, capable of careful formal arguments on efficient means and, at its substantive best, on rights and procedures. But how does reason, thus narrowed, discuss, as it once did, not merely means but ends—including intuition of ends as a human good? Even defenders of the pluralistic democratic liberal theory for society (as I am) can become alarmed that the discussion of "goods," not merely "rights," is relatively impoverished in modern liberal political theory. Some of the contemporary debate on cloning sometimes reads as if the hands are still the hands of John Stuart Mill but the unintended and subconscious voice is that of Dr. Mengele.

There must be better ways to visions of the human good than most liberal democratic theory presently allows. If reason is rendered merely technical, art is sure to become marginalized and religion privatized. Of course, in a pluralistic, democratic society, everyone is welcome to live with her or his vision of the good. But preferably they should live on what Adorno called a "reservation of the spirit." For the public debate too often excludes all public debates on intuitions and visions of the good (or "ends") and thereby the use of all the cultural and symbolic resources of art and religion, except of course as "private" visions of private individuals or communities. Indeed, even without the aid of either art or religion, all of us presumably have learned in the last ten years at least this much from the shocking revelations of the extent of child abuse and spousal abuse: We do in fact share a repulsion, a moral outrage at such conduct as unacceptable for anyone claiming to be a human being respectful in the most fundamental human sense of other human beings.

Fortunately, the feelings and intuitions of the good in art now have distinguished public defenders in such thoughtful philosophers as Iris Murdoch, Martha Nussbaum, Charles Taylor, even, at times Richard Rorty. But the resources of religions on visions of the good can seem a far more dangerous choice for entry into the discussion. Of course, given the ambiguous history of religion in every culture, this makes some sense. And given that many of the best religious thinkers have confined their attention to clarifying the religious vision of a particular tradition for the sake of that tradition alone, this reluctance to discuss religion in the public realm also makes some sense.

However, if we are to find out if we share any basic values (visions of the good) at all about what is human about a human being, the religions can and should be viewed as traditions of great and subtle complexity on these very issues and, at their best, as ancient and highly developed depositories of rare wisdom for any open-minded inquirer. If we are to hold, for example, that any re-

sponsible understanding of human being precisely as human must include some acknowledgment of our embodied, relational, and responsible character as human beings, then we may well want to consider the following examples from religious traditions.

1. On the necessary embodiment of the human being as a self, there are few wiser traditions (even the Aristotelian) than the Jewish tradition in its extraordinary and unbroken defense of the reality of human embodiment for authentic humanity. The book of Genesis alone, for example, is clearly as wise a text as our culture possesses on how human beings precisely as humans are embodied, and how they cannot be viewed as merely autonomous minds and wills. The Rabbinic, Kabalistic, and contemporary Jewish reflection—Reform, Conservative, and Orthodox—bears such subtle and persuasive analysis of the reality of eros as embodied, of mind as embodied, of will as embodied in the innate bonds constituting a people, that we ignore these classic Jewish discussions at the price of impoverishing ourselves as a society. Among the religions, possibly only Taoism provides so rich a resource for reflection of the full implications of our embodiment for our humanity as Judaism does.

2. On the intrinsic relationality of every person, there are a few wiser, centuries-long traditions of reflections than the Catholic social justice tradition. In Catholic theory, there is no concept of the modern possessive individual, even in the recent and strong Catholic defense of individual human rights (especially in Pope John Paul II's writings). The central Catholic category for the human is usually the dignity of the person—and the "person" is always understood as an intrinsically relational reality. There is no such reality, for Catholic reflection, as a human person without an intrinsic relationship to other persons, to the community, to nature, and to god. Nor, as John Courtney Murray argued, was there for the American founders and their appeals to "self-evident truths." Once again, to ignore the complexity and subtlety of arguments in the Catholic tradition of reflection on the reality of the human per-

son as relational and the unreality of the "possessive individual" is to impoverish the public discussion on the nature of human beings as human.

3. In the Reformation traditions, moreover, the classic "Protestant principle" of critique and suspicion is strong. Where else in the history of the religions can one find such useful reflections on the self's propulsion to self-delusion? Where else does one find contemporary ethical reflection like Paul Ramsey's or Reinhold Niebuhr's or James Gustafson's on how technology and science, however necessary and admirable, never remove such basic human drives as power, pride, and greed? Indeed, this prophetic principle and its explicit appeal to some notion of a responsible self is central to all prophetic traditions. Recall for example, Martin Luther King, Jr.'s brilliant use of biblical motifs for a genuinely public discussion of the just and loving society. This prophetic vision of justice lives in all the great monotheistic traditions from the prophets of the Hebrew Bible through the Reformers of Christianity to the amazing single-mindedness and purity of will of so many Islamic traditions. Today we need the prophetic principle, above all, to keep reminding ourselves, as the classic prophets always did, that justice for the poor, the oppressed, the marginal of society is the true moral test of the genuine civilization of that society. If human cloning becomes (as it easily and unintentionally could without constant vigilance and reflection—and prophetic outcry) merely another luxury item for the powerful, the rich, the talented, the beautiful, we have, as Amos, Isaiah, and Jeremiah would not hesitate to say, damned ourselves as a people.

As such thinkers as Franklin Gamwell have argued with care, moreover, the question of God can and should become, on commonly available grounds of public reason, a question for any inquirer in the public realm. But even before that further question of God is addressed publicly, the resources of the religions on understanding shared intuitions on the embodied, relational, justice-driven character of human beings as human beings can and should

be part of the wider public debate on human cloning. Of course the use of the Western monotheistic religions' visions of the human good should not exclude but encourage inquiry into alternative visions of the human good in the tragic visions of the West, in the great philosophies and works of art—popular and elite—of the ancient, medieval, and modern periods. All are public resources. It is weirdly self-impoverishing to ignore that cultural fact.

Of course, we must also be open to learn from other religious traditions as well on the human good: the remarkable insights of the Taoist traditions, especially on the body; the unparalleled wisdom of the Buddhist traditions, especially on our relationships to nonhuman creatures and our need to cease clinging to our possessive egos; the clarity of the Confucian tradition and its exceptional insight into our responsibilities to past and future generations; the rich complexity of the Hindu traditions on the reality of the erotic in all spiritual quests for humanity; the wisdom of such indigenous traditions as our own native American spiritual traditions on our human selves in community not only with our fellow humans but also with nature and the cosmos.

These examples of resources from the religions are so briefly stated here, I admit, that they may, at the moment, seem more like "hints and guesses" than the needed lengthy description and defense of their intuitions and visions of the human good of the religious traditions. But like any suggestive examples, they may at least serve to remind us of some of the resources we do, in fact, already possess, if we are wise enough to employ them. Fortunately, on the debate on the possibility of human cloning we are not yet at what too often passes as public debate on visions of the good: shouting matches masquerading as debates; ever more clever marketing devices for new consumer goods (including cloning?); scientific, philosophical, artistic, and religious monologues unwilling to hear one another. At least bumper stickers have not yet replaced reflection on the possibility of human cloning.

There is still time for the communal discussion to be demand-

ing, clear, and inclusive. Ultimately no one of us will be able to avoid the literally awe-full questions that the possibility of human cloning provokes for any thoughtful person: What do we ultimately mean by a human being? For myself, I remain profoundly suspicious of human cloning as even a possibly positive contribution to the human good. But everything I know and sense about my own relative ignorance on certain aspects (and not only technical scientific ones, but also the many ethical issues relevant to this debate) also leads me to acknowledge my own need to listen, hear, and learn from others. Surely I am not alone in this sensed need. If we cannot discuss reasonably and openly the unavoidable question evoked by the possibility of human cloning—"What is a human being?"—then we might as well all fold up our tents and return to whatever private reservation of the spirit we inhabit. For then we would have to admit that there is no genuine public realm where all can and must meet on those questions that necessarily involve us all.

PART IV
Law and Public Policy

The Constitution and the Clone

Cass R. Sunstein

"My decision to clone myself should not be the government's business, or Cardinal O'Connor's, any more than a woman's decision to have an abortion is. Cloning is hugely significant. It's part of the reproductive rights of every human being."

—Randolfe Wicker, head of the Cloning Rights United Front of New York, *New York Times Magazine,* May 25, 1997, at 18.

It is some time in the future. Federal and state laws forbid the practice of cloning human beings; but a number of American citizens are claiming that the Constitution guarantees a "right to clone." Some infertile couples contend that cloning provides their "best option for having children." Some couples who have lost their first child are seeking a biologically identical replacement via cloning. Some homosexual groups are insisting on a right to clone.

An especially prominent case was brought by Kristina Martin and Ronald Martin. Kristina is 38 and Ronald is 42; Ronald is infertile. Kristina seeks to carry Ronald's cloned child. In a case brought by the Martin and several other married couples, a court of appeals held that the Constitution protects the right to clone. The constitutional issue has come before the Supreme Court of the United States.

But now there is a fork in the road: two possible but very different paths for constitutional law. Path A contains the Supreme Court's reasoning in its dramatic decision firmly recognizing a constitutional right to reproductive privacy, including the right to clone. Path B summarizes the Supreme Court's reasoning in its unambiguous denial of any such right. There are intersections between the two divergent paths. The reasoning of the two Supreme Courts has been organized to allow comparisons between the two paths—and to facilitate choices between them.

Kristina Martin and Ronald Martin, et al. v. Martin Ballinger, Secretary of Health and Human Services, et al.

On Petition for Writ of Certiorari to the United States Court of Appeals for the Eighth Circuit

No. 99-1099.

Justice Monroe delivered the opinion of the Court.

In this case American citizens seeking to clone human beings have challenged federal and state prohibitions on cloning. The plaintiffs are married couples. They argue that these prohibitions violate their right to free reproductive choice.

The plaintiffs make two arguments. They argue, first, that the right to clone is part and parcel of the right of reproductive privacy. They claim that this right is akin to the rights to use contraception and to have an abortion, firmly recognized under our prior cases. They therefore urge that the right to clone qualifies, under the due process clause of the Fifth and Fourteenth Amendments, as a "fundamental interest," which may be invaded only if the government can satisfy "strict scrutiny," by showing the most compelling of justifications.

The plaintiffs argue, second, that even if the right to clone does not qualify as a "fundamental interest," the legal prohibition on

cloning is unconstitutional, because the government cannot show a "rational basis" for the restriction. The plaintiffs claim that the government has no legitimate reason for interfering with private decisions about whether to have a child via cloning.

The government makes several arguments in response. It urges that the right to clone is very different from the right to use contraceptives or to have an abortion, and that it does not qualify as a fundamental right under the Constitution. The government also claims that there are compelling reasons to ban human cloning even if the right to clone does qualify as a fundamental right. Finally, the government insists that there is a "rational basis" for restricting human cloning, to prevent a wide range of social harms.

We reject the government's arguments and hold today that under the Constitution as it has come to be understood, there is a constitutional right to clone. The Court's cases firmly recognize the individual right to control reproduction—to decide whether or not to have a child. This right lies at the very heart of the constitutional right of "privacy"; it is part of the liberty protected by the due process clause of the Fifth and Fourteenth Amendments.

To be sure, the government can override that right if it has an extremely good reason for doing so. But in the context of cloning, the government's arguments are far too weak. Certainly the government cannot satisfy the "strict scrutiny" standard that governs this Court's review of restrictions on fundamental rights. Indeed, we do not believe that the government's interests are strong enough to overcome "rational basis" review, the most deferential standard the Court now uses.

I

There is an acknowledged constitutional right to some form of individual control over decisions involving reproduction. In *Griswold v. Connecticut,* 381 U.S. 479 (1965), this Court held that a state could not ban a married couple from using contraceptives. In the

Court's view, a right of "privacy" forecloses state interference with that decision. In *Eisenstadt v. Baird,* 405 U.S. 438 (1972), the Court extended *Griswold* to invalidate a law forbidding the distribution of contraceptives to unmarried people. In the key passage of its opinion, the Court said, "If the right of privacy means anything, it is the right of the individual, married or single, to be free from unwarranted governmental intrusion into matters so affecting a person as the decision whether to bear or beget a child." And in *Roe v. Wade,* 410 U.S. 113 (1973), the Court held that there is a constitutional right to have an abortion. This decision the Court strongly reaffirmed in *Casey v. Planned Parenthood,* 505 U.S. 833 (1992).

On the other hand, we have held that there is no general right against government interference with important private choices. Thus in *Washington v. Glucksberg,* 116 U.S. 2021 (1997), we held that under ordinary circumstances, there is no general right to physician-assisted suicide. We emphasized that this right is quite foreign to the traditions of American law and policy, which strongly discourage suicide, assisted or otherwise.

These cases clearly establish a basic principle: The Constitution creates a presumptive individual right to decide whether and when to reproduce. The precise dimensions of this right will inevitably change over time. Of course new technologies are expanding the methods by which reproduction is possible. New technologies have been especially prominent in the last decades, and undoubtedly scientific progress will continue, producing unforeseeable developments. The Constitution provides the basic right, which is itself constant; but the specific content of the right necessarily changes with relevant technology.

We think it very plain that the government would need an exceptionally powerful justification to ban couples with serious fertility problems from using methods other than sexual intercourse to produce a child between husband and wife. It has become quite ordinary for couples to use new methods and technologies, and governments have generally refrained from interfering with indi-

vidual freedom to choose. A governmental ban on in vitro fertilization, to take one example, would have to be powerfully justified, certainly if the ban prevented couples from having children in the only way they could. Cloning is of course a new technology. But for some couples, including the plaintiffs here, it is the only or the best reproductive option. If the government wishes to limit or restrict that choice, it must come up with an exceptionally strong justification.

II

The closest precedent for our decision today is *Roe v. Wade,* reaffirmed in *Casey v. Planned Parenthood,* and these decisions strongly support a right to clone. In fact the argument for a right to clone is far stronger, in many ways, than the argument for a right to abortion. Cloning produces life where abortion destroys it. Abortion is contested on the ground that it destroys the fetus, which many people consider to be equivalent to, or nearly equivalent to, a human being. If there is a right to abort fetal life, there must be a parallel right to create life. Of course the morality of abortion, like that of cloning, is socially contested. *Roe* demonstrates that the fact that people have moral reservations, whether or not inspired by religion, is by itself an insufficient reason to allow interference with a decision about whether to bear or beget a child.

In any case the right to have an abortion reflects a judgment that the choice about whether to reproduce lies with the individual, not the government. That judgment strongly supports the plaintiffs' claim here.

III

If a ban on cloning is subject to the most stringent forms of constitutional review, it is clear that the ban cannot be upheld. The government's interests are speculative in the extreme. The government

notes that there is a risk of psychological harm to the clone, who will know that it is the genetic equivalent of someone else, with a known life; perhaps this knowledge will be hard to bear. We acknowledge that psychological harm may occur. But psychological harm is a risk in many settings, and it is not a reason to allow the government to control reproductive choices, to ban adoption, or (for that matter) to outlaw twins, for whom there is in any case no decisive evidence of trauma.

The government argues that it fears the outcomes of unsuccessful medical experiments; it says that children with various physical defects are likely to occur. This too is possible, especially at the early stages, but it is a reason for regulation, not for prohibition. The government refers as well to the need for a large stock of genetic diversity. The interest in a large gene pool is, we may acknowledge, compelling; but it is utterly implausible to think that the existence of cloning, bound to be a relatively unusual practice, will compromise the genetic diversity of mankind.

Finally, the government attempts to justify its ban with the legal equivalent of tales from science fiction or horror movies—thus, the government refers to dozens or even hundreds of genetically equivalent people, or of clones of especially abhorrent historical figures. The government fears that narcissistic or ill-motivated people will produce armies of "selves." We think it plain that these fanciful speculations, far afield from the case at hand, do not justify a total ban. If problems of this kind arise, they should be controllable through more fine-tuned regulations. The government's emphasis on unlikely scenarios of this kind simply confirms our belief that the government has been unable to find a "compelling" interest to override the presumptive right to control one's reproductive processes.

IV

Even if the right to clone did not qualify as a fundamental interest, we believe that a wholesale ban on cloning would be unconstitu-

tional, because it cannot survive rational basis review. In the end the government's justifications are best understood as a form of unmediated and highly emotional repugnance—produced not by evidence, arguments, or reality, but by the simple novelty of the practice under review.

Repugnance frequently accompanies new technological developments; and repugnance tends to underlie the worst forms of prejudice and irrationality. We need not repeat the details about our nation's long-standing practices of discrimination on the basis of race and sex—now understood to violate our deepest constitutional ideals—in order to establish the point. Nor should it be necessary to stress that the most solemn obligation of this Court is to uphold constitutional principles against popular prejudice and irrationality, which often take the form of "repugnance." And to the extent that the ban on cloning has foundations in religious convictions, it should be unnecessary to say that religious convictions, standing alone, are not, in a pluralistic society, a sufficient basis for the coercion of law. It does not deprecate religious conviction to say that its appropriate place is not in the statute books, and to emphasize that religious arguments must have secular equivalents in order to provide the basis for law.

V

Our conclusions are fortified by a simple, widely recognized point: A ban on cloning will simply drive the practice of human cloning both abroad and underground. At this stage in our history, it is altogether clear that prohibitions on cloning will not operate as prohibitions, but will simply force people who are determined to clone to act unlawfully or in other nations. Thus, the prohibition at issue here cannot be supported by the government's justifications, which would lose what little force they have if the prohibition cannot operate in practice as it does on paper.

We hold, in sum, that the right to clone, however novel as a

matter of technology, is part and parcel of a time-honored individual right to control the circumstances and event of reproduction; that the government has pointed to no sufficient justification for overriding that fundamental right; and that on inspection, the government's grounds for concern dissolve into a simple statement of repugnance and disgust, lacking scientific or ethical foundations and fed mostly by imaginative literature. Because they invade the right to privacy in its most fundamental form, legal bans on cloning violate the due process clause of the Constitution.

The judgment of the court of appeals is affirmed.

It is so ordered.

Kristina Martin and Ronald Martin, et al. v. Martin Ballinger, Secretary of Health and Human Services, et al.

On Petition for Writ of Certiorari to the United States Court of Appeals for the Eighth Circuit

No. 99-1099.

Justice Winston delivered the opinion of the Court.

In this case a group of American citizens seeking to clone human beings have challenged federal and state prohibitions on cloning. The plaintiffs are married couples. They argue that these prohibitions violate their right to free reproductive choice.

The plaintiffs make two arguments. They argue, first, that the right to clone is part and parcel of the right to reproductive privacy, closely akin to the rights to use contraception and to have an abortion, recognized under our prior cases. They therefore urge that the right to clone qualifies, under the due process clause of the Fifth and Fourteenth Amendments, as a "fundamental interest," which may be invaded only if the government can satisfy "strict scrutiny," by showing the most compelling of justifications.

The plaintiffs argue, second, that even if the right to clone does not qualify as a "fundamental interest," the legal prohibition is unconstitutional, because the government cannot show a "rational basis" for the restriction. The plaintiffs claim that the government has no legitimate reason for interfering with private decisions about whether to have a child via cloning.

The government makes several arguments in response. It urges that the right to clone is very different from the right to use contraceptives or to have an abortion, and that it does not qualify as a fundamental right under the Constitution. The government also claims that there are compelling reasons to ban human cloning even if the right to clone does qualify as a fundamental right. Finally, the government insists that there is a "rational basis" for restricting human cloning, to prevent a wide range of social harms.

We accept the government's arguments and hold today that under the Constitution as it is now understood, there is no constitutional right to clone. The Court's cases recognize an individual right to control reproduction, as part of the liberty protected by the due process clause of the Fifth and Fourteenth Amendments. But it is facetious, at best, to say that anything in our precedents recognizes an individual right to replicate oneself through the new technology of cloning.

To override the individual interest in replicating other human beings, the government needs only a "rational basis." But the government has far more than this. We believe that the government has exceptionally powerful grounds for controlling cloning. Indeed, the government's justifications are strong enough to override the individual's interest even if the government needs to overcome "strict scrutiny," the least deferential standard the Court now uses.

I

There is an acknowledged constitutional right to some form of individual control over decisions involving reproduction. In *Griswold*

v. Connecticut, 381 U.S. 479 (1965), this Court held that a state could not ban a married couple from using contraceptives. In the Court's view, a right of "privacy" forecloses state interference with that decision. In *Eisenstadt v. Baird,* 405 U.S. 438 (1972), the Court extended *Griswold* to invalidate a law forbidding the distribution of contraceptives to unmarried people. In the key passage of its opinion, the Court said, "If the right of privacy means anything, it is the right of the individual, married or single, to be free from unwarranted governmental intrusion into matters so affecting a person as the decision whether to bear or beget a child." And in *Roe v. Wade,* 410 U.S. 113 (1973), the Court held that there is a constitutional right to have an abortion. This decision the Court strongly reaffirmed in *Casey v. Planned Parenthood,* 505 U.S. 833 (1992).

On the other hand, we have held that there is no general right against government interference with important private choices. Thus in *Washington v. Glucksberg,* 116 U.S. 2021 (1997), we held that under ordinary circumstances, there is no general right to physician-assisted suicide. We emphasized that this right is quite foreign to the traditions of American law and policy, which strongly discourage suicide, assisted or otherwise.

These cases clearly establish a basic principle: The Constitution creates a presumptive individual right to decide whether and when to reproduce. Thus, government cannot prevent people from choosing not to have a child, and we agree with the plaintiffs that serious issues would also be raised by (for example) a legal requirement of abortion, or a restriction on the number of children a married couple might have. But the constitutional right is far from unbounded. It lies in a specific judgment about *reproduction,* understood by our traditions as a distinctive human interest with a distinctive human meaning.

Our traditions rebel against the idea that the state, rather than the individual, can make the decision whether a person is to bear or beget a child. But it defies common sense to suggest that *repli-*

cation falls in the same category. No tradition supports a right to replicate. This is not merely a matter of technological limitations. The human meaning of replication, of creating genetically identical beings, is fundamentally different from that of reproduction, and replication is to many people horrifying. Centuries of culture, of myth and literature, confirm this basic fact. It is not the business of this Court to say whether replication of human beings should or should not be permitted. But when the people of the country, and their elected representatives, conclude that it should be banned, no fundamental right is invaded. We require only a rational justification.

II

The plaintiffs rely most fundamentally on *Roe v. Wade,* but there is an enormous difference between the right to clone and the right to an abortion. The Court has come to see that the decision in *Roe* turned in large part on the interest in equality on the basis of sex. As a matter of history, governments have denied the right to abortion because they seek to preserve women's traditional role. Moreover, the denial of the right to have an abortion tends to fortify that traditional role and thus to undermine equality on the basis of sex. No equality interest supports the right to clone. With respect to sex equality, cloning is a very complex matter—reasonable people have set forth competing views—and we do not believe that it is plausible to argue that the right to clone finds a justification in principles of equality on the basis of sex.

There is a further point. *Roe v. Wade* did not create a general right to decide whether to have a child through whatever technological means may be available. It is far narrower than that: an outgrowth of cases establishing a right to decide whether to reproduce, a time-honored right in Anglo-American law. The right to replicate stands on much weaker ground.

III

Even if the ban on cloning were subject to the most stringent forms of judicial review, it would be upheld. Physical difficulties and even deformities are highly likely. The government has an exceptionally strong interest in protecting young children against disease and disability, and both of these are likely products of experiments in human cloning. The government has pointed to considerable evidence of this risk, and this Court is in no position to second-guess the scientific evidence.

It is highly likely as well that the practice of cloning would have undesirable effects on the "people" who result. There is some evidence of psychological difficulties faced by human twins; the practice of cloning will inevitably risk far more severe problems from people who know that they are genetic equivalents of people with known lives, including known problems, known successes, and known failures. Similarly, the government reasonably fears that the parent-child relationship, between genetic equivalents, would be unrecognizable, and permeated by difficulties of various sorts. It may well be that especially wealthy people, or especially narcissistic people, would fund large numbers of replications of themselves. Who would rear the resulting children? With what motivations? The government has the strongest possible reasons to fear the outcomes of such a situation.

There is a further consideration. The government has an extremely powerful interest in preserving the stock of biological diversity. Widespread cloning could compromise that interest to the detriment of humanity as a whole. We think that these points confirm our belief that the government has a wide range of compelling interests sufficient to override any presumptive right to clone.

IV

If the decision whether to clone does not qualify as a fundamental right, the only question is whether the government's ban is "rational." Certainly it qualifies as such. As we have indicated, the government might reasonably believe that there would be adverse psychological effects on "clones." It might believe that the process of cloning human beings would result in physical deformities for the "products" of the relevant scientific practices. It might even believe that the existence of clones would have adverse psychological effects on many children and even adults who might fear that they would be cloned against their will. All of these speculations are reasonable.

This Court does not sit to second-guess reasonable judgments by the elected representatives of the American people, especially when there is no defect in the system of democratic deliberation that gave rise to the law under review. And it should not be necessary to say that the religious convictions that may underlie legal bans on cloning are not, in a pluralistic society, at all troublesome from the standpoint of constitutional democracy, where everyone's convictions are entitled to count.

Our conclusions are not undermined in the least by the possibility that people determined to defy the law will do so, either here or by seeking refuge abroad. It is not an argument against the criminal law that criminal prohibitions may be violated or circumvented. If bans on human replication do not operate in practice as they do on paper, Congress and the legislatures of the several states are entitled to respond as they choose.

We hold, in sum, that the right to clone has no basis in our constitutional traditions, which involve human reproduction, not replication; that the government has ample grounds for restricting individual choice in light of the novelty of the relevant technology and its unpredictable and potentially damaging effects on the most

basic human values and in particular on those involved in the relevant "experiments." Because they do not implicate the right to privacy or any other constitutionally protected interest, legal bans on cloning are entirely consistent with the due process clause of the Constitution.

The judgment of the court of appeals is reversed.

It is so ordered.

On Not Banning Cloning for the Wrong Reasons

Laurence Tribe

Most of the interesting issues about cloning in general, and human cloning in particular, involve shades of gray—not "either/or" but "how": How should the evolution and deployment of this fascinating but disturbing new technology be funded and controlled? How should the human experimentation that would precede its routine availability for the genetic replication of people as opposed to sheep or calves be conducted and regulated? How should domestic and international regulatory efforts mesh? Interesting though such questions are, they are not my focus here. Rather, I want to address the strictly binary question: Should human cloning be forbidden altogether? Although I offer no definitive answer to that inquiry, I explore what I have come to regard as a particularly forceful objection to any regime of prohibition in this technological realm—an objection centered on how the very *fact* of prohibition, and the social meanings likely to attend it, might be expected to reshape, in strikingly negative ways, the structure of social relations and the status of the human lives that those social relations in turn affect.

As it happens, this isn't my first attempt to address these questions. The first time around, I had only recently completed law school and a pair of judicial clerkships and had just begun my career as a teacher of law building on a one-year stint directing a study of technology assessment for the National Academy of Sciences. Maybe a bit too eager to use that technology-focused expe-

rience as a springboard for my musings about emerging advances in biomedical science and its applications, I seem to have been predisposed to view significant technological changes in the most portentious terms—and to pay somewhat less attention to the social and cultural impacts of the legal regimes through which new technologies are either facilitated or forbidden. Now, after a long period of reflection about the structure of law generally, and of constitutional law in particular, I guess I'm more attuned to the effects of legal rules themselves—and of legal prohibition as an especially consequential "technology" in its own terms. And so it is, as the brief essay that follows will hopefully make plain, that I'm a lot more dubious now than when I first explored this terrain about the wisdom of banning the cloning of human beings.

In my first crack at this subject—taken at a time when most people didn't take the prospect of human (or, indeed, of mammalian) cloning seriously enough to warrant careful analysis—my thinking took the form of a series of articles about the need to assess and channel new biomedical and electronic technologies not solely in instrumental terms—that is, not solely in terms of their "costs" and "benefits" as measured on existing scales of value—but in intrinsic terms as well. In those articles, I urged the importance of assessing at least the most basic new technologies, especially those operating directly on the human mind or body, in terms of how their development and use might alter "the ends—and indeed the basic character—of the individuals and the communities that choose them."[1] The articles focused in particular on what struck me as the paradigm case of a technology requiring assessment in such intrinsic terms—a reproductive method that seemed to lie not very far ahead: the "perfection of cloning technology for human beings."[2] My evaluation of that reproductive technology stressed the fragility of purely consequentialist arguments against such a development.[3] Any "on balance" assessment against allowing at least the selective use of such a technology, grounded in the estimate that any such use would inflict greater cost than benefit in

terms of "our" values, would be vulnerable to potent rebuttal—(1) in terms of the necessarily inconclusive nature of any such estimate; (2) in terms of the question-begging character of appeals to shared values where how "we" should value various outcomes is anything *but* shared; and (3) in terms of the doubtfulness of assuming that the choice of how an individual or a couple should be permitted to reproduce is properly to be made through collective political processes. If we ask whether the concrete gain to the individual or couple and their child-to-be is outweighed by the less tangible loss to their community and perhaps to future generations, we may be hard-pressed to explain why that balance is the state's rather than the individual's to strike. And alleged losses to the child in question are particularly tough to factor into the cost/benefit calculus when the alternative to that child's clonal creation is something as stark as nonexistence. How awful to be a clone? How awful not to *be* at all?

In those early writings, without ever coming out four-square for a ban on human cloning, I suggested that the strongest case for nipping human cloning in the bud, or for banning its use on a global basis once such use became feasible (and perhaps for banning particular forms of research and development thought likely to lead in an imminent way to the feasibility of human cloning, although efforts to forbid the generation of supposedly dangerous knowledge might well be deemed intolerable in terms of freedom of inquiry), would probably take an intrinsic rather than instrumental form. My argument was that cloning human beings might well constitute "a fundamental threat to the concept and the reality of the human person as a unique and intrinsically valuable entity, conscious of its own being and responsible for its own choices."[4] The essay quoted the physician-philosopher Leon Kass, expressing agreement with his suggestion that "to 'lay one's hands on human generation is to take a major step toward making man himself simply another one of the manmade things.' "[5] And the essay went further. To conceive of the changes that would be wrought by permitting such a tech-

nology to be deployed "as a selection in terms of a 'given' value framework," I claimed, "begs the question presented" by the technology's use, for "[a]t stake are not merely alterations in the 'costs' and 'benefits' associated with implementing existing preferences and values but alterations in the very structures of human thought and reality on which all value premises and the choices that embody them—all the frames of reference for defining one thing as a 'cost' and another as a 'benefit'—must ultimately be based."[6] Many others before and since—with ideological orientations as different as those of Karl Marx[7] and Leon Kass[8]—have likewise made much of how every major choice among technologies is likely to reconstitute the choosers, both as developers and as users, in often profound ways.

This recap of my earlier work reflects no sense of self-congratulation, but a spirit of confession. For the truth is that, twenty-five years after first seeking to apply to the example of human cloning the insight (by no means original with me) that certain technologies might reconstitute society too deeply to yield to merely instrumental analysis, my primary impulse is to say that my "yes" answer to the truly basic question of whether human cloning must be perceived as a threat to the very meaning of human individuality was probably wrong. No doubt human cloning is deeply unsettling to many, perhaps most, of us. But would its advent jeopardize something truly essential? My answer today is: maybe—but maybe not. Who was I—who is anyone—to forecast *which* technologies will over time generate transformations sufficiently deep, and sufficiently worthy of shared condemnation, that we may confidently favor the outright prohibition of those technologies, predicating such prohibition on our prediction that the technologies we urge banning would otherwise deform the human project?

It's certainly not a matter of technological manifest destiny—not a matter, that is, of assuming that anything people are technically capable of doing ought, for that reason alone, to be permitted. It's not even a matter of positing a basic human right—or, in American law,

a federal constitutional right—to reproduce oneself through whatever means become technically possible. Whether courts should declare such a right, and what its limits might be, is a subject for another essay. It's simply a matter of humility: My point is less to make a federal case out of it than to suggest a far more tentative attitude. How can any of us feel so confident that the meaning of humanity will be degraded by human cloning in any and all circumstances that we are prepared to shut down altogether the potentially humane possibilities of this admittedly (for most of us) most distasteful, perhaps even diabolical, method of reproducing human life?

Perhaps some technological possibilities—those that would significantly alter the genetic or at least biological composition of the human species as a whole, or those that would "marry" humanity with its humanly developed systems for processing and exchanging information so as to create human-computer hybrids that might have to be regarded as new species—would genuinely reshape humanity itself, and would accordingly require all who debate the pros and cons of the underlying choices to grapple with the truly ultimate questions of good and evil posed by proposed changes in "human nature." Whether to permit the genetic blending, for experimental or other purposes, of human beings with chimps or with computer chips—whether to allow the generation of chimeras or of cyborgs—might pose questions of this deep character. Does human cloning pose those questions? Some of the thinkers with whose work on this topic I agreed in the 1970s argue that it does; they have reacted to the now far more imminent prospect of human cloning essentially by reiterating and elaborating their earlier convictions as to the nightmarish, nature-altering character of such a technology.[9] Although I continue to think those misgivings point to real problems and to issues far too profound to be ignored, I have come to believe that objections of the sort that writers like Kass put forth—objections that rest ultimately on an aversion to patterns of human interaction and behavior that the

observer deems "unnatural"[10]—are themselves at *least* as serious a source of danger as are the technologies that provoke them. We *may* have more to fear than fear itself—but when fear of the unnatural drives a campaign to ban some innovation, then that very fear may be more fearsome than the innovation that spawns it.

It's not that the amorphous and often hard-to-articulate character of such fears or objections is *itself* proof of their misguided character. Wisdom often outpaces our ability to capture its essence in verbal formulas, and those who automatically dismiss deeply felt misgivings as insubstantial or as irrationally sentimental whenever we have not (yet) been able to capture those misgivings in a rigorous argument underestimate the profundity of human intuition—and overestimate the power of cold logic. On the other hand, the difficulty of capturing in crisp and tightly analytical form the visceral unease one might feel at the deployment of a given technology should not be confused with a sign that this unease *must* be well-grounded, that it must reflect a wisdom too deep for words. Unease should count for a great deal; but it must not count for everything.

When that unease focuses on the sense that a proposed act or technical development is incompatible with what the opponent of that act or development deems the essence of human nature or of the human condition, the alarm bells ought to go off loud and clear. It is no coincidence, it seems to me, that the latest eloquent assault on cloning by Leon Kass is embedded in an essay that describes "[c]loning" as "the perfect embodiment of the ruling opinions of our new age," in which "the sexual revolution" has made it possible for us to "deny in practice, and increasingly in thought, the inherent procreative teleology of sexuality itself," in which, once "sex has no intrinsic connection to generating babies, babies need have no necessary connection to sex," and in which, "[t]hanks to feminism and the gay rights movement, we are increasingly encouraged to treat the natural heterosexual difference and its preeminence as a matter of 'cultural construction.' "[11] The Kass crescendo ends with this

observation: "Thanks to the prominence and the acceptability of divorce and out-of-wedlock births, stable, monogamous marriage as the ideal home for procreation is no longer the agreed-upon cultural norm. For this new dispensation, the clone is the ideal emblem: the ultimate 'single-parent child.' "[12] So there we have it: Cloning is the technological apotheosis of Murphy Brown and Ellen DeGeneres, the biomedical nemesis of Dan Quayle, Phyllis Schlafly, and Pat Robertson.

I say that this linkage—between passionate opposition to human cloning as a lawful option, and emotion-charged objection to supposedly "unnatural" ways of living and loving and parenting—is no coincidence precisely because the cloning objection being addressed here, like the objections to such practices as surrogate motherhood or gay marriage and gay adoption, takes the form of an irreducible appeal to human nature, whether or not divinely ordained, as the normative source of the case for legal prohibition. Much has, of course, been written about the virtues and vices of such appeals in other social and moral contexts. Here, my focus is on the special problems inherent in claims that a particular method of *creating human beings* is unacceptably unnatural and hence ought to be forbidden as evil. (Let's put to one side objections to various courses of action, presumably including the creation of embryos designed to be discarded, that might have to be undertaken as part of any research and development program leading to the perfection of the reproductive method in question; a case for banning such embryo-manipulating behavior on the ground that it constitutes unethical experimentation on human beings without their consent might well be convincingly advanced quite apart from the supposed case against any use of the particular reproductive method whose perfection the course of experimentation might bring about. Once the contested reproductive technique has finally been developed—outside the United States, perhaps—objections to the experiments that were needed to produce it are likely to be irrelevant, leaving us with the core question of whether the mode of

human reproduction, having been developed, ought to be made criminal.)

As we analyze any proposed decision to outlaw a particular way of making babies, it's vital to keep in mind that, just as physical or biomedical technologies may in some circumstances "reconstitute" the societies that choose them by altering the preferences and even the values of those societies, so too there are significant constitutive dimensions in any society's decisions to accept a line of argument against deploying a given technology, and then to employ the institutional "technology" of domestic legal prohibition (presumably coupled with international agreements designed to make the prohibition meaningfully enforceable) in an effort to prevent the technology in question from ever being used. It is not only *constitutional* law but *all* of law that has important constitutive effects, and those effects may be particularly dramatic when the technology of law—including the legal practices, arguments, and institutions that support and surround a decision to criminalize a particular physical or biomedical technology—is deployed in an effort to prevent that physical or biomedical technology from being used. Even when that contested technology would operate to do something other than create a human child—when it operates, for instance, to abort a developing embryo (as with RU 486, say) or to induce addiction to a pleasurable substance (as with the nicotine delivery system of a cigarette)—employing the counter-technology of criminalization may well have, as all are aware, the many "costs" associated with black markets generally. Whether one thinks of coat-hanger, back-alley abortions before 1973,[13] or of the concern with how an FDA ban on nicotine in cigarettes might encourage addicts to resort to a contraband market, a standard part of the policy analysis surrounding choices between legalization and criminalization entails addressing the consequences of imperfect (often grossly imperfect) enforceability.

When the technology at issue is *a method for making human babies*—whether that method differs from a society's conventional

and traditionally approved mode because of some socially constructed "fact" such as the marital status or kinship relation or racial identity of a participant, or differs in a more intrinsic way as in the case of in vitro fertilization, or surrogate gestation, or cloning so as to achieve asexual reproduction with but a single parent—applying the counter-technology of criminalization has at least one additional, and qualitatively distinct, social cost. That cost, to the degree any ban on using a given mode of baby making is bound to be evaded, is the very considerable one of creating a class of potential outcasts—persons whose very *existence* the society has chosen, through its legal system, to label as a misfortune and, in essence, to condemn.

Even the simple example of what the "politically correct" call nonmarital children and what others call illegitimates (or, more bluntly, bastards) powerfully illustrates the high price many individuals and their families are forced to pay for a society's decision to reinforce, through outlawing nonmarital reproduction and discriminating against nonmarital offspring, particular norms about how children ought to be brought into the world. How much higher would that price be when the basis on which the law decides to condemn a given baby-making method (like cloning) is not simply a judgment that the particular pairing of parents was for some reason to be frowned upon to the point of prohibition, but the far more personalized and stigmatizing judgment that *the baby itself*—the child that will result from the condemned method—is morally incomplete or existentially flawed by virtue of its unnaturally man-made and deliberately determined (as opposed to "open") origin and character? That judgment may begin with sympathy or even pity for the innocent baby's anticipated predicament as a child whose single parent is the baby's identical twin and whose very being may express and embody parental expectations with which no child should be burdened. But even if the judgment begins with sympathy, its very structure entails an enormous risk that it will end in condemnation, in some version of original sin. At first the ob-

ject of a pity that may be justified (but might also be misplaced—are not many *non*-clones even more cruelly burdened by parental expectations?), the human clone—in a world where cloning is forbidden as unnatural—is likely in the end to become the object of a form of contempt: the contempt that the (supposedly) spontaneous, natural, and unplanned would tend to feel toward the (supposedly) manufactured and allegedly artificial.

Laws against highly personal activities, conducted in private and involving no "victim" in the usual sense—sexual prostitution, for instance—generate, as we have noted, black markets in which such laws may be circumvented, in turn generating contraband substances or practices. That is bad enough—though not necessarily a decisive reason to opt for legalization in any given context, from the use of narcotic drugs to the sale of body parts. What is far worse is any situation in which the "contraband" takes the form of human beings. In any such situation, the upshot may be a particularly pernicious form of caste system, in which an entire category of persons, while perhaps not labeled untouchable, is marginalized as not fully human.

Even if one could (unrealistically) posit perfect enforceability of a worldwide ban on human cloning, so that the set of contraband persons would be empty, the social costs of prohibition—whatever one may think of claims that there is an individual "right" to reproduce by this or, indeed, any other particular method—would be far from zero. For the arguments supporting the iron-clad prohibition of human cloning we have hypothesized could not easily be cabined within that single context. Such arguments would almost invariably rest on, and if acted upon would reinforce, the notion that it is unnatural, and intrinsically wrong, to sever the conventional links between heterosexual unions sanctified by tradition and the creation and upbringing of new life. Witness the argument by Leon Kass, only the most eloquent of a familiar genre. And the entrenchment of that essentialist notion, its deeper embedding in our culture and our law, is in turn anything but costless. It is most

assuredly not costless for lesbians, gay men, persons gay or straight with genetically transmittable diseases, and others whose sexual or other orientations or capacities draw them into unconventional patterns of intimate relationship—and unconventional modes of linking erotic attachment, romantic commitment, genetic replication, gestational mothering, and the joys and responsibilities of parenting.

Nor is the entrenchment of the essentialist vision costless for the culture of the wider community, straight as well as gay: A society that bans acts of human creation that reflect unconventional sex roles or parenting models (surrogate motherhood, in vitro fertilization, artificial insemination, and the like) for no better reason than that such acts dare to defy "nature" and tradition (and to risk adding to life's complexity) is a society that risks cutting itself off from vital experimentation and risks sterilizing a significant part of its capacity to grow. This is not necessarily a conclusive argument against banning human cloning, nor does it purport to be. But it is an argument that I hope creates something like a *presumption* against any such ban—an argument one must reckon with and ultimately overcome if such a ban is to be given serious consideration.

In sum, much as one might deplore as shallow and perhaps disgusting the impulse to create genetic "copies" of deceased loved ones—or, maybe even worse, of oneself or of one's heroes—one must be at *least* as suspicious of the impulse to forbid such cloning altogether—and of the legal apparatus through which that impulse would be effectuated—when that impulse is embedded in a picture of human nature, and of human possibility, that is, in the end, neither altogether human nor genuinely humane.

Endnotes

1. L. Tribe, "Technology Assessment and the Fourth Discontinuity: The Limits of Instrumental Rationality," 46 *So. Cal. L. Rev.* 617, 642 (1973) (hereinafter, "The

Fourth Discontinuity"); see also L. Tribe, "Ways Not To Think About Plastic Trees: New Foundations for Environmental Law," 83 *Yale L. J.* 1315 (1974); L. Tribe, "Policy Science: Analysis or Ideology?" 1 *Philosophy & Public Affairs* 66 (Fall 1972); L. Tribe, "Legal Frameworks for the Assessment and Control of Technology," 4 *Minerva* 243, 254–55 (1971).

2. "The Fourth Discontinuity" at 643.

3. *Id.*

4. *Id.* at 648.

5. *Id.* at 649, quoting L. Kass, "Making Babies—The New Biology and the 'Old' Morality," 26 *Public Interest* 18, 49 (Winter 1972).

6. "The Fourth Discontinuity" at 650. For a similar theme in constitutional law and theory, see L. Tribe, "Constitutional Calculus: Equal Justice or Economic Inefficiency," 98 *Harv. L. Rev.* 592 (1985); cf. L. Tribe, "The Curvature of Constitutional Space: What Lawyers Can Learn from Modern Physics," 103 *Harv. L. Rev.* 1 (1989).

7. See "The Fourth Discontinuity" at 650 n. 116.

8. See L. Kass, "The Wisdom of Repugnance," *New Republic* (June 2, 1997), pp. 17–26.

9. E.g., L. Kass, in "The Wisdom of Repugnance," supra note 8.

10. E.g., L. Kass, in "The Wisdom of Repugnance," supra note 8 at 17 ("Dolly was, quite literally, made. She is the work not of nature or nature's God but of man, an Englishman, Ian Wilmut, and his fellow scientists."); *id.* at 20 (considering "the deeper anthropological, social and, indeed, ontological meanings of bringing forth new life . . . cloning shows itself to be a major alteration, indeed, a major violation, of our given nature as embodied, gendered and engendering beings—and of the social relations built on this natural ground"); *id.* at 21 ("A sexual reproduction, which produces 'single-parent' offspring, is a radical departure from the natural human way, confounding all normal understandings of father, mother, sibling, grandparent, etc., and all moral relations tied thereto.").

11. L. Kass, in "The Wisdom of Repugnance," supra note 8 at 18.

12. *Id.*

13. Prior to *Roe v. Wade,* 410 U.S. 113 (1973), the states were free to criminalize nearly all abortions; most did just that.

The Demand for Human Cloning

Eric A. Posner and Richard A. Posner

The news that a sheep ("Dolly") had been created by cloning adult nonreproductive tissue[1] has given rise to speculation that it may soon be feasible to create human beings in the same way. In fact, substantial technical obstacles remain to be overcome,[2] but no doubt they will be in time. The prospect of human cloning is ferociously controversial.[3] The controversy presupposes that if human cloning were safe, reliable, and permitted, there would be a demand for it. For if there would be no demand, why worry? More realistically, if the demand would be slight, or limited to situations that do not provoke acute concern on the part of people who worry about human cloning, there would be no reason to incur the bother and expense of prohibiting it out of fear of monstrous social consequences.

We therefore limit our discussion to the demand for human cloning. We assume that a safe and effective procedure will be developed that enables a man or a woman to produce a perfect genetic copy of himself or herself (or of his or her child—or of anyone, for that matter), a copy that would bear the same genetic relation to the cloned individual that one identical twin bears to the other. We ask, Who will want to take advantage of this procedure, and with what effects: In economic terminology, we focus on the private benefits and social costs of human cloning. We do not consider the demand for cloning in countries in which the demand for

children is much greater, and the status of women much lower than in the United States and its peer countries. Nor do we consider the moral and legal issues presented by cloning, such as whether cloning should be permitted without the permission of the person cloned and who would have parental rights over the clone of a person involuntarily cloned. These are not absurd questions; cloning need not be an invasive procedure, since a person sheds many cells every day, any of which might be cloned.

Nor do we attempt to factor into our analysis the sheer "weirdness" of human cloning, a consideration that might be thought to depress the demand. Not only is this consideration analytically intractable, but it is probably only transitional. A product or service that is new and rare tends to be thought of as weird, and its diffusion is resisted. But if it is a source of potentially substantial net benefits, its use will spread, and when some critical mass is reached, the aversion will drop away and a more rapid diffusion will begin.

We are tempted to put to one side the case in which a couple clones its dying child in order to produce a closer replacement than it would get by having another child in the usual way, or in which an infertile couple clones one of the partners in lieu of adoption or (if it is a heterosexual couple and the man is the infertile one) of artificial insemination, or in which cloning is used because one of the partners has a serious genetic disease or weakness. In these situations—situations of "reproductive failure" in a broad sense—cloning might seem to be simply a substitute for the other methods of obtaining a child that do not involve sexual intercourse between the parents. If the demand for human cloning were limited to these situations, the procedure might not seem worthy of greater controversy than in vitro fertilization of long-frozen ova. (Not that modern reproductive technology is uncontroversial; our point is only that human cloning considered merely as an alternative reproductive technology need not raise particularly novel issues.) Yet we shall see later that this may be mistaken—that cloning

the infertile could have the radical consequence of eventually eliminating sexual reproduction. The critical difference between cloning and other reproductive technologies is not that cloning involves choosing what genes one's child shall have; such choices are within the horizon of reproductive technology wholly apart from the Dolly trick of cloning an adult nonreproductive cell. The critical difference is that the other methods require fertility and cloning does not, or more precisely that cloning does not require that the biological parent be fertile but only that there be a womb, not necessarily the genetic parent's womb, capable of incubating the clone embryo.

Since gene selection is not limited to cloning, what we have to say about the demand for cloning may well have implications for other reproductive technologies. But we shall generally ignore those implications. Comparison with in vitro fertilization and the other now-familiar techniques for overcoming problems of fertility must not be allowed to obscure the fundamental point that the demand for human cloning would in all likelihood not be limited to cases of "reproductive failure," broadly construed to include the child who dies before reaching adulthood and the parent who fears transmitting a bad gene. The amplification of this point is the main contribution of this essay.

The principal reason not to expect the demand for human cloning to be limited to cases of reproductive failure lies in evolutionary biology. A gene's frequency depends on the rate at which the organisms that are carrying the gene reproduce themselves. In the word "themselves" is the key to understanding the genetic appeal, as it were, of cloning. In sexual reproduction, a gene of one of the parents has only a 50 percent chance of being reproduced; with cloning, it is 100 percent. We might incautiously expect, therefore, an evolved preference for cloning, similar to the evolved preference of most people for their children (who have on average 50 percent of each parent's genes) over their nephews (who have on average 25 percent of each uncle's or aunt's genes). Yet we do

not find a preference for cloning. The reason is that reproduction by cloning was not an available choice for human beings during the period in which the genetic makeup of the human race—the basis of our instinctual preferences and aversions—reached its present state. The likely reason that this choice did not evolve is that the reshuffling of the genes with every generation, which we get with sexual reproduction, provides protection against co-evolving parasites.[4] From the standpoint of inclusive fitness, the benefits apparently exceed the costs, for "natural" human cloning is limited to the rare case of identical twins.

The fact that a particular course of conduct might increase the frequency of one's genes doesn't mean that it will be undertaken. Otherwise the demand to be a donor to a sperm bank would be much greater than it is, for it is an extremely cheap way for a man to increase the frequency of his genes. Since there were no sperm banks in the period in which human beings evolved to their present state, a proclivity to donate to such banks has never evolved. Likewise there is no innate proclivity to clone oneself; but equally important, there is no innate aversion to cloning oneself, as there is to heights, which were, as cloning was not, a feature of our distant ancestors' environment.

The absence of an instinctual aversion is important because sexual desire is not the only evolved mechanism for stimulating reproduction. People love children, particularly their own; so adoption is rarely considered a perfect substitute for having natural children, even though the natural route will often be more costly for the mother. Parents enjoy noticing physical and mental resemblances between their children and themselves and thinking of their children as conferring upon themselves a kind of immortality. This narcissistic tendency, which we call evolved rather than acculturated because of its universality and its importance to reproductive fitness—people who don't have a strong preference for their own children are unlikely to produce many descendants—is likely to make some people, perhaps a great many people, desire perfect ge-

netic copies of themselves. Very few people prefer to be the parents of the biological child of another person even if that child is greatly superior to what they themselves could produce, unless they have a deadly genetic defect. Adoption is a last resort.[5] Some people might therefore prefer to have a child that was entirely their own, rather than only half their own, from a genetic standpoint. This preference would be a logical extension of the well-documented tendency in animal species and primitive human communities to assist relatives in proportion to the fraction of shared genes.[6] That proportion reaches 100 percent for clones and identical twins.

In short, why share your genes if you don't have to? We are not likely to shudder at the thought of cloning ourselves, given the absence of an instinctual fear of cloning. As for danger from coevolving parasites, modern medicine has largely banished that concern. Moreover, if it is a danger, it is one to the health of the human race as a whole rather than to that of an individual faced with choosing between sexual reproduction and cloning; the clone is unlikely to be more susceptible to infectious disease than his parent.

There are cultural as distinct from biological answers to the question, Why share your genes if you don't have to? but they would not convince everybody to follow the traditional route if cloning were cheap. One answer is through sexual reproduction you may produce someone even better than yourself, with the improvement compensating for the dilution of your genes in the next generation. This answer will appeal especially to people whose success in life exceeds what one would have predicted from knowing their genetic endowment. These people can "buy" the superior genes of a spouse with the financial resources or social prestige that is the fruit of their worldly success. Such a purchase is especially attractive from the standpoint of reproductive fitness when the purchaser has some genetic defect that will limit the reproductive capabilities of his clone.

Another answer to the question, Why dilute your genetic legacy?, is that it is a price of marriage—you will have to give your spouse a share of "your" children's genes. If this is an attractive trade, presumably because you put a high value on marriage or the particular marriage partner, it means that, as in the previous example, the dilution of your genes is compensated.

Both examples illustrate the important point that our genetic endowment does not completely determine our behavior. So from the fact that cloning would often be a way of maximizing the number of copies of our genes in the next generation it cannot be inferred that the demand for cloning will be great, even if the monetary cost is modest. Specifically, the demand for human cloning is likely to be concentrated in people who have "good" genes (by which we mean genes that make it more likely that a person will have good physical and mental health, high intelligence, or other prized talents, energy, and physical attractiveness, not necessarily genes that maximize reproductive fitness) *and* would not derive great benefits from marriage. These will sometimes, perhaps often, be the same people. Good genes as we have defined them are positively correlated with worldly success, that is, what makes them "good" in a society such as ours. The more successful a person is, the better able he will be either to marry on his own terms or to get along without being married at all. Some of these people will want to marry anyway; but others will not. Already we observe many people choosing not to marry. There would be more—and with a tilt not observed today toward the genetically and financially privileged—if human cloning were feasible and cheap. Cloning would thus be "anti-marriage," and, even if cheap, would benefit mostly rich men and women.

In stressing "normal narcissism" as a spur to cloning in cases where there is no problem of reproductive failure, we may have seemed to overlook a simpler point, that cloning provides a method of quality control or assurance. If we think of reproduction as the "purchase" of a child by its parents, the "product" cannot be ob-

served before it is purchased or its qualities ascertained with any confidence. Cloning overcomes this uncertainty—or does it? The prospective parent may not be certain how many of his own qualities are due to his genes and how many to randomly favorable environmental factors that are unlikely to be duplicated in the upbringing of his clone child. He can reduce this uncertainty by mating with a person who has similar qualities, since the probability that the qualities of both persons are the product of luck rather than genes is less than the probability that the qualities of one of the two persons are.

From what we have said so far, it should be apparent that analyzing the demand for cloning and the social effects if the demand is allowed to be satisfied is difficult and involves many imponderables, even if the supply of cloning services is unproblematic. Intuition is not a reliable guide to estimating the consequences of cloning. Consider the most "obvious" of these consequences: an increase in the birth rate. By providing an alternative to sexual reproduction that some people might prefer, cloning would reduce the total costs of producing children. Yet the number of children might not increase. Cloning does not just reduce the cost of having a child, for example, to a person for whom sexual reproduction might be impossible or unappealing; it produces a different *kind* of child, namely, an identical twin of the parent. Someone who considered this kind superior to a child produced by sexual reproduction might decide to have fewer children, substituting perceived quality for quantity.[7] This would be especially likely if people generally prefer to have a child of their own sex, since cloning will produce that every time. Indeed, it seems plausible that people who cloned themselves would generally want to have just one child. The second child would be identical to the first, and a mixture of clones and sexually produced children might engender serious tensions. It is possible, therefore, that cloning would lead to a reduction rather than an increase in the birth rate.

We need a model to help us sort through these issues.

A Model of the Demand for Human Cloning

We begin by assuming that people seek to maximize their children's welfare,[8] viewed as an increasing function of the child's genetic endowment.[9] Imagine a society consisting of ten people, all adults. For simplicity, assume that everyone is of the same sex and can mate with anyone else and that each person has one child either by cloning or in the usual way; if the latter, the couple has exactly two children, to preserve the ratio of one adult to one child. Each person can be ranked from 1 to 10, with person 1 having the least desirable genetic endowment and person 10 the highest. A child is assumed to have the average genetic endowment of its parent(s); therefore, if a person clones himself, his child will have the same genetic endowment as he. Implicitly this assumes, but plausibly if we confine our attention to just a few generations, that the environment is not changing radically. If it is, the clone may be less well adapted than the sexually produced child, because the clone's missing parent may have genes better adapted to the new environment.

Table 1 reveals the payoffs under alternative reproductive regimes: a regime in which mating is the only option, a regime in which one may mate or be cloned, and a regime in which only people with a genetic endowment greater than 7 may clone themselves. This last option approximates a world in which the genetically best endowed are also the wealthiest and only the wealthiest people can afford to be cloned.

To understand the payoffs under mating, observe that 10 will marry 9, giving their child a genetic endowment of 9.5. This leaves 8 to marry 7, 6 to marry 5, . . . 2 to marry 1. Under cloning, 10 will clone himself because the payoff (10) exceeds the payoff from marrying 9 (9.5).[10] While 9 would rather marry 10 than clone himself, 10 is no longer available. But 9 would rather clone himself (and obtain a 9 child) than marry 8 and obtain for his (their) child

TABLE 1

Genetic Endowment of Offspring Under Alternative Reproductive Regimes

Parent	Reproductive Regime		
	Mating	*Cloning*	*Cloning* >*7*
1	1.5	1	0.0
2	1.5	2	2.5
3	3.5	3	2.5
4	3.5	4	4.5
5	5.5	5	4.5
6	5.5	6	6.5
7	7.5	7	6.5
8	7.5	8	8.0
9	9.5	9	9.0
10	9.5	10	10.0

an endowment of only 8.5. This process will continue all the way to 1, who must clone himself because there is no one left for him to mate with. When only the genetically best-endowed people can clone themselves (the last column in the table), all the less well endowed mate with each other unless, as in 1's case, no one is left for him to mate with.

The model suggests the possibility that the option to clone oneself could drive out sexual reproduction (except for the occasional contraception failure) and thus the mixing of genes over generations. The genetically best-endowed people in the model clone themselves because they do not want to mix their genes with people at the next level down. The people at the next level down do not want to mix their genes with the people below them, so they clone themselves as well. And this continues all the way to the least well endowed. Cloning would not completely displace sexual reproduction, however, unless it was possible to determine people's genetic endowments accurately, the preference for maximizing

one's children's genetic endowments overrode all other preferences, and cloning was not much more costly than sexual reproduction.[11]

Notice that the availability of free cloning would not necessarily help the genetically best endowed at the expense of the least endowed, as one might expect. It would make 10 better off, 9 worse off, 8 better off, 7 worse off, and so on. The availability of free cloning would make the least well endowed (types 1–5) worse off as a group only if they would otherwise marry the best endowed (types 6–10). They would not. The well endowed would generally marry each other, in order to provide the best genetic endowment for their children, and this would leave the least endowed to marry each other.[12] Therefore, the availability of cloning would make some well endowed better off and others worse off and some poorly endowed better off and others worse off.

Even if cloning were expensive, so that only people with a genetic endowment (and, we are assuming, corresponding wealth) greater than 7 could afford it, the best endowed might not be made better off or the least endowed worse off. The availability of expensive cloning would make 9 worse off because it would allow 10 to remove himself from the marriage pool, eliminating 9's chance of obtaining some of 10's genes for his offspring. It would also make 7 worse off because 8 would clone himself. But 7 could no longer marry 8 and so would have to marry 6, and this would make 6 better off than under either alternative regime.

A risk-neutral person, evaluating the regimes behind the veil of ignorance, would thus be indifferent between no cloning and free cloning but would prefer either regime to expensive cloning because the average payoff for the first two regimes is 5.5 and for the third regime is 5.4. But this (slight) difference arises only because we have assumed that an odd number of people can afford to clone themselves in a society consisting of an even number of people, so that person 1 cannot have any children. This is an artifact of the example.

A risk-averse person might prefer the no-cloning regime to the free-cloning regime and the free-cloning regime to the expensive-cloning regime. For notice that in the table the distribution of payoffs widens as one moves from left to right. People might fear cloning because they do not like the idea that one could be born into a world in which one's children are certain to inherit one's bad genes, as opposed to one in which some mixing is likely. The advantage of mixing to the risk-averse person is that he gains more from avoiding the worst result (having the worst genes and passing them on unmixed) than he loses from not being able to achieve the best result (having the best genes and passing them on unmixed). But he would have to weigh this gain against the fact that the no-cloning regime forces him to bear the risk of infertility. If you're infertile, only through cloning can you transmit your genes to the next generation.

We can enrich the model by assuming that a child's welfare is an increasing function of his wealth (including the value of his education prior to adulthood and gifts and bequests from the parent afterward) as well as of his genetic endowment. We assume diminishing marginal utility both of genetic endowment and of wealth, so that an equal amount of each produces more welfare than do unequal amounts.

Imagine that society consists of 100 people, each of whom can be located within a 10-by-10 matrix, with genetic endowment on one axis and wealth on the other. Each person is assumed to have a unique genes-wealth pair, so that, for example, (1,1) denotes a poor person with bad genes and (10,10) a rich person with good genes. The average child produced in the usual way will have the average of his parents' genetic endowments, so that, for example, the mating of (10,10) and (2,4) will produce on average a (6,7), and for simplicity we'll now drop the qualification "on average" and assume that every child has the average of his parents' endowments. We define a person's welfare as the sum of the logarithms of each of his endowments to reflect the diminishing marginal utility of

each. For example, welfare for (9,1) is 0.95, whereas for (5,5) it is 1.40.

Under these assumptions and in a regime of no cloning, the very highly endowed will marry each other and the least endowed will marry each other, but rich people with bad genes will marry poor people with good genes. (10,10) does best by marrying (9,10) or (10,9), while (1,9) does better by marrying (9,1) than by marrying (5,5), and (5,5) does better by marrying (6,4) than by marrying (9,1). The match between (10,10) and (9,10) produces a child with endowments of (9.5,10) and welfare, therefore, of 1.98. The match between (1,9) and (9,1) produces a child with endowments of (5,5) and welfare of 1.40, and the match between (5,5) and (6,4) produces a child with endowments of (5.5,4.5) for a welfare of 1.39, while a match between (9,1) and (5,5) produces a child (7,3) with welfare of 1.32.

In a regime of free cloning, people with equal endowments would clone themselves (those on the high end by choice, those on the low end because no one would marry them), although people with unequal endowments would continue to marry each other. The results would not be much different in a regime of expensive cloning. Again, the high equals would clone themselves; the unequals, even if wealthy, would marry; but this time the low equals would have to marry each other rather than clone. Sexual reproduction would continue to be preferred by many people. People with good genes but little wealth would want to "trade" their genes for money in order to have the wherewithal to support and financially endow their offspring, while wealthy people with poor genes would want to trade their money for genes. Both types of trade require sexual reproduction. Yet on fairly ordinary assumptions about what people desire in their children, many people—all the equals—would clone themselves, and as a result the amount of genetic mixing would decline. And since people who had both great wealth and superb genes would no longer have to spread

their wealth and genetic material in order to have children, cloning might foster the emergence of a genetic and financial elite.[13]

The Model Further Enriched

We can enrich the model further by asking, What if people could have as many children as they wanted? In a regime in which cloning is feasible and permitted, rich people with good genes who wanted to maximize the welfare of each child would have just one clone and no other children. The reason is that wealth, as distinct from genes, must be spread (though not necessarily evenly) among multiple children whether they are clones or the products of sexual reproduction. But if instead rich people wanted to maximize the chance that their genes would survive for many generations, the best strategy might be either to have multiple clones, because the extra genetic copies are cheap and only the wealth must be divided, or to have a few clones and a few ordinary children because a sexual partner with an overall poorer genetic endowment may still have some superior genes. A few people might wish to clone other people besides themselves or their children,[14] but we shall ignore this possibility. Nothing in our analysis depends on whether all people who want to clone want to clone themselves. A recent poll revealed that 6 percent of the respondents wanted to clone themselves, and apparently none wanted to clone anyone else.[15]

To the extent that cloning increased the demand for children by offering superior opportunities for maximizing one's influence on the gene pool, inequalities of wealth would decline because rich people would have more children among whom to divide their wealth. This possibility should moderate concern that cloning would increase disparities in wealth, genetic endowment, and overall welfare. But as we noted earlier, it is by no means certain that cloning would result in more children. Moreover, cooperation

among clones, facilitated by genetic identity, which should reduce friction (as seems to be the case with identical twins), might enable the wealth of a family to grow faster than the number of members.

Let us consider differences between the sexes in the demand for clone. Cloning would benefit women more than men,[16] and so the demand for clone would presumably be greater among women. Cloning would allow them to have children later in life, enabling them to invest more in their market skills earlier.[17] Women while pregnant or taking care of the children would be less dependent on men for support. As a result, there would be fewer marriages; unmarried women would become wealthier relative to men; married women would have greater bargaining power in marriage. These effects would be multiplied when the woman had great wealth, good genes, or both. Wealth would allow her to raise the child alone, and good genes would make her less likely to find a man with equally good genes. Her benefits from marriage and sexual reproduction would be small.

Although the availability of cloning would benefit women with good genes and good market skills, it is less clear that it would benefit other women. On the one hand, cloning would hurt women by reducing men's demand for women's fertility. Because a man could have himself cloned and pay for help in raising the child, he could satisfy his desire to reproduce himself without enlisting the participation of a woman, save as the incubator of the clone fetus.[18] This would hurt women who lacked wealth or good genes, since such a woman would not be able to compensate the man for sharing his children's genes with her by forgoing cloning. On the other hand, cloning would benefit women by reducing their dependence on men's fertility. Because a woman could have herself cloned and pay for household help, she could satisfy her desire to reproduce herself without enlisting the aid of a man. This option would be available to poor women if welfare paid for the costs of raising clone children. Moreover, cloning by wealthy women would increase the demand for womb rental by poor women, since there

would be little reason for a wealthy woman to carry her clone fetus herself, especially with no husband to help out.

Gillian Hadfield argues that women and girls (maybe at the urging of their parents) invest in skills that are complements to the skills ordinarily possessed by men because women with complementary skills are more desirable marriage partners than women with redundant skills.[19] As evidence, she points out that in all societies men and women specialize in different kinds of work, but that with some exceptions for work requiring great strength there is little cross-cultural consistency in the kind of work that men and women do. The availability of cheap cloning would reduce the importance for women of having complementary market skills. Girls would no longer be as likely to invest in complementary education; they would invest in whatever education would maximize their lifetime earnings independently of a husband's career. The result would be an even more rapid entry of women into areas of the workforce traditionally dominated by men than we are observing today.

Human cloning might thus portend an accelerating breakdown in the traditional roles of men and women and facilitate the emergence of a class of wealthy and powerful women—both disturbing prospects to men and women who hold traditional views of sex roles.

To summarize the discussion to this point, cloning would benefit mainly wealthy women with good genes and to a lesser extent wealthy men with good genes. One would therefore expect, if human cloning were feasible and permitted, a growing concentration of wealth and highly desired heritable characteristics at the top end of the distribution of these goods and fewer marriages there. Although the rest of the population distribution would be made relatively worse off as a group, many people within that part of the distribution would be made better off, including people with incurable infertility.

But the model is still too abstract. Wealth, genetic endowment,

risk aversion, fertility, and sexual difference are not the only important variables bearing on the demand for and consequences of cloning. Here is a mundane but frightening point: The demand for cloning would be disproportionately concentrated in people whose narcissism exceeded normal bounds, and, more generally, in people who today are prevented from (or rather impeded in) reproducing by being unmarriageable, usually because of severe personality disorders. Normal people want to mate with other normal people, not with people who are psychotic; and psychotics themselves probably do not want to mate with other psychotics, and often do not want to mate or associate with anyone, since difficulty of establishing personal relationships is a symptom of a disordered personality.[20] Extreme narcissists in particular would probably not want to marry anyone, save on terms intolerable to any self-respecting person[21]—especially another narcissist! Other types of men and women who today have difficulty finding mates include mentally retarded people, people with serious physical disabilities, convicted felons, homosexuals, pedophiles, and sociopaths. Men despairing of or rejecting marriage (or simply wanting to have more children than is feasible through sexual reproduction in a society that outlaws polygamy) who wanted to clone themselves would still have to rent a womb, and that would create some constraint, even though the necessity of finding a mate would be eliminated. Women who cloned themselves would be self-sufficient; they would have merely to bear the cost of pregnancy. Concern about clones carrying defective genes and raised by disordered persons might engender pressure for governmental screening of people who wanted to clone themselves, thus raising the spectre of eugenic regulation. This would be an example of how technology, by eliminating a social or biological barrier to an activity, can increase the optimal scope of government.

Persons with extraordinary talents having a large genetic component, such as champion athletes and world-class musicians, might be tempted to clone themselves. If so, then over time the eco-

nomic rents obtained by persons who have scarce and highly valued genetic endowments would decline—an income-equalizing effect of cloning. An esoteric but important class of potential demanders for cloning are dictators, who might believe that problems of succession would be lessened if a clone were waiting in the wings. Imagine if when Stalin died, a fifty-year-old Stalin clone had been Stalin's designated successor; imagine if today Fidel Castro had a fifty-year-old clone.

An important variable in the demand for human cloning is the desire of most people to marry. As we noted earlier, they are unlikely to be able to do so if they are "gene selfish." In addition, most people do not seek to produce a child who is *merely* financially and genetically well endowed, but one who is happy, and most people believe that happier children have two parents. What is more, because of economies of scale and specialization within the household, it is less than twice as expensive for a couple to raise two children than for a single parent to raise one. Against these points it can be noted that the desire to marry is in part a function of the desire for children. The more the desire for children can be satisfied by alternative arrangements, the less demand there will be for marriage. And cloning can be reconciled with marriage and dual parenting in the following way: The married couple can decide that rather than producing two children sexually they will each clone. This is not a perfect solution for them. Because a person is more closely related to his or her clone than to his or her sexually reproduced children, and *a fortiori* than to his or her spouse's clone, to whom indeed he or she is not related at all, each spouse may have difficulty thinking of himself or herself as a parent of both children; so dual cloning may not produce dual parenting.

We can put this differently. The man who "sells" his wife a genetic half-interest in "his" children gets in return more than someone who will take a share (maybe the lion's share) in the rearing of the children. He gets a child rearer who has a superior *motivation* to do a good job precisely because of the genetic bond. Altruism is

a substitute for market incentives, and the man can take advantage of this substitute by giving his wife a genetic stake in the children.[22] So marriage and sexual reproduction would remain for many, probably for most, persons a superior alternative to cloning, even if cloning were not only lawful but also very cheap.

Many people, moreover, want to have children that differ from them in important (genetic) respects. They wish to improve their stock, which they cannot do by cloning themselves, or to hedge against the risk that their own genes are not as good as they think. Even if they are preoccupied with, or driven subliminally by their genes to maximize, their inclusive fitness, they can do this as well by having two children, each of whom shares half their genes, as by having two children, one of whom shares all their genes and the other (the spouse's clone) none.

And it is impossible to know whether people would find cloning an attractive option until we know what a clone would be like. A clone might seem disappointingly different from his parent, or eerily similar; in either case, people might prefer sexual reproduction. And we have not taken into account possible social responses to cloning. If cloning led to an extraordinarily unequal distribution of wealth, society might respond by imposing highly progressive taxes. It might even place an excise tax on cloning. Then adverse effects on wealth distribution would not be compelling arguments against the availability of cloning—unless the costs of social measures to reduce the distributive effects of cloning were great, which they might be.

In a discussion of an imagined but no longer unforeseeable reproductive technology that would allow a husband and wife to choose which of their genes to give to their child, Thomas Schelling points out that people might compete over characteristics.[23] They might, for example, choose taller children in the hope of giving them competitive advantages. But their hope would be dashed because all children would become taller, assuming many other parents also had a preference for tall children. Because cloning gives

people less power over the genetic characteristics of their children, the danger of such a zero-sum competition is less. But the general point still holds. To the extent that genetic endowment is a positional good, competition over it does not produce social gains; in contrast, competition in the market produces social gains because market goods are, for the most part, nonpositional, at least if envy is ignored.

Schelling's point raises the general question of the effect of cloning on the clones themselves. Earlier we assumed that parents want to maximize their children's welfare. This is an unrealistic assumption. Rational parents want to maximize their own welfare, and thus their children's only to the extent that the children's welfare enters into the parents' utility function. So we cannot assume, at least when people have a choice between cloning and sexual reproduction, that their children's welfare will be maximized by the choice made.

Setting to one side biological uncertainties that we assume will eventually be dispelled,[24] the clone will be a perfectly normal human being, as normal as an identical twin. But the vertical relation of genetic identity has different implications from the horizontal relation. Take the case in which a married couple decides to have two clones, one of each spouse, rather than producing children sexually. If the clones then clone themselves, the original husband and wife will have the same genetic relationship to their grandchildren as to their children, while their children will have no genetic relationship to each other and also their grandchildren no genetic relationship to each other. If the (unrelated) children marry each other and coproduce a child, the original husband will have a closer relationship with his grandchild than with the cloned child he has through his wife. Or suppose a husband and a wife coproduce a child and then clone the child while he is still an infant. Is the clone the child's sibling or the child's child? Is he the father's child or the father's grandchild? If the clone grows up and clones himself, the original husband and wife will have the same genetic

relationship to their grandchild as they have to their child. In these examples, cloning might run up against the deep-seated incest taboo, though this is speculative.

In the Very Long Term

We consider, finally, some highly speculative long-term effects of human cloning. One is that it might reduce the genetic diversity of the human race by facilitating eugenic breeding. Imagine: Parents coproduce a child, who at the age of three manifests signs of great precocity. They clone this child rather than coproduce another child. Or parents have two children and clone the better-looking or more intelligent one. Fertile parents who share a common genetic defect or infertile parents who have genetic defects may choose to clone superior relatives or, indeed, to purchase the right to clone other people who have desirable genes, although that tendency will be retarded by the preference for own over adopted children. Because cloning involves a smaller genetic gamble than does a combination of sperm and egg of even highly desirable strangers, cloning would be preferred to artificial insemination or surrogate motherhood by those attracted to the idea of selective breeding. To the extent that selection was in favor of a few widely desired features, and against the widely undesired, human genetic diversity would decrease, with obvious risks to human adaptability to unforeseeable changes in the environment that might make currently undesirable traits more valuable and currently desirable traits less valuable.

In cultures in which boys are valued more than girls, parents might decide to clone the father or, having coproduced a son, to clone that son rather than risk having daughters. Over time, sex ratios could change dramatically.[25] This process may be self-correcting in the long run, because girls will become more valued offspring as the ratio of males to females rises. Even so, the in-

evitable lags in the self-correcting process might cause grave social dislocations and incite demands for intrusive government regulation of reproductive decisions,[26] for which we now have ample precedent in East Asia. Asked to correct an undesirable sex ratio, government would have to choose some legal instrument. Maybe it would tax the cloning of men but not the cloning of women, or tax cloning but not coproduction. Since wealthier people would have more clones than poorer people, a tendency accelerated by the tax, wealthier people would have relatively more boys. And once it became acceptable for the government to influence cloning, could interest groups resist using the government to encourage the cloning of some people (geniuses?) but not others (the genetically defective)? We would then be in the much-feared world of eugenic regulation.

Earlier we showed that cloning might have a tendency to crowd out sexual reproduction. The more people clone, the fewer people are available for sexual reproduction; the pool of potential reproductive partners shrinks, and it becomes more difficult to produce a superior child by reproduction than by cloning. A different path of crowding out is opened if we consider the possible long-term consequences of even the relatively benign public policy with which we began this essay: permitting only infertile couples to clone themselves. Currently, mutant genes that interfere with sexual reproduction cannot be propagated; infertile people do not have offspring. When cloning becomes available, the genes that enable sexual reproduction will lose their survival advantage over genes that interfere with sexual reproduction. Imagine a society consisting of 50 men and 50 women. Assume that in every generation 2 percent of the people (for simplicity, one man and one woman) are infertile because of a condition that is heritable. Assume everyone marries and the average couple has 2.04 children (for example, 48 couples have two children and one couple has 4 children). In a world without cloning, the genes of the infertile people will not be reproduced, and every generation will replace itself by producing

100 children. Now suppose that cloning becomes available. Each generation's infertile couples will have on average 2.04 (cloned) children, who will be infertile (for we are discussing cases in which infertility is caused by an inherited defect). So while the first generation will consist of 98 fertile people and 2 infertile people, the second generation will consist of 98 fertile people and 4 infertile people, and the third generation of 98 fertile people and 6 infertile people. In five generations clones would constitute almost 10 percent of the population; eventually they would be dominant.[27]

It is not clear whether sexual reproduction would eventually disappear. On the one hand, random mutations would interfere with sexual reproduction but would not interfere with the cloning of infertile people—a crucial asymmetry. And as the percentage of fertile people fell, the costs of matching would rise because the population of potential mates would be small. On the other hand, the mixing of genes that results from sexual reproduction may enhance survival, even under the environmentally gentler conditions brought about by modern medicine.

As long as clones must be incubated in human wombs (which may not be for long, for artificial wombs are being developed), infertile men and women would generally (depending on the nature of the woman's infertility) have to pay fertile women[28] to bear their clones. If as a result these women did not reproduce themselves, infertility would spread even more rapidly than in our numerical example. It is true that if infertile individuals married fertile individuals and the couple decided to have only the fertile partner cloned, the genes for infertility would not be reproduced. But it is more likely that the infertile partner would demand that at least one child be his or her clone; the preference for costly and painful reproductive technologies over adoption attests to the importance that people attach to genetic reproduction (what we earlier discussed as normal narcissism). So each infertile person might make clones of himself or herself without matching up with anyone else,

or might marry another infertile person and share the burden of raising two clones.

People can clone themselves faster than they can produce children through sexual reproduction, which imposes a delay of more than nine months between children. Because of the strong incentives of modern women to delay childbearing until late in life, this might give cloning a great advantage over sexual reproduction. Perhaps great enough to increase the birth rate of the infertile over the fertile, assuming cloning were practiced only by the former. To take an extreme example, if infertile couples clone themselves once (that is, produce two clones) in the time that a fertile couple takes to have one child, and if time between births is the only constraint on reproduction, then starting in our world of 100 people of whom 2 are infertile, infertile clones would outnumber fertile people in about five generations.

Our estimates of the possible effects of cloning on fertility are, of course, highly sensitive to the percentage of persons having *heritable* infertility. The percentage is not known. It is undoubtedly only a small fraction of all persons who are infertile, because genes that cause infertility are maladaptive and hence highly likely to be selected out in the course of evolution. The number of persons with fertility problems, heritable or nonheritable, is unknown, because only people who are trying and failing to have a child (and not all of them) seek medical attention for such problems. Infertility, moreover, is often a function of the couple, each member of which might be fertile with another sexual partner. It has, however, been estimated that at least 20 percent of fertility problems are male and that 10 to 20 percent of these are genetic.[26] Assuming a like percentage of genetic female infertility problems (for which, however, we have not been able to find any substantiation), 10 to 20 percent of all fertility problems are genetic. The higher figure may be consistent with the estimate we used earlier, that 2 percent of couples have heritable fertility problems. An estimated 7.1 percent

of married couples have fertility problems,[30] and this is clearly an underestimate, not only because noncomplainers are not counted but also because people who know themselves to be infertile are less likely to marry. On the other hand, fertility problems often merely delay rather than prevent conception and birth, and often are treatable; so 2 percent may be too high after all. But since random genetic mutations can cause a fertile person to become infertile, while it is extremely unlikely that a random mutation would cause an already infertile person to become fertile, it may not be crucial whether 2 percent or 0.2 percent or even 0.002 percent of the population is afflicted with mutations that impair infertility. Infertility will spread like a virus, merely at different rates, and eventually drive off fertility.

The spread of infertility through cloning might be even more rapid if, as realism requires, "reproductive failure" were defined broadly enough to encompass the situation of a homosexual couple, for whom cloning might be an attractive alternative to adoption, artificial insemination (if it is a lesbian couple), or surrogate motherhood (if it is a male homosexual couple). Assuming that all or most homosexual orientation is genetic,[31] the fraction of homosexual genes in the gene pool would be increased if cloning resulted in a disproportionate increase in reproduction by homosexuals, who might be thought of as "functionally" infertile to the extent that they do not reproduce sexually. But this depends on the transmission path of the homosexual gene. If the gene predisposing to male homosexuality is through the female line,[32] then male homosexuals will not transmit the gene to their clones.

Is the spread of infertility throughout the population something to be feared, when, by assumption, people are able to reproduce using cloning technologies? As noted earlier, the evolutionary advantage of sexual over asexual reproduction is that the mixing of genes protects future generations against coevolving parasites. If everyone cloned himself, future generations would have the same genetic diversity as the current generation; so parasites that evolved

the capacity to crack the immunological defenses of members of the current generation would pose a threat to the members of future generations who were their clones. And if some people cloned themselves more than others, future generations would have less genetic diversity than the current generation. Genetic diversity, like vaccination, is a barrier to the spread of parasites. Like the person who refuses to be vaccinated, the person who clones himself or herself does not internalize all the costs of his or her behavior. Unless medical technology evolves as quickly as parasites do, over time the human race could find itself increasingly vulnerable to disease.

Conclusion

Our exploration of the likely demand for human cloning has been strictly that—exploratory. The demand is impossible to estimate; it depends on too many variables of uncertain strength. But the analysis does provide a rational basis for the widespread disquiet that the prospect of human cloning has aroused. Some of that disquiet has religious or emotional foundations that our analysis does not touch; some of it reflects an unreasoning fear of change. But consider: The most sympathetic demanders for human cloning, the infertile, may, over time, if allowed to clone, drive out sexual reproduction. The least sympathetic demanders, extreme narcissists and other psychotics and misfits, will be among the most enthusiastic for cloning, and their cloning too will feed on itself to the extent that the disorder that makes them unmarriageable is hereditary.[33] The point is not that cloning frees each sex from dependence on the other, though it does (women more clearly than men, however, since a womb is still necessary), but that it eliminates the barrier to reproduction that is created by the need to find another person willing to mate with you. That barrier is a screen against reproduction by people with serious maladjustments.

Cloning may also aggravate inequalities in genetic endowment and in wealth, undermine the already imperiled institution of marriage, alter the sex ratio, and create irresistible pressures for eugenic regulation. This is on the one hand. On the other hand, some of the frightening effects of cloning may be offsetting: If, as we speculate, cloning will increase the wealth and power of women, the demand for daughters may rise, canceling out a preference for sons that cloning might enable parents to indulge. And some of the effects are so long run that technological advances of the very kind that have given us cloning may eliminate them: Long before the population becomes dominated by infertile and narcissistic clones, infertility and extreme narcissism may be as passé as smallpox. In other words, fertility technology and psychiatric medicine may advance as rapidly and as far as cloning technology. Perhaps, then, despite the concerns discussed in this paper, only the very cautious will want to prohibit human cloning.

Endnotes

1. See I. Wilmut *et al.*, "Viable Offspring Derived from Fetal and Adult Mammalian Cells," 385 *Nature* 810 (1997), and for a popular treatment Ruth Macklin, "Human Cloning? Don't Just Say No," *U.S. News & World Report,* March 10, 1997, p. 64. The technique involves replacing the nucleus of an ovum with the nucleus of a cell of the animal to be cloned. The ovum is then implanted in a womb, where it grows into a baby in the normal way. When we speak of "cloning" in this essay we mean the method by which Dolly was created, that is, by the cloning of adult nonreproductive tissue from a single animal or human being. The possibility of cloning an adult human being gives new meaning to the term "single parent."
2. See "Whatever Next?" *Economist,* March 1, 1997, p. 79.
3. See, for example, Leon R. Kass, "The Wisdom of Repugnance: Why We Should Ban the Cloning of Humans," *New Republic,* June 1, 1997, p. 17. For an earlier treatment, when cloning was foreseen but not yet within reach, see Paul Ramsey, "Shall We Clone a Man?" in *Fabricated Man: The Ethics of Genetic Control*, ch. 2 (New Haven: Yale University Press, 1970).

4. See William D. Hamilton, "Sex versus Non-Sex versus Parasite," 35 *Oikos* 282 (1980); Robert Trivers, *Social Evolution* 322–330 (Menlo Park: CA: Benjamin/Cummings Publishing, 1985).
5. See, for example, Linda S. Williams, "Adoption Actions and Attitudes of Couples Seeking In Vitro Fertilization: An Exploratory Study," 13 *Journal of Family Issues* 99 (1992), and studies cited there.
6. See, for example, Matt Ridley and Richard Dawkins, "The Natural Selection of Altruism," in *Altruism and Helping Behavior: Social, Personality, and Developmental Perspectives* 19 (J. Philippe Rushton and Richard M. Sorrentino, eds.; Hillsdale, NJ: L. Erlbaum Associates, 1981); Trivers, note 4 above, chs. 3, 6, 15.
7. On the quantity-quality tradeoff in children, see Gary S. Becker, *A Treatise on the Family* 145–154 (enlarged ed.; Cambridge, MA: Harvard University Press, 1991).
8. The assumption is obviously unrealistic, implying as it does that, beyond some age, parents would transfer all their wealth to their children and starve. We relax the assumption later.
9. Another unrealistic, temporary assumption: It abstracts from other constituents of welfare, such as financial resources, not due solely to one's genetic makeup.
10. Notice the assumption that 10 *knows* he's a 10. If there is uncertainty about one's genetic fitness, one may decide to hedge one's bets by mating with someone of similar qualities, as we noted earlier.
11. Another threat posed by cloning to the future of sexual reproduction is considered later in the essay.
12. On the tendency to positive assortative mating, see Becker, note 7 above, at 112–118. With the breakdown in the United States of traditional cultural barriers to marriage between persons otherwise alike (such as barriers against crossing religious or ethnic lines), assortative mating is increasingly likely to take a genetic form. Yet even when such barriers are insurmountable, assortative mating along genetic lines takes place behind the barriers, that is, within the segmented groups.
13. The Hardy-Weinberg Equilibrium, in which gene frequencies remain unchanged from generation to generation, assumes random mating. See, for example, Eli C. Minkoff, *Evolutionary Biology* 142–144 (Reading, MA: Addison Wesley, 1983); Mark Ridley, *Evolution* 87–90 (Boston: Blackwell Scientific, 1993). That is not a realistic assumption for human beings.
14. Humbert Humbert, for example, might have wanted to clone Lolita.
15. "Clone the Clowns," *Economist,* March 1, 1997, p. 80.
16. This is the general effect of technological improvements in reproduction. See Richard A. Posner, "Separating Reproduction from Sex," in *Sex and Reason,* ch. 15 (Cambridge, MA: Harvard University Press, 1992).
17. Although they can get the same result by freezing their eggs and hiring a surro-

gate mother to incubate them, there is still the problem of obtaining sperm to fertilize them. The woman may not want to go to the bother of finding a man with good genes to be the father. She can avoid the bother by going to a sperm bank, but then she is taking a genetic gamble.

18. A current in ancient Greek thought represented by Aeschylus and Aristotle. They believed that *all* children were the father's clone—that the woman's role in reproduction was limited to incubation.

19. Gillian K. Hadfield, "A Coordination Model of the Sexual Division of Labor" (unpublished, University of Toronto Law School, 1996).

20. See, for example, American Psychiatric Association, *Diagnostic and Statistical Manual of Mental Disorders* 638–642 (4th ed.; Washington, DC: American Psychiatric Association, 1994).

21. See, for example, Arnold Rothstein, *The Narcissistic Pursuit of Perfection* 87 (New York: International Universities Press, 1980).

22. Important evidence for this is the enormously increased risk of child abuse by stepparents compared to parents. See Martin Daly and Margo Wilson, *Homicide* 83–93 (New York: A. de Gruyter, 1988).

23. Thomas C. Schelling, *Micromotives and Macrobehavior,* ch. 6 (New York: Norton, 1978).

24. These are lucidly described in the *Economist* article, note 2 above. For example, it is uncertain whether a mammal cloned from nonreproductive tissue would have a normal lifespan; the clone's biological age might be the sum of its and its parent's chronological ages.

25. See Schelling, note 23 above, at 197–203.

26. *Id.* at 202–203.

27. *Cf.* Michael Bliss, *The Discovery of Insulin* 245 (Chicago: University of Chicago Press, 1982): "Because insulin enabled diabetics to live and propagate, and because the disease had a strong hereditary component, the effect of the discovery of insulin was to cause a steady increase in the number of diabetics."

28. Fertile in the sense of being able to carry a fetus to term; they might be infertile in the sense of being unable to produce an egg. The discussion in text assumes that all women are either fertile or infertile in both senses.

29. D. M. de Kretser, "Male Infertility," 349 *Lancet* 787 (1997).

30. Joyce C. Abma *et al.*, "Fertility, Family Planning, and Women's Health: New Data from the 1995 National Survey of Family Growth," 23 *Vital Health Statistics,* no. 19, p. 7 (Centers for Disease Control and Prevention, May 1997).

31. For a summary of the evidence, which however is largely limited to male homosexuality, see Richard A. Posner, "The Economic Approach to Homosexuality," in *Sex, Preference, and Family: Essays on Law and Nature* 173, 186, 191 n. 26 (David M. Estlund and Martha C. Nussbaum, eds.; New York: Oxford, 1997).

32. See Dean H. Hamer *et al.*, "A Linkage between DNA Markers on the X Chromosome and Male Sexual Orientation," 261 *Science* 321 (1993).
33. One can also envisage a demand for clones on the part of people who want a source of "spare parts" for organ transplants and other medical needs.

The authors thank Héctor Acevedo-Polanco, Emlyn Eisenach, Sorin Feiner, Gertrud Fremling, Dan Kahan, Leo Katz, William Landes, Martha Nussbaum, Charlene Posner, Reed Shuldiner, Robert Trivers, and participants in the University of Chicago's Workshop on Rational Models in the Social Sciences for many helpful comments on a previous draft of this essay, and Acevedo-Polanco, Feiner, and Brady Mickelsen for helpful research assistance.

A Rush to Caution: Cloning Human Beings

Richard A. Epstein

What Me Worry?

Few announcements have provoked more rapid public fascination and academic dismay than the news story in the *Observer* on February 23, 1997: Ian Wilmut and his colleagues at the Roslin Institute had successfully cloned Dolly, a sheep from a cell drawn from her (as it were) mother's mammary glands. That successful cloning clearly represented a major and somewhat unexpected technical breakthrough, and since that day further advances have followed rapidly. On July 25, 1997, the *New York Times* reported that a team led by Dr. Wilmut and Dr. Keith Campbell had been able to create a lamb that had a human gene in every cell of its body.[1] That result was quickly topped by news that a Wisconsin biotech company had been able to clone three identical calves from fetal calf tissue, using processes that it claimed were more efficient and reliable than those used by the Wilmut group.[2]

My own position, which I shall develop here, is that these new developments call for no immediate legal response: Watchful waiting is far preferable to hasty or ill-conceived legislation whose unanticipated consequences are likely to do more harm than good. First, do no harm, is as good a principle now as it has ever been. But inaction leaves political actors on the sidelines, where they be-

long but not where they would like to be. So it was all too predictable that the first reports on cloning whipped into action a powerful coalition of the bioethical and legal professions. Various nations across the world, and several states in the United States took the first steps toward a ban on cloning human beings, and, somewhat more diffidently, research that could lead to the cloning of human beings. President Clinton responded to the whiff of crisis first by imposing a temporary ban on federal funding of cloning research, and then by asking President Harold Shapiro of Princeton University to head a distinguished review team of the National Bioethics Advisory Commission (NBAC) to chart the legal and political responses to cloning after taking into account the ethical and religious concerns raised about the practice. The report was duly prepared within 90 days and issued these two recommendations:

- A continuation of the current moratorium on the use of federal funding in support of any attempt to create a child by somatic cell nuclear transfer [i.e., cloning].
- An immediate request to all firms, clinicians, investigators, and professional societies in the private and nonfederally funded sectors to comply voluntarily with the intent of the federal moratorium. Professional and scientific societies should make clear that any attempt to create a child by somatic cell nuclear transfer and implantation into a woman's body would at this time be an irresponsible, unethical, and unprofessional act.[3]

In addition, the NBAC recommended that any legislation prohibiting cloning should contain a sunset clause of between three and five years—an eternity in the field of biotechnology. The NBAC also urged that the regulations in question "be carefully written so as not to interfere with other important areas of scientific research."[4] It then enigmatically suggested that "if the legislative ban

is ever lifted," the twin protections of independent review and informed consent be used to protect the human subjects who participate in preliminary research trials on cloning. From the tone of the report the "ever" suggests that "never" is the preferred position of most of the ethicists and theologians who have anxiously considered the problem.

Why adopt this position in preference to watchful waiting? The usual justifications examine the various ramifications of cloning. One set of objections is quickly proving to be transitory, namely, that the practice is too dangerous to be conducted on human beings today. The second set of objections—those favoring "never"—promise a more permanent ban: a wide set of religious and ethical misgivings that promise to become more, rather than less, insistent as the techniques of cloning are improved.

But "why?" is a question that should be asked in a second way: Why impose the ban *now?* The NBAC's report spends a good deal of time on the merits of human cloning, but it spends far less time thinking through the logic of research bans, whether induced by government decree or moral persuasion. That issue is worth a few comments here. My basic position is that our rush toward caution is not warranted by the factual information, practical doubts, religious convictions, or moral intuitions invoked to sustain it. I plan to get at this issue by taking a slight detour. I shall examine what I consider to be the basic conditions for banning any practice, and thereafter apply these standards to human cloning. I do not wish at present to commit myself to a position that cloning should be forever legal. Still less do I wish to commit myself to a view that some vision of untrammeled reproductive rights places human cloning on some preferred constitutional plane that defeats any and all government efforts to regulate or forbid the practice. Rather my point is merely one of practical philosophy: The presumption of liberty of action counsels waiting, not rushing, to impose any legal prohibitions on human cloning research.

The Basic Framework

It is always dangerous business to set out a writer's basic framework in a few short paragraphs, but I do so to orient the reader.[5] I think that the rights and wrongs of human action are not determined by one grand insight, but come from a set of successful approximations that move us cautiously but surely toward some social ideal. The first step on this journey is that individuals are ordinarily entitled to do what they want. Now that someone (the actor) benefits, the presumption of free action can be overridden only by showing negative consequences to other individuals. Even here, however, a lot depends on the nature of the supposed harm: killing, raping, and maiming are one thing; individual harm from open competition is quite another. The former should galvanize the state into action. The latter should provoke a collective yawn, because over the long run competitive harms are inseparably linked to the competitive benefits that on net advance human welfare. So until we run into monopoly power, the case for liberty of action remains intact.

The analysis thus far presupposes that we can accurately track the consequences of individual actions or practices, so that the major social task is to divide legal from illegal conduct. Our task becomes more complex when we don't know the actual consequences of these actions or practices. At this point we—and here it is the collective "we" to which I refer—are forced to separate forbidden from permitted actions. But we are unable to make the division on the intrinsic quality of certain types of acts: What matters is how things turn out in individual cases. *X* is about to drive an automobile. Surely we should stop him if we know he is going to crash into a house or run over a pedestrian. Yet surely we should bid him fond farewell if we know he will arrive safely at his destination. But what should we do when we are unclear whether his journey will end in disaster or success?

At this point, it is best to examine a range of factors to identify the occasions and ways to apply collective force. One factor, obviously, is the expected cost of the feared harm, which, roughly speaking, is defined as the probability that harm will occur to some individual, multiplied by its anticipated severity. The greater the likelihood of harm, and the greater its expected severity, the stronger the case for banning the action in question. But we also have to consider a second type of error, that of banning activity that might prove harmless or even beneficial: What is the expected probability of a successful outcome, multiplied by the social gain that comes from its occurrence? Even armchair estimates of the relevant variables remind us that life has few certainties. For a start, at least we should resist any rule that bans all activities whose expected costs of harm are greater than zero, wholly without regard to the offsetting benefits: Nothing would ever get done, and we would also starve, unless we could somehow ban starvation as well. Both benefits and costs count in reaching some sensible *final* position on banning.

From that simple observation many nettlesome complications follow. One factor worth looking at is the distribution of gains and losses between persons. Self-inflicted harms usually present little reason for legal intervention: Nature's feedback mechanism is strong enough to stop most self-destructive conduct. It is harm to others, not harm writ-large, that provokes social concern. Now the soundness of any ban depends in large measure on what will happen if no ban is imposed. If the individual actor is on the hook for money damages, the case for banning those activities is weakened: The risk of financial loss will have some of the cautionary effects of self-inflicted injury. To be sure, it takes a bothersome lawsuit to make the damage payment stick, but against institutional defendants with substantial assets, that threat is real. So the basic rule is where damage actions look as though they are effective, then the case for a ban is correspondingly weakened.

More importantly, we should always be alert to choices in the

size and scope of the proposed ban. We could ban everyone from driving a car; we could ban only those who are under sixteen years old; or we could also ban people over sixteen years old who have not passed a test, or who have committed serious traffic violations. Where a more restrictive ban is possible in the future, we should be cautious about imposing the ban today. Better to let the useful activity go forward, and then select the spots in which to impose the ban. In addition, we can mix partial bans, licenses, and damage actions to get the right levels of driving, hopefully by the right people. These principles, moreover, generalize to cover not only driving cars, but also clearing swamps, building apartment houses, and spraying disinfectants. Risk is endemic to all activities; even so—or better, precisely so—we should only shut down those activities that hold a high risk of substantial peril or harm. The strategy will backfire on occasion, and some actions will take place that we will regret in the fullness of time. But the simple fact that we have automobile accidents offers no justification for banning cars, and the occurrence of high-profile oil spills gives no reason for banning oil tankers from the high seas, although it might justify routing them out of environmentally sensitive areas. Deciding what bans to impose and who should implement them is part science and part art. Some judgment calls are close, but throughout all the initial presumption should always be set in favor of liberty of action: Be careful and go slow with the ban.

Banning or Waiting?

How does this framework carry over to the distinct issue of cloning? To answer that question we have to identify and weigh the relevant variables on both sides of the ledger: the harms that might occur, and the probability of their occurrence, versus the benefits that could be obtained and the probability of their occurrence.

The difficulties hit us at the first step. The implicit assumption

of the earlier model was that the relevant harms fell into certain definable classes: bodily injury or death to persons; damage to private property, or even to public lands and waters. But cloning presents none of the customary forms of harm that have been the target of legal action. Indeed the term "identifiable harm" seems sadly out of place for the diffuse set of perils at stake. Indeed I find it something of a mystery why cloning is said to give rise to some natural and widespread human revulsion which, if we follow Leon Kass, should serve as us our moral lead.[6] I confess some curiosity about how it would all work out and a little edginess about the worst-case scenarios. But we should keep this in perspective. Cloning does not belong on a list with assault, incest, illegitimacy, debauchery, deformity, depravity, or neglect. What we have is the creation of one new person whose genetic component is identical to that of another human being, alive or dead. What, we may ask, is the harm in all that?

The simple, hard-line answer sticks with the narrowest conception of harm and concludes nothing at all. That approach makes our decisions easy, perhaps too easy: Cloning should never be banned. Once we are certain that the practice in question involves no harm (as defined) to other persons, then the expected losses are zero: Offense, or even revulsion, toward cloning, and the satisfaction, or even curiosity, that others might attach to it are both ignored. So long as someone wants to undertake the activity, its expected gains are positive. This uncluttered libertarian view thus ends the matter: If there is no threat of future damages, then there is no case for a present ban.

The most cursory review of the NBAC report indicates that its perplexities begin exactly where this simple libertarian approach ends. The somewhat depressive report contains a menu of real and fancied harms that cannot be ignored. Start with the question of psychological harms. We have the newly cloned infant who is now told that he is genetically identical with some other human being—perhaps his "father" or "mother" (whose quotation marks need no

explanation), or perhaps some public personage of great intellectual, athletic, or artistic merit. What would we expect his reaction to be to his subordinate and derivative place? Here the implicit assumption of the anti-cloning forces is that the distressed newcomer would have been in some sense better off if he had never been born: This situation reminds me of the unhappy experience I had in the Yale Law School moot court competition in arguing with a straight face that a child with severe damages from German measles contracted during pregnancy would have been "better off" never having been born at all.[7] But rather than try to plumb these philosophical depths, I will take the criticism as asking, Why invest in a cloned individual when we could find someone else who did not have to carry this psychological baggage around for all the days of his life?

So now the issue about the burdens heaped on the new person is just empirical. How heavy is the load? I confess to substantial ignorance on the question. Today we know of lots of people who are clones of each other: the entire class of identical twins, some of whom were reared together and others who were reared apart. And here the evidence is decidedly mixed. Some twins might lack the space that comes from being one of a kind. On the other hand, many twins report that they enjoy a special kinship that comes from knowing that another person shares their moral, aesthetic, and emotional presuppositions. It helps to get rid of the loneliness in facing the world. My own casual research led me to a story in the August 1997 issue of *Marie Claire,* which features two male identical twins who met and married two female identical twins at a twins convention in Twinsberg, Ohio, and then set up house together as a foursome.[8] Apparently no psychological baggage here. Clearly some twins rejoice in their twinned state. But recall that the question is not whether we would prefer to be a singleton or twin. It is whether we should ban cloning right now.

Perhaps the bonding between natural identical twins is not decisive on the issue of psychological harms. These twins are of the

same age: One does not have to live in the shadow of those who have gone before, and that element could well bring about a certain level of gloom and frustration. Who could hope to live up to an older identical clone, or keep a sense of optimism and independence if that person should suddenly suffer a deadly disease or commit some heinous act? it might be hard to make plans for one's own future, when we have uncommon insight as to what it will be. The NBAC quotes the philosopher Hans Jonas who warns against cloning as violative of the right to ignorance, a right which I for one would gladly waive about tomorrow's closing stock prices. The philosopher Joel Feinberg is mentioned as speaking about the right to an open future, and the philosopher Martha Nussbaum is taken to defend the importance of separateness of persons.[9]

These sound like very lofty concerns. But how are they likely to play out in practice? Everyone concedes that the genetic identity of two individuals predisposes them to act in parallel ways. Will the clone of Michael Jordan regard life as a failure if he does not reach the basketball heights of, as it were, his genesake? But before becoming excessively gloomy on the subject, note that other outcomes are possible. The children of successful parents often have greater confidence in their own ability to succeed. Perhaps the clone would say, "Look, with my genes I have a real advantage over those other children of distinguished parents who face the strong tendency of regression toward the mean." The future holds lots of uncertainties even for people who know their genetic complement. Some people might like to have a leg up on others who are struggling to figure out their own identities. Perhaps the clone would have, dare one suggest it, the psychological edge.

Either result is, in my view, possible once we recall the determinants of personal identity and success. The new individuals are genetic twins of their single ancestor, but different people. As the NBAC stresses, the thought that we could clone "a team of Michael Jordans, a physics department of Albert Einsteins, or an opera chorus [no soloists?] of Pavarottis, is simply false."[10] We do not have to

indulge in speculation about multiple cloning to see why no copy of the parent is likely to be just that person. The basic explanation is almost too simple: Human behavior is a function of genetic endowment interacting with social and environmental forces. Those who reach the top at anything need a fair bit of luck to do it. A twisted ankle at age four, a disagreeable science teacher in third grade, a sore throat in winter could throw the best-endowed clone permanently off the fast track, or result in the development of some previously ignored talent. Major differences in uterine environment (which separates the clone from the identical twin) are enough to account for big differences in personality and intelligence;[11] differences in diet and care, in fad and fashion, in occupation and education should also yield perceptible differences between "ancestor" and clone and preclude exact duplication of personality. Given the confluence of change and determination, similarity and difference, who can confidently predict the psychological response, positive or negative, of the cloned person to his second-chair status, with or without counseling?

There is of course no direct evidence, but perhaps a parallel provides some food for thought. Cloning is but one of many high-tech methods of reproduction. Other methods also torment bioethics today.[12] We also have artificial insemination (father or donor), in vitro fertilization, and surrogate parenthood. And we know how to manipulate the contents of individual cells early in the reproductive process. Are we aware of any major social and psychological damage to the offspring of these practices? Here we actually do have some evidence, and it speaks to the adaptability of human beings, not to their psychological fixations.

Moving further afield, surrogacy involves the artificial insemination (not strictly necessary for the practice to survive) of a woman who is paid to nurture an unborn to birth and then turn it over to the biological father and his own spouse. Sounds pretty weird. The literature contains many abstract philosophical denunciations of how this dangerous form of commodification—how I

hate this use of the word!—will lead to the impoverishment of these young lives.[13] But the evidence does not seem to support that conclusion. Professor Lori Andrews did her own informal survey of surrogacy and found that the women hired as surrogates were able to explain the position quite comfortably to their own children and to get on with their lives.[14] Obviously, the practice is not for all. Yet it is by allowing persons to sort themselves out by contract, and to hold them to the contracts that they make, that the institution seems to have flourished.[15] The stability of the contractual arrangement is not dispositive of the position of the children born to these arrangements. But the critics of surrogacy have not presented any evidence that the children born of these surrogate arrangements show any special psychological problems. Given the resources of their parents, and their determination to go through with this procedure, my guess is that these children will usually be reared in circumstances that children naturally conceived in less fortunate circumstances would envy. The calls for ban in surrogacy have met with partial success. Yet it is far less clear that they have been justified by any showing of psychological harm to any of the relevant parties.

That lesson should carry over to the cloning case. My speculations could be morally obtuse; or the finely honed anxieties of the philosophical and theological elites could be unrepresentative of how most people will respond to the practice of cloning if it comes their way. The variation in human responses is likely to be wide, and I have some confidence at least that the people who will make themselves candidates for cloning (either by using their cells or carrying the child) are more likely to be well equipped for the emotional ride than those who recoil from the practice and thus keep their distance.

So we have lots of uncertainty about the matter, and that is precisely why it is so problematic to justify a ban on harm-prevention grounds. The usual legal standard requires clear evidence of serious harm, at the least. Here we do not come close to meeting it.

If we were to wait a bit, and see what happens, then we could form our judgments with greater knowledge as to how the practice did impact the lives of the newly cloned and their immediate families. At that point, we might learn things that support the worse fears of the opponents of cloning, and if so, then we can use hard evidence, not abstract fears, to decide what form of ban (whole or partial, conditional or absolute) to impose on the practice. It may turn out that the only clones who have trouble are those of a person who assumes the role of parent, or those of sports figures, or whatever. If so, the narrower ban could be tailored to the abuse. Knowledge, not ignorance, could guide our deliberations. No one says that this course of action is risk-free. It could well be that matters turn out well at the beginning and the harms begin only years later when many clones have been born. But again the point cuts both ways. To treat these fears as decisive is to say that we can never have cloning unless we have certain knowledge of the future. That cost could be high as well. Our task is to minimize error, not to cling to the status quo.

The same pattern of argument carries over to other concerns. Cloning surely makes it difficult to maintain the usual social roles of parent, sibling, grandparent, nephew, and niece. And we could easily join Leon Kass and others who brood about the level of disconnectedness that comes by awkwardly shoehorning this new person into a set of relationships created by nature and instituted by countless cultures over thousands of years. Again, it may seem presumptuous to respond so cavalierly to these epic themes, but still it is worth suggesting in a small voice that most human beings have the internal flexibility to adapt to this novel situation. We know that adoptions take children out of their natural families and place them in very different settings; interracial adoptions are still more dramatic, and yet many of these adoptions are the source of the most profound satisfaction to parents and child alike.[16] Are resourceful parents and a responsive legal system wholly unequal to the challenge?

Furthermore, we do not have to quibble over legal issues that can be resolved right now. If the question is whether the child is person or object: Person is the emphatic answer, with rights equal, as both child and citizen, to those of any other child however conceived and wherever raised. It is here that separateness matters. We can make it clear by statute and by agreement, if not by birth, that the woman who gives birth to a cloned child must agree to raise it as her own, for better or for worse. We can demand that her husband take on the obligations of its father. For single women, we might be forced to do without a father, as we now do when these women adopt or give birth to their own children. The conscious assumption of these obligations is no small matter, and leads people to reconsider their actions before they undertake them.

No one can guarantee that fixing the legal position will ensure an ideally affective and emotional upbringing. But no abstract concerns should allow the best to become the enemy of the good. Lots of children born within ordinary families come into horrific social settings. Forcing couples and single women to think hard about the legal position should encourage desirable social practices that assimilate the cloned child to traditional patterns of childrearing; my guess is that the child will worry less about cosmic identity and more about sports or fashion. So long as that outcome is not improbable, we should hesitate before banning the practice on the strength of unsubstantiated fears that it will miscarry. So, on this score too the ban is premature: Lesser precautions, many easily implemented, can reduce some of the risk, and allow the experiment to be played out a bit longer.

The proponents of the ban find it easy to think of other forms of harm. Human beings who evolve by sexual reproduction have a diversity that could not be achieved by asexual reproduction, which is why all higher forms of life are built around these sexual differences. That diversity has strong benefits for the overall survival of the human race: To put all of our eggs (quite literally) in one basket violates this fundamental norm of diversification. In good times

the undiversified species will flourish, but in bad times the species could be wiped out, so that good times will never come again. To follow the apt language of the financial analyst: Diversification of the portfolio gives us the best hedge against the uncertainty of the future.

Yet I can see no reason to fault cloning on grounds of incomplete diversification. Cloning is not the same practice as inbreeding: The guess is that any clones will come from successful individuals, not failures, and we should not expect to see with each passing generation the rise of recessive traits that will cripple the species. Nor is it clear how much, if at all, cloning could reduce diversity. The cloned individual will in all probability mate with other persons of his or her own age. Cloning thus opens up new possibilities for unique genetic combination as it forecloses others. I doubt that anyone could find any appreciable difference in the composition of the gene pool even if cloning becomes a widespread practice.

Finally, here lies the rub. What makes anyone think that cloning will become widespread even if legalized? My guess is that it will make some dent on human reproductive practices in a few desperate cases. But in the grand scheme of things, the impact is likely to be slight. It is too quickly forgotten that allowing cloning does not require anyone to clone. The opponents of cloning may, and should, raise their theological and ethical arguments to all who will listen, and inveigh against the practice with all the passion they can summon. (I am happy to report that they will be able to persuade me not to partake in the grand experiment in any role.) In all likelihood, given the sense of professional opinion, they will have some success with others: Even Wilmut and his fellow cloners are more interested in using cloning for genetic experimentation in agriculture and livestock than in making human beings. We know that cloning humans presents certain risks, even though it already seems possible to do better than 1 successful cloning in 277 attempts, the success rate with Dolly. No matter how great the advances, the process will likely remain delicate so that, just a guess,

the odds of successful completion will be well below 50 percent. If the law forces individuals to bear the costs of their own vanity, then price itself will deter many from striking out in this novel direction. We can expect to see few takers given the other available alternatives. Why therefore worry about the effects on biodiversity of a practice that is not likely to affect even 1 person in a million? For those of us who want to worry, start with illegitimacy, foster care, abuse, neglect, and starvation, where some intelligent human intervention might improve what has become a baleful situation.

In response it could be asked, If the likelihood of cloning is so low then why object to the ban at all? Few will be inconvenienced and the greater certainty in the legal and social environment will work to the long-term advantage of us all. But the balance of convenience runs clearly in the opposite direction. No ban costs little to enforce: We do not have to draft regulations that "carefully distinguish" between the research practices that are banned and those that can continue. We do not have to worry about the international cooperation that is necessary to make sure that the practice does not take hold in Scotland, or for that matter, Singapore or Qatar. And we do not have to worry about the possibility that the ban will, in spite of our best intentions, prevent the kind of practices that give very little reason for concern. Already I have been told that biotech companies that have no corporate interest in getting into the human cloning business are concerned by the overbreadth of the potential legislation, which could interfere with their own more focused efforts to develop new treatments for various genetic disorders. And they should be. The bills introduced in the House and Senate this past March had the virtue of being short; they had the greater vice of being wholly uninformative. One bill provides: "It shall be unlawful for any person to use a human somatic cell for the process of producing a human clone."[17] Another bill is still broader in scope: "No Federal funds may be used for research with respect to the cloning of a human individual."[18] It of-

fers no definition of what counts as "research," even if it does offer a definition of what counts as cloning.[19] The pithy nature of the bill will require supplementation through regulation, but why assume that bureaucrats and administrators will issue regulations that take a narrow view of their power?

Here is one example. Suppose that some great benefit from cloning comes not with Michael Jordan, but with work with infertile couples. Suppose that they are able to produce fertilized eggs, and that these for some reason have to be reproduced. Suppose further that cloning might help in this process. If so, then we have a ban that surely overshoots its mark. This cloning is not of a present human being. We do not have to worry about individual autonomy, unrooted individuals, preordained futures, psychological deprivation, or biodiversity. If the cloning works we have a new unique child with two traditional biological parents. The placement of the child is where we want it, even if it reached that end by a devious path. Who knows whether this path will prove viable, but introducing the ban may well knock it out.

So wait, and learn. If it should come to pass that some horror stories occur, then we can think of more focused responses, just as we do in so many other areas of life. Let ten thousand impressionable members of the same Girl Scout troop decide that they want to carry the precise likeness of their favorite (and willing) heartthrob; then even I would think that a narrow ban on (to use the pejorative term) "trafficking" might be appropriate. Let some famous rock star auction off cells ripe for cloning, and perhaps I could be persuaded to go along with the tidal wave of sentiment that would call for stopping the practice (or at least allowed for a cooling-off period), perhaps even before the first sale took place. But that is just the point. If we can wait, then we can focus, and if we can focus then we can eliminate the chaff without knocking out the wheat. So my advice is to continue the debate while we allow the research to go on full steam ahead. The new information should allow us to

make better decisions, but only if we take a more level-headed and less angst-driven approach to the problem than seems to have dominated the gloomy NBAC. The end of the human race is not at hand; so for the time being, relax.

Endnotes

1. Gina Kolata, "Lab Yields Lamb with Human Gene," *New York Times,* July 25, 1997, at A12.
2. Ronald Kotulak, "Move over Dolly: U.S. Firm Clones in New Way," *Chicago Tribune,* August 8, 1997, at 1.
3. NBAC, Report ("Cloning Human Beings," 1997) at 108–109. (Hereafter called NBAC.)
4. *Ibid.* at 109.
5. For the longer account, see Richard A. Epstein, *Simple Rules for a Complex World* (Cambridge, MA: Harvard University Press, 1995).
6. Leon Kass, "The Wisdom of Repugnance," *New Republic,* June 2, 1997, at 17.
7. The case was *Gleitman v. Cosgrove,* 49 N.J. 22, 227 A.2d 689 (N.J. 1967).
8. See Lucy Broadbent, "Twin Set," *Marie Claire,* August 1997, at 40.
9. NBAC at 67–68. Nussbaum is clearly misunderstood. Her position is only that all individuals deserve dignity and respect of their own. She takes no position on whether there is anything objectionable in having two persons with identical genetic profiles.
10. NBAC at 33.
11. See Sharon Begley, "Wombs with a View," *Newsweek,* August 11, 1997, at 61.
12. Gina Kolata, "Scientists Face New Ethical Quandaries in Baby-Making," *New York Times,* August 19, 1997, at B7.
13. See, e.g., Elizabeth Anderson, *Value in Ethics and Economics* (Cambridge, MA: Harvard University Press, 1993).
14. Lori Andrews, "Beyond Doctrinal Boundaries: A Legal Framework for Surrogate Motherhood," 81 *Va. L. Rev.* 2343 (1995).
15. Richard A. Epstein, "Surrogacy: The Case for Full Contractual Enforcement," 81 *Va. L. Rev.* 2305 (1995).
16. See Janny Scott, "Orphan Girls of China at Home in New York," *New York Times,* August 19, 1997, at A1, on the adoption of Chinese girls by middle-aged New York professional couples.
17. H.R. 923 (introduced March 5, 1997).
18. S. 368 (introduced February 27, 1997).

19. "(b) *Definition*—For purposes of this section, the term 'cloning' means the replication of a human individual by the taking of a cell with genetic material and the cultivation of the cell through the egg, embryo, fetal, and newborn stages into a new human individual." *Ibid.*

I should like to thank L. Rex Sears and Michael Maimin of the Law School Class of 1999 for their valuable assistance in preparing this article.

On Order

Barbara Katz Rothman

Cloning is about control. It's about introducing predictability and order into the wildly unpredictable crapshoot that is life. If normal procreation is the roll of a hundred thousand dice, a random dip in the gene pool, cloning is a carefully placed order. And that's where it gets interesting: It is *order* both in the sense of predictability and control, and in the sense of the market, an order placed, a human being on order.

In a perfect world, we could think about the value of the first form of order, the value of predictability and control in procreation, without thinking about the second form of order, the power of the market. In our world, the two are hopelessly, endlessly entangled. I personally am not convinced that predictability and control are really achievable in human procreation, nor am I convinced that they would be good things to achieve. But those points are at least open for debate, for discussion. I am completely convinced that market forces are an evil in human procreation.

That leaves me in the funny kind of place I often am with the new technologies of procreation: Thank goodness they don't work terribly well. The only thing that could make them worse would be if they got better.

Predictability has its limits in procreation. Think for a moment about identical twins, "nature's own clone" as it were. Identical is a funny word. It means they're the same. And so they are, strikingly

so, which is why people noticed that they are a particular kind of twin. Identical twins arise from the same fertilized egg. One zygote becomes two people. Or even more rarely, three. At the moment of zygotic zero, when the egg and the sperm join, the twins are not only identical, they are one and the same. Very soon after that they split and go their separate ways.

If the splitting occurs within the first three days, they each develop their own placentas. If splitting occurs a bit later, between the fourth and the eighth day, they, each within its own amniotic sac, share a placenta. If the splitting is later still, they will share a single sac too. And later than that, the twins themselves may be joined, "Siamese" twins, two people in a more-or-less shared body.[1]

How identical are identical twins? Right there, in the very same woman, nestled in the very same womb, they go their separate ways, experiencing life differently. Genetic changes take place as the eternal splitting and building of cells occur. Mutations can occur differently in each. One could be born a boy, with the full X,Y chromosomes; the other, missing the Y chromosome in many of its cells, a girl. A girl, with one X and no second sex chromosome, a condition known as Turner's syndrome, can be the "identical" twin of her brother, grown of the same fertilized egg.[2]

And even without dramatic mutations occurring, twins are not the same baby twice. At birth they do not weigh the same: Their rates of growth can be very different. Placed here or there, in the same womb in the same woman in the same environment, they're not having the same experience. *Here* isn't *there,* and nothing is ever the same.

They don't even have the same "genetic" diseases. Type I diabetes, for example, has been traced to a gene located on the small arm of the sixth chromosome. One variation of that gene, one allele, "causes" autoimmune diabetes. In one twin. In one identical twin the gene causes diabetes and in the other the same gene does not cause diabetes. If one twin has type I diabetes, the chances of an identical twin having it are only 30 percent.[3] More than two-

thirds of the time the identical twin will not have this "genetic" disease. Some genes are more powerful, in which case the odds of a shared disease or trait go up; some are less powerful, and the odds go down. Diseases, traits, characteristics—two people, two individuals from one fertilized egg. You can't predict which will be which, how it will play itself out over time.

You can't get away from the idea of chance. Start with the same egg and the same sperm forming the same zygote in the same woman, and one twin gets sick and asks "Why me?" Clone the same cell and each person produced will be different from the source of the cell, and different from each other. No matter how much we want to control, to predict, to answer that question of "Why?" the answer sometimes really is just *because,* luck, chance.

That is *not* what we used to think science was about. Physicists have had to come to terms with that uncertainty, raising it to a principle. Classic physics thought that you could know it all, "that our cosmos is governed by mathematically precise laws at all scales, from inside of an atom to the totality of the universe."[4] And then chance raised its head, and "the positions and movement of the invisible atoms that make up all objects were now lost in a probabilistic blur. While the universe remained determinate, the revised mathematical constructs of physics—more accurately reflecting the way atoms behave—could no longer promise completely predictable events and objective, universal knowledge."[5] You can't, it seems, know it all.

Predictability and control are forever slipping out of our hands, crumbling as we touch them. When you're working with small herds of sheep, say, cloned to produce some expensive, exotic protein in their milk for medicinal purposes, a certain percentage of error is to be expected, accounted for. It is accounted for in two senses: It is part of the "account" or narrative of what might happen. (Shit happens!) And it is accounted for in the ledger books, an anticipated expense. Most of the errors that can be expected will

not matter: Only a few will affect the single and sole purpose for which the sheep were cloned: the production of that protein in their milk.

With people, the accounting gets a lot more complicated, in both senses. Errors are not to be written off, and our expectations are rarely so narrowly confined.

We—those of us who have been around the track a few times—know how this latest "advance" in human procreative technology is going to be brought to us, marketed to us. It is going to be the solution to some heartrending problem. There's going to be a very good reason to do it the first time: some irreplaceable bone marrow donation, or some man who is the very, very, very last of his family, preferably made so by some cataclysmic political tragedy like the Holocaust. The guy will have absolutely, totally, no sperm whatsoever. Or maybe it will be . . . But I don't want to do this, don't want to give anybody any ideas.

For that first time, any success will probably be success enough. Later though, if we begin to make cloning routine, offer it as a service at the growing number of fertility clinics, the expectations will be more specific and at the same time more generalized. People will want to predict and control the kinds of children they are creating, or why bother using the technology?

And the "kinds of children" they might create are understood to be products of the nucleus of the cell from which they are created. Genetics—not just as a science or a set of technologies, but genetics as an ideology, as the way we are more and more thinking about life—is the descendent of classical patriarchal thinking. In a patriarchy, a father-based kinship system, men are the source of life; women the vessels. Life on earth is the product of the many and varied seeds of the earth; human life is the product of the seeds of man. The earth itself, in this thinking, is only the place, the location, where seeds are planted. The very words we use for earth—dirt, soil—indicate the disdain in which location is held relative to

the glorious, powerful life-giving seed. In our more enlightened, modified patriarchy, women are also recognized as having seeds, but the primacy of the seed remains. Seeds count.

The idea of cloning suggests that the essence, the true essential quality, the very thing that makes a being itself—what once might have been called the soul—lies in the nucleus of its cells. Everything else is reduced to environment, background, ground, earth, dirt.

To hear the talk of the geneticists, one would think that the contents of that cell nucleus, the hundred thousand or so segments of DNA that constitute the "genes," are themselves the miracle of life. All life-forms begin in DNA; all life then is DNA; and maybe all life is, is DNA. They—the geneticists who have pushed to translate the full length of DNA into the letters GCAT so that it can be "read" and "mapped"—sound religious, awestruck, overwhelmed by the power and the majesty of the DNA: It's the Bible, the Holy Grail, the Book of Man. Those are their very words. Our fate, James Watson tells us, lies not in our stars but in our genes.

On a more mundane, work-a-day level, the DNA is called a code, an encyclopedia, an instruction kit, a program, and most often, a blueprint. Well, sure. I started out as a little cell with a nucleus of DNA and here I am. Those must have been plans in there.

But it took about fifty years to get where I am now, and I think that's worth thinking about. When you have the code or the plans for a person, you don't have the person. If you take my very DNA and clone it, make copies, and let those copies grow into people, it will take fifty years for them to get where I am now. And a lot happens in those fifty years.

If I want to build a cabin, and I have a blueprint, I could gather a bunch of people and machines and do it in a few days, or I could work with hand tools by myself on weekends for the next ten years. A blueprint doesn't have time or growth built into it and so a blueprint isn't really a good analogy for DNA.

A recipe might make more sense if we want analogies. Baking bread, for instance, combines making something with growth, the growth of the yeast that gives bread its rise. I've baked a lot of bread in my time, and I've learned that the same recipe under different circumstances results in different breads. Use a flour from a wheat grown in one part of the country and you have a different mineral composition and a slightly different taste than if you use flour from a wheat grown somewhere else. Bake on a humid day and you get a heavier bread from the same recipe than on a dry day. Bake on a hot day and the bread rises faster and has bigger air holes. Bake the same bread every day for a week, and no two loaves will be exactly the same: The web, that distinctive pattern of holes, will vary from loaf to loaf. Bake it in different pans or in different ovens, and you'll have differently textured crusts.

I've also made a couple of babies in my life. And while I understand about the DNA and the plans and the blueprints and all that, I also remember the rituals of avoidance. I read the ingredients on every food package before I used it, hesitating to put things I couldn't pronounce into the growing body of my baby. I avoided coffee, and cat litter dust, and, by the time of the second pregnancy when the rules had changed, alcohol. I read books about fetal development until I decided it was totally incapacitating: How could I possibly walk down the subway steps, cross a street and breathe exhaust fumes, even get out of bed, on arm-bud development day? All that blueprint following wasn't happening somewhere else. It was happening in my belly, day after day after day after day.

It's that element of time that seems so strangely absent in the discussion of cloning and DNA, in the thinking of genetic determinists. One of the Nobel laureates in genetics likes to hold up a compact disk at his lectures and say "This is you." As if the genes that were there at the moment of zygotic zero when I began fifty years ago, and the me that stands here now, were one and the same.

In the talk of the geneticists, time seems to exist only in terms of evolution, of progress, not in its daily, processual, experienced way, the time in which I bake a bread, grow a baby.

A blueprint is always located in a place and in a time. The same DNA, the same genes, will make a tall person or a short one, depending on the nutrition available during growth. One could have all the symptoms of copper deficiency because of an error in the gene to use copper—or because of a copper-deficient environment. Someone noticed the brittle wool of sheep grazing on copper-deficient land and identified the inability to metabolize copper as the cause of the genetic disease that has among its symptoms, brittle hair. The same DNA will produce sheep with lush wool in one place, and short unusable wool in another. The same DNA, dipped out of the same gene pool, will produce the short people of my grandparents' generation or the tall ones of my children's. Monday's bread is lighter than Tuesday's; Tuesday's crust is crispier than Wednesday's.

And what does the market introduce into this? What do we get when we take these variable processes of growth and time and turn them over to the forces of the market? Wonderbread: a nearly perfectly predictable bread.[6]

I cannot afford to do what my great-great-grandmother did out of necessity, bake my own bread, any more than I could afford her uncontrolled fertility. I can't afford the time. Home-baked bread, like eight children, is a luxury well beyond the likes of me. I almost always buy my bread, baking only for a treat, for a holiday, for the occasional pleasure of it. I can afford to buy a more customized bread than Wonderbread: at the bakery, at the farmer's market. I am buying the services of the baker, considerably more industrialized than what I could do at home, somewhat less industrialized than the factory supplying my supermarket. And sometimes, when I'm rushed or broke, I do grab those plastic wrapped loaves off the shelf.

Could people ever be mass-produced like supermarket loaves?

I don't actually think so, but the image frightens. The factories toss all the errors—the loaves that come out misshapen, that failed to rise evenly, that are burnt a bit or are underdone. It happens. They take that into account. It is part of their quality-control program.

The current technologies of procreation introduced first quantity control and more recently, and increasingly, quality control.[7] Prenatal screening and testing with the expectation of selective abortion are a form of quality control, avoiding the production of children we claim we can no longer afford to raise. The choice of quantity control, the choices offered to us by (relatively) safe and (relatively) effective contraception, eventually lost us the choice of not controlling the quantity of our children: Who could really afford the eight children my great-grandmother bore? And so it is with quality control: The introduction of that choice may ultimately cost us the choice not to control the quality, the choice of taking our chances in life's great, glorious, and terrifying roll of the hundred thousand dice.

Cloning may well eventually be offered to us as a way of avoiding the tragedy of prenatal diagnosis and selective abortion, the grief of deliberately ending a wanted pregnancy because of the kind of child it would produce.[8] Cloning may eventually—and eventually isn't as long a time as it used to be—be offered to us as a way of inserting predictability and control earlier in the process. Placing order in procreation: Placing our orders.

I don't think they'll be able to get that level of control, because I don't think life lives in that nucleus. If the DNA is a bible, it's capable of being read in a lot of different ways. My friend Eileen Moran says, "Think of the DNA as a musical score, notes on a page, but capable of nuanced interpretations." Is it possible that this static thing, this string of ACGTs, these notes on the page, *is* life? Or is life the way in which those notes are played?

And what is a bread? Is it the recipe? The ingredients? The process? Or isn't it all of those, the end product of a complex interaction played out over time?

And what are our children? Not seeds grown up, DNA transcribed, but also the product of a complex interaction played out over time.

So I'm not *that* worried about cloning. I don't think it can ever work terribly well. Not well enough to bank on.

References

1. Pritchard, Jack A., and Paul C. MacDonald. *Williams Obstetrics.* 16th ed. New York: Appleton Century Crofts, 1980, p. 640.
2. *Ibid.,* p. 644.
3. Burr, Chandler. *A Separate Creation: The Search for the Biological Origins of Sexual Orientation.* New York: Hyperion, 1996, p. 220.
4. Pollack, Robert. *Signs of Life: The Language and Meanings of DNA.* Boston: Houghton Mifflin, 1994, p. 150.
5. *Ibid.,* p. 150.
6. My appreciation to Maren Lockwood Carden for showing me where the bread-baking analogy was headed.
7. My appreciation to Roslyn Weinman for this insight and this wording.
8. For a fuller discussion of the difficulties and consequences of prenatal screening—for which cloning may be offered as the solution—see Barbara Katz Rothman, *The Tentative Pregnancy: How Amniocentesis Changes the Experience of Motherhood.* New York: W. W. Norton, 1993.

Recommendations of the Commission

National Bioethics Advisory Commission

With the announcement that an apparently quite normal sheep had been born in Scotland as a result of somatic cell nuclear transfer cloning came the realization that, as a society, we must yet again collectively decide whether and how to use what appeared to be a dramatic new technological power. The promise and the peril of this scientific advance was noted immediately around the world, but the prospects of creating human beings through this technique mainly elicited widespread resistance and/or concern. Despite this reaction, the scientific significance of the accomplishment, in terms of improved understanding of cell development and cell differentiation, should not be lost. The challenge to public policy is to support the myriad beneficial applications of this new technology, while simultaneously guarding against its more questionable uses.

Much of the negative reaction to the potential application of such cloning in humans can be attributed to fears about harms to the children who may result, particularly psychological harms associated with a possibly diminished sense of individuality and personal autonomy. Others express concern about a degradation in the quality of parenting and family life. And virtually all people agree that the current risks of physical harm to children associated with somatic cell nuclear transplantation cloning justify a prohibition at this time on such experimentation.

In addition to concerns about specific harms to children, people

have frequently expressed fears that a widespread practice of somatic cell nuclear transfer cloning would undermine important social values by opening the door to a form of eugenics or by tempting some to manipulate others as if they were objects instead of persons. Arrayed against these concerns are other important social values, such as protecting personal choice, particularly in matters pertaining to procreation and childrearing, maintaining privacy and the freedom of scientific inquiry, and encouraging the possible development of new biomedical breakthroughs.

As somatic cell nuclear transfer cloning could represent a means of human reproduction for some people, limitations on that choice must be made only when the societal benefits of prohibition clearly outweigh the value of maintaining the private nature of such highly personal decisions. Especially in light of some arguably compelling cases for attempting to clone a human being using somatic cell nuclear transfer, the ethics of policy making must strike a balance between the values society wishes to reflect and issues of privacy and the freedom of individual choice.

To arrive at its recommendations concerning the use of somatic cell nuclear transfer techniques, the National Bioethics Advisory Commission (NBAC) also examined long-standing religious traditions that often influence and guide citizens' responses to new technologies. Religious positions on human cloning are pluralistic in their premises, modes of argument, and conclusions. Nevertheless, several major themes are prominent in Jewish, Roman Catholic, Protestant, and Islamic positions, including responsible human dominion over nature, human dignity and destiny, procreation, and family life. Some religious thinkers argue that the use of somatic cell nuclear transfer cloning to create a child would be intrinsically immoral and thus could never be morally justified; they usually propose a ban on such human cloning. Other religious thinkers contend that human cloning to create a child could be morally justified under some circumstances but hold that it should be strictly regulated in order to prevent abuses.

The public policies recommended with respect to the creation of a child using somatic cell nuclear transfer reflect the Commission's best judgments about both the ethics of attempting such an experiment and our view of traditions regarding limitations on individual actions in the name of the common good. At present, the use of this technique to create a child would be a premature experiment that exposes the developing child to unacceptable risks. This in itself is sufficient to justify a prohibition on cloning human beings at this time, even if such efforts were to be characterized as the exercise of a fundamental right to attempt to procreate. More speculative psychological harms to the child, and effects on the moral, religious, and cultural values of society may be enough to justify continued prohibitions in the future, but more time is needed for discussion and evaluation of these concerns.

Beyond the issue of the safety of the procedure, however, the NBAC found that concerns relating to the potential psychological harms to children and effects on the moral, religious, and cultural values of society merited further reflection and deliberation. Whether upon such further deliberation our nation will conclude that the use of cloning techniques to create children should be allowed or permanently banned is, for the moment, an open question. Time is an ally in this regard, allowing for the accrual of further data from animal experimentation, enabling an assessment of the prospective safety and efficacy of the procedure in humans, as well as granting a period of fuller national debate on ethical and social concerns. The Commission therefore concluded that there should be imposed a period of time in which no attempt is made to create a child using somatic cell nuclear transfer.

Within this overall framework the Commission came to the following conclusions and recommendations:

I. The Commission concludes that at this time it is morally unacceptable for anyone in the public or private sector, whether in a research or clinical setting, to attempt to create a child using somatic

cell nuclear transfer cloning. We have reached a consensus on this point because current scientific information indicates that this technique is not safe to use in humans at this time. Indeed, we believe it would violate important ethical obligations were clinicians or researchers to attempt to create a child using these particular technologies, which are likely to involve unacceptable risks to the fetus and/or potential child. Moreover, in addition to safety concerns, many other serious ethical concerns have been identified, which require much more widespread and careful public deliberation before this technology may be used.

The Commission, therefore, recommends the following for immediate action:

- A continuation of the current moratorium on the use of federal funding in support of any attempt to create a child by somatic cell nuclear transfer.
- An immediate request to all firms, clinicians, investigators, and professional societies in the private and nonfederally funded sectors to comply voluntarily with the intent of the federal moratorium. Professional and scientific societies should make clear that any attempt to create a child by somatic cell nuclear transfer and implantation into a woman's body would at this time be an irresponsible, unethical, and unprofessional act.

II. The Commission further recommends that:

- Federal legislation should be enacted to prohibit anyone from attempting, whether in a research or clinical setting, to create a child through somatic cell nuclear transfer cloning. It is critical, however, that such legislation include a sunset clause to ensure that Congress will review the issue after a specified time period (three to five years) in order to decide whether the prohibition continues to be needed. If state legislation is enacted, it should also contain such a sunset provision. Any such legislation or associated regulation also ought to require that at some point prior to the expiration of the sunset period, an appropriate oversight

body will evaluate and report on the current status of somatic cell nuclear transfer technology and on the ethical and social issues that its potential use to create human beings would raise in light of public understandings at that time.

III. The Commission also concludes that:

- Any regulatory or legislative actions undertaken to effect the foregoing prohibition on creating a child by somatic cell nuclear transfer should be carefully written so as not to interfere with other important areas of scientific research. In particular, no new regulations are required regarding the cloning of human DNA sequences and cell lines, since neither activity raises the scientific and ethical issues that arise from the attempt to create children through somatic cell nuclear transfer, and these fields of research have already provided important scientific and biomedical advances. Likewise, research on cloning animals by somatic cell nuclear transfer does not raise the issues implicated in attempting to use this technique for human cloning, and its continuation should only be subject to existing regulations regarding the humane use of animals and review by institution-based animal protection committees.
- If a legislative ban is not enacted, or if a legislative ban is ever lifted, clinical use of somatic cell nuclear transfer techniques to create a child should be preceded by research trials that are governed by the twin protections of independent review and informed consent, consistent with existing norms of human subjects protection.
- The United States Government should cooperate with other nations and international organizations to enforce any common aspects of their respective policies on the cloning of human beings.

IV. The Commission also concludes that different ethical and religious perspectives and traditions are divided on many of the im-

portant moral issues that surround any attempt to create a child using somatic cell nuclear transfer techniques. Therefore, we recommend that:

- The federal government, and all interested and concerned parties, encourage widespread and continuing deliberation on these issues in order to further our understanding of the ethical and social implications of this technology and to enable society to produce appropriate long-term policies regarding this technology should the time come when present concerns about safety have been addressed.

V. Finally, because scientific knowledge is essential for all citizens to participate in a full and informed fashion in the governance of our complex society, the Commission recommends that:

- Federal departments and agencies concerned with science should cooperate in seeking out and supporting opportunities to provide information and education to the public in the area of genetics, and on other developments in the biomedical sciences, especially where these affect important cultural practices, values, and beliefs.

This is the unabridged text of chapter 6 of the NBAC report on human cloning (June 1997).

PART V

Fiction and Fantasy

World of Strangers

Lisa Tuttle

My mother and I were not related.

For a long time I never noticed, although our differences were many and obvious. Throughout infancy, she was simply my world, and I had no reason to question it. I didn't know what was normal, and I was not unhappy.

It was only after I went to school and began to look around me and question what I saw that the oddity of my family situation became apparent. I could not help noticing the difference between me and my mother, and the other parents when they came to collect their children from school. Like me, most of the children at my exclusive, very expensive school had single parents. But unlike me, they were all precisely matched. Day after day as I watched the fathers walking away with their miniature selves, the mothers so happy with their identical little daughters, I felt more and more powerfully the strangeness of my situation. Why didn't my mother have a little girl? I was a boy—so where was my father?

I worried that it meant there was something wrong with me. My mother never commented on it; could it be she hadn't noticed? That she didn't know? For a long time I hugged my fears to myself and said nothing, but one day, inevitably, it came bursting out and I demanded, "Am I adopted?"

"Darling Nicky! Of course not! Why should you think such a thing?"

I began cautiously. "Well, I don't look like you."

"Lots of children don't look like their parents."

"Not at *my* school."

My mother might have saved herself some grief—or at least put off the day of reckoning—if she'd simply sent me off to the local school. Among the poor and ordinary the two of us wouldn't have stood out like the freaks we were, and it might have been years before I thought to question my origins.

She shook her head. "Nicky, you're not adopted. You know I'm your mother. You know I gave birth to you—you've seen the video!"

I remembered; I'd watched it often with a sickened fascination. The groaning, crying woman in labor was undoubtedly my mother, so who else could that slimy, bloody baby be but me? I nodded. "Then who's my Dad?"

A little line appeared between her eyes, and her mouth got tight. "Who *have* you been talking to, Nicky? You don't have a father!"

I did know some basic biology, garnered from school, CD-ROMs, and television. I knew about cloning: the nice, modern way of continuing a species. I also knew how animals reproduced, when left to themselves, and that most of the world's human population, through poverty, ignorance, superstition, or sheer perversity, continued to breed in that messy, animal way—but not people like us! No wonder she was offended. But I was offended, too, that she should think I was stupid enough to believe that I'd been cloned like all my friends, when it was so obviously impossible.

"What's the matter?" I taunted, "Did you forget his name? You're not religious and you're not poor, so I guess that leaves stupid. Was I an accident?"

I had never seen such a murderous expression on the face of my usually adoring mother. For a split second I thought she would hit me. And I deserved to be hit. What I suggested was outrageous. I could hardly believe my mother had ever had real-life sex with another person. She certainly hadn't since I was born. Cuddles with

me, and a weekly full-body massage from a professional masseur were her only physical intimacies with others. Probably, like most adults, she indulged in virtual sex with the equipment in her bedroom—but at that time of my life I knew nothing of such things.

Then her anger passed, and she stared at me sadly. "You don't know what you're saying. Poor Nicky, has this been worrying you? I'm sorry. . . . I promise you, you were no accident. You were very much planned. And you were cloned."

"Do you think I'm stupid? Look at me! I'm nothing like you! I'm a boy—I have dark, curly hair—there's no way I'm your clone!"

"No—listen to me—you're not *my* clone, but you are. . . . I cloned you from a man—the man I loved—and I carried you in my womb for nine months—"

I didn't want to hear about her womb. "Is he dead?" I demanded. "My original. My father. Is he dead? Is that why you have me?"

"No. I'm not sure. I don't know. Oh, Nicky, you're not really old enough to understand. . . ."

"I am so! You have to tell me—it's not fair—he's my real parent, not you. I should be living with him, not you. You have to tell me why I'm not."

She tried to be firm, but she could never resist me for long when I was determined to have my way, and also, I think, after so many years of secrecy, she needed to share her secret.

"I loved him," she said. "I really loved him. That's the important thing for you to understand; that's why I did it. I would have done anything for him, would have been whatever he wanted—but he didn't want me, that was the problem. He loved sex, and novelty, and the excitement of new beginnings. After about a month he'd had enough of me, he wanted to move on. I wouldn't have stopped him taking other lovers, if that was what it took to make him happy. I told him so. I wouldn't interfere. I'd learn to live on whatever he had to spare, as long as he would spare me something. But he didn't even want to have me around. I bored him, he said."

And she bored me. I didn't care what grown-ups got up to in the name of sexual love; what did that have to do with *me?*

"I can't expect you to understand," she went on. "I hardly understand myself. It all seems so long ago. . . . I was a different person before you were born, Nicky. Being your mother has changed me."

"But you're not my mother," I objected. "We're not related. There's absolutely nothing of you in me at all."

"Oh, Nicky, there's more to motherhood than a genetic link! Of course I'm your mother, in all the ways that matter. I love you. I've always taken care of you. I carried you for nine months before you were born—"

"Any cow could have done that," I pointed out.

"But a cow would have had to been *made* to do it. A cow wouldn't have done it for love, or even have understood what was happening inside her. Nicky, the only reason you exist at all is because I loved you. Because I wanted you to be. Genetically, we're not related, that's true. But I couldn't love you any more if you were my own flesh and blood."

I pestered her for the name of my real parent, but she wouldn't tell me. The discussion was closed.

But the damage had been done. She had told me enough for me to draw two conclusions: My mother was a criminal, and she loved someone else, not me.

If my father was dead, there would be no reason not to tell me his name. I thought that the same would be true if for some, unimaginable reason he had *allowed* her to keep his cloned child. If she had, as I first imagined, reneged on a mutual agreement—if he had hired her womb and she had run away with me once I was safely implanted—I was sure she would not have gotten away with it. My father, with the full force of the law behind him, would have tracked her down and got me back, if not before my birth, then certainly after. I knew, with every ounce of certainty in my body (which was, after all, exactly the same as *his* body), that my father

would never give up until he found me, and I was just as certain that my so-called mother would not have been able to cover her tracks well enough to confuse him for long. She wasn't even bright enough to tell me a convincing lie about my origins. She didn't live like a hunted person; I was sure she had never feared pursuit.

Which left only one remaining possibility: that she had cloned a man without his permission or knowledge.

The "why" was a baffling mystery. She said she loved my father, yet she had done the most hateful thing imaginable. Because I couldn't trust what she told me, I set about trying to find answers on my own.

From her personal computer I dredged up traces of old journals, notes she'd written to herself, and, although I still found it hard to comprehend, a picture began to emerge.

I'd be his friend, his helper, his servant—I'd be whatever he wants. I'd change my sex for him if it would help. Since he says it won't, I'll abjure sex. After all, it's little enough. If I can't have him, I don't want anyone else inside my body. He doesn't understand: He thinks love is sex. But I can live on less and find it more. I can sublimate, quite happily. His voice in my ear, the sight of him filling my vision, will thrill and sustain me.

I can't live without him. Somehow, I must have him.

It'll never be over for me, as long as I live. He needn't touch me, if he finds me so distasteful; he doesn't even have to talk to me, not even look at me, if only he'll let me draw near, warm myself at the fire of his being.

I lay in his bed, inhaling the scent of him. It was mingled with that of his latest lover, as were the secretions dried on the sheets, but that doesn't matter. I know what is his well enough to filter out the other.

In the old days they'd have burned me as a witch, I thought, as I gathered up the hairs from his brush and comb. But in the old days they'd have un-

derstood my passion, my love for him, as nobody does today. It doesn't matter what he does to me or says—I'll always love him.

He ordered me out of his house. He's had the locks changed. He warned me he'll get an injunction to stop this "harassment." Afraid that I'd never see him again, afraid I'd never have another chance, I struck him in the face, my fingers curved into claws, raking his flesh. I left a line of raised welts. I drew blood. He cursed me, but I'd got what I wanted, beneath my nails.

His name was nowhere to be found, only her obsession with him, the why and the how of her crime. She'd stolen skin cells from the man she'd been pursuing, then run away and created her own personal, infant replica.

At that moment of understanding I left behind my babyish love and need for her. No child, it might be argued, ever asks to be born, but in my case it was much worse. My mother had not given life; she had stolen it. From that day, I despised her. This was the first, profound turning point of my life.

The second came nearly a decade later.

I was living in San Francisco, where I'd gone when I'd left home because I knew my mother had lived there as a young woman, and it seemed likely that was where she'd met my father. He might have moved on, of course, but I had no other leads, and in any case I needed a place where I could live without interference, where I could lose myself and survive.

It was the right choice. I looked older than I was and I was quick to adapt to whatever was expected. Now set free from the pretence of being *her* child, I could be anyone, just another ordinary stranger, struggling to get by.

Then one day I walked into the café where I'd been working as a waiter for the past two months, and saw *myself* sitting at a table, drinking an espresso.

It was worse than seeing a ghost. I felt as if a bucket of cold water had just been poured down my back. I gulped and shivered.

He looked straight back at me with narrowed eyes. He was trying to look calm, but when I got closer I could see he was trembling all over like a horse restrained from bolting.

I sat down across from him. That took all my nerve. There are legends, although at the time I'd never heard them, that to meet your own double is a harbinger of death. I don't know if he knew that. For what seemed a long time we simply stared at each other. Then he said, "They told me my identical twin was working here. I didn't believe it, but they were right. Who *are* you?"

"Who are *you?*" I spoke angrily, because I already knew he wasn't going to give me the answer I wanted, and for a second I thought he was going to argue. Then he gave in, with an impatient movement of his mouth. "As if you didn't know. Charles Nicholas Weller, the second. Don't ever call me 'Junior.' I go by Chaz. Yourself?"

"Nick."

"How old are you?"

"Eighteen." The reply came automatically. I had been saying it for so long I hardly knew if it was true.

He looked startled. "But you're older than me. I was just sixteen last month. *You* should be 'the second.' Father never mentioned you."

Father. The word burned like a hot coal. How I had longed to be able to say it to someone. For years I had dreamed of this fateful meeting, of coming face to face with my double on the street, in a park or a café, and being able to address him as my father. And now the meeting had happened, and it was all wrong. Not my father, but my father's son, the one he must love best of all. Like the woman who had pretended to be my mother, this boy was in the way, blocking me off from the one relationship that mattered.

"He doesn't know I exist," I said. "I've been looking for him, but I never even knew his name."

"But how—?" Chaz's fear had gone, and he gazed at me in fascination, mouth hanging open slightly, looking like a boy who's just been told the facts of life.

"It's a long story," I lied. "I'd rather tell it just once, to both of you. I'm sure he'll want to meet me. . . ."

I wasn't sure at all. In all my dreams my father had been a man on his own, aware of something missing from his life and ready for me to step in and fill the gap. But, as he already had a son, what would he want with me?

"Sure," said Chaz, so eagerly that it was obvious he felt too secure in his father's love to fear an interloper. "Sure he will. Wow, isn't this something? Just wait till Dad sees you! Come on, brother!"

We left the café together. I didn't even bother telling anyone there that I'd quit.

Ever since I'd become aware of what was wrong in my life, I'd been fascinated, maybe even obsessed, by the subject of fathers and sons. I'd done a research project on it at school, going beyond the simple biological facts into the deeper cultural and psychological importance of the relationship.

Motherhood, by comparison, is unproblematic. Women have it easy. All throughout history even the poorest, ugliest woman could get a child if she really wanted one—if she was barren, there were usually plenty of unwanted children around to be fostered. These days, of course, she can carry her own clone to term.

Long, long ago, perhaps, women were worshipped for their powers of fertility. The children who issued forth from their wombs were gifts from the gods, or ancestors reborn, and had no connection to the men of the tribe at all. However, once the male contribution to reproduction was recognized, it quickly came to assume the dominant role. Throughout most of recorded history it was generally assumed that a child belonged 100 percent to the father, as if it was entirely his seed, or his clone; the woman was no

more than the house in which the little sperm-homunculus could live and grow.

It's no wonder, really, that men in the past treated women so badly. Imagine what it would be like if you couldn't build or buy your own house, if you could only have a home by begging or forcing someone else to take you in? Think of women as the ones who had the houses. Deprivation doesn't make for nice people. The only way a man could ensure that his children got born was by totally possessing a woman, and keeping her locked away from other men who might want to use her to house their own offspring.

Not until 1960—coincidentally around the same time as the development of really effective contraception, and the women's liberation movement—was it incontestably, scientifically proved that every child was created half by the mother, half by the father. As women were finally granted equality with men, in all areas of life, the pendulum swung wildly the other way. Once upon a time, children had belonged wholly to their fathers. If a woman left her husband, even if a divorce was granted, she had to leave her children behind. Even in the case of the father's death, *his* family had more rights over the fate of the children than their mother did. By the 1970s, legislation rapidly changed this, to recognize that children belonged equally to both parents. But when push came to shove, or into a court of law, the woman's half-share was generally given precedence. Men's paternity could be proved beyond a doubt by genetic testing, but rather than giving him the right to his own child, paternity usually did nothing more than establish his monetary responsibility. Equal ownership is a con. It doesn't work. As King Solomon proved long ago, there are no shares in a child; it's all or nothing. And as men in the past instinctively recognized, either a woman owns her own body—and the children who come out of it—or a man does. As the old saying has it, "A man cannot serve two masters." Nor a child two parents.

Human cloning set men—and women—free. We don't have to fight each other any more. Now men have the same, inalienable

right as women. We can reproduce ourselves. We can have our own children.

That, more or less, is how I ended my class presentation, all those years ago. I got an A-plus. I still remember the applause from my classmates.

Yet the freedom I proclaimed then was not yet as actual as I made it sound: When Chaz was an infant, men were still dependent on women for the gestation period, although at least use of women in this way could be a relatively straightforward, commercial transaction. The development of a completely satisfactory artificial womb lagged, perhaps because there was no perceived demand. There were always plenty of women willing to rent out their wombs; it wasn't as profitable as regular prostitution, perhaps, but some women preferred it. Another possibility was animal wombs: Dairy cows were fine, and farmers were always on the lookout for extra sources of income. But some studies suggested possible developmental delays, or later psychological problems in the cowborn. A few men were dedicated—or mad—enough to actually give birth to their own children, but the failure rate (including parental, as well as infant, mortality) was significant and the major surgery involved for a one-time event remains daunting to this day.

Charles Nicholas Weller devoted himself to his forthcoming fatherhood like an ancient scholar to his holy task—but he wasn't mad. He had the injections necessary to allow him to nurse his child for up to six months, and he took great care in choosing the woman whose womb he would rent. He paid extra to ensure she was surrounded by positive environmental influences throughout her confinement. He visited her apartment every day in order to speak to his unborn child, carefully constructing a prenatal bond. Birth was, of course, by cesarean section, with the carrier under total anesthetic: She never so much as glimpsed the baby who was delivered into his father's waiting arms, laid on his naked, swollen breast to suck.

I winkled all these details out of Chaz as he drove us out to his

father's beautiful bayside home, and I burned inside with the single, jealous thought: That baby could have been me. *Should* have been me.

"Dad!" Chaz shouted as we entered through the glass-walled conservatory at the side of the house. "Hey, Dad, I'm home! You'll never guess what!"

I felt a murderous, infantile rage that encompassed both Chaz and my mother. This was my birthright, stolen from me.

And then Charles Nicholas Weller walked in, and my whole world shifted on its axis. Suddenly, everything changed.

I no longer hated my poor, mad, sad mother, for it seemed she was no longer the wicked witch, but a good fairy in disguise: If she had not kidnapped me, I'd never have known this happy ending.

I looked at Charles Nicholas Weller, my original, and my mouth went dry. I could feel (in my imagination) the tiny hairs lifting on the back of his neck. Of course, he hadn't been expecting me. But neither had I expected my own response. His blue eyes looked into their reflection in mine, and my penis swelled and stiffened. I wanted to fall down and worship at the feet of this god; I wanted to fling myself on this man.

All my envy of Chaz evaporated. I wouldn't have stood in his shoes for all the world. I didn't want to be this beautiful man's son—I wanted to be his lover.

His eyes widened as if he'd read my thoughts. I looked at his trousers and saw his desire before, I think, he knew it himself.

"Chaz," he said, in a strained voice, still looking at me. "What is this? *Who* is this?"

"It's obvious, isn't it?" said Chaz. "But he hasn't said *how.*"

I told him my mother's name. This drew a blank at first—it must have been years since he'd thought of her—but then he touched his face, fingers tracing where her nails had raked, the very point of my origin.

"Oh," he said softly. "Son, please believe me, I had no idea. If I had, son—"

"No," I said, softly but emphatically. "I'm *not* your son. I'm yours, but not your *son.* I want you, but not to be my father."

He stared at me for a moment, bewildered, grappling with his feelings—I know, I had the same feelings—and then, gradually, rising through the bafflement in his eyes, I saw his desire. He wanted me. Not as a man wants a child, but as he yearns for his other half, the missing part that will make him ecstatically whole.

Chaz broke into our charged silence, whining like a child. "Hey, what is this? I thought this guy was going to tell us his story?"

"Sure," I said, backing off. "Of course."

"What am I thinking of? We're not very hospitable, keeping you standing out here like this! Come into the family room. Chaz, go get us some drinks, please. What would you like, uh . . . ?"

"Nick," I told him. "Call me Nick. A beer would be great, or a soft drink. Whatever."

It was obvious to both of us what we wanted and what would happen later that night, but we were both grown-ups. We knew how to behave. Charles was careful not to lay a finger on me until Chaz had gone off to his bedroom, and it was as well he was so careful, because the moment his flesh brushed mine we couldn't stop ourselves rushing together in the futile yet strangely satisfying struggle to merge completely.

All our care to tread lightly around Chaz's feelings was pointless. We might just as well have made love in front of him. He hates me, and blames me for his lost happiness. All his life he's had his father to himself, and he obviously imagined him as a sexless being whose whole satisfaction was bound up in his son's happiness. Children don't like to think of their parents as sexual beings.

But Chaz is not a child anymore. He's older than I was when I left home. There's no point in telling him now, because he's still too young to appreciate the long view, but, far from taking anything away from him, my arrival has paved the way for his future happiness.

"It's disgusting!" he hissed at me that first day, when he realized his father and I were lovers. "Shouldn't be allowed! It's incest!"

But of course it's not. Sex between Chaz and Charles would be unthinkable, a corruption of the father-son relationship. But Charles is not my father. Not in a biological sense, and not in a social or cultural sense, as I was raised by someone else in complete ignorance of his existence. It's idiotic to talk about crimes against nature in this context. We're not part of nature, Charles and I; we've transcended it, remade it.

We are the forerunners of a new race. It was for this that I was born. Being so happy, we long to share our happiness with everyone. And we will, but it can't happen overnight. We've already planned for Chaz's future, though: Without his knowledge, Charles has had him cloned, and set aside some safe investments to ensure that the boy is raised in good circumstances, completely anonymously, by foster parents. Once he's reached sexual maturity he'll be told who he really is, and Chaz will be informed of his existence.

When they meet, nature—our new-formed nature—will take its course. By then, any lingering resentment he may feel towards me will be washed away on the tide of happiness. Someday, after we are all dead, no doubt, everyone will make such arrangements for the happiness of their descendants, and the world of strangers into which I was born will have become a world of lovers.

Flourish Your Heart in This World

Felicia Ackerman

L*aurel* knows she is not supposed to play favorites, but she cannot help liking Mrs. Noll better than the other hospice patients. Mrs. Noll is someone Laurel would like even if it weren't a professional duty, someone Laurel would be happy to spend time with at a party. Now Laurel is sitting at Mrs. Noll's bedside, in the intricately carved teak armchair Mrs. Noll has brought from home. The chair is unupholstered and the wood is slippery, but it is surprisingly comfortable. "Did you get this chair in India?" Laurel asks.

Mrs. Noll nods, smiling. Although she is seventy and dying, she is still vaguely beautiful, with her blue eyes and thick white hair—a marvel in this place where most of the patients (Laurel keeps forgetting to call them guests) have had chemotherapy. "My husband and I got the chair and the rug on our twentieth-anniversary trip to Asia, and that"—she gestures at the framed calligraphy-and-goldleaf Malory quotation on the wall—"was his first-anniversary present to me. It is lovely to be able to have so many of my own things with me here. It makes up for all the psychobabble."

"I know." The homelike atmosphere—you can bring your own furniture, redecorate your own private room, and one woman has even brought her parakeet—is of course a major selling point for this residential hospice. Sometimes this reminds Laurel of the Richard Armour book that says college dormitories have a home-

like atmosphere, especially for people who come from homes with hundreds of bedrooms, each of which is occupied by a stranger. But she has to admit that this is a much pleasanter place to die than the hospital where she used to work. That's why she works here now. And there aren't hundreds of bedrooms here, just thirty-four.

"And the coverlet is from Nepal," Mrs. Noll is saying. "I have no regrets about my travels. They were worth it."

"I know," Laurel says again, although she also knows that without the Asian trip, not only these exotic items but Mrs. Noll herself would not be here. "Hepatitis," Mrs. Noll said at the intake interview six weeks ago. "Hardly the worst thing you could pick up in Asia. It takes twenty-five years to destroy your liver, and for most of that time, there are almost no symptoms. And once people learn that your cirrhosis of the liver comes from unhealthy travel rather than unhealthy drinking, they become a lot nicer. Fascinating, isn't it?" she added, winning Laurel's heart on the spot.

Now Mrs. Noll is inching her way up against her silk-covered pillows, inching her way farther into the sunlight that, streaming through the curtain, is making a lacy pattern on her face. "Have you heard anything more from your cousin in California?" she asks.

"I talked to her last night. She says that when you're actually doing it, you don't go around thinking, Isn't this weird, I've gotten myself cloned. You're just pregnant."

"When did they first clone a person, a couple of years ago?"

"A little more. 2003. It's still pretty experimental."

"How very interesting." Mrs. Noll sounds interested, which is part of her charm. Of course, the social workers are paid to be interested in the patients, not the other way around, but why shouldn't you like someone who takes an interest in what you say? And who often has a box of chocolates invitingly open on her night table—Mrs. Noll no longer eats chocolates, but she likes to watch other people enjoy them. Laurel takes a chocolate-covered cherry, feeling the slithery sweetness spread through her mouth. She is about to say that Juliana, who has always gotten everything she

wanted except a baby, is now getting to have the baby too. But Mrs. Noll is saying, "I suppose I'm a hopeless reactionary. But I still think it's unnatural. Like going to a Mercicenter instead of a hospice. Cloning, suicide—people have to control everything nowadays. At my age I figure I have the right to be a reactionary if I want to be."

"You certainly do," Laurel says.

"I wanted children at first, but my husband and I grew to be very glad it was just the two of us."

"Juliana spent eight years trying to get pregnant," says Laurel. "I don't think she would ever have gotten to be glad. She's not much for adjustment. She's used to getting what she wants."

"I believe in taking life as it comes," Mrs. Noll says placidly. "Hardly a fashionable attitude for a woman these days. Unless she's seventy and dying in a hospice," she adds, her tone without rancor.

Laurel feels ridiculous saying "I know" for the third time, but in fact she does know. Seeing Mrs. Noll here, dying serenely but with flair, makes Laurel recognize the insidious contagiousness of the hospice mentality. How lovely it would be, she often thinks, how lovely to stop struggling to find a man who could love a woman who never had much verve and is now thirty-six and fading, to stop hoping for a stroke of good fortune to change her life, just to accept, accept, lie back in a perpetual warm bubble bath of acceptance. But only part of her feels that way. The other part can't bear to abandon her dreams.

"You don't like your cousin, do you?" Mrs. Noll's voice is weakening; her eyes are closing.

"Well," says Laurel, "I got off to a bad start. Juliana lived across the street from me until I was eighteen, and she had a bigger house, a bigger wardrobe, a swimming pool in her backyard, and a red BMW. Would you like someone like that?"

"As a teenager?" Mrs. Noll murmurs. "I doubt it."

"And all those fancy trappings couldn't hide the fact that underneath it all, she was prettier and smarter than I was."

Mrs. Noll's eyes snap open, as if she has received a sudden infusion of energy. "I suppose nowadays they would say you should sign up for one of those self-image therapy weekends."

"So I can think I'm as pretty and smart as my Stanford-physics-professor cousin who has blond hair she can sit on?"

Mrs. Noll laughs, thrilling Laurel with how momentarily vigorous she sounds. "Oh, you are delightful," Mrs. Noll says, "especially as compared with the general run of people around here."

Laurel feels as if she has stepped into a pool of sunlight.

"And you can be attractive." Mrs. Noll's voice, kind as ever, has taken on an appraising tone. "All you need is lipstick and just a bit of moss-green eyeshadow and maybe blusher. You should also start wearing richer colors, to bring out the rich auburn highlights in your hair."

"What rich auburn highlights in my hair?"

"The highlights you will have when you start using an auburn rinse, which is something else you should be doing."

Laurel is actually considering following this advice. She puts her hand on Mrs. Noll's shoulder, recalling how last week Mrs. Noll said, "When you had thirty-eight years of marriage to a wonderful husband, the last thing you want is to have your hand held by a hired professional, but of course, it's different with you, dear."

A moment later there is a knock on the door, and then Ellen Lefferts, the hospice director, is walking into the room, pulling up a chair, and sitting down by the bed. "I hear you had a bad night," Ellen says.

"Only for a bit," says Mrs. Noll. "Nicole came and gave me a shot right away. The symptom relief here is very effective."

"That's what we're here for," Ellen says.

"Thank you."

"I also stopped by to invite you to our support group that will be meeting at three in the solarium." Ellen leans forward; she is wearing a blue cotton dress with sprigs of coral flowers.

"No, thank you."

"Are you sure?"

Mrs. Noll nods.

"I hope you will let us know as soon as you are ready to talk about your feelings. We're caring for the complete you."

"Thank you."

As she is leaving, Ellen asks Laurel to stop by the office before going home for the day.

"How I wish there were some tactful way to get it across to her that while I'm quite happy to die serenely, like a good hospice poster child, I don't want to talk about it," Mrs. Noll says, almost as soon as Ellen has left and closed the door behind her. "It's not an interesting subject. Besides, some things are private."

"We're caring for the complete you," Laurel says with a grin.

"Oh, well," says Mrs. Noll. "I suppose we shouldn't be too hard on her. When I think of how terrible I felt when I came here and how comfortable this place has managed to make me, I'm ready to forgive her anything. Well, almost anything. I hope she isn't giving you trouble for spending too much time with me."

"Oh, no," Laurel lies.

"Good. Let me see your hands."

"My hands?"

"I had thought perhaps some coral nail polish. The flowers on her dress gave me the idea." All at once, Mrs. Noll looks exhausted. She is sinking back against the pillows, but she manages to say, "We're caring for the complete you," before drifting off to sleep.

* * *

Ellen's office is full of plants. There is a thicket of pink begonias on the mantelpiece and an herb garden on the windowsill. There are two African violets in green flowerpots on the desk. A potted avocado tree is threatening to burst through the ceiling. Plants are the main decoration throughout the hospice building. Maybe Ellen has read that plants symbolize the cycle of nature, the passing of the old

and the coming of the new. Or maybe she just likes plants. She is certainly good at growing them; the thicket of begonias is the most luxuriant Laurel has ever seen. Above it, a placard proclaims, "Medicine should be high-touch, not high-tech." Laurel figures this is not the place to mention Juliana.

"Did Minnie talk to you yesterday about the party?" Ellen is asking.

Minnie is Mrs. Noll's cousin and her only visiting relative, a retired nurse who began visiting recently and comes on Thursdays, dressed in tennis whites on her way to the courts. This strikes Laurel as tactless, but Mrs. Noll doesn't seem to mind, although she privately calls Minnie "Minnie Mouse." Minnie even looks a trifle mouselike, with her bright eyes, sleek gray hair, and perky features. "What party?" Laurel says.

Ellen rests her elbows on her oak desk, steeples her hands, and explains that Minnie will be having a sixtieth birthday party a week from Sunday. Most of the extended family will be there. It will be an opportunity for Mrs. Noll to reconcile with relatives she's been estranged from for years. But she is resisting the idea of going. "If you would talk with her and try to get at the root of the problem."

"Well," says Laurel, "if she doesn't want to go, I don't see what there is to talk about."

Ellen sharpens the steeple and reminds Laurel that patient plus family is the unit of hospice care.

"Mrs. Noll is dying." Laurel turns her head, with the result that she is staring into an African violet. "I'm not going to push her to do something she doesn't want to do just to make her relatives happy."

"It's not just to make her relatives happy." Ellen has unsteepled her hands, which now lie flat on her desk. "People die more peacefully when they are at peace with their families."

If Mrs. Noll were any more peaceful, you could package her and sell her as a tranquilizer, Laurel is tempted to say. Then it oc-

curs to her that Mrs. Noll might enjoy a new opportunity to poke mild fun at Ellen's ideas about good adjustment. "Okay," she says. "I'll talk to her. I'll do it."

* * *

"You did it!" says Mrs. Noll when Laurel comes in after the weekend.

"Do you like it?"

"The hair is perfect and the lipstick is fine too. But the eyeshadow is all wrong. Oh, I don't blame you, dear. I blame myself. I should have seen that you needed golden brown, to complement your new auburn hair."

"How about this?" Laurel opens her purse and takes out her little palette of eyeshadows—mauve, two greens, and mahogany.

A few minutes later, she is looking into Mrs. Noll's silver-backed mirror at her new mahogany eyelids and, since Mrs. Noll has gotten her to intensify the lipstick, brighter lips. Still no competition for Juliana, and maybe the effect is rather conspicuous, but why not?

"Tell me what you've been up to, aside from a makeover for the complete you," says Mrs. Noll.

"Well, I promised Ellen I would talk to you about Minnie's birthday party."

"What?"

"She thinks you will be more at peace if you are at peace with your family."

"Tell her if I were any more at peace, I'd be dead already."

Laurel looks at her hands. The coral nail polish has already begun to chip. "Juliana's invited me to visit in about seven weeks, after the baby is born."

"I thought you didn't like her."

"I can't really dislike her. She's too nice. Anyway, a friend of hers will be at Stanford for a mini-course. She thinks he and I might like each other. She wants to—"

"That's marvelous."

"I'm not sure I want to go." But then Laurel realizes Mrs. Noll might suspect the reason—Laurel doesn't want to risk being away when Mrs. Noll dies—so, keeping her eyes focused on the embroidered Nepalese coverlet, she launches into an account of the contagiousness of the hospice outlook and how she seems to be losing what little get-up-and-go spirit she ever had. "Not that I'd tell Ellen that," she adds. "She's always talking about how the terminally ill can be an inspiration to us all. But I doubt this is the kind of inspiration she has in mind."

Laurel looks up, expecting Mrs. Noll to be amused. But Mrs. Noll looks horrified. "You mustn't—all this acceptance is fine for a dying old lady like me whose husband is dead and whose life is over. But a young person like you who has never had an abiding love . . . You must take this opportunity, Laurel, flourish your heart in this world."

"What?"

"Flourish your heart in this world. It's from the Malory passage on the wall. Get up and read it. You might as well become familiar with it. I have left it to you in my will."

Laurel's eyes fill with tears.

"Read it, dear," Mrs. Noll says gently. "And you must try not to cry when you are wearing eye makeup."

Laurel walks over to the wall. "Therefore, like as May month flowereth and flourisheth in many gardens, so in likewise let every man of worship flourish his heart in this world," she reads aloud after a moment.

" 'Worship' meant honor in the fifteenth century. A man of worship was an honorable man. Won't that be a nice thing to hang in your living room?"

Laurel, working her way through the difficult calligraphy and unfamiliar phrasing, starts to giggle shakily.

"What's so funny?"

"But the old love was not so; men and women could love to-

gether seven years, and no licours lusts were between them, and then was love, truth, and faithfulness," Laurel reads aloud.

" 'Licours lusts' meant sexual pleasures," says Mrs. Noll. "What is funny about that?"

Laurel stifles a mental image of a man walking into her living room and seeing a wall-hanging that says he should go seven years without lusts. She turns around. Mrs. Noll is smiling, her eyes half-closed. Probably the passage reminds her of her husband, although Laurel doubts they waited seven years to have sex.

"I guess you don't read fashion magazines, with their articles about how long to wait before sleeping with a new man," she says, sitting back down at Mrs. Noll's bedside. "On the third date, or the fourth, or if you're really conservative, maybe wait a few months. I don't recall any of them saying seven years. But of course I'll put it up in my living room. I want to. I can't tell you how much I . . ." She swallows hard.

"Perhaps this will help you attract a better sort of man. At any rate," Mrs. Noll says sleepily, "the main thing for now is to get you to California. I'll go to Minnie's birthday party if you'll go to Juliana. I'll visit my cousin if you'll visit yours. Is it a deal?"

"Yes," says Laurel. "It's a deal."

* * *

Her side of the deal didn't turn out so badly, Mrs. Noll tells Laurel on Tuesday of the following week. "They were all terribly sweet to their dying old relative, partly out of pity and no doubt partly because they're all hoping to be remembered in my will."

Laurel glances out the window. The day is bright and blue, with pink and yellow flowers swaying in the hospice garden, the kind of day that would bring hope to anyone, even a dying old lady and an aging unloved social worker.

"I'm going to have some fun," Mrs. Noll continues. "People who are after a dying old woman's money deserve to be toyed with. That's why I agreed to stay through yesterday so I could spend

more time with some relatives I hadn't seen in decades. Minnie's also invited me to a luncheon this Thursday for her granddaughter, and I agreed to go if I feel up to it. And if I'm being unfair and all she wants is the pleasure of my company," Mrs. Noll's voice is fading, but her expression is still alert, "well, that's all she's going to get. Have you made your plane reservations for California? Have you practiced saying, 'Oh, she looks just like you'?"

* * *

"Oh, she looks just like you," Laurel is saying six weeks later. "You'd better not commit a crime tomorrow, or she might get arrested."

Juliana beams, leaning back in her lawn chair, and runs a finger down the baby's round pink cheek. Juliana's cheekbones are high. Her hair is golden, and the baby is almost bald. Ten-day-old Beatrice Parker-Denison looks about as much like her mother as like Laurel. But if genes settle the matter, in thirty-six years Beatrice will have her mother's shining hair and perfect cheekbones. And Juliana will be seventy-two. Maybe still vaguely beautiful, like Mrs. Noll, but nothing to compare with the youthful version. Laurel has heard people say you have to be very egotistical to get yourself cloned. Now it strikes her the opposite is true. Generous and non-competitive, that's what you have to be—imagine bringing someone into the world who will be genetically just like you, but as you age, decades younger.

Paul, Juliana's husband, is standing behind her lawn chair and dangling a red ball on a string above Beatrice, the way Laurel earlier saw him dangle a toy in front of the family cat. "Look at this," he says. "A family in their backyard, what could be more natural? I wish that patient of yours who says cloning is unnatural could see this, Laurel."

"Everything that is usual appears natural. That's what Vicky always said," says Dan, opening a can of beer. "Of course, she got it from John Stuart Mill."

Laurel tries to catch Juliana's eye, but Juliana is blissfully ab-

sorbed in the baby. As absorbed as Dan apparently is in Vicky. But at least Juliana's daughter is alive. Dan's wife Vicky has been dead for seven years, but except for the past tense, he talks about her as if she has just gone out to the supermarket. Vicky liked teaching middle school because no matter how ruthless the pecking order was, the girls were so young you could always tell yourself that someday the last would be first. Vicky didn't like wine and wasn't interested in learning to like it; Vicky said she worked at her work, she wasn't going to work at her fun. Vicky once had a pet swan. Laurel thinks she would have liked Vicky. But she can't imagine how she is supposed to attract a man who still sees himself as Vicky's husband.

"Vicky—" Dan begins again.

Beatrice shrieks. Good for you, Laurel says silently. "Excuse me," says Juliana and gets up, carrying Beatrice into the house.

Laurel hesitates, then follows. Juliana is sitting on a loveseat in the living room, a towel draped over her chest, breast-feeding Beatrice. Laurel is surprised. She had a vague idea that in California breast-feeding would be as public as politics.

"So what do you think?" Juliana asks.

"She's beautiful."

"I mean about Dan."

"Dan?" Laurel sits down in a green velvet armchair that turns out to be even softer than it looks. "I think if he gets involved with me, he'll be committing adultery. Why are you trying to fix me up with someone who's still in love with his wife?"

"Widowers who were happily married make ideal husbands."

"No, they *made* ideal husbands. If widowers want to get married again, it means they love marriage, not their wives. True love," Laurel picks up a pretzel stick from a bowl on the coffee table and holds it aloft like a scepter, "does not look for replacements."

Juliana giggles. "What've you been reading, *Riveting Romances*?"

"Malory. Mrs. Noll has got me reading him. People in Malory's world don't look for replacements."

"You can't really believe—"

"I really believe Dan isn't looking for a replacement. Neither did Mrs. Noll. She wouldn't be so serene about dying if her husband were still alive." Laurel gazes straight ahead. The opposite wall has a mural of wildflowers. "Too bad Vicky died too long ago for Dan to clone her."

"So he could marry an infant? Besides, he wants Vicky, not a clone."

"Then why do you think he'd want me?"

"You have a lot in common. You're both so romantic. No one can mourn forever."

Oh yes, they can, Laurel wants to say. But Beatrice is falling asleep, and Juliana also seems to be shutting down, her face at once peaceful and exhilarated as she looks at her daughter, as though falling in love and assured of reciprocation. Mrs. Noll grew to be happy to be childless, happy to flourish her heart entirely unto her husband. Probably Dan, who is also childless, was the same way. Probably he was as wonderful a husband as Mrs. Noll's was. If only . . . Laurel is tired too, jet-lagged. She feels as if she is sinking into the field of flowers on the wall. She can almost smell the flowers; then she realizes there is a vase of roses on the end table. Juliana's plushy cat, blue-gray like Dan's eyes, is rubbing against Laurel's ankle. How soft. Everything seems to be conspiring to make her fall in love. But she doesn't want to be like the women in Malory's world who fall in love with Lancelot because he is so devoted to Guinevere and they want all that devotion for themselves. They can't see that going after someone because of the stability he shows in his devotion to someone else is a losing proposition. If he shifts his devotion to you, he no longer has the stability that attracted you in the first place. Anyway, she barely knows Dan.

Laurel has an impulse to telephone Mrs. Noll and find out how she is, but it is too late and she is too sleepy.

* * *

The next morning Laurel awakens with an urge to giggle. Imagine, she was practically ready to fall in love with a total stranger just because he still loved his dead wife and Juliana's living room smelled of roses. That's what reading Malory will do to you, she envisions Mrs. Noll saying. Why not give her a chance to say it right now? And why not give her a chance to hear that Juliana's daughter doesn't look like an unnatural clone, she looks like a baby? Laurel picks up the receiver to call Mrs. Noll, only to be interrupted by the cat, who has come into the guest room, bounded onto the bed, and is now inserting her velvety blue-gray body between Laurel's mouth and the receiver, purring loudly. Three times Laurel pushes her away, but the cat keeps returning like a velvet boomerang. Laurel is so absorbed in trying to keep her mouth at the receiver that it is a while before it strikes her that the rings are not being answered. She hangs up, tries again, waits ten minutes, and tries a third time.

Maybe she's just out of her room, Laurel tells herself, don't get upset. But on the other hand, why not? People in Malory's world get upset all the time. They don't worry about being well adjusted. And Mrs. Noll is rarely out of her room anymore. In the past month, she has gotten weaker, although the hospice doctor predicts a couple of months more for her. He has admitted he can't be sure. Laurel will have to sound calm if she is going to call Ellen. Ellen thinks Laurel is too involved with Mrs. Noll, just as most people would think Dan is too involved with the memory of his dead wife. Where do they keep the rule book? Laurel picks up the receiver again, concentrating so hard on how calm she is going to sound that it is not until the telephone starts to ring that she realizes the cat is still on the bed.

"Ellen Lefferts."

"Hello. This is Laurel." She tries to push the cat away.

"This is a terrible connection. Do you hear buzzing on the line?"

"It's just a ca—Yes, it's a terrible connection." The purrs are

rising like tidal waves. Laurel scoops up the cat and plops her on the floor. "Is Mrs. Noll all right?"

"I have such good news." The good news is that Mrs. Noll has gone back to Minnie's for a few days. Minnie is a retired nurse, remember? Isn't Laurel glad she persuaded Mrs. Noll to go to the birthday party? Isn't it wonderful when terminal illness leads to family reconciliation?

Laurel gazes out the guest room window, which overlooks the backyard. Juliana is lying in a hammock, with Beatrice on her stomach. Juliana's husband is pushing the hammock back and forth. And in the room, the cat is purring the loudest purrs Laurel has ever heard.

"Yes," she says, "wonderful."

* * *

And if Merlin could have enchanted him into believing I was Vicky, we would have lived happily ever after, Laurel is rehearsing in her mind eight days later as she knocks on the door of Mrs. Noll's room, her first stop in the hospice on the day after returning from California. Knock before entering; that's a rule of what Ellen calls hospice philosophy. Give our guests the courtesy you would give a guest in your own home.

"Come in," says a man's voice.

Laurel's first thought is that it must be the hospice doctor. But the doctor would not be lying in the bed instead of Mrs. Noll. He would not be the reason the room now has none of Mrs. Noll's possessions, no teak armchair, no embroidered Nepalese coverlet, no Asian rug. No framed Malory passage. And the doctor is not an elderly black man with a fringe of white hair and a benign pedagogical expression, as if he has been reading fables to children.

"Good morning," says the man. "You must be Laurel."

* * *

"She's as well as can be expected. She has gone to live with Minnie. She'll be there until the end, so she can die surrounded by her loved ones." Sitting under a hanging basket of ferns that is a new addition to her office, Ellen sounds as pleased as if Mrs. Noll has been cured and is off for a trip around the world.

Laurel presses her palms together. First the jet lag, then the fear, and now this. "I can keep on as her social worker. I want to. I don't mind the extra work."

"She won't be using home hospice care. The family wants to take care of her themselves." Ellen steeples her hands. "Minnie used to be a nurse, you know."

* * *

Of course, it is only because she felt so close to Mrs. Noll that Laurel feels so bereft now. Patients have chosen to leave this residential hospice before. Some go home to die. Occasionally people even leave because they have a remission, although Laurel can count on her eyeballs the number of times this has happened. Then there are the ones they're not supposed to think about, the ones who leave the hospice to go to Mercicenters, pleasant facilities like hospices, except that at the end of a lovely day or two, you get free poison with your tea. Or they'll bring it to your home. Like hospices, Mercicenters have home care for people who prefer to die at home. Our role is to make our guests comfortable enough with *us* that they don't feel the need to turn to *them,* Ellen likes to say.

Mrs. Noll would never turn to *them,* would she? She scorns the idea. She thinks it's unnatural. But if the nausea got out of control . . . Laurel forces the thought away, but it keeps moving in and out of her consciousness, like a floater drifting across her visual field, until finally, as soon as she gets home, she telephones Minnie.

Ten rings. Twelve rings. No answer. Three occurences of this pattern in half an hour, and it's like being back in Juliana's guest room except for the absence of purrs. Don't get upset. Well, why

not? People in Malory's world . . . Eventually, at a quarter after nine, Minnie answers the telephone, and Laurel launches into her prepared speech. "Is this Minnie Larson? This is Laurel from the hospice. I was wondering how Mrs. Noll is doing."

"She's doing as well as can be expected," Minnie says.

"I wonder if I could say hello to her?" Laurel draws a pair of concentric circles on her notepad.

"I'm afraid she's past that. She's quite disoriented. But at least she isn't suffering. We're keeping her comfortable."

Laurel's throat feels scraped. "Maybe I could come and visit?"

"I'm afraid she wouldn't recognize you, dear. But thank you so much for calling. She liked you very much, you know."

Not until several minutes after hanging up does it occur to Laurel to wonder why, if Mrs. Noll is so disoriented, she was left alone in the house for over three hours.

* * *

To find out if a particular person has died recently in your city, you can log on to the department of vital statistics at City Hall. Laurel remembers this from a murder mystery she read last month. But Mrs. Noll is not listed. So she hasn't died at a Mercicenter, with Minnie tactfully concealing it from the hospice. What else might Minnie be concealing? You could hardly expect to find Mrs. Noll's death listed if Minnie is concealing it in order to get her Social Security checks. But it wasn't her Social Security checks that Mrs. Noll said Minnie was interested in. It was her will. What if Minnie has gotten Mrs. Noll to make a will in her favor, and now Mrs. Noll is bound and drugged? Or maybe Mrs. Noll has become so weak and disoriented that Minnie has no need of rope or drugs to feel safe leaving her home alone. Or maybe Laurel reads too many murder mysteries. Maybe Minnie is taking perfectly good care of Mrs. Noll and just had her telephone unplugged for a few hours so as not to be disturbed.

All through the following morning, through the staff meeting and the session with the gentlemanly new occupant of Mrs. Noll's room, Laurel is making plans. At lunchtime she telephones Minnie. No answer. Then she drives to a jewelry store, where she buys a pair of garnet earrings she can always keep for herself if no one answers Minnie's door.

"I found an earring wedged behind the night-table drawer. I figured it must be Mrs. Noll's," Laurel rehearses in her mind fifteen minutes later as she pulls up in front of Minnie's house. The curtains are closed, a magazine sticks out of the mailbox, and no car is in the driveway. She walks down the marigold-bordered path and rings the doorbell. She waits five minutes, rings again, waits another five minutes, then bangs the knocker as loudly as she can. She puts her ear to the door. Still no sound from within. Of course, Mrs. Noll may be unable to scream. But Laurel is beginning to suspect there is no one inside the house.

* * *

"Maybe Minnie was taking a bath," Juliana is saying late that evening.

"And yesterday she just happened to have her phone unplugged until nine-fifteen?" Laurel shifts the receiver to her other ear. "Look, I went back today after dark, and still no one answered the door, and the porch light was on but the house was all dark inside. Even in back—I drove around the block. I think Mrs. Noll isn't there anymore."

"But—"

"Juliana, could you do something about the cat? I can hardly hear you." Laurel takes a sip of water. "I can't talk to Ellen," she continues after Juliana has removed the cat. "She'd probably say I need to go to a support group for stressed hospice professionals."

"Maybe you do. But that won't help you find out whether your suspicions are right. What you need," says Juliana, "is to go to the police."

Laurel stares at her hands. In memory of Mrs. Noll, she is still

wearing coral nail polish. In memory of? Where did that come from? "I don't know if they'd get involved. Anyway, I'd prefer something less official and more discreet. So if it turns out to be nothing, Minnie won't have to know. Maybe I'll investigate a little more on my own."

"Be careful," Juliana says.

* * *

Three times during the next week, Laurel takes one of the earrings to Minnie's on her lunch hour. She drives past the house three evenings after dark. No one answers the doorbell at lunchtime, and in the evening there is never light in more than one place. Surely Minnie is out during the day and alone here at night? The vital statistics department still has no listing of Mrs. Noll's death. Laurel is now desperate enough to call the police department of missing persons. Mrs. Noll, however, does not qualify as a missing person just because she is missing to Laurel.

"She's seventy and dying," Laurel protests.

"There's no evidence of foul play. Nothing for us to investigate. Even dying seventy-year-olds are entitled to their privacy."

Laurel has to admit that the last part sounds like something she might say to Ellen. But that Saturday, after calling Juliana, describing what she is about to do, and ending, "If I don't call you back today, call the police," she drives over to Minnie's and rings the doorbell.

Minnie looks so different in her old slacks, T-shirt, and no makeup that Laurel probably would not have recognized her on the street. Apparently, it's mutual. Minnie is blinking and saying, "Yes?" in a pleasant but puzzled way.

"I'm Laurel. The hospice social worker. I think Mrs. Noll left an earring. . . ."

How odd Minnie's expression looks, strained and almost pitying. Pinpoints of fear rise within Laurel like a fireworks display. "Is she alive?" she asks abruptly.

"Come in." Minnie steps back from the door. "I suppose I might as well tell you now."

"When did she die?" Laurel whispers.

"She is not dead."

Laurel does not remember walking through the hall and into the living room, but now she is seated on a sofa opposite a tapestry wall-hanging. "Is she still here?"

"She never was here," Minnie says, "and she's not my cousin."

* * *

Laurel does not try to sort out her thoughts until she is walking back down the marigold-bordered path. First comes relief, relief plus elation, because Mrs. Noll is not dead. Is maybe not even dying anymore. Is flourishing her heart, not to mention her liver, in this world. Laurel has a wild urge to laugh; then the second reaction sets in. Betrayal. The sweet old lady with her old-fashioned ideas about natural and unnatural, the sweet old lady serenely dying in a hospice, was a fake. What else was a fake? All that warmth and interest —did Mrs. Noll come to see Laurel just as a dupe? Laurel could hardly ask Minnie that, but she did inquire about Mrs. Noll's husband.

"Yes, she loved him very much," Minnie said, as she poured iced tea into Laurel's glass, "but that doesn't mean she was ready to die. You hospice people are all so apt to believe terminally ill people are ready to die."

Only the ones who come to us, Laurel answers silently now as she gets into her car. They don't have to come to us if they don't want to. But Mrs. Noll did want to, at first. Laurel turns on the radio to an oldies station. "Stop! In the name of love," floats into the car. Laurel cannot stop. She cannot stop thinking about how Mrs. Noll came to the hospice so weak and nauseated that she really was ready to die. But after a few weeks of the comfort care the hospice is so proud of, she felt better, so much better that she began

having second thoughts. And when Laurel started to talk about Juliana . . .

Laurel turns the corner, drives several blocks, then turns another corner. She is driving aimlessly. Take the adventure, Malory says. Mrs. Noll took the adventure. Like most of the patients, she had her own telephone. No one in the hospice ever knew what calls she made. So she called the university medical center, a hundred and thirty miles away, just to see. Then she called her old friend Minnie Larson, not a retired nurse at all, but a part-time accountant.

How Laurel fell for Mrs. Noll's sympathetic interest in her and in Juliana! But Mrs. Noll was making plans. For a long time she had been ready to die; she hadn't been looking into last-ditch experimental treatments. But the university medical center staff told Mrs. Noll there was a brand-new possibility, a new kind of transplant, still experimental, but with no worries about organ rejection or waiting lists for scarce livers where a seventy-year-old would rank near the bottom. The procedure involved cloning her and making the cloned embryo cells turn into liver cells instead of developing into a fetus. So in a way the cloned embryo was sacrificed. So was the truth. You can't stay in a hospice if you're awaiting a transplant. Laurel knows this. It's right in the rules. Hospice philosophy means palliative care. If you want to take a chance on a life-extending experimental treatment, go somewhere else. Ellen would not have dumped Mrs. Noll on the street, of course. But there would have been a transfer to a nursing home for the six weeks between the cloning and the transplant, and who could be confident of finding a space in such a pleasant facility on such short notice? The hospice is so comfortable, and the symptom relief is so good.

"You have to understand, her life and her comfort were at stake," Minnie said, taking a gingersnap. "You know how important comfort is when you're so ill. She had no other choice."

No other choice but this elaborate deception? Well, Minnie ad-

mitted, looking embarrassed for the first time, perhaps it didn't have to be quite so elaborate. But deception is hard to keep in bounds. Hasn't Laurel ever found that? Minnie conceded that perhaps Mrs. Noll went too far, perhaps she even started to enjoy creating her own little world. But she needed an excuse for the preliminary sessions at the university hospital while they ran tests, evaluated her case, and finally harvested the cells from inside her cheek. That was what Mrs. Noll was up to when the hospice staff, so eager to facilitate a family reconciliation, thought she had gone to Minnie's birthday party and then to the luncheon for Minnie's granddaughter. Ironic, Minnie added, because although new life was being created, there would be no birth. Of course, a lot of people would think that is terrible, but Minnie and Mrs. Noll both think *they're* terrible, especially the ones who think it is all right to have an abortion because you don't want to have a child, but not to produce an embryo on purpose because you want to try to save your own life. And what did Laurel think? Minnie asked.

But Laurel, sitting stiffly on Minnie's sofa, was not thinking about embryos at all. She was thinking about deception and betrayal. She is thinking about that now as she finds herself driving alongside a golf course she has never seen before; she is out of the city by now. First relief, then knowledge of betrayal—where has she previously encountered this pattern? In stories about wives, of course, wives who are afraid something dreadful has happened when their husbands don't come home one night, and it turns out something dreadful has happened, but not to the husbands. To the wives. The husbands are happily with other women. Laurel's face feels singed. How unwholesome Ellen would find all this, perfect proof that Laurel is too involved and needs help whether she wants it or not. But this thought raises Laurel's spirits. It makes her feel unconventional and daring, instead of pathetic. Who is Ellen to say whom Laurel should flourish her heart unto? Laurel turns the car again, and soon she is driving along a country road beside a field of wildflowers like the mural in Juliana's living room, like the May in

Malory's world, when hearts begin to blossom and to bring forth fruit. Laurel's heart is beginning to bring forth fruit right now. Why shouldn't Mrs. Noll grasp at a second chance at life? And why suppose she was using Laurel? Maybe she was trying to protect Laurel by not letting her in on the deception. Maybe she was afraid Laurel would lose her job if she went along with the deception and Ellen found out. Maybe she was right. Laurel's hands are gripping the steering wheel; she sees her coral fingernails—a memorial, no, a tribute, to Mrs. Noll. Surely all that warmth and interest was no fake. All at once, Laurel has the thrill of relief again, but now it is relief plus triumph, as if she and Mrs. Noll have carried off the deception together. Laurel's talk of Juliana was what got Mrs. Noll thinking about cloning, after all. Surely she would be delighted to see Laurel. Laurel does not have to be back at the hospice until Monday. She can drive to the university tomorrow and appear in Mrs. Noll's hospital room with an armful of flowers. Maybe she should take along her copy of Malory, but on second thought, that won't be necessary. Mrs. Noll has undoubtedly brought her own.

My Clone

C. K. Williams

Brow still fused to brow, brain to brain, one of us, I can't tell which, is crying; then an anguishing *release.* This is how my clone comes to me; not elaborated in some mute womb, but wrenched entire from my matter and my mind.

Because what my clone means, at the end, is doubling, multiplying, self-replication, as a person or a species; all its science finally tends towards that, our desire is that, our fear is that.

The first thing I imagine with him is my fear. To see oneself naked before one's naked self. The human dream, the human dread.

The next thing I imagine is his going, his dying, his suicide. He kills himself, does away with what he is, because I so oppress him; he can bear no longer my oppression, bear no more the "life" I've given him.

He kills himself because he knows that what I ask of him is irresolvable. To be as wounded as I am, as scarred: to have suffered all I have, just as I have.

I hear him telling me I didn't really want a thing of flesh and blood. That I'd really dreamed of something of a substance other than myself, generated from the tissues of imagination, from an unsmelted crystal of my unconscious. Something from a myth: centaur, mino-

taur, half-dream, half-human, which would answer all my ancient quandaries. Oedipus, or angel.

Perhaps he was right, perhaps I did feel something like regret, and fear again, when I reached out to him and my hand passed through him.

But still, to kill himself? Yet I know why. Because I ask of him: to be more serious than I am, more courageous, potent, virtuous. Especially virtuous, because he doesn't have the wounds I have to keep him from being so.

I imagine that he'll say to me: then you worried whether I'd be sensitive enough to even be as virtuous as you. You wondered whether human good might be too related to your pathological accumulation of pain. Your hoarding of your wrongs. He'll say: perhaps you didn't *want* me to be "good"; if I were, I might disprove too much.

The inward scars, the failures, losses, disappointments that slash the lining of the heart. How, without them, would he have been enough like me to *indicate* enough, to *mean* enough?

Your fear, he'd say, that I'd *absorb* you, that I'd steal that tiny quantum of eternity which you conceive is yours. Your fear that I'd *replace* you, with no one ever suspecting. How can I exist when what I represent to you is worse than death?

The wounds of pastness, the wounds of never being ready for the wounding, wound of wondering or of wishing for the end of wounding.

I imagine I become afraid that he'd be *more* than me, just as much as ever me, but more focused, less susceptible to all the flinchings and feintings which are the residue of all I've lived. With greater *ardor,* he'd exist, with greater *force.* He wouldn't be bedeviled by my prudence, wouldn't have to flail through all my apprehensions.

How wearisome, he says, your dialectics are. These lurches out towards knowledge, these tremblings back to ignorance and fear.

Perhaps my fear is grounded in the way he fits my most intense desires: to have a matrix for the self that absolutely matches self. That everlasting human passion to have family, nature, culture, earth, precisely made to fit me, *bent* to fit me, *crushed* to fit me.

Your rule of being, he'd say: is me and me and me. Like-minded, like-bodied, even like-divinitied.

What he might represent is the possibility of that impossibility: in his likeness to me, he'd embody how malignant our ambitions are.

And the way you change your mind ten times a minute. How was I supposed to learn to split myself in half, or ten, to have the wars against myself you want consciousness to be? The way, he'd say, you face forward every moment with ever gleaming hopes for better outcomes to your striving. Don't you, in your mind, he'd say, reproduce one self after another, each you think better than the last? And this hypothetically improved identity which you cast out before yourself: surely, at least sometimes, don't you become him? Aren't you then, in your mind at least, your own multiplying double, *your own clone?*

I could never clear my conscience of my feeling he was more *disposable* than I am. That finally it was this he'd been created for. Is it this that would torment him?

Your fear of mindless masses of me, he'd tell me, our eyes fixed, shoulders rigid. Our duplicability, replaceability: automatons, all primed to cast ourselves into oblivion for masters who have somehow gained control of us, who would steal our minds, our labor, bodies, lives. How dangerous those whose lives are stolen. Won't they do any evil? Toil and war, deception and control. Another of your agonizing fears, he'd say, but what else is human history? Master, slave. War and toil.

But I *need* you, I might tell him: you are me now, you can't do away with me.

You do away with one another. All your genocides, your holocausts, your hatreds: what were they but reducing others to their genetic stuff? Kike-clone, nigger-clone, Spic and Chink and Mick. How much, he'd say, is actually disposable to you: how much, even of your selves, you throw carelessly away.

Sometimes it occurred to me that I was taking vengeance on existence through him. Its uncertainties, its impossibilities. Perhaps my real desire was to prove that all the quandaries of consciousness were valid, no matter how much self-inflicted. We had made with him the antithesis to quandary: that which comes to birth exactly from self-consciousness, the part of self that always stands aside beholding, registering the self, even in its quandary, even in its pain.

Don't worry, he would say, my dying won't affront me as yours will you; I won't feel something's *stolen* from me, as you do. Death will still remain a human treasure.

Is there anything I could impart to him other than despair?

You want perfection, he would tell me, you human creatures, but not too much of it, not enough of anything that possibly might change your nature. You so love your nature, the way you're so defined by your biologic past: you meant me to sublimate this for you.

Your ambition, he would say, so outstrips your moral force, yet your ambitions are what you cultivate. What am I, he would say, but one more instance of your rhetoric, of your pathetic illusion-making?

But the *spirit,* I might ask him: is the human spirit nothing more than all the false equations, false confusions, anxieties, misapprehensions, horrid histories, of which it seems to be composed? Is there nothing past all that? Are we merely monsters?

Always you conceived of *me,* he'd say, as monster: because I represent the illusion of perfectibility you believed should be in spirit, yet never is. And that illusion is an abnegation of what you think is worthiest in you. You'd like to think that what can't be stated in a formula about you is precisely what you are, yet you can't keep yourself from generating formulae.

But why really must you leave me?

You said yourself, he'd tell me, it's the wounds, because by definition I can't have your wounds, and so by definition must affront you, disappoint you. You define yourself by character, and character by aberrations from a norm. Don't I represent a norm? Aren't I meant to *be* a norm? To the degree that I develop an identity, I become more threatening to you: a generated self, a monster. I'm so circumscribed by all your notions of monstrosity that I can hardly move. And yet without your wounds, I have no reason to.

I'd thought, I'd say, that because of how we'd made you, with our minds, that you'd have access with *your* mind to mysteries that denied us. I had thought you'd stand out in the night and hear the chording of the stars which to us are silent; I'd thought you'd hear the octaves that unfold from cell to cosmos.

Oedipus and angel: how much you wished of me, a creature generated from such contaminated wants.

Perhaps we wanted you to rectify our foolishness, our weakness. Perhaps we thought that if the definition of the species changed, we would love each other more. Perhaps what we wished from you was *love.*

Self-veneration.

To complete ourselves in love by means of you.

Not an angel, but a minotaur, a monster.

I imagine rending sadness. That I ask him not to go, and yet he goes.

But what will be your legacy to us?

Self-love. Self-loathing.

And what of us will you take with you?

Loathing. Love.

Little C

Martha C. Nussbaum

He seized her by the arm, unable to speak. Trembling, she tried to run after Jeannie and Jeannette, but he drew her back as if by force, and made her return with him. And Madeleine, seeing how his will gave him the daring to resist hers, understood, far better than by any words, that it was no longer her child, the foundling boy, it was François her lover who was walking by her side.

GEORGE SAND, *François de Champi*

You weren't there any more. I don't know why, but I know you were gone, just not there any more, and I was frozen with grief. (You know how it would be. I was eating lots of salad, running four miles a day, writing several articles—but still, my heart was a heavy cold block.)

Then, one day, our friends at the institute told me that they had a surprise for me. They had seen how unhappy I was, and they wanted to bring me something. I heard my apartment doorbell ring. I opened the door to the elevator. There, nestling in a purple laundry basket, surrounded by rushes and daffodils, wrapped in a green plaid pajama top, was the baby clone. He looked up at me with the defiant smile of baby Hercules getting ready to throttle the

serpents. His hands were already big enough to hold a tennis racket, and his thighs showed signs of promise.

Little C.

I picked him up and embraced him, declaring that henceforth he would live with me in my house as my very own child.

How I loved Little C. I would hold him so hopefully in my arms, thinking that he would soon become you. When his eyes turned from baby blue to a deeper gray-blue with flecks of yellow, a wonderful joy began to seep into my heart. I never tired of nursing him (through medical advances this was possible). I felt the baby lips around my nipple, and I imagined, as the milk flowed out, how the new sensation would please you. How eagerly I watched his hands wave in the air, describing ever more articulate and commanding gestures.

I gave Little C many baths. His legs pounded the water with rebellious strength, and he laughed with defiance as he covered me with water.

Often, in the late afternoon, Little C lay beside me as I rested, and made his happy baby gurgling noises. "Very good, Little C," I said.

But I also teased him, saying, "When are you going to talk about your own ideas, about global redistribution, and the shortcomings of utilitarianism? Move along quickly, Little C, for there is something lacking in this relationship."

I examined the different parts of his body, so white and soft, growing bigger under my care and nutrition. And I teased him again, saying, "Very good, Little C, but where is the lovely large body of which I am especially fond? Move along more rapidly, Little C."

In the early evening we sat at the window overlooking the lake, and we watched the evening light grow paler, the flecks of gold changing to swirls of rose and gray. Little C lay contented in my arms, and I sang to him my favorite songs, such as "Caro mio ben,"

and "Rêve d'Amour." Knowing you well, I watched for signs of boredom; but Little C listened to the end, contentedly gurgling.

As time went on, Little C got bigger and more wonderful. He walked at ten months, and very soon he showed a quickness and poise beyond his years. His strong legs pounded the floor as he ran, and I could see the muscles in his thighs growing rapidly. I moved to a house with a large yard, so that Little C could run and jump. A natural athlete, I told my colleagues at the institute, who were not surprised. They smiled at the extravagance of my maternal praise.

As Little C played, I would watch his movements closely, to see whether he had begun to develop that sloping posture, right shoulder slightly lower than left, by which I could recognize you three miles off or from the air at 10,000 feet. The shoulder slopes a little as if its heavier muscles are pulling it down, and the back twists ever so slightly to the right, portending grim prospects for the opponent. I would think I saw its signs, although Little C had never been on a tennis court. (Indeed, at that time he showed a strong preference for youth soccer.) I loved the light in his multicolored eyes, the jutting defiance of his jaw, the deft and rapid movements of his feet.

When Little C was eight, I began to take him with me to the opera. It is only an experiment, I told myself, and I will stop it if he shows any signs of boredom. How happy I was that Little C reacted well. First *Hansel and Gretel,* and soon even *The Magic Flute,* although he expressed disapproval of its images of racial and sexual inequality. We spent blissful intermissions together discussing the two principles of global justice with reference to Monostatos and the Queen of the Night. (Little C did not use that philosophical language, of course, but I noted with pleasure that he seemed to gravitate naturally toward the core ideas.) Soon Little C was asking to be taken to the opera on a regular basis.

"See," I imagined myself saying to you, "Little C likes classical music a great deal, and opera most particularly. So it wasn't in the genes, was it? The principles of global justice were in the genes, but the anti-opera principle was not." And I couldn't wait for him to develop a taste for Verdi, and even perhaps Wagner. Life looked very promising at that time.

As mothers go, I tended to the Proustian. I would promise Little C a bedtime kiss, and when, like Marcel, he implored me to stay longer and read to him, I would come into his room and read for hours. Among our favorite books was George Sand's *François le Champi,* the book Marcel's mother reads to him when she stays up with him all night. Little C was entranced by the story of the young miller's wife who finds a foundling boy in the field and decides to bring it up as her own child. He especially loved the part where Madeleine, looking at the poor cold wretched abandoned boy, asks him what his name is. "They call me François the foundling." "François le Champi." At that name (so indicative, had he known it, of his own condition), Little C's eyes grew bright with joy, and he liked to repeat the name in French, Champi, as if it were his own. "Then, Little C," I continued, "Madeleine looked at the little Champi with a gaze full of compassion. She picked him up, and announced that henceforth he would live in her house as her very own child."

And that was the manner in which I revealed to Little C his strange origin. One day, "You, my love," I told him, "are that Champi. For I found you: not in a field, but at my door, lying in a purple laundry basket, surrounded by rushes and daffodils, wrapped in a green plaid pajama top. You had as excellent a smile as baby Hercules getting ready to throttle the two serpents, and your thighs already showed signs of their current strength. I picked you up in my arms and embraced you, announcing that henceforth you would live in my house as my very own child." After that, Little C never tired of hearing that story. He requested it almost every day.

At this time concern for propriety made me refrain from revealing to Little C the ending of Sand's narrative. How the miller's wife, abandoned by her husband, grows very close to the foundling boy. And how one day, after years of intimate domestic life, she notices that the Champi is a grown man, and amazing in beauty. How he shows adult defiance of her will, and seizes her in a passionate embrace. No, I concealed those portions of the book, and ended my readings with the Champi's boyhood. But after Little C went to sleep, I read to myself, frequently, the scene where Madeleine and François embrace, and she recognizes, with joy, feeling the power of a mature and independent will, that the child she has raised as her own will henceforth be her lover and her husband. While Little C slept, I would look out at the moon over the black lake, and think of the happiness in store.

One day when Little C was ten, he said to me, "Mother, green is such a beautiful color. Why do you never wear green dresses?" Astonished, I replied, "What a ridiculous question. Because you hate green." But I was wrong, for Little C did not hate green. So I got out the green Armani suit that was hanging in my closet unused when you were there, and the green silk shell that looks so nice under several jackets, and I wore them for Little C's pleasure, and for my own. And I thought, with a softly sinking feeling in my stomach, "Why does Little C like green? Surely I look better in blue."

Then one day, shortly after this, I said, "Little C, please clean up your room." And, since I asked very gently, giving no incentives for defiance, Little C obeyed. And every day from then on, without my even having to ask, the room was clean. Papers in neat piles on the desk, books on the shelf, socks in the laundry, pajamas hung up on a hook behind the door, cups and plates neatly stacked in the dishwasher. I watched with approval and gentle encouragement. And the ice of grief began to grow again in my heart.

People from the institute, who knew the story of Little C, came

to marvel at the room, as at a wonder. Some approved of the alteration. The institute's chief economist, fastidious, felt himself released from a long-standing disgust. Our director, too, was relieved and gratified. But others—your philosopher friends in the global justice project—began to sneak behind my back and say, "Little C, it's okay to leave your socks on the floor." "Little C, this half-empty of Diet Coke looks really great turned upside down on your desk." "Little C, let's get out some papers and pile them up on the floor." But Little C said, "My mother asked me always to keep my room clean." And so he would refuse them. And they, too, began to grieve.

How, I thought, had I produced a child so pliable, so lacking in willfulness? Had I nursed him too often? Bathed him too tenderly? Sung too many soft French love songs? Where was my heroic child, fit to leap over all obstacles, including those imposed by his mother? Could it be that the secrets of making love to you were so well known to me, while the secrets of producing you were unknown completely?

At this time, my heart began to alter. Oh I was a good mother still, and I did the things that good mothers do. But the wild hopefulness and joy slowly drained out of our daily interactions. I did not sing or read as often to Little C, even though the knowledge of his individuality made it rational to sing all the more, since he seemed inclined to cultivate the musical talents that you spurned. In lieu of singing, I arranged for piano lessons, and Little C duly became a fine musician.

I no longer looked for the rightward slope in the shoulder. I noted that, in fact, Little C had a definite preference for soccer. He showed no inclination for either tennis or any other racket sport. For my part, I could not find much enthusiasm for soccer, a game I have always disliked. Little C's deft motions up and down the field began to bore me, since I saw no daring in them.

Or perhaps it was the body of Little C that failed to hold my in-

terest, so skinny and light, with neither muscular shoulders nor thighs of any substance.

During this same period a change also came over Little C. His multicolored eyes grew more subdued, losing their flashes of yellow light. His humor, once so wild and extravagant, subsided, as if beneath a weight. His running, though indeed exceedingly deft, lost the edge of exuberance that made people speak of rare athletic gifts.

Instead, as he grew into a tall boy of twelve and then thirteen, he poured his emotions into the piano, practicing for hours, with a gloomy intensity that astonished those who had previously known him. From Bach fugues and Mozart sonatas, he moved on, seeking pensive solemn music, music of lost love and a world of unavailable ease and grace. Satie, Debussy, Ravel—a world of pale moonlight, where the joy is so distant that it exists only in fantasy. The house vibrated with the haunting notes of "La Cathédrale Engloutie," as the cathedral, buried under the ocean floor, rises gloriously into the light for one moment—and sinks again beneath the waves.

Occasionally, charmed by the music itself, I allowed myself to sing while Little C played. Songs of Duparc and Fauré, songs with lines such as "Exiled from a golden sky where your beauty flourishes." And "Beyond the roof, how blue, how calm, the sky is." I felt as I sang that I could see your face through the music, and at those moments I loved Little C for bringing you closer. Little C was happy then. Increasingly, he sought out the piano.

Through his music he won much acclaim. People spoke of a rare poetic sensibility in one so young.

A time came when Little C was seventeen, and due to leave home shortly, to continue his musical studies at Juilliard. For although he was a fine academic student, he cared deeply for nothing but music, and he could not be truly happy unless he was playing something delicate and sad. The night before his departure for New York, we went for a last celebratory evening, mother and son, at the opera.

By chance, they were performing *Don Carlo,* and we sat together in silence through the Fontainebleau scene. Elisabetta and Carlo, finding that they are fated to be mother and son rather than lovers, sang of the horrible pain of their renunciation. "L'hora fatale è suonata," the fateful hour has sounded, and love is doomed forever. Yes, I thought. Doomed to be mother and son, forever.

In the intermission, Little C stood beside me, and I smiled up at him. By now, he was six foot three, although he retained his skinny tense physique and, being an athlete no longer (since he feared injury to his hands), he still had no shoulders to speak of. His multicolored eyes gleamed with a quiet, no longer a heroic light. We analyzed the performance, as was our habit.

Then Little C looked at me with the grave sadness that had by now become his characteristic expression.

"Mother," he said to me, "I see that I do not make you happy."

"It is true that I am not happy, Little C," I said to him. "But it has nothing to do with you."

"I have always tried so hard to please you, Mother," he said. "But no matter what I do or say, you are always just a little sad, and your eyes look at me as if you are thinking of something else."

"That is true, Little C," I said. "It is not your fault, but it is the truth."

"What are you thinking about, Mother, when that sad lost expression comes into your eyes? I wish I could know, because perhaps then I would be able to make you happy."

"It is a long long story, Little C, and you cannot know it."

"And that baby in the laundry basket, surrounded with rushes and daffodils, wrapped in a green plaid pajama top. Am I that baby?"

"You are indeed that baby. My Champi. My Little C."

"Why, then, do you not love me the way Madeleine loved her grown François?"

"Because each story has its own ending, and no person is exactly like any other."

"Am I then less lovable than François was?"

"You are the best Little C the world has ever known. Now let us go and take our seats. The intermission is almost over, and the second act is very fine."

Contributors' Notes

Felicia Ackerman is professor of philosophy at Brown University, as well as a writer whose short stories, many of which deal with issues in medical ethics, have appeared in ten magazines and one O. Henry Awards collection.

Dan Brock is the Charles C. Tillinghast, Jr., University Professor; professor of philosophy and biomedical ethics; and director of the Center for Biomedical Ethics, at Brown University.

Richard Dawkins is the Charles Simonyi Professor of Public Understanding of Science at Oxford University. His latest book is *Climbing Mount Improbable* (1997), published by W. W. Norton.

Wendy Doniger is the Mircea Eliade Professor of the History of Religion at the University of Chicago. She is the author of *Other Peoples' Myths, The Implied Spider,* and several Penguin translations from the Sanskrit.

Andrea Dworkin is the author of *Pornography: Men Possessing Women, Intercourse, Life and Death,* and the novels *Mercy* and *Ice and Fire.*

Jean Bethke Elshtain is the Laura Spelman Rockefeller Professor of Social and Political Ethics at the University of Chicago. She is the author, most recently, of *Democracy on Trial* (1995) and *Augustine and the Limits of Politics* (1996). She is also a contributing editor to the *New Republic.*

Richard A. Epstein is the James Parker Hall Distinguished Service Professor of Law at the University of Chicago.

William N. Eskridge, Jr., is professor of law at Georgetown University Law School and the author of *The Case for Same-Sex Marriage, Dynamic Statutory Interpretation,* and *Cases and Materials in Legislation: Statutes and the Creation of Public Policy* (with Philip Frickey).

Stephen Jay Gould is the author of sixteen books, including, for Norton, such international bestsellers as *Ever Since Darwin, The Panda's Thumb, Bully for Brontosaurus, Wonderful Life,* and *Eight Little Piggies,* and most recently, for Random House, *Questioning the Millennium.* Winner of the American Book Award for Science and of the National Book Critics Circle Award for *The Mismeasure of Man,* he teaches geology, biology, and the history of science at Harvard University.

George Johnson is a science correspondent for the *New York Times* writing from Santa Fe, New Mexico. His books include *Fire in the Mind: Science, Faith, and the Search for Order, In the Palaces of Memory: How We Build the Worlds Inside Our Heads, Machinery of the Mind: Inside the New Science of Artificial Intelligence,* and *Architects of Fear: Conspiracy Theories and Paranoia in American Politics.*

William Ian Miller is a professor of law at the University of Michigan. He is the author of *The Anatomy of Disgust* (1997), *Humiliation* (1993), and *Bloodtaking and Peacemaking* (1990).

The National Bioethics Advisory Commission (NBAC) was created by executive order of President Clinton in October 1995 to offer recommendations to the National Science and Technology Council, as well as to any government agencies concerned with human biological and behavioral research, on the ethical treatment of human research subjects. The NBAC was also charged with considering the issues that human genetics research raised and any other significant bioethical issues they or the Congress or the public identified. The order encouraged the Commission to hold hearings, develop reports, commission papers, and form subcommittees as needed. The Commission's members are: Harold T. Shapiro, President of Princeton University; Patricia Backlar, Research Associate Professor for Bioethics at Portland State University; Arturo Brito, Assistant Professor of Clinical Pediatrics at University of Miami School of

Medicine; Alexander M. Capron, Henry W. Bruce Professor of Law and University Professor of Law and Medicine at University of Southern California Law Center; Eric J. Cassell, Professor of Public Health at Cornell Medical College; R. Alta Charo, Associate Professor of Law and Medical Ethics at University of Wisconsin Schools of Law and Medicine; James F. Childress, Kyle Professor of Religious Studies and Professor of Medical Education at University of Virginia; David R. Cox, Professor of Genetics and Pediatrics at Stanford University School of Medicine; Rhetaugh G. Dumas, Vice Provost Emerita and Dean Emerita and Lucille Cole Professor of Nursing at University of Michigan; Laurie M. Flynn, Executive Director of National Alliance for the Mentally Ill; Carol W. Greider, Associate Professor of Molecular Biology and Genetics, Johns Hopkins University School of Medicine; Steven H. Holtzman, Chief Business Officer, Millennium Pharmaceuticals; Bette O. Kramer, Founding President, Richmond Bioethics Consortium; Bernard Lo, Director, Program in Medical Ethics, University of California, San Francisco; Lawrence H. Miike, Director, State Department of Health, Hawaii; Thomas H. Murray, Professor and Director, Center for Biomedical Ethics, Case Western Reserve School of Medicine; and Diane Scott-Jones, Professor of Psychology, Temple University.

Martha C. Nussbaum is Ernst Freund Professor of Law and Ethics at the University of Chicago, with appointments in the Law School, the Philosophy Department, and the Divinity School. Among her books are *The Fragility of Goodness, Love's Knowledge,* and *For Love of Country* (ed.).

Adam Phillips is principal child psychotherapist in the Wolverton Gardens Child and Family Consultation Center in London and a member of the Guild of Psychotherapists. He is the author of *On Kissing, Tickling, and Being Bored* and *On Flirtation,* and has edited such volumes as *Charles Lamb: Selected Prose, Richard Howard: Selected Poems,* and *A Philosophical Enquiry* by Edmund Burke.

Eric A. Posner is professor of law at the University of Chicago.

Richard A. Posner is chief judge of the United States Court of Appeals for the Seventh Circuit, senior lecturer at the University of Chicago Law School, and the author of *Sex and Reason.*

Barbara Katz Rothman is professor of sociology at the City University of New York. Her books include *The Tentative Pregnancy,* and the forthcoming *Of Maps and Imaginations: Confronting the Human Genome.*

Edward Stein is the author of *Without Good Reason: The Rationality Debate in Philosophy and Cognitive Science* (Oxford, 1996) and the editor of *Forms of Desire: Sexual Orientation and the Social Constructionist Controversy.* His book *Sexual Desires: Science, Theory, and Ethics* is forthcoming in 1998 from Oxford. He has also written many articles on philosophy and on lesbian and gay studies.

Cass R. Sunstein is the Karl N. Llewellyn Distinguished Service Professor of Jurisprudence in the Law School and Department of Political Science at the University of Chicago. He is the author of *Free Markets and Social Justice* (1997), *Legal Reasoning and Political Conflict* (1996), and *Democracy and the Problem of Free Speech* (1993).

David Tracy is Distinguished Service Professor at the University of Chicago and the Andrew T. and Grace McNichols Professor of Catholic Studies at the Divinity School of the University. He is also a member of the Committee on Social Thought. His books include *Plurality and Ambiguity: Hermenueutics, Religion, Hope.*

Laurence Tribe is the Tyler Professor of Constitutional Law at Harvard University, a fellow of the American Academy of Arts and Sciences, holder of numerous honorary degrees, author of many books and articles, and a leading advocate before the Supreme Court, where he has argued and won many landmark cases.

Lisa Tuttle, an American living in Scotland, is the author of many short stories in the field of science fiction, fantasy, and horror. She has also written several novels, including *Windhaven* (co-authored with George R. R. Martin) and, most recently, *The Pillow Friend,* as well as books for children and the nonfiction *Encyclopedia of Feminism.*

C. K. Williams's most recent books of poetry are *Selected Poems* and *The Vigil.* He teaches at Princeton University.

Ian Wilmut was awarded the Ph.D. from the University of Cambridge for research on the Deep Freeze Preservation of Boar Semen. Subsequent re-

search in Cambridge led to the birth of the first calf from a frozen embryo ("Frosty" in 1973). His work at the Animal Breeding Research Organization has been concerned with developing techniques of multiple ovulation/embryo transfer in sheep and cattle, and he was a joint leader of the team that produced transgenic sheep at Roslin. Over the past five years, his research has been focused on the factors regulating embryo development in sheep after nuclear transfer, work leading to the first birth of live lambs from embryo-derived cells and then to the birth of lambs derived from fetal and adult cells, most famously, Dolly.